The I

Cap

D1464189

the Winelands & the Garden Route

written and researched by

Tony Pinchuck and Barbara McCrea

ROUGH
GUIDES

NEW YORK · LONDON · DELHI

www.roughguides.com

Contents

Going wild in Cape Town colour section following p.80

Cape colonial colour section following p.144

Colour maps following p.336

Cape Town

◄◄ Lion's Head and Camps Bay ◄ Camps Bay beach

Introduction to

Cape Town

the Winelands & the Garden Route

Cape Town's setting is simply stunning. The Mother City – as the oldest city in South Africa is affectionately nicknamed – is perched on a rugged tail of land at Africa's tip, pounded by two thundering oceans and dominated by iconic Table Mountain. With enough heart-pumping activities, from abseiling to paragliding, as well as more relaxed outings to beaches, vineyards and museums, the city easily fills an extended visit. But many, if not most, visitors venture further afield – into the Winelands to sample South Africa's celebrated wines and, much further east, out along the Garden Route, whose enticements include some of the best land-based whale-watching in the world, crashing seascapes, dappled forests and, at its culmination, lions and elephants in the best game reserve in the southern half of the country.

Cape Town has a rich urban texture too, immediately apparent in its diverse **architecture**. An indigenous Cape Dutch style, rooted in the Netherlands, finds its apotheosis in the wine estates, which were themselves brought to new heights by French refugees in the seventeenth century; Muslim slaves, freed in the nineteenth century, added their minarets to the centre's skyline; and the English, who invaded and freed these slaves, introduced Georgian and Victorian buildings. In the tightly packed terraces of the Bo-Kaap quarter and the tenements of District Six, the coloured descendants of slaves evolved a unique, evocatively Capetonian brand of jazz, which is well worth catching live. Indeed great sounds, along with high standards of accommodation, smart restaurants, laid-back cafés and a vibrant gay scene, make visiting Cape Town a truly cosmopolitan experience.

But despite a reputation for greater **liberalism** and racial tolerance during the apartheid era than the rest of the country, Cape Town has paradoxically been the slowest city in South Africa to embrace post-apartheid multiracialism. Ever since the mid-seventeenth century when Jan van Riebeeck, leader of the first whites to settle in South Africa, thought of digging a canal across the Cape Peninsula to cut it off from the rest of Africa, Cape Town has stood aloof from the rest of the country. For 350 years Cape Town's white establishment endeavoured to maintain an illusion that the city was somehow really European, despite its location.

Under apartheid, black (as opposed to coloured) South Africans were actively excluded from the Western Cape, which is why today **Africans** are still a minority in the Mother City, though they constitute the overwhelming majority in South Africa. For most Capetonians, living in crowded **townships** and **shanty-towns**, poverty and sky-high crime rates are part of everyday life.

Fact file

• Founded 350 years ago, Cape Town is the **legislative capital** of South Africa, the seat of **parliament** and the capital of the **Western Cape** province.

• The city's **population** is just over three million, of whom half are coloured (people of mixed race); 26 percent black; 23 percent white; and the remainder of Asian descent. This is a young city, demographically – a third of Capetonians are under 14.

• Of South Africa's eleven official languages, the three main ones spoken in Cape Town and the Western Cape are **Afrikaans** (the mother tongue of many whites and coloureds), **Xhosa** (the language of most blacks) and **English** – the effective lingua franca.

• Almost 40 percent of Cape Town's households live around or below the official poverty line, set at a household income of R1600 a month.

• The Western Cape is both an agricultural and industrial area. The province's top five exports are fruit; wine, beer and spirits; fish; iron and steel; and machinery.

▶ Viewpoint on Table Mountain

What to see

Table Mountain, frequently mantled by its "tablecloth" clouds, is the solid core of Cape Town, dividing the city into distinct zones, with public gardens, wilderness, forests, hiking routes, vineyards and desirable residential areas. To its north lies the **city centre**, home to the city's most important museums and galleries, as well as featuring a buzzing street life – buskers, hawkers and market traders. In the adjacent **Bo-Kaap** Muslim quarter, colourful terraces and restaurants serving local curries add piquancy to the city's heart. A stone's throw from the centre, the **V&A Waterfront** is Cape Town's most popular spot for shopping, eating and drinking in a highly picturesque setting among the piers and quays of a working harbour. It's also the embarkation point for catamarans to **Robben Island**, the notorious site of Nelson Mandela's incarceration. The rocky shore west of the Waterfront is occupied by the inner-city suburbs of **Green Point**, **De Waterkant** and **Sea Point**, whose main drag is lined with some of the peninsula's oldest and best restaurants, while their back streets are crammed with backpacker lodges, B&Bs and hotels. Equally good for accommodation, but leafy and upmarket in comparison, the **City Bowl suburbs** gaze down from the Table Mountain foothills across the central business district to the ships in Duncan Dock.

South from Sea Point, a coastal road traces the chilly **Atlantic seaboard** under the heights of the Twelve Apostles and past some of Cape Town's most expensive suburbs and spectacular beaches. Further south, past Hout Bay, the road merges with the precipitous **Chapman's Peak Drive**, ten dramatically snaking kilometres of Victorian engineering carved into the western cliffsides of the Table Mountain massif, high above the crashing waves. To the east, across Table Mountain, the exceptionally beautiful **Kirstenbosch National Botanical Gardens** creep up the lower slopes, as do

the **Constantia Winelands** a little further south, while the middle-class **southern suburbs** stretch down the peninsula as far as Muizenberg. The Metrorail line, the only viable public transport down the length of the peninsula, cuts through these suburbs and continues along the **False Bay seaboard**, passing through villagey **Kalk Bay**, with its intact harbour and working fishing community, and **Fish Hoek**, which has the best bathing beach along the eastern peninsula, before the final stop at the historic settlement of **Simon's Town**.

Most visitors see only the areas that were classified under apartheid as "white" and which still remain relatively safe and salubrious. But the townships of the **Cape Flats** to the east of the city can be visited on guided tours, and if you really want to get under the skin of the African areas, you can enjoy the hospitality of any of several B&Bs in Xhosa homes.

Away from the city, an hour's drive east of the Cape Flats into the Western Cape interior, are the beautiful **Winelands**, with elegant examples of Cape Dutch architecture, wonderful wines and excellent restaurants. Southeast of Cape Town you can take the picturesque coastal route, winding around massive sea-cliffs, to reach Hermanus, the largest settlement on the **Whale Coast**, and a fabulous spot for shore-based whale-watching.

The Two Oceans Aquarium

Cine city

When *U-Carmen eKhayelitsha* took top prize at the prestigious Berlin Film Festival in 2005, Cape Town was for once being admired for showing its grittier face on film. A local reworking of Bizet's opera, the movie was shot entirely in Xhosa in the Mother City's largest black area. But it's more commonly for the beauty of the city and its environs – the slatey mountains, the mile upon mile of gorgeous coastline and the vineyards – as well as the guaranteed sunshine and the cut-price (but highly skilled) crews, that international filmmakers adore Cape Town; these and its chameleon-like ability to re-create anything from French boulevards to hectic New York traffic.

Cape Town was astonishingly able to stand in for 35 diverse locations for the 2005 Nicolas Cage movie *Lord of War*, including Bolivia, Beirut, Berlin, the Caribbean, Sierra Leone, Indonesia, Odessa and New York City.

Thousands of permits to film in Cape Town are issued every year, mostly for international commercials. Until recently, feature films shot here have been forgettable affairs involving equally unmemorable actors, but increasingly Capetonians have been spotting Hollywood names in bars along the glittering Atlantic seaboard beaches, among them Juliet Binoche, Samuel L. Jackson, Jean-Claude Van Damme, Daniel Craig, Salma Hayek and Morgan Freeman. Star-gazing could become an increasingly common pastime on the peninsula once the R450-million Dreamworld Film City studios, intended to clinch Cape Town's status as the filmmaking capital of Africa, are completed.

After Cape Town, the best-known tourist feature of the Western Cape is the **Garden Route**, a drive along the N2 from Cape Town all the way to Port Elizabeth in the Eastern Cape. The Garden Route can be driven in a day, but to cover it so quickly would mean missing its essence, which lies off the road, in its coastal towns, lagoons, mountains and ancient forests on the stretch between **Mossel Bay** and **Storms River Mouth**. The highlight along here is the **Tsitsikamma National Park**, where the dark Storms River opens spectacularly into the Indian Ocean. Public transport along the Garden Route is better than anywhere in the country, partly because the route is a single stretch of freeway, and tour operators along the way have begun turning it into the country's most concentrated strip for packaged **adventure sports** and **outdoor activities**. The ultimate destination at the eastern end of the Garden Route is **Addo Elephant National Park**, where sightings of elephants are virtually guaranteed, and there's a chance of seeing lions, buffaloes and rhinos, among other wildlife.

When to visit

Cape Town has a **Mediterranean climate**, the warm dryish summers balanced by cool wet winters. Come prepared for hot days in winter and cold snaps in summer: pack at least one short-sleeved garment during the cooler months and a jumper and jacket whatever time of year you come. The **southeaster**, the cool summer wind that blows in across False Bay, forms a major obsession for Capetonians. Its fickle moods can singlehandedly determine what kind of day you're going to have, and when it gusts at over 60kph you won't want to be outdoors, let alone on the beach. Conversely, its gentler incarnation as the so-called **Cape Doctor** brings welcome relief on humid summer days, and lays the famous cloudy tablecloth on top of Table Mountain. The **Garden Route** falls within overlapping weather systems and as a result has rain throughout the year, falling predominantly at night, which brings forth the verdure from which the region draws its name.

For sun and swimming, the best time to visit Cape Town and the Garden Route is from **October to mid-December** and **mid-January to Easter**, when it's light till well into the evening and there's an average of ten

▲ Flower sellers on Adderley Street

hours of sunshine a day. From mid-December to mid-January, the whole region becomes congested as the nation takes its annual seaside holiday. In Cape Town, this is major party time, with plenty of major festivals and events; if this is when you plan to visit, arrange accommodation and transport well in advance, and expect to pay considerably more for your bed than during the rest of the year.

Despite its shorter daylight hours, the **autumn** period, from April to mid-May, has a lot going for it: the southeaster drops and air temperatures remain pleasantly warm and the light is sharp and bright. For similar reasons the **spring** month of September can be very agreeable, with the added attraction that following the winter rains the peninsula tends to be at its greenest. Although spells of heavy rain occur in **winter** (June and July), it tends to be relatively mild, with temperatures rarely falling below 6°C. Glorious sunny days with crisp blue skies are common, and you won't see bare wintry trees either: indigenous vegetation is evergreen and gardens flower year round. It's also in July that the first migrating **whales** begin to appear along the Southern Cape coast, usually staying till the end of November.

▼ Market stalls

Climate

	Jan	Feb	Mar	Apr	May	Jun	Jul	Aug	Sep	Oct	Nov	Dec
Cape Town												
Temperature												
max (°C)	26	27	25	23	20	18	18	18	19	21	24	25
min (°C)	16	16	14	12	9	8	7	8	9	11	13	15
max (°F)	79	80	78	73	69	65	65	65	67	70	74	77
min (°F)	60	60	58	53	48	46	45	46	48	51	56	59
Rainfall												
mm	15	17	20	41	69	93	82	77	40	30	14	17
inches	0.6	0.7	0.8	1.6	2.7	3.7	3.2	3.0	1.6	1.2	0.6	0.7
Tsitsikamma National Park												
Temperature												
max (°C)	23	22	21	20	19	18	17	17	17	19	20	22
min (°C)	17	17	16	14	12	10	10	10	11	13	14	16
max (°F)	73	72	70	68	66	64	63	63	63	66	68	72
min (°F)	63	63	61	57	54	50	50	50	52	55	57	61
Rainfall												
mm	77	70	81	80	86	75	78	111	66	83	78	60
inches	3.0	2.8	3.2	3.1	3.4	3.0	3.1	4.4	2.6	3.3	3.1	2.4

22

things not to miss

It's not possible to see everything that Cape Town and the Garden Route have to offer in one trip – and we don't suggest you try. What follows is a selective and subjective taste of the highlights, including outstanding national parks, spectacular wildlife, thrilling adventure sports and beautiful architecture. They're arranged in five colour-coded categories to help you find the very best things to see, do and experience. All entries have a page reference to take you straight into the guide, where you can find out more.

01 **Seafood** Pages **114** & **133** • With two oceans to fish from, Cape Town offers a real feast for seafood lovers. Head to Kalk Bay to sample today's catch.

02 **V&A Waterfront** Page **73** • Find out why a huge harbourside shopping mall is Cape Town's most popular tourist destination.

03 **Cape Point** Page **119** • One of the most dramatic viewpoints in the country, the treacherous rocky promontory south of Cape Town has seen many ships come to grief since the fifteenth century.

04 **Cape minstrels** Page **106** • Every January 2, minstrel bands parade through the streets in a carnival harking back to the days of slavery at the Cape.

05 **Elephants** Page **272** • Just beyond the eastern end of the Garden Route is Addo Elephant National Park, the largest game reserve in the southern half of the country, with some three hundred pachyderms to marvel at.

06 **Sandboarding** Page **155** • One of the newest and most exciting challenges for adrenaline junkies is trying to stay on your board as you slalom at speed down some of the peninsula's tallest dunes.

07 **Penguins** Page **117** • Boulders Beach has one of only two mainland African penguin colonies in the world.

09 **Cape Town International Jazz Festival** Page **38** • Local musos come into their own at the most important jazz event of the year.

08 **The Bo-Kaap** Page **60** • The streets of Cape Town's oldest residential area are filled with colourful Cape Dutch and Georgian architecture.

10 Kirstenbosch National Botanical Gardens Page

93 • One of Cape Town's three most popular attractions, Kirstenbosch is the first botanical garden to have earned World Heritage status.

11 Mother City Queer Projects Page 158 • Dress as

outrageously as possible for the biggest ball of the year – Cape Town's straight-friendly gay party.

12 Canopy tours Page 248 •

Swing through the treetops among the arboreal giants of South Africa's tallest indigenous forest.

13 Ocean safaris Page 240 •

Take to the waves for incomparable encounters with several of the whale and dolphin species that frequent South African waters.

14 South African National Gallery Page **63** • Get to grips with South African contemporary art in the middle of The Gardens.

15 Winelands Page **167** • The Western Cape's wine estates combine stunning scenery, Cape Dutch architecture and some fine and affordable vintages.

16 Sundowners Page **105** • Relax with a tipple at Clifton on the Atlantic Seaboard and watch the sun turn into a molten orb as it sinks into the ocean.

17 Storms River Mouth Page **246** • The Garden Route's most dramatic coastline, where the Storms River thrusts out from a gorge to meet the crashing surf – best seen from the suspension footbridge at the mouth.

18. Township tour Page 101

• Witness the reality of daily life for most Capetonians in one of the city's sprawling townships.

19. Table Mountain cableway Page 82

• The most spectacular way to ascend Cape Town's famous flat-topped peak is also the easiest – the revolving cable car.

20. Chapman's Peak Drive Page 108

• Take a spin along the sinuous road that traces the precipitous cliff edge of the Atlantic seaboard, affording some of the most sublime views on the peninsula.

21. De Hoop Nature Reserve Page 200

• Monumental dunes and whales by the dozen make this one of the most compelling reserves in the Western Cape.

22. Robben Island Page 77

• Visit the notorious offshore jail where some of South Africa's most famous figures, including Nelson Mandela, were incarcerated.

Basics

Basics

Getting there

Most overseas visitors to Cape Town travel there by air, either on a direct flight or via Johannesburg, which is connected to Cape Town by frequent domestic flights. A nonstop flight from the UK or North America makes the twelve-hour-plus journey a little more bearable, but it can be cheaper to fly via mainland Europe or Africa.

Airfares always depend on the **season**, with the highest prices and greatest demand occurring in June, July, August, December and the first week of January. Prices drop during the "shoulder" season in May and September. You get the best prices during the low season in October, November and the last three weeks of January till March.

Flights from the UK and Ireland

From London there are nonstop flights with British Airways, South African Airways and Virgin Atlantic to Cape Town. Flying time from the UK is around twelve hours and average high/low scheduled direct fares from London are £850/650, but you can save up to £200 by flying via mainland Europe, Africa or Asia, and enduring at least one change of plane.

From the Republic of Ireland a number of European carriers fly to South Africa via their hub airports, while in high season there are direct charter flights to Cape Town operated by Slattery's Sun (see the listing under "Tour operators" on p.25).

Flights from the US and Canada

From the US Delta Airlines flies direct four times a week from New York (JFK) to Cape Town, with a refuelling stop in Dakar, Senegal. There are also daily nonstop flights from **Washington** and one-stop flights from New York via Dakar to **Johannesburg** operated by South African Airways (SAA), which take around fifteen hours. Most other flights stop off in Europe or the Middle East and involve a change of plane. From Canada you don't have much of a choice, with daily services from **Toronto** and **Vancouver** to

Johannesburg operated by British Airways and by Northwest/KLM changing planes in London and Amsterdam.

On the nonstop flights from the US to Jo'burg, expect the high/low season **fare** to start from $2700/1350 for a round trip, depending on season; you might save $100–200 if you fly via Europe. Fares from Vancouver to Jo'burg start at Can$2500.

There are dozens of daily connecting flights between Jo'burg and Cape Town on South Africa's domestic airlines (see p.30 for more details). By far the biggest is **South African Airways** (SAA) with several smaller airlines, of which the most significant is **British Airways Comair** and its budget subsidiary **Kulula.com**. Other no-frills airlines include **Nationwide**, **1Time** and **Mango**.

On SAA and its associates, expect to pay just under R1500 for a one-way tourist-class **fare** from Johannesburg to Cape Town, although generally this price will already be included if you've bought a ticket through to Cape Town.

Flights from Australia and New Zealand

There are flights **from Sydney**, which take fourteen hours, and **Perth**, just under twelve hours, to Johannesburg, with onward connections to Cape Town; New Zealanders have to fly via Sydney. South African Airways (SAA) and Qantas both serve South Africa from Australia. Some Asian, African and Middle Eastern airlines fly to South Africa via their hub cities, and tend to be less expensive, but their routings often entail more stopovers.

Southern Africa is not a cheap destination for travellers from Australia and New Zealand. **Fares** start at around Aus$2000 for a return

Fly less – stay longer! Travel and climate change

Climate change is the single biggest issue facing our planet. It is caused by a build-up in the atmosphere of carbon dioxide and other greenhouse gases, which are emitted by many sources – including planes. Already, flights account for around three to four percent of human-induced global warming: that figure may sound small, but it is rising year on year and threatens to counteract the progress made by reducing greenhouse emissions in other areas.

Rough Guides regard travel, overall, as a global benefit, and feel strongly that the advantages to developing economies are important, as are the opportunities for greater contact and awareness among peoples. But we all have a responsibility to limit our personal "carbon footprint." That means giving thought to how often we fly and what we can do to redress the harm that our trips create.

Flying and climate change

Pretty much every form of motorized travel generates CO_2, but planes are particularly bad offenders, releasing large volumes of greenhouse gases at altitudes where their impact is far more harmful. Flying also allows us to travel much further than we would contemplate doing by road or rail, so the emissions attributable to each passenger become truly shocking. For example, one person taking a return flight between Europe and California produces the equivalent impact of 2.5 tonnes of CO_2 – similar to the yearly output of the average UK car.

Less harmful planes may evolve but it will be decades before they replace the current fleet – which could be too late for avoiding climate chaos. In the meantime, there are limited options for concerned travelers: to reduce the amount we travel by air (take fewer trips, stay longer!), to avoid night flights (when plane contrails trap heat from Earth but can't reflect sunlight back to space), and to make the trips we do take "climate neutral" via a carbon offset scheme.

Carbon offset schemes

Offset schemes run by **climatecare.org**, **carbonneutral.com**, and others allow you to "neutralize" the greenhouse gases that you are responsible for releasing. Their websites have simple calculators that let you work out the impact of any flight. Once that's done, you can pay to fund projects that will reduce future carbon emissions by an equivalent amount (such as the distribution of low-energy light bulbs and cooking stoves in developing countries). Please take the time to visit our website and make your trip climate neutral.

ⓦ www.roughguides.com/climatechange

---

flight from Sydney to Johannesburg, and a flight to Europe with a stopover in South Africa, or even a RTW ticket, may represent better value than a straightforward return.

Airlines, agents and operators

Online booking

ⓦ www.expedia.co.uk (in UK), ⓦ www.expedia .com (in US), ⓦ www.expedia.ca (in Canada)
ⓦ www.lastminute.com (in UK)
ⓦ www.opodo.co.uk (in UK)
ⓦ www.orbitz.com (in US)
ⓦ www.travelocity.co.uk (in UK),

ⓦ www.travelocity.com (in US), ⓦ www .travelocity.ca (in Canada)
ⓦ www.zuji.com.au (in Australia), ⓦ www.zuji .co.nz (in New Zealand)

Airlines

Air France US ☎ 1-800/237-2747, Canada ☎ 1-800/667-2747, UK ☎ 0870/142 4343, Australia ☎ 1300/390 190, SA ☎ 0861/340 340; ⓦ www.airfrance.com.
Air Namibia US ☎ 1-800/NAMIBIA, UK ☎ 0870/774 0965, Australia ☎ 02/9244 1841; ⓦ www.airnamibia.com.na.
British Airways US & Canada ☎ 1-800/AIRWAYS, UK ☎ 0870/850 9850, Republic of Ireland ☎ 1890/626 747, Australia ☎ 1300/767 177,

NZ ☎09/966 9777, SA ☎114/418 600;
@www.ba.com.
Cathay Pacific US ☎1-800/233-2742, Canada
☎1-800/2686-868, UK ☎020/8834 8888,
Australia ☎13 17 47, NZ ☎09/379 0861, SA
☎11/700 8900; @www.cathaypacific.com.
Delta Airlines US & Canada ☎1-800/221-1212,
UK ☎0845/600 0950, Republic of Ireland
☎1850/882 031 or 01/407 3165, Australia
☎1300/302 849, NZ ☎09/977 2232; @www
.delta.com.
Emirates US & Canada ☎1-800/777-3999, UK
☎0870/243 2222, Australia ☎03/9940 7807, NZ
☎05/0836 4728, SA ☎0861/363 728; @www
.emirates.com.
Gulf Air UK ☎0870/777 1717, Republic of Ireland
☎0818/272 828, Australia ☎1300/366 337, SA
☎11/268 8909; @www.gulfairco.com.
Iberia US ☎1-800/772-4642, UK ☎0870/609
0500, Republic of Ireland ☎0818/462 000, SA
☎011/884 5909; @www.iberia.com.
KLM (Royal Dutch Airlines) See also Northwest/
KLM. US & Canada ☎1-800/225-2525, UK
☎0870/507 4074, Republic of Ireland ☎1850/747
400, Australia ☎1300/392 192, NZ ☎09/921
6040, SA ☎11/961 6727; @www.klm.com.
LTU International Airways US & Canada
☎1-866/266-5588, SA ☎0860/359 588;
@www.ltu.com.
Lufthansa US ☎1-800/3995-838, Canada
☎1-800/563-5954, UK ☎0870/837 7747,
Republic of Ireland ☎01/844 5544, Australia
☎1300/655 727, NZ ☎0800/945 220, SA
☎0861/842 538; @www.lufthansa.com.
Malaysia Airlines US ☎1-800/5529-264, UK
☎0870/607 9090, Republic of Ireland
☎01/6761 561, Australia ☎13 26 27, NZ
☎0800/777 747, SA ☎11/8809 614; @www
.malaysia-airlines.com.
Nationwide Airlines US ☎1-866/686-6558, UK
☎0870/300 0767, SA ☎0861/737 737;
@www.flynationwide.co.za.
Northwest/KLM US ☎1-800/225-2525, UK
☎0870/507 4074, Australia ☎1300/767 310;
@www.nwa.com.
Olympic Airways US ☎1-800/223-1226, Canada
☎1-416/964-2720, UK ☎0870/606 0460, Australia
☎02/9251 2044; @www.olympic-airways.com.
Qantas US & Canada ☎1-800/227-4500, UK
☎0845/774 7767, Republic of Ireland ☎01/407
3278, Australia ☎13 13 13, NZ ☎0800/808 767
or 09/357 8900, SA ☎11/441 8550; @www
.qantas.com.
Singapore Airlines US ☎1-800/742-3333,
Canada ☎1-800/663-3046, UK ☎0844/800 2380,
Republic of Ireland ☎01/671 0722, Australia

☎13 10 11, NZ ☎0800/808 909; SA ☎11/880
8560 or 11/880 8566, @www.singaporeair.com.
South African Airways (SAA) US & Canada
☎1-800/722-9675, UK ☎0870/747 1111,
Australia ☎1800/221 699, NZ ☎09/977 2237,
SA ☎11/978 1111; @www.flysaa.com.
Swiss International Airlines US ☎1-877/3797-
947, Canada ☎1-87755-97947, UK ☎0845/601
0956, Republic of Ireland ☎1890/200 515,
Australia ☎1300/724 666, NZ ☎09/977 2238,
SA ☎0860/040 506; @www.swiss.com.
TAP (Air Portugal) US & Canada ☎1-800/221-
7370, UK ☎0845/601 0932, Australia & NZ
☎02/9244 2344, SA ☎11/455 4907;
@www.flytap.com.
Virgin Atlantic US ☎1-800/821-5438, UK
☎0870/380 2007, Australia ☎1300/727 340, SA
☎11/340 3400; @www.virgin-atlantic.com.

Agents and operators

Abercrombie & Kent UK ☎0845/0700 611,
@www.abercrombiekent.co.uk; Australia
☎1300/851 800, NZ ☎0800/441 638,
@www.abercrombiekent.com.au. Classy operator
whose packages feature Cape Town, the Winelands
and the Garden Route.
Adventure Center US ☎1-800/228-8747 or
510/654-1879, @www.adventurecenter.com. Wide
variety of affordable South African packages including
"soft adventure" options.
Africa Travel Centre UK ☎020/7387 1211,
@www.africatravel.co.uk. Experienced Africa
specialist with a variety of tailor-made itineraries; acts
as agent for many South Africa-based overland
operators.
Bales Worldwide UK ☎0870/241 3208,
@www.balesworldwide.com. High-quality
escorted tours that include Cape Town and the
Garden Route.
Classic Safari Company Australia ☎1300/130
218 or 02/9327 0666, @www
.classicsafaricompany.com.au. Luxury tailor-made
safaris to southern Africa, including the Western and
Eastern Cape provinces.
Cox & Kings US ☎1-800/999-1758, @www
.coxandkingsusa.com. Stylish operator with classic
luxury journeys, including a twelve-day Cape Town to
Johannesburg excursion and deluxe safaris.
Destinations Republic of Ireland @01/855 6641,
@www.destinations.ie. Specialist in long-haul
destinations, including South Africa.
ebookers UK ☎0800/082 3000, Republic of
Ireland ☎01/488 3507, @www.ebookers.com,
@www.ebookers.ie. Low fares on an extensive
selection of scheduled flights and package deals.

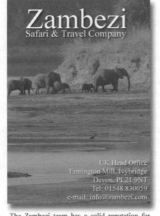

Avoid Guilt Trips

Buy fair trade coffee + bananas ✓

Save energy – use low energy bulbs ✓
– don't leave tv on standby ✓

Offset carbon emissions from flight to Madrid ✓

Send goat to Africa ✓

Join Tourism Concern today ✓

Slowly, the world is changing.
Together we can, and will, make a difference.

Tourism Concern is the only UK registered charity fighting
exploitation in one of the largest industries on earth: people forced
from their homes in order that holiday resorts can be built,
sweatshop labour conditions in hotels and destruction of the
environment are just some of the issues that we tackle.

Sending people on a guilt trip is not something we do. We know as
well as anyone that holidays are precious. But you can help us to
ensure that tourism always benefits the local communities involved.

Call 020 7133 3330
or visit **tourismconcern.org.uk** to find out how.

*A year's membership of Tourism Concern costs just £20 (£12 unwaged)
– that's 38 pence a week, less than the cost of a pint of milk, organic of course.*

Fighting
Exploitation
in Tourism

TourismConcern

Exodus UK ℡ 0870/950 0039, ⊛ www.exodus.co
.uk. Small-group adventure tour operator with plenty
of South Africa offerings, include trips in and around
Cape Town, excursions to the country's wildlife
reserves and activity packages that include horse-
riding, kloofing (canyoning), mountain biking and
surfing.

Expert Africa UK ℡ 020/8232 9777, ⊛ www
.expertafrica.com. Small-group tours for independent
travellers, as well as tailor-made trips. Specialist in
good-quality accommodation/flight deals, and
particularly strong on Cape Town, the Garden Route
and the rest of the Western Cape.

Explore Worldwide UK ℡ 0870/333 4001,
⊛ www.explore.co.uk. Good range of small-group
South Africa tours, treks, expeditions and safaris,
staying mostly in small local hotels and taking in Cape
Town, the Winelands and the Garden Route.

Joe Walsh Tours Republic of Ireland ℡ 01/676
0991, ⊛ www.joewalshtours.ie. Long-established
general budget fares and holidays agent with beach
and safari packages to South Africa.

Journeys International US ℡ 1-800/255-8735
or 734/665-4407, ⊛ www.journeys-intl.com.
Small-group trips with a range of packages in the
Western Cape, several of which are specifically
tailored to families.

Kumuka Expeditions US ℡ 1-800/517-0867,
⊛ www.kumuka.com; UK ℡ 0800/389 2328,
⊛ www.kumuka.co.uk; Australia ℡ 1800/667 277,
⊛ www.kumuka.com.au. Five-week journeys from
Nairobi to Cape Town and short tours around South
Africa using local operators.

Kuoni Travel UK ℡ 01306/747 002, ⊛ www.kuoni
.co.uk. Award-winning major tour operator running
flexible package holidays to South Africa including the
Western Cape. Especially good deals for families.

Maupintour US ℡ 1-800/255-4266, ⊛ www
.maupintour.com. A one-week Cape Town and
Winelands package, plus a ten-day package involving
luxury travel on the Rovos train (see p.29) and visits to
Kruger and the Victoria Falls in Zimbabwe.

North South Travel UK ℡ 01245/608 291,
⊛ www.northsouthtravel.co.uk. Friendly, competitive
travel agency, offering discounted fares worldwide.
Profits are used to support projects in the developing
world, especially the promotion of sustainable tourism.

Oasis Overland UK ℡ 01258/471 155, ⊛ www
.oasisoverland.co.uk. One of the smaller overland
companies, often running budget trips through Africa.

Okavango Tours and Safaris UK ℡ 020/8343
3283, ⊛ www.okavango.com. Top-notch outfit with
on-the-ground knowledge of sub-Saharan Africa,
offering fully flexible and individual tours across the
country.

Peregrine Adventures Australia ℡ 1300/791
485, ⊛ www.peregrine.net.au. Specialist small-
group programmes that include a variety of wildlife
packages and a one-week Western Cape Experience.

Rainbow Tours UK ℡ 020/7226 1004, ⊛ www
.rainbowtours.co.uk. Knowledgeable and sensitive
South Africa specialist whose trips emphasize
eco-friendly and community-based tourism, with
accommodation in good-value guesthouses, game
lodges and independent hotels.

Safari Consultants UK ℡ 01787/888 590,
⊛ www.safari-consultants.co.uk. Individually tailored
and fairly upmarket holidays across southern Africa,
with particular expertise in activity-based holidays,
including walking safaris.

Slattery's Sun Republic of Ireland ℡ 1890/200
525, ⊛ www.slatterys.com. Cheap charter flights
from Dublin to Cape Town and a vast range of South
African itineraries that take in Cape Town, Kruger
National Park and Zululand.

STA Travel US ℡ 1-800/781-4040, UK
℡ 0871/230 0 040, Australia ℡ 134 STA, NZ
℡ 0800/474 400, SA ℡ 0861/781 781, ⊛ www
.statravel.com. Worldwide specialist in independent
travel; also student IDs, travel insurance, car rental,
rail passes, and more. Good discounts for students
and under-26s.

Trailfinders UK ℡ 0845/058 5858, Republic of
Ireland ℡ 01/677 7888, Australia ℡ 1300/780 212,
⊛ www.trailfinders.com. One of the best-informed
and most efficient agents for independent travellers.

Travel Bag UK ℡ 0800/804 8911, ⊛ www
.travelbag.co.uk. Discount deals worldwide.

Tribes UK ℡ 01728/685 971, ⊛ www.tribes.co.uk.
Unusual and off-the-beaten track, fair-trade safaris
and cultural tours in South Africa.

Twohigs Republic of Ireland ℡ 01/648 0800,
⊛ www.twohigs.com. Long-haul specialist offering
South Africa packages.

USIT Republic of Ireland ℡ 01/602 1904, ⊛ www
.usit.ie. Specialist in student, youth and independent
travel, offering flights and online hostel room bookings
in a number of towns in South Africa.

Wilderness Travel US ℡ 1-800/368-2794,
⊛ www.wildernesstravel.com. Hiking, cultural and
wildlife adventures, with a sixteen-day package taking
in Cape Town, the Garden Route and Kruger.

Wildlife Worldwide UK ℡ 0845/130 6982,
⊛ www.wildlifeworldwide.com. Tailor-made trips for
wildlife and wilderness enthusiasts, including a
Garden Route self-drive package and excursions
taking in national parks and the winelands.

World Travel Centre Republic of Ireland ℡ 01/416
7007, ⊛ www.worldtravel.ie. Competitive fares to
South Africa.

Arrival

Cape Town International Airport lies on the Cape Flats, 22km east of the city centre. A bureau de change is open to coincide with international arrivals; there are also ATMs here and a basic tourist information desk. The major car-rental firms have desks inside the international terminal. Prebooking a vehicle is essential, especially during the week when there is a big demand from domestic business travellers, and over the mid-December to mid-January and Easter peak seasons.

An airport shuttle (☎021 462 0272 or 082 360 9956, ✉airportshuttle@new.co.za) operates from the airport to anywhere in the city; the **fare** into the city centre is R150 for the first person and R50 for each additional passenger. An alternative is the similarly priced Magic Bus (☎021 505 6300), which must be **booked** a day ahead; the bus will meet you at the airport and take you anywhere on the peninsula. Metered **taxis** operated by Touch Down Taxis, the company officially authorized by the airport, rank in reasonable numbers outside both terminals and charge about R180 per person for the trip into the city. There's a **hotel** at the airport, *Road Lodge* (☎021 934 7303; R355), useful if your flight is weirdly timed; you can walk to it from the terminal buildings and it's not too pricey.

Getting around

The Golden Acre shopping complex, at the junction of Strand and Adderley streets in the heart of Cape Town, can be a confusing muddle, but this is where all rail and bus transport (both intercity and from elsewhere in the city) and most minibus taxis converge – if you use public transport at all, you're bound to find yourself here at some stage. Everything you need for your next move is within two or three blocks of here, including tourist information (see p.48).

City transport

Although Cape Town's city centre is compact enough to get around on foot, many of the attractions are spread along the considerable length of the peninsula. To make the most of your visit the best option by far is to rent a car. Otherwise, **Rikkis** (☎0861 745 547) are cheaper than **taxis**, or you could take a **tour**,

English/Afrikaans street names

Many towns along the Garden Route have **bilingual street names** with English and Afrikaans alternatives sometimes appearing along the same road. Often the Afrikaans name will bear little resemblance to the English one, something it's worth being aware of when trying to map read. In Cape Town you'll also find Afrikaans direction signs; for example signs for the airport will sometimes use the Afrikaans word "Lughawe".

For a list of Afrikaans terms you may encounter on signage, see "Language", p.307.

or make do with the pretty skeletal public transport system.

Inner-city areas west of the centre are better served by **buses** than other central suburbs, but transport north along the Atlantic coast is negligible. There is, however, a **train** service cutting through the southern suburbs and continuing all the way down to Simon's Town. It's fairly reliable and well used, though the rolling stock, which is gradually being upgraded, is looking a little battered.

Note that using public transport **after dark** is potentially risky. If you're forced to do so, take sensible precautions, such as travelling in a group (especially women) and avoiding third-class carriages on trains; otherwise, make every effort to take metered taxis at night.

Buses

The only frequent and reliable **bus** services are those from the centre to the Waterfront and Sea Point; infrequent buses also go down the Atlantic seaboard to Camps Bay and Hout Bay, and there are a couple to Kirstenbosch. Don't attempt to catch a bus to the southern suburbs: the train is much quicker and more efficient.

The principal bus station is the **Golden Acre bus terminal**, off Strand Street, wedged between Golden Acre Shopping Centre, the station and the Grand Parade. Buses depart from here to Green Point, Sea Point, Camps Bay and Hout Bay, while services for the Waterfront leave from Adderley Street outside the station. Note that the buses aren't numbered; you identify them from the destination on the front. All but the Waterfront buses are intended for use by workers, with services beginning at 6.30am, and ending at 6.30pm. The Waterfront buses

also start early, but continue until 10.30pm, and have the greatest frequency.

Tickets are sold by the driver: state your destination to the driver, and pay when you get on. A single ticket from the city costs around R5 to Sea Point, or about R8 to Camps Bay. Weekly and monthly tickets are also available. For **timetables**, enquire at the Golden Arrow **information booth** (toll-free ☏0800 65 64 63) at the Golden Acre bus terminal. It's advisable to check bus times and points of departure at the booth.

Useful city-bus routes

City centre to Waterfront Cape Town station–Riebeeck St–Buitengragt St–Waterfront. Mon–Fri every 10min, Sat & Sun every 15min.
City centre to Sea Point Golden Acre terminal–Mouille Point–Main Rd Green Point–Main Rd Sea Point. Mon–Sat 20 daily.
City centre to Hout Bay Golden Acre terminal–Lower Plein St–Darling Rd–Adderley St–Green Point–Sea Point–Camps Bay–Hout Bay beach–Hout Bay harbour. Mon–Sat 6 daily, Sun 3 daily; 1hr.
City centre to Kirstenbosch Golden Acre terminal–Mowbray–Kirstenbosch at 7.30am, 12.35pm and 3.35pm, returning at 9.35am and 3.30pm only.
V&A Waterfront to Sea Point V&A Waterfront–Mouille Point–Green Point–Three Anchor Bay–Beach Rd Sea Point. Daily every 20min.

Taxis, minibus taxis and Rikkis

In Cape Town and elsewhere in South Africa, the term **"taxi"** is used to refer to conventional metered cars as well as jam-packed minibuses. In Cape Town, it's also used to refer to the more upmarket minibuses called Rikkis.

Metered taxis, regulated by the Cape Town Municipality, don't cruise up and down looking for fares. You find a taxi at

The City Sightseeing Bus

The open-top, hop-on/hop-off Cape Town **City Sightseeing Bus** (☎021 511 6000, ⓦwww.sightseeing.co.za) is also an extremely useful, if slightly expensive (R100 per person per day), means of negotiating the city-centre sights and the Atlantic seaboard beaches. You can get on and off throughout the day wherever you please along the route. **Departures** (daily: April, Sept & Oct half-hourly 9.30am–3pm; May–Aug hourly 9.30am–2pm; Nov–March every 20min 9.30am–3.30pm & until 5pm Dec–Feb) are from the **V&A Waterfront** outside Two Oceans Aquarium. The **route** is circular and takes in the Clock Tower at the Waterfront; the Cape Town Convention Centre on the Foreshore; the city centre (buses stop at Cape Town Tourism in Strand Street, the South African Museum, the South African Jewish Museum, the Castle of Good Hope and the Gold Museum); the City Bowl suburbs; the lower cableway station (for the cable car up Table Mountain) and the Atlantic Seaboard from Camps Bay to Sea Point, before returning to the Waterfront. The bus also visits Kirstenbosch National Botanical Gardens.

the ranks around town, including at the Waterfront, the train station and Greenmarket Square, or you can phone to be picked up (see p.164). Taxis must have the driver's name and identification clearly on display and the meter clearly visible. Fares work out at around R10 per kilometre, expensive compared with other forms of transport, though definitely worth it at night, when metered taxis are the safest way of getting around.

Minibus taxis are cheap, frequent and bomb up and down the main routes at tearaway speeds. They can be hailed from the street – you'll recognize them from the hooting, loud music and touting – or boarded at the central taxi rank, adjacent to the train station. Once you've boarded, pay the *guardjie* (assistant), who sits near the driver, and tell him when you want to get off. Fares should be under R8 for most trips. As well as crazed driving, be prepared for pickpockets working the taxi ranks.

Rikkis are minibus taxis aimed principally at tourists (Mon–Fri 6.30am–midnight, Sat & Sun 24hr). Carrying a maximum of eight passengers, they are small open-backed vehicles, covered by a canopy but open at the rear; you need to book them by telephone (☎0861 745 547). In Cape Town, Rikkis zip about the City Bowl, the Waterfront and the Atlantic seaboard as far as Camps Bay, and go to Kirstenbosch (R80 for four passengers), as well as providing the cheapest transport to the airport (R150 for a group of four).

Shuttle buses

A growth area in Cape Town are **shuttle buses**, which have to be booked, and which will pick you up from your accommodation. In some cases they run to a schedule, or can be chartered. They tend to be cheaper than metered taxis and take you door to door. One of the most useful services, organized in collaboration with Cape Town Tourism, runs on demand from the city centre and Waterfront visitor centres (during opening hours), going to Kirstenbosch National Botanical Gardens (R50 one-way), and also to the Table Mountain lower cableway station and other points of interest.

Reliable operators you can charter include Sun Tours & Shuttle (☎021 797 4646), which offers a 24-hour service between any two points on the peninsula, including the city to the airport (R250 for the first three passengers, then R60 per additional person).

Trains

Cape Town's suburban train service is run by **Metrorail** (timetable information ☎0800 656 463). The only route likely to be useful to tourists is the relatively reliable if slightly run-down line going through the southern suburbs and all the way down to False Bay seaboard from Cape Town station. Three other lines run east from Cape Town to Strand (through Bellville), to the Cape Flats, and to the outlying towns of Stellenbosch and Paarl; however, the journeys aren't recommended, as they run through some less salubrious areas of the Flats.

The service to the **False Bay seaboard** is undoubtedly one of the great urban train journeys of the world. It reaches the coast at Muizenberg and continues south to Simon's Town, sometimes so spectacularly close to the ocean that you can feel the spray and peer into rock pools. The stretch of the line to Fish Hoek is well served, with several trains an hour (Mon–Fri 5.10am–7.30pm every 15min, Sat 6.20am–6.45pm every 20min, Sun 5.50am–6.30pm roughly hourly, though more frequently during the summer). Services to Simon's Town go every 40–60 minutes. Even on these popular and tourist-friendly trains, though, never board an empty carriage.

Trains run overground, and there are no signposts to the stations on the streets. If you're staying in the southern suburbs, ask for directions at your accommodation. Tickets must be bought at the station before boarding. You're best off in the first-class carriages, which are reasonably priced (for example, Cape Town–Muizenberg is R10 one-way); curiously, there's no second class. Third class tends to be more crowded, and in the mornings can ring out with the harmonies of domestic workers singing their way to clean houses.

Intercity buses

Baz Bus operates an extremely useful hop-on/hop-off service daily between Cape Town and Port Elizabeth in both directions, via Mossel Bay, George, Knysna, Plettenberg Bay, Storms River and Jeffrey's Bay, with other stops possible along the N2. The service is aimed squarely at backpackers, with buses stopping off at hostels en route. The Cape Town–Port Elizabeth fare is R970 one-way, though there are also better-value seven-, fourteen- and 21-day passes costing R1020, R1920 and R2600. Bookings can be made directly (see opposite) or through hostels or the Baz offices at the central tourist offices in Cape Town. The only drawback of using the Baz buses, apart from occasionally erratic timing, is that the people you'll meet on them will almost exclusively be other backpackers, rather than locals.

South Africa's three established **intercity bus** companies are Greyhound, Intercape and Translux; between them, they reach most towns in the country. Travel on these buses (commonly called **coaches**) is safe, good value and very comfortable, the vehicles invariably equipped with air conditioning and toilets. Fares vary according to distances covered and the time of year, with peak fares corresponding approximately to school holidays; at other times you can expect about thirty percent off. As a rough indication you can expect to pay the following fares for one-way journeys from Cape Town: to Paarl, R100 (a 50km trip); Mossel Bay, R130 (389km); Port Elizabeth, R210 (738km).

Greyhound, Intercape and Translux intercity buses leave from around the interlinked complex in Cape Town's centre that includes the train station and **Golden Acre** shopping mall. Note that Intercape and Translux arrive on the northeast side of the station, off Adderley Street, while Greyhound arrives on the northwest side in Adderley itself.

Translux, Greyhound and Intercape also operate the no-frills budget buslines **City to City**, **Cityliner** and **Budgetliner** respectively, whose schedules and prices are listed on their main websites. There is also a host of small private companies about which information is thin on the ground; your best bet is to enquire at the bus station the day before you travel.

Intercity bus companies

Baz Bus ☎ 021 439 2323, ⊛ www.bazbus.com.
Greyhound ☎ 083 915 9000, ⊛ www.greyhound .co.za.
Intercape ☎ 0861 287 287, ⊛ www.intercape.co.za.
Translux ☎ 0861 589 282, ⊛ www.translux.co.za.

Intercity trains

The only rail service between Cape Town and the Garden Route is operated by **Rovos Rail** (☎ 021 421 4020, ⊛ www.rovos.co.za), which runs luxury trains between Cape Town and George (R5250 one-way for two sharing a suite), worth considering if you want to travel in plush surroundings – often through wonderful scenery – and don't mind paying through the nose for the privilege.

For details of intercity rail services between Cape Town and Durban or Pretoria, contact **Spoornet** (☎086 000 8888, ⓦwww .spoornet.co.za). It's worth noting that travelling by train is just about the slowest way of getting around South Africa: the journey from Cape Town to Johannesburg, for example, takes around 27 hours – compared to around eighteen hours by bus.

The above trains leave from the **train station** at the bottom of Adderley Street in the city centre.

Domestic flights

Driving the Garden Route in one direction – say out from Cape Town – and flying back from Port Elizabeth is a good (and commonly taken) option, especially if time is short. The flight takes just over an hour and fares compare favourably with the money you'll spend covering the distance in a rental car, stopping over at places en route. You'll generally have no trouble picking up a ticket for under R600 one-way, and the fare can be as little as R400 one-way, particularly if you're able to book well ahead.

By far the biggest airline offering domestic flights is **South African Airways** (SAA), with its associates **SA Airlink** and **SA Express** (reservations for the three are through SAA). There are a number of smaller airlines, of which the most significant are **British Airways Comair** and its budget subsidiary **kulula.com**.

None of the airlines offers discounts for students or pensioners, though, subject to availability, hefty discounts can be expected for booking two weeks ahead on SAA or BA Comair.

South African domestic airlines

1Time ☎0861 345 345, ⓦwww.1time.co.za.
Budget flights on a network that covers Johannesburg, Cape Town, Port Elizabeth, East London, Durban and Bloemfontein.
British Airways Comair ☎0860 435 922
ⓦwww.ba.com/travel/home/public/en_za. Flights from Johannesburg to Cape Town, Port Elizabeth and Durban; and Cape Town to Durban.
kulula.com ☎0861 585 852, ⓦwww.kulula.com.
Budget flights from Johannesburg to Cape Town, Durban, Port Elizabeth and George; and between Cape Town, Port Elizabeth and Durban.

Mango ☎0861 162 646, ⓦwww.flymango.com.
Cheap flights from Johannesburg to Cape Town and Durban; and from Cape Town to Jo'burg, Durban and Bloemfontein on SAA's budget airline.
Nationwide ☎0861 737 737, ⓦwww
.flynationwide.co.za. Flights from Johannesburg to Cape Town, Nelspruit (for Kruger National Park), Durban, Port Elizabeth and George; Cape Town to Port Elizabeth and Durban; and between Port Elizabeth and Durban.
South African Airways ☎0861 359 722,
ⓦwww.flysaa.com. Together with SA Airlink and SA Express, SAA serves the major hubs of Johannesburg, Cape Town and Durban.

Driving and cycling

Cape Town has good roads and several fast freeways that, outside peak hours (7–9am & 4–6pm), can whisk you across town in next to no time. The obvious landmarks of Table Mountain and the two seaboards make orientation straightforward, particularly south of the centre, and some wonderful journeys are possible. The most notable are the drives along the Atlantic seaboard to Hout Bay and **Chapman's Peak Drive**, a narrow, winding, cliff-edge road with the Atlantic breaking hundreds of metres below; and around the **Cape Point** section of the Table Mountain National Park, via the False Bay seaboard.

National roads (with an "N" prefix) and **provincial roads** (with an "R" prefix) in the rest of the Western Cape are of a generally high standard. The only time you're likely to encounter adverse conditions is during school holidays, particularly the Easter and December breaks, when the N1 and N2 become fairly congested, nerves fray, alcohol is copiously consumed and drivers' behaviour deteriorates accordingly.

Filling stations are frequent on the major routes of the country, and usually open 24 hours a day. Off the major routes, though, stations are less frequent, so fill up whenever you get the chance. Stations are rarely self-service; instead, poorly paid attendants fill up your car, check oil, water and tyre pressure if you ask them to, and often clean your windscreen even if you don't. A tip of at least R5 is always appreciated.

Regulations and driving tips

You drive on the **left-hand side**; **speed limits** range from 60kph in built-up areas

Cape Town parking

Car parks are dotted all over the place in Cape Town. To park on the street you pay one of the attendants who carry electronic ticketing devices. If you want to park in peace, head for one of the multistorey parking garages – there's one attached to the Golden Acre complex, and another at the north end of Lower Burg Street. Almost anywhere you park, bar the garages, you'll be expected to tip the **car guards** who purportedly look after parked vehicles and (whether you need help or not) direct you in and out of parking spots.

to 100kph on rural roads and 120kph on highways and major arteries. In addition to roundabouts, which follow the British rule of giving way to the right, there are four-way stops, where the rule is that the person who got there first leaves first, and you are not expected to give way to the right. Note that traffic lights are called **robots** in South Africa.

The only real challenge you'll face on the roads is **other drivers**. South Africa has among the world's worst road accident statistics – the result of reckless driving, drunken drivers (see p.41) or defective, overloaded vehicles. Keep your distance from cars in front, as domino-style pile-ups are common. Watch out also for overtaking traffic coming towards you. Overtakers often assume that you will head for the hard shoulder to avoid an accident (it is legal to drive on the hard shoulder, but be careful as poor South Africans frequently walk on it). If you do pull into the hard shoulder to let a car overtake, the other driver will probably thank you by flashing the hazard lights. If oncoming cars flash their headlights at you, it probably means that there is a speed trap up ahead.

Driving in and around Cape Town presents a few peculiarities all of its own. An unwritten rule of the road on the peninsula is that minibus taxis have the right of way – and will push in front of you without compunction. Don't mess with them: their vehicles are bigger than yours, they may carry handguns and will routinely run through amber lights as they change to red – as will many Capetonians.

Take care approaching a **freeway** in Cape Town: the on-ramps frequently feed directly into the fast lane, and Capetonians have no compunction in exceeding the 100kph freeway and 120kph highway

speed limits. Furthermore, there's often little warning of branches off to the suburbs, only the final destination of the freeway being signed. Your best bet is to plan your journey, and make sure you know exactly where you're going.

Foreign **driving licences** are valid in South Africa for up to six months provided they are printed in English. If you don't have such a licence, you'll need to get an International Driving Permit before arriving in South Africa (available from national motoring organizations). When driving, make sure you have your driving licence and passport on you at all times.

Motoring organizations

South Africa

Automobile Association (AA) ☎0800 01 01 01, ⓦwww.aasa.co.za.

UK

AA ☎0870/600 0371, ⓦwww.theaa.com.
RAC ☎0800/550055, ⓦwww.rac.co.uk.

Republic of Ireland

AA Travel ☎01/617 9988, ⓦwww.aaireland.ie.

US and Canada

American Automobile Association (AAA)
☎1-800/222-4357, ⓦwww.aaa.com. Each state has its own club – check the phone book for local details.
Canadian Automobile Association (CAA)
☎613/247-0117, ⓦwww.caa.ca. Each region has its own club – check the phone book for local details.

Australia and New Zealand

AAA Australia ☎02/6247 7311, ⓦwww.aaa .asn.au.
New Zealand AA ☎0800/500 444, ⓦwww.nzaa .co.nz.

Car and bike rental

Given Cape Town's scant public transport, **renting** a vehicle is the only convenient way of exploring the Cape Peninsula, and needn't break the bank. There are dozens of competing car-rental companies to choose from (see below). To get the best deal, either pick up one of the brochures at Cape Town Tourism office or look in the *Yellow Pages*.

Aroundabout Cars (see below), an independent national rental company based in Cape Town, offers great package deals and flexible pricing; the rate can be as low as R150 per day with unlimited mileage. It offers one-way rental (to drive down the Garden Route and fly back from Port Elizabeth, for example), but as with all rental agencies, there is an additional charge for this.

Competitive **motorhome** deals are offered by Drive Africa (see below) and if you're planning to be on the road for three months or longer, consider its rental-purchase agreement, under which you buy a car and the company guarantees to buy it back for an agreed price.

For **motorbike rental**, Le Cap Motorcycle Hire, B9 Edgemead Business Park, on the corner of Link Way & Southdale Road, Edgemead (☏072 259 0009, ⊛www.lecap .co.za), provides all the necessary gear and rents out serious bikes (from R400 daily, plus R1/km; weekly rental available).

For **cyclists**, one of the most popular – and hair-raising – road routes is along the narrow hairpins of Chapman's Peak Drive, which offer stupendous views of the Atlantic. There are also a number of dedicated mountain-biking routes in the peninsula's nature reserves. Mountain bikes are available from Rent 'n' Ride, 243 Main Rd, Three Anchor Bay (☏021 434 2382; R85 a day including helmet and lock; R1000 credit card deposit required), and Downhill Adventures, Shop 1 Overbeek Building, corner of Kloof and Orange streets (☏021 422 0388, ⊛www.downhilladventures.co.za), which offers similar rentals for R100 a day, and seven days' rental for the price of six.

Rental agencies

Alamo US ☏1-800/462-5266, SA ☏0800 011 323; ⊛www.alamo.com.

Aroundaboutcars ☏0860 422 4022, ⊛www .aroundaboutcars.com.
Auto Europe US & Canada ☏1-888/223-5555, ⊛www.autoeurope.com.
Avis US & Canada ☏1-800/331-1212, UK ☏0870/606 0100, Republic of Ireland ☏021/428 1111, Australia ☏13 63 33 or 02/9353 9000, NZ ☏09/526 2847 or 0800/655 111, SA ☏0861 021 111; ⊛www.avis.com.
Britz Australia ☏1800/331 454, NZ ☏0800/831 900, SA: Johannesburg ☏011 396 1860, Cape Town ☏021 982 5107; ⊛www.britz.com. One of the biggest rental outlets for camper vans and 4WDs.
Budget US ☏1-800/527-0700, Canada ☏1-800/268-8900, UK ☏0870/156 5656, Australia ☏1300/362 848, NZ☏0800/283 438, SA ☏0861 016 622; ⊛www.budget.com.
Dollar US ☏1-800/800-3665, Canada ☏1-800/229 0984, UK ☏0808/234 7524, Republic of Ireland ☏1800/575 800, SA: Johannesburg ☏011 390 3454, Cape Town ☏021 936 2121; ⊛www.dollar.com.
Drive Africa ☏ 021 447 1144, ⊛www .driveafrica.co.za.
Europcar US & Canada ☏1-877/940 6900, UK ☏0870/607 5000, Republic of Ireland ☏01/614 2800, Australia ☏393/306 160, SA ☏0800 011 344, ⊛www.europcar.com.
Hertz US & Canada ☏1-800/654-3131, UK ☏020/7026 0077, Republic of Ireland ☏01/870 5777, NZ ☏0800/654 321, ⊛www.hertz.com.
Holiday Autos US ☏866-392/9288, UK ☏0870/400 4461, Republic of Ireland ☏01/872 9366, Australia ☏299/394 433, SA ☏11 2340 597, ⊛www.holidayautos.co.uk. Part of the lastminute .com group.
Imperial ☏0861 131 000, ⊛www .imperialcarrental.co.za.
National US ☏1-800/CAR-RENT, UK ☏0870/400 4581, Australia ☏0870/600 6666, NZ ☏03/366 5574, SA ☏0800 011 323; ⊛www.nationalcar.com.
SIXT US ☏1-877/347-3227, Republic of Ireland ☏1850/206 088, UK ☏0800/4747 4227, SA ☏011 396 1080; ⊛www.e-sixt.com.
Suncars UK ☏0870/500 5566, Republic of Ireland ☏1850/201 416; ⊛www.suncars.com.
Tempest SA ☏0860 031 666, ⊛www .tempestcarhire.co.za.
Thrifty US & Canada ☏1-800/847-4389, UK ☏01494/751 500, Republic of Ireland ☏01/844 1950, Australia ☏1300/367 227, NZ ☏09/256 1405; ⊛www.thrifty.com.
Vineyard Car Hire ☏021 761 0671, ⓔvineyardcarhire@iafrica.com. Vehicles from as little as R290 a day (including 300km per day free), cheaper if you take the vehicle for a week or more.

Tours

A growing number of small companies offer niche cultural tours of the Cape Town area. The most popular of these are townships tours, which can safely get you around the African and coloured areas that were created under apartheid. Apart from this, a number of other outfits, listed below, can help you scratch beneath Cape Town's surface. Almost all these companies will pick you up from your accommodation and drop you off again at the end of the day.

Besides the companies listed below, Cape Town Tourism offers a **city walking tour** (Mon–Fri 11am & 1.30pm; R100), which covers the main sights and lasts an hour. There's a Bo-Kaap walk on Tuesdays and Thursdays at 9.30am (R75).

Tour operators

Day Trippers ☏ 021 511 4766, ⓦ www .daytrippers.co.za. Cycling from Scarborough into the Table Mountain National Park, with hikes down to Cape Point and a picnic, as well as tours to the usual sights such as the Winelands (all R425). The peninsula day-trip includes Hout Bay, with the option of a boat trip to Duiker Island to see the seals and Boulders Beach for the penguins.

Grassroute Tours ☏ 021 706 1006, ⓦ www .grassroutetours.co.za. Half-day trips (R350) include a visit to African and coloured townships, and walking tours of the Bo-Kaap, covering the *kramats* (Muslim

shrines). A day tour (R525) features a visit to Robben Island, with the cost of the ferry and island tour included in the price.

Hylton Ross Tours ☏ 021 511 1784, ⓦ www .hyltonross.com. Offers all major guided tours in and around Cape Town including Cape Winelands, townships, whale-watching and four-day Garden Route tours.

Our Pride ☏ 021 531 4291 or 082 446 7974, ⓦ www.bonanitours.co.za. Highly recommended tours on which you get to meet the people of the Bo-Kaap and District Six as well as the African townships and squatter camps. A full-day Winelands or Cape Point tour will cost R500, and half-day Gospel tours, which take in church services, are available.

Touch Africa Tours ☏ 021 705 3201 or 083 400 2090, ⓔ atouch@iafrica.com. Personalized tours of all the places of interest and beauty in and around Cape Town, with trips focusing on the Winelands, townships and local culture. Also offers tours and safaris anywhere in South and Southern Africa.

Health

You can put aside most of the health fears that may be justified in some parts of Africa; run-down hospitals and bizarre tropical diseases aren't typical of Cape Town and the Garden Route, and malaria isn't an issue here. All tourist areas boast generally high standards of hygiene and safe drinking water. The only hazard you're likely to encounter, and the one the majority of visitors are most blasé about, is the sun.

Public **hospitals** are fairly well equipped but are facing huge pressures, under which their attempts to maintain standards are unfortunately buckling. Expect long waits

and frequently indifferent treatment. Private hospitals or clinics, which are well up to British or North American standards, are usually a better option for travellers. You're likely to get more personal treatment and the costs are nowhere near as high as in the US – besides which, the expense shouldn't pose a problem if you're adequately insured.

Dental care in South Africa is well up to British and North American standards, and is generally no more expensive. You'll find dentists in Cape Town and most smaller towns, listed under "Dentists" in the main body of the telephone directory; doctors are listed under "Medical".

Inoculations

No specific inoculations are compulsory if you arrive in South Africa from the West. A yellow fever vaccination certificate is necessary if you've come from a country or region where the disease is endemic, such as Kenya, Tanzania or tropical South America.

The Hospital for Tropical Diseases in London advises that you ensure your polio and tetanus vaccinations are up to date. In addition, it recommends a course of shots against **typhoid** and an injection against **hepatitis A**, both of which can be caught from contaminated food or water – though this is extremely unlikely in the region covered by this guide.

If you decide to have an armful of jabs, start organizing them **six weeks** before departure. If you're going to another African country first and need the yellow fever jab, note that a yellow fever certificate only becomes valid ten days after you've had the shot.

Medical resources for travellers

UK & Ireland

Hospital for Tropical Diseases Travel Clinic ☎020/7387 4411 or 0845/155 5000, ⓦwww .thehtd.org. Reliable, up-to-date health briefings on South Africa and what precautions you should take. Also sells travellers' health products.
MASTA (Medical Advisory Service for Travellers Abroad) ☎0870/606 2782 or ⓦwww.masta.org. Online health briefs and details of UK clinics.
Travel Medicine Services ☎028/9031 5220. Travel advice before you leave.
Tropical Medical Bureau ☎1850/487 674, ⓦwww.tmb.ie. Advice on inoculations and other health issues relating to South Africa.

US & Canada

Canadian Society for International Health ⓦwww.csih.org. Extensive list of travel health centres.
CDC ⓦwww.cdc.gov/travel. Official US government travel health site.
International Society for Travel Medicine ⓦwww.istm.org. A list of travel health clinics throughout the world.

Australia & New Zealand

Travellers' Medical and Vaccination Centres ☎1300/658 844, ⓦwww.tmvc.com.au. Lists travel clinics in Australia and New Zealand.

Stomach upsets

Stomach upsets from food are rare. Salad and ice – the danger items in many other Third World countries – are both perfectly safe. As anywhere, though, don't keep food for too long, and be sure to wash fruit and vegetables as thoroughly as possible.

If you do get a **stomach bug**, the best cure is lots of water and rest. Papayas – the flesh as well as the pips – are a good tonic to offset the runs. Otherwise, most chemists should have name-brand anti-diarrhoea remedies, such as Lomotil.

Avoid jumping for **antibiotics** at the first sign of illness. Instead keep them as a last resort – they don't work on viruses and they annihilate your gut flora (most of which you want to keep), making you more susceptible next time round. Most tummy upsets will resolve themselves if you adopt a sensible fat-free diet for a couple of days, but if they do persist without improvement (or are accompanied by other unusual symptoms), then see a doctor as soon as possible.

The sun

The **sun** is likely to be the worst hazard you'll encounter in southern Africa, particularly if you're fair-skinned. The dangers of over-exposure to the sun, including the risk of skin cancer, are something white South Africans haven't yet caught onto, and locals still regard their tans as more important than their health.

Short-term effects of **overexposure** to the sun include burning, nausea and headaches. This usually comes from overeager tanning, which can leave you looking like a lobster. The fairer your skin, the slower you should take tanning. Start with short periods of exposure and **high protection sunscreen** (at least SPF 15), gradually increasing your time in the sun and decreasing the factor of the sunscreen. Many people with fair skins, especially those who freckle easily, should take extra care, starting with a very high factor screen (SPF 25–30) and continue using at least SPF 15 for the rest of their stay. There's no shame in smearing sensitive areas of your face with total block cream.

Overexposure to the sun can cause sunburn to the surface of the eye, inflammation of the cornea and can result in serious short- and long-term damage. Good **sunglasses** can reduce ultraviolet (UV) light exposure to the eye by fifty percent. A **broad-brimmed hat** is also recommended.

The last few measures are especially necessary for **children**, who should ideally be kept well covered at the seaside. Don't be lulled into complacency on cloudy days, when UV levels can still be high. UV-protective clothing is available locally, but it's best to buy before you arrive. If you don't come with this gear, make sure children wear T-shirts at the beach, and use SPF 30 sunscreen liberally and often.

Bites and stings

Bites and stings in South Africa are comparatively rare. **Snakes** are present, but hardly ever seen as they move out of the way quickly. The sluggish puff and berg adders are the most dangerous, because they often lie in paths and don't move when humans approach. The best advice if you get bitten is to note what the snake looked like and get yourself to a clinic or hospital. Most bites are not fatal and the worst thing you can do

is to panic: desperate measures with razor blades and tourniquets risk doing more harm than good.

Tick-bite fever is occasionally contracted from walking in the bush, particularly in long wet grass. The offending ticks can be minute and you may not spot them. Symptoms appear a week later – swollen glands and severe aching of the joints, backache and fever. The disease will run its course in three or four days. Ticks you may find on yourself are not dangerous, just repulsive at first. Make sure you pull out the head as well as the body (it's not painful). A good way of removing small ones is to smear Vaseline or grease over them, making them release their hold.

Scorpion stings and **spider bites** are painful but almost never fatal, contrary to popular myth. Scorpions and spiders abound, but they're hardly ever seen unless you turn over logs and stones. If you're collecting wood for a campfire, knock or shake it before picking it up. Another simple precaution when camping is to shake out your shoes and clothes in the morning before you get dressed.

Rabies is present throughout southern Africa. Be wary of animals and go immediately to a clinic if bitten. Rabies can be treated effectively with a course of injections.

Sexually transmitted diseases

HIV/AIDS and venereal diseases are widespread in southern Africa among both men and women, and the danger of catching the virus through sexual contact is very real. Follow the usual precautions regarding safer sex. There's no special risk from medical treatment in the country, but if you're travelling overland and you want to play it safe, take your own needle and transfusion kit.

The media

With two rather parochial daily English-language newspapers, plus a few magazines devoted mainly to entertainment and tourism, Cape Town's media are unlikely to blow anyone away. Radio and TV are dominated by South Africa's national broadcasters, with a few local radio offerings that include a talk station, a pioneering black community station and several others that play sounds from classical to pop.

Newspapers and magazines

Cape Town has two fairly boring daily English **newspapers**, owned by the same company: the **Cape Times** comes out on weekday mornings, while the afternoon **Cape Argus** also comes out during the week, but has Saturday and Sunday morning editions. The content of both papers is dominated by local news, with a smattering of national and international coverage. In addition there's the national **Business Day**, which is the best daily source of hard countrywide and international news.

Unquestionably the country's intellectual heavyweight ("heavy" being the operative word) is the **Mail & Guardian**, which comes out on Friday; it benefits enormously from its association with the London *Guardian* (from which it draws most of its international coverage). South Africa's **Sunday Times** can attribute the fact that it has the biggest circulation in the country – roughly half a million copies – to its well-calculated mix of solid investigative reporting, gossip, material from the British press and salacious rewrites of stories lifted from foreign tabloids. The **Sunday Independent**, part of the same stable as Britain's *Independent* newspapers and their Irish counterparts, projects a more thoughtful image than the *Sunday Times*, but is beginning to look a bit thin, with almost all its foreign news lifted from its sister papers. The **Sowetan**, targeted at a mainly black Jo'burg audience, is widely available across the country and provides a less exclusively white perspective on South African issues.

The best sources of **events listings** in Cape Town are the relatively unprepossessing supplements that appear in the mainstream press at the weekend. The *Top of the Times* supplement comes with Friday's *Cape Times*, and the *Good Weekend* pullout with the Saturday *Cape Argus*, but best of the bunch is the *Mail & Guardian*'s "Friday" supplement, which injects some attitude into its reviews and listings.

Both local papers and international publications such as *Time*, *Newsweek*, *The Economist* and the weekly overseas editions of the British *Daily Mail*, the *Telegraph* and the *Express* are available from corner stores and newsagents (especially the CNA chain).

Television

The South Africa Broadcasting Corporation's three TV channels churn out a mixed bag of domestic dramas, game shows, soaps and documentaries, filled out with lashings of familiar imports. **SABC 1**, **2** and **3** share the unenviable task of trying to deliver an integrated service, while having to split their time between the eleven official languages. English turns out to be most widely used, with SABC 3 broadcasting almost exclusively in the language, while SABC 2 and SABC 1 spread themselves thinly across the remaining ten languages, with a fair amount of English creeping in even here.

A selection of sports, movies, news and specialist channels are available to subscribers to the **M-Net** satellite service, which is piped into many hotels. South Africa's first and only free-to-air independent commercial channel **e.tv** won its franchise in 1998 on the promise of providing a showcase for local productions, a pledge it has signally failed to meet – its output has substantially consisted of uninspired and uninspiring imports.

There is no cable TV in South Africa, but **DSTV** (🌐www.dstv.co.za) offers a **satellite television** subscription service with selection of sports, movies, news and specialist channels, some of which are piped into hotels.

Radio

Given South Africa's low literacy rate and widespread poverty, it's no surprise that **radio** is its most popular medium. The SABC operates a national radio station for each of the eleven official language groups. The English-language national service, **SAfm** (104–107FM, 🌐www.safm.co.za), is of a generally decent standard, but perhaps too heavily laden with dull phone-in shows; its best offerings are the morning (5.30–8am) and evening (4–6pm) news programmes.

Cape Town stations include **Cape Talk** (567AM, 🌐www.capetalk.co.za), which puts out wall-to-wall chatter consisting of news, reviews, discussions and phone-ins of varying quality; and **Bush Radio** (89.5FM, 🌐www.bushradio.co.za), one of South Africa's first community stations, which attempts to actively involve members of Cape Town's black community, who were denied a voice under apartheid. Apart from hosting debates about significant issues to the community and broadcasting informative social documentaries, Bush Radio also pumps out great local music. A number of other local stations are devoted to 24-hour music, the most succesful being Heart **Radio** (109.4FM), which targets high-income black and coloured listeners in the Mother City with its hip mix of cool jazz fusion, funk, soul and R&B. Somewhat staid by comparison is **Fine Music Radio** (101.FM, 🌐www.fmr.co.za), which politely broadcasts the classics and a smattering of respectable jazz.

Festivals

Many of the Western Cape's events take place outdoors in summer, and make full use of the city's wonderful setting. They include the **Coon Carnival** (the name is widely used despite the pejorative connotations), a unique event rooted in the city's coloured community, while the **Kirstenbosch Summer Sunset Concerts**, which run from late December to early April, are a must. Winter tends to be quiet, but it does herald the arrival of calving whales, and in their wake the **Hermanus Whale Festival** in September, which packs out this small southern Cape settlement.

Tickets for many of the events listed below are available from Computicket (see p.164).

January

The Coon Carnival Jan 2 and the following three Saturdays. South Africa's longest and most raucous annual party, the Coon Carnival (aka the Cape Minstrel Carnival), brings over ten thousand spectators to Green Point stadium. It starts on Jan 2 for the Tweede Nuwe Jaar or "Second New Year" celebrations – an extension of New Year's Day unique to the Western Cape. Central to the festivities are the brightly decked-out coloured minstrel troupes that vie in singing and dancing contests. Tickets are best reserved through Computicket – you won't get such a good view if you buy tickets at the gate on the day. For more, see the box on p.106.

Maynardville Shakespeare Festival Mid-Jan to mid-Feb; more info on ☎021 421 7695. A usually imaginative production of one of the Bard's plays is staged each year in the beautiful setting of the Maynardville Open Air Theatre in Wynberg.

February

Cape Town Pride Pageant 🌐www.capetownpride.co.za. Series of gay-themed events over two weeks, kicking off with a pageant at which Mr and Mrs Gay Pride are crowned and taking in a bunch of parties and a street parade.

March

Cape Argus Pick'n Pay Cycle Tour First half of the month; ⓦ www.cycletour.org.za. The largest and arguably most spectacular, individually timed bike race in the world, with 30,000 participants on the 105km course – much of it along the ocean's edge – draws many thousands of spectators along the route. You can pick up entry forms from Pick'n Pay supermarkets, cycle shops or enter online. Book early as it is heavily subscribed.

Cape Town International Jazz Festival Last weekend of the month; ⓦ www.capetownjazzfest .com. Initiated in 2000 as the Cape Town counterpart of the world-famous North Sea Jazz Festival, this event has now come of age and acquired a local identity. Notable past performers have included Courtney Pine, Herbie Hancock, and African greats such as Jimmy Dludlu, Moses Molelekwa, Youssou N'Dour, Miriam Makeba and Hugh Masakela. Day/ weekend passes cost R300/440 from Computicket.

Klein Karoo Nasionale Kunstefees Last week of the month; ⓦ www.kknk.co.za. South Africa's largest Afrikaans arts and culture festival packs out the Karoo dorp of Oudsthoorn with festival goers, turning the otherwise dozy town into one big jumping, jiving party. If you don't understand Afrikaans, you'll still find enough English offerings as well as dance, music and other performance to keep you busy.

April

Two Oceans Marathon Second half of the month; information and entry forms from Old Mutual Two Oceans Marathon, PO Box 2276, Clareinch 7740 ☏ 021 671 9407, ⓦ www.twooceansmarathon.org .za. Another of the Cape's big sports events, this is in fact an ultra-marathon (56km), with huge crowds lining the route to cheer on the participants.

July

Knysna Oyster Festival First two weeks of the month; ⓦ www.oysterfestival.co.za. A fortnight of carousing and oyster-eating in all its forms along the Garden Route, kicked off with a road-bike race and closed with the Knysna Marathon.

September

Cape Town International Comedy Festival ⓦ www.comedyfestival.co.za. Africa's largest comedy festival showcases local and international acts in six separate programmes that include family-friendly mainstream performances, street theatre and the "Danger Zone" – risque sets that sail close to the

wind. And if your Afrikaans is up to it, you can take in humour in the new "Bek Lash" (tongue-lashing) programme.

Hermanus Whale Festival ⓦ www.whalefestival .co.za. To coincide with peak whale-watching season, the southern Cape town of Hermanus (see p.188) stages a week-long annual festival of arts and the environment towards the end of the month. Activities include plays, a craft market, a children's festival and live music.

November

Cape Town World Cinema Festival Ten days in the middle of the month; ⓦ www.sithengi.co.za. Exciting showcase of films from the developing world, with an emphasis on Africa and specifically South Africa. Material is also sourced from Latin America, Asia and the Black Diaspora and includes movies by independent directors from Europe and North America. Screenings take place at venues all over Cape Town.

Kirstenbosch Summer Sunset Concerts Every Sun from end of the month to early April; ☏ 021 799 8999, ⓦ www.sanbi.org/frames/whatsonfram .htm. Among the musical highlights of the Cape Town calendar are the popular concerts held on the magnificent lawns of the botanical gardens at the foot of Table Mountain. Performances begin at 5.30pm and cover a range of genres, from local jazz to classical music. Come early to find a parking place, bring a picnic and some Cape fizz – and enjoy. Tickets available at the gate.

Out in Africa South African Gay & Lesbian Film Festival ⓦ www.oia.co.za. Purportedly the most popular movie festival in the country screens gay- and lesbian-themed international and local productions over the first fortnight of the month.

December

Mother City Queer Projects Early in the month (see p.158). A hugely popular party attracting thousands of gay revellers, for which a vast venue is chartered. Outlandish get-ups, multiple dance floors and a mood of sustained delirium make this event a real draw.

Carols by Candlelight at Kirstenbosch Cape Town ☏ 021 799 8783. The botanical gardens' annual carol-singing and Nativity tableaux – staged on the Thursday to Sunday before Christmas – is a Cape Town institution, drawing crowds of families with their picnic baskets. The gates open at 7pm and the singing kicks off at 8pm.

Parks, reserves and wilderness areas

The region covered by this book is punctuated at either end by a major national park: at the western extreme is the Table Mountain National Park, a patchwork of wilderness that covers the full extent of the Cape Peninsula; and at the eastern end is Addo Elephant National Park which, apart from the pachyderms, is also home to lions, buffaloes, leopards and rhinos – the only such major game reserve in the southern half of the country.

Between the two lie a series of rewarding provincial reserves and national parks, many of which are worth incorporating into any journey across the Southern Cape. In addition to the two already mentioned, among the top wilderness areas in the country are **De Hoop Nature Reserve**, with its massive dunefields and its status as one of the best places in the world for land-based whale watching; and the **Tsitsikamma National Park**, which attracts large numbers of visitors for its ancient forests, cliff-faced oceans and the dramatic Storms River Mouth.

Top parks and wildlife areas

PARK	PRINCIPAL FOCUS	DESCRIPTION & HIGHLIGHTS	DETAILS
Addo Elephant National Park	Endangered species	The only Big Five national park in the southern half of the country, known for its three-hundred-strong elephant herd	p.272
Agulhas National Park	Marine and coastal ecology	Rugged southernmost tip of Africa with rich plant biodiversity and significant archeological sites	p.198
De Hoop Nature Reserve	Marine mammals and coastal fynbos	Whales, massive dunes, *fynbos* and spectacular coastline	p.200
Goukamma Nature and Marine Reserve	Marine and coastal ecology	River and estuary with some of the highest vegetated dunes in South Africa	p.223
Robberg Marine and Nature Reserve	Rocky headland ecology	Hikeable promontory that is a fine example of the interaction of plant and animal life on southern coastal headlands and a good place to spot seals at work	p. 240
Table Mountain National Park (formerly Cape Peninsula National Park)	The natural areas of the peninsula	Boasts extraordinarily rich and diverse flora and fauna that lives in the wild areas forming a large part of Cape Town, including Table Mountain, the Boulders Beach penguin colony and the Cape of Good Hope	Chapters 3 & 6
Tsitsikamma National Park	Marine and coastal	Cliffs, tidal pools, deep gorges and evergreen forests; offers snorkelling, scuba and forest trails	p. 244
Wilderness National Park	Marine and coastal	Lakes, rivers, lagoons, forest, *fynbos*, beaches and the sea	p.222

All the national parks mentioned in this guide fall under the aegis of **South African National Parks** (**SANParks**; PO Box 787, Pretoria 0001; street address 643 Leyds St, Muckleneuk, Pretoria; ☎012 343 9111, ⓦwww.sanparks.org). A few other reserves mentioned, including De Hoop and Goukamma, are run by **Cape Nature Conservation** (general enquiries: CNC Cape Town Tourism Desk, Pinnacle Building, Castle and Burg streets, ☎021 426 0723 or 021 423 9611, ⓦwww.capenature.org.za). Only a few national parks and CNC wilderness areas are game reserves; the chart on p.39 details what to expect from the major parks.

Entry fees and accommodation

National parks charge a **conservation fee** which is usually **payable daily**. At most this comes to R80 per day for foreign visitors (R40 for children), though citizens of the Southern Africa Development Community (SADC; includes Angola, Botswana Congo, Lesotho, Malawi, Mauritius, Mozambique, Namibia, South Africa, Swaziland, Tanzania, Zambia and Zimbabwe) pay half the adult foreigner's rate. South African residents pay a quarter of the adult foreigner's rate.

In the case of Table Mountain National Park there is a daily conservation fee of R55 (children R10), which applies to all visitors. Entry into Cape Nature Conservation reserves generally costs around R25 (children R12.50) a day per person, irrespective of nationality.

Most national parks and some of the Cape Nature Conservation reserves have **accommodation**, which generally has a pleasantly rustic atmosphere in keeping with the wilderness surrounds. Units vary from cottages at De Hoop Nature Reserve that go for R350 for two people a night, to pretty comfortable, fully-equipped en-suite cottages and chalets at Wilderness, Tsitsikamma and Addo Elephant national parks that cost around R500–600 a night for a couple. Some reserves have family units that sleep four or more, and you'll find **camping facilities** at virtually all the reserves.

You can **book** park accommodation in advance (to stay in high season, do so several months in advance) through SANParks if the park in question is managed by them or, in the case of a Cape Nature Conservation site, through the park itself (details in the guide and on its website). Note that if you try booking for South African National Parks over the phone you could well be in for a long wait; contacting them online is recommended.

Crime and personal safety

Despite horror stories of sky-high crime rates, most people visit South Africa without incident; be careful, but don't be paranoid. This is not to underestimate the issue – crime is probably the most serious problem facing the country. However, once you realize crime is disproportionally concentrated in the poor African and coloured townships, its scale becomes less daunting.

Protecting property and "security" are major national obsessions, and it's difficult to imagine what many South Africans would discuss at their dinner parties if the problem disappeared. A substantial percentage of middle-class homes subscribe to the services of armed private security firms. The other obvious manifestation of this obsession is the huge number of alarms, high walls and electronically controlled gates you'll find, not just in the suburbs, but even in less deprived areas of some townships.

Guns are openly carried by police – and often citizens. In many high streets you'll spot firearms shops rubbing shoulders with places selling clothes or books, and you'll come across notices asking you to deposit your weapon before entering the premises.

If you fall victim to a **mugging**, you should take very seriously the usual advice not to resist, and do as you're told. The chances of being mugged can be greatly minimized by using common sense and following a few simple rules, listed in the box on p.42.

Drugs and drink-driving

Dagga (pronounced like "dugger" with the "gg" guttural, as in the Scottish pronunciation of "loch") is cannabis in dried leaf form. South Africa's most widely produced and widely used drug, it is fairly easily available and the quality is generally good – but this doesn't alter the fact that it is illegal.

Strangely, for a country that sometimes seems to be on one massive binge, South Africa has laws that prohibit drinking in public – not that anyone pays any attention to them. The **drink-drive laws** are routinely and brazenly flouted, making the country's roads the one real danger you should be concerned about. People routinely stock up

their cars with booze for long journeys and even at filling stations you'll find places selling liquor. Levels of alcohol consumption go some way to explaining why, during the Christmas holidays, over a thousand people die in an annual orgy of carnage on the roads. However, concerted attempts are being made to deal with the problem, including the widely publicized Arrive Alive campaign and the confiscation of the vehicles of drunk drivers and drivers travelling well over the speed limit.

Sexual harassment

South Africa's extremely high incidence of **rape** doesn't as a rule affect tourists. In fact women are very unlikely to need to fend off the unwanted attentions of men. However, at heart the majority of the country's males, regardless of race, hold on to fairly sexist attitudes. Sometimes your eagerness to be friendly may be taken as a sexual overture – always be sensitive to potential crossed wires and unintended signals.

Women should take care while travelling on their own, and should avoid hitchhiking or walking alone in deserted areas. This applies equally to Cape Town, the countryside or anywhere after dark. Minibus taxis should be ruled out as a means of transport after dark, especially if you're not exactly sure of local geography.

The police

For many black South Africans, the **South African National Police** (SANP) still carry strong associations of collaboration with apartheid and a lot of public relations work has still to be done to turn the police into a genuine people's law enforcement agency. Poorly paid, shot at (and frequently hit),

Safety tips

In general:
- try not to look like a tourist.
- dress down.
- don't carry a camera or video openly in cities.
- avoid wearing jewellery or expensive watches.
- leave your designer shades at home – they are sometimes pulled off people's faces.
- if you are accosted, remain calm and cooperative.

When on foot:
- grasp bags firmly under your arm.
- don't carry excessive sums of money on you.
- don't put your wallet in your back trouser pocket.
- always know where your valuables are.
- don't leave valuables exposed (on a seat or the ground) while having a meal or drink.
- develop an awareness of what people in the street around you are doing.
- don't let strangers get too close to you – especially people in groups.
- in big cities, travel around in pairs or groups.

On the road:
- lock all your car doors, especially in cities.
- keep rear windows sufficiently rolled up to keep out opportunistic hands.
- never leave anything worth stealing in view when your car is unattended.

On the beach:
- take only the bare essentials.
- don't leave valuables, especially cameras, unattended.
- safeguard car keys by pinning them to your swimming gear, or putting them in a waterproof wallet or splash box and taking them into the water with you.

At ATMs:
Cash machines are favourite hunting grounds for sophisticated conmen. Never underestimate their ability and don't get drawn into any interaction at an ATM, no matter how well spoken, friendly or distressed the other person appears. If they claim to have a problem with the machine, tell them to contact the bank. Don't let people crowd you or see your personal identification number (PIN) when you withdraw money; if in doubt, go to another machine. Finally, if your card gets swallowed, report it without delay.

underfunded, badly equipped, barely respected and demoralized, the police keep a low profile. If you ever get stopped, at a roadblock for example (one of the likeliest encounters), always be courteous. And if you're driving, note that under South African law you are required to carry your **driving licence** at all times.

If you are robbed, you will need to report the incident to the police, who should give you a case reference for insurance purposes – though don't expect too much crime-cracking enthusiasm, or to get your property back.

Travel essentials

Costs

The most expensive thing about visiting South Africa is getting there. Once you've arrived, you're likely to find it a relatively inexpensive destination. How cheap you find South Africa will depend partly on exchange rates at the time of your visit – in the decade after becoming fully convertible (after the advent of democracy in South Africa) the rand has seen some massive fluctuations against sterling, the dollar and the euro.

When it comes to **daily budgets**, your biggest expense is likely to be accommodation. If you're willing to stay in backpacker lodges and self-cater, you should be able to get by on under £15/$30/€20 a day. If you stay in B&Bs and guesthouses, eat out once a day, and have a snack or two you should budget for at least double that. In luxury hotels and game lodges, expect to pay upwards of £100/US$200/€150 a day. Extras such as car rental, outdoor activities, horse-riding and safaris will add to these figures substantially. While most **museums** and **art galleries** impose an entry fee, it's usually quite low: only the most sophisticated attractions charge more than £1/$2/€1.50.

Electricity

South Africa's **electricity** supply runs at 220/230V, 50Hz AC. Sockets take unique round-pinned plugs; see ⓦ www.kropla.com for details. Most hotel rooms have sockets that will take 110V electric shavers, but for other appliances US visitors will need an adaptor. It's worth noting that because it failed to build new power stations ten years ago, South Africa now has a shortage of electricity and power cuts of up to two hours are a real possibility at any time.

Entry requirements

Nationals of the EU, the US, Canada, Australia and New Zealand don't require a **visa** to enter South Africa. As long as you carry a passport that is valid for at least six months and with at least two empty pages you will be granted a temporary visitor's permit, which allows you to stay in South Africa for up to ninety days. All visitors should have a valid return ticket; without one, you may be required to pay the authorities the equivalent of your fare home (the money will be refunded after you have left the country). Visitors may also need to prove that they have sufficient funds to cover their stay.

Applications for **visa extensions** must be made at one of the main offices of the Department of Home Affairs, where you will be quizzed about your intentions and your funds. In Cape Town, go to 56 Barrack St (☎ 021 462 4970). The Department also has offices in a number of towns – check in the telephone directory or on its website (ⓦ www.home-affairs.gov.za/regions.asp), and make sure that the office you're intending to visit is able to grant extensions.

South African diplomatic missions abroad

Australia Corner of State Circle and Rhodes Place, Yarralumla, Canberra, ACT 2600 ☎ 02/6272 7300, ⓦ www.sahc.org.au.
Canada 15 Sussex Drive, Ottawa, Ontario K1M 1M8 ☎ 613/744-0330, ⓦ www.southafrica-canada.ca.
Netherlands Wassenaarseweg 40, 2596 CJ, The Hague ☎ 070/392 4501, ⓦ www.zuidafrika.nl.
New Zealand c/o the High Commission in Australia.
UK Consular Section, 15 Whitehall, London SW1A 2DD ☎ 020/7925 8900, ⓦ www.southafricahouse.com.
US 3051 Massachusetts Ave NW, Washington, DC 20008 ☎ 202/232-4400, ⓦ www.saembassy.org. Consulates: 333 E 38th St, 9th floor, New York, NY 10016 ☎ 212/213-4880, ⓦ www.southafrica-newyork.net; 6300 Wilshire Blvd, Suite 600, Los Angeles, CA 90048 ☎ 323/651-0902, ⓦ www.link2southafrica.com.

Insurance

It's wise to take out an **insurance policy** to cover against theft, loss and illness or injury prior to visiting South Africa. A typical travel insurance policy usually provides cover for the loss of baggage, tickets and – up to a certain limit – cash or cheques, as well as cancellation or curtailment of your journey. Most of them exclude so-called **dangerous sports** unless an extra premium is paid: in South Africa this can mean scuba diving, whitewater rafting, windsurfing, horse-riding, bungee jumping and paragliding. In addition to these it's well worth checking whether you are covered by your policy if you're hiking, kayaking or game viewing on safari, all activities people commonly take part in when visiting South Africa. Many policies can be chopped and changed to exclude coverage you don't need – for example, sickness and accident benefits can often be excluded or included at will. If you do take **medical coverage**, ascertain whether benefits will be paid as treatment proceeds or only after you return home, and if there is a 24-hour medical emergency number. When securing **baggage cover**, make sure that the per-article limit will cover your most valuable possession. If you need to make a claim, you should keep receipts for medicines and medical treatment, and in the event you have anything stolen, you must obtain an official statement from the police.

Rough Guides has teamed up with Columbus Direct to offer you **travel insurance** that can be tailored to suit your needs. Products include a low-cost **backpacker** option for long stays; a **short break** option for city getaways; a typical **holiday package** option; and others. There are also annual **multi-trip** policies for those who travel regularly, with variable levels of cover available. Different sports and activities (trekking, scuba diving, abseiling, etc) can usually be covered if required. See our website – Ⓦwww.roughguidesinsurance .com for eligibility and purchasing options. Alternatively, UK residents should call ☎0870/033 9988; US citizens should call ☎1-800/749-4922; Australians should call ☎1-300/669 999. All other nationalities should call ☎+44 870/890 2843.

Internet

Finding somewhere to access the **Internet** will seldom be a problem in South Africa:

cybercafés are found even in relatively small towns, and most **backpacker hostels** and hotels have Internet and email facilities. If you are carrying your own computer or palm-top device you'll also be able to take advantage of the wireless hotspots at a small (but growing) number of cafés and accommodation.

Mail

The deceptively familiar feel of South African post offices can lull you into expecting an efficient British- or US-style service. In fact, **post** within the country is slow and unreliable, and money and valuables frequently disappear en route. Expect domestic delivery times from one city to another of about a week – longer if a rural town is involved at either end. **International airmail** deliveries are often quicker, especially if you're sending or receiving at Johannesburg or Cape Town – the cities with direct flights to London. A letter or package sent by surface mail can take anything up to six weeks to get from South Africa to London.

Most towns of any size have a **post office**, generally open Monday to Friday 8.30am to 4.30pm and Saturday 8am to 11.30am (closing earlier in some places). The ubiquitous private **PostNet** outlets (Ⓦwww .postnet.co.za) offer many of the same postal services as the post office and more, including **courier services**. Courier companies like Federal Express (☎0800 033 339, Ⓦwww.fedex.com/za) and DHL (☎0860 345 000, Ⓦwww.dhl.co.za) are more expensive and available only in the larger towns, but far more reliable than the mail.

Stamps are available at post offices and also from newsagents, such as the CNA chain as well as supermarkets. Postage is relatively inexpensive – it costs about R4 to send a postcard by airmail to anywhere in the world, while a small letter costs about R5 to send. You'll find **poste restante** facilities at the main post office in most larger centres, and in many backpackers' hostels.

Maps

Numerous decent **foldout maps** of Cape Town are available, both abroad and from South African bookshops and the CNA chain of newsagents. Typically these cover the city centre, the City Bowl Suburbs and the Atlantic Seaboard as far as Sea Point in some detail, with a schematic map of the whole Cape Peninsula on the reverse.

If you're planning to explore beyond the confines of the city centre, you'd do well to invest in one of the detailed **street atlases**, available at the ubiquitous CNA and at most South African bookshops. MapStudio publishes two such books, one of which is good for the centre and most of the suburbs, but doesn't cover Simon's Town, and a more comprehensive one which covers all the peninsula's streets and also provides coverage of the Winelands towns. MapStudio also publish the *Official Visitor's Guide to the Cape Peninsula*, which is cheaper and far more slender than the street atlases and consists of a selection of the street maps that are most likely to be needed by tourists.

For explorations along the **Garden Route**, or anywhere else in the Western Cape, MapStudio's *Western Cape Tourist Atlas* is worth considering. It provides selective street maps of Cape Town and gives street layouts of many of the province's smaller towns, as well as a motoring atlas of the whole province.

For **hiking**, Peter Slingsby's series of five large-scale Cape Peninsula National Park maps is invaluable, available from the bigger CNA outlets and at most decent bookshops. These comprehensively cover the Table Mountain National Park, which runs down the peninsula from the city centre in the north to Cape Point in the south, showing all the hiking trails and the access points from the southern suburbs.

Money

South Africa's currency is the **rand** (R), often called the "buck", divided into 100 **cents**. Notes come in R10, R20, R50, R100 and R200 denominations and there are coins of 5, 10, 20 and 50 cents, as well as R1, R2 and R5. At the time of writing, the **exchange rate** was hovering at just around R14 to the pound sterling, R7 to the US dollar, R10 to the euro and R6 to the Australian dollar.

In Cape Town, you'll find banks all over the place, while along the Garden Route, Whale Coast and R62 all but the tiniest settlement will have a **bank** where you can **change money** swiftly and easily. **Banking hours**

are Monday to Friday 9am to 3.30pm, and Saturday 9am to 11am; the banks in smaller towns usually close for lunch. In major cities, some banks operate bureaux de change that stay open until 7pm. Outside banking hours, some hotels will change money, although this entails a fairly hefty commission. You can also change money at branches of American Express and Rennies Foreign Exchange (ⓦ www.bidvestbank.co.za).

Cards and traveller's cheques

Credit and debit cards are the most convenient way to access your funds in South Africa. Most international cards can be used to withdraw money at **automatic teller machines** (ATMs), open 24 hours a day in the cities and elsewhere. Ask your bank which option you should choose for your card when the machine asks for the account type (cheque, savings, transmission or credit). Plastic can come in very handy for hotel bookings and for paying for more mainstream and upmarket tourist facilities, and is essential for car rental. Visa and Mastercard are the cards most widely accepted in major cities.

Traveller's cheques make a useful backup as they can be replaced if lost or stolen. American Express, Visa and Thomas Cook are all widely recognized brands; both US dollar and sterling cheques are accepted in South Africa.

Traveller's cheques and plastic are useless if you're heading into remote areas, where you'll need to carry **cash**, preferably in a very safe place, such as a leather pouch or waist-level money belt you can keep under your clothes.

Opening hours and holidays

The working day starts and finishes early in South Africa: shops and businesses generally open on weekdays at 8.30am or 9am and close at 4.30pm or 5pm. In small towns, many places close for an hour over lunch. Many **shops** and businesses close around noon on Saturdays, and most shops are closed on Sundays. However, in every neighbourhood, you'll find small shops and supermarkets where you can buy groceries and essentials after hours.

Some establishments have summer and winter opening times. In such situations, you can take winter to mean April to August or September, while summer constitutes the rest of the year.

School holidays in South Africa can disrupt your plans, especially if you want to camp, or stay in the national parks and the cheaper end of accommodation (self-catering, cheaper B&Bs, etc), all of which are likely to be booked solid during those periods. If you do travel to South Africa over the school holidays, book your accommodation well in advance, especially for the national parks.

The longest and busiest holiday period is **Christmas (summer)**, which for schools stretches over most of December and January. Flights and train berths can be hard to get from December 16 to January 2, when many businesses and offices close for their annual break. You should book your flights – long-haul and domestic – as early as six months in advance for the Christmas period. The inland and coastal provinces stagger their school holidays, but as a general rule the remaining school holidays roughly cover the following periods: **Easter**, mid-March to mid-April; **winter**, mid-June to mid-July; and **spring**, late-September to early October. Exact dates for each year are given on the government's information website: @ www .info.gov.za/aboutsa/schoolcal.htm.

Phones

South Africa's telephone system, operated by the state monopoly, **Telkom**, generally works well. Public phone booths are found in every city and town, and are either coin- or card-operated. While **international calls** can be made from virtually any phone, it helps to have a phone card, as you'll be lucky to stay on the line for more than a minute or two for R20. Phone cards come in R15, R20, R50, R100 and R200 denominations, available at Telkom offices, post offices and newsagents.

Mobile phones (referred to locally as cell phones or simply cells) are extremely widely used in South Africa, with more mobile than land-line handsets now in use in the country. The competing networks – Vodacom, MTN, Cell C and VirginMobile – cover all the main areas and the national roads connecting them.

You can use a GSM/tri-band phone from outside the country in South Africa, but you will need to arrange a **roaming agreement** with your provider at home; be warned this is likely to be expensive. A far cheaper alternative is to buy a **local SIM card** which replaces your home SIM card while you're in South Africa. (For this to work, you'll need to check that your phone hasn't been locked to your home network.) The local SIM card contains your South African phone number, and you pay for airtime with **prepaid cards**. Very inexpensive starter packs (R100 or less) containing a SIM card and some airtime can be bought from the ubiquitous mobile phone shops and a number of other outlets, including supermarkets and the CNA chain of newsagents and supermarkets.

Calling home from South Africa

To dial **out of South Africa**, the international access code is ☎00. Remember to omit any initial zero in the number of the place you're phoning.
Australia ☎61
Republic of Ireland ☎353
New Zealand ☎64
UK ☎44
US & Canada ☎1

Taxes

Value-added tax (VAT) of fourteen percent is levied on most goods and services, though it's usually already included in any quoted price. Foreign visitors can claim back VAT on any goods over R250. To do this, you must present an official tax receipt for the goods, a non-South African passport and the purchased goods themselves, at the airport just before you fly out. You need to complete a VAT refund control sheet (VAT 255) which is obtainable at international airports. For further information contact the VAT Refund Administrator (☎011 394 1117, @ www .taxrefunds.co.za).

Time

There is only one **time zone** throughout the region, two hours ahead of GMT year round. If you're flying from anywhere in Europe, you shouldn't experience any jet lag.

South African public holidays

Many shops and tourist-related businesses remain open over public holidays, although often with shorter opening hours. Christmas Day and Good Friday, when most of the country shuts down, are the only exceptions. The main holidays are:

New Year's Day January 1
Human Rights Day March 21
Good Friday, Easter Monday
  variable
Freedom Day April 27
Workers' Day May 1

Youth Day June 16
National Women's Day August 9
Heritage Day September 24
Day of Reconciliation December 16
Christmas Day December 25
Day of Goodwill December 26

Tipping

Ten to fifteen percent of the tab is the normal **tip** at restaurants and for taxis – but don't feel obliged to tip if service has been shoddy. Keep in mind that many of the people who'll be serving you will be black South Africans, who rely on tips to supplement a meagre wage on which they support huge extended families. Porters at hotels normally get about R5 per bag. At South African garages and filling stations, someone will always be on hand to fill your vehicle and clean your windscreen, for which you should tip around R5. It is also usual at hotels to leave some money for the person who services your room. Many establishments, especially private game lodges, take (voluntary) communal tips when you check out – by far the fairest system, which ensures that all the low-profile staff behind the scenes get their share.

Tourist information

Cape Town and the Garden Route are experiencing a boom in tourism, and you should have no difficulty finding information about the region over the Internet as well as maps, books and brochures before you leave. The best source of information about the city itself is **Cape Town Routes Unlimited** (@www.tourismcapetown.com), which markets Cape Town and the Western

Any South African land line has a ten-digit number incorporating the old three-digit area code at the start. Calling a land line requires you to dial all ten digits even if the number you're dialling has the same area code as yours.

Cape, including the Garden Route. Cape Town Tourism has two excellent **information bureaus**: the city-centre visitor centre (Mon–Fri 8am–6pm, Sat 8.30am–2pm & Sun 9am–1pm; ℡021 487 6800), at the corner of Burg and Castle streets, a five-minute walk two blocks west of the station; and the Clocktower Precinct visitor centre (daily 9am–9pm; ℡021 405 4500), in a fabulous office at the V&A Waterfront next to the Nelson Mandela Gateway to Robben Island. Both centres operate comprehensive accommodation and activity **booking services**, have a swanky coffee shop, a book shop and cybercafé, as well as lots of brochures and very cheap city maps. Bookings for national parks can also be made here.

Along the **Garden Route**, nearly every town has some sort of **tourist office** – sometimes connected to the museum, municipal offices or library – where you can pick up local maps, lists of B&Bs and travel advice. They are generally open Monday to Friday 8.30am to 5pm, with many offices also open on Saturdays and Sundays. Some offices in smaller towns close between 1pm and 2pm, while in the bigger centres some have extended hours.

In this fast-changing country, the best way of finding out what's happening is often by word of mouth, and for this **backpacker hostels** are invaluable. If you're seeing South Africa on a budget, the useful noticeboards, constant traveller traffic and largely helpful and friendly staff you'll encounter in backpacker hostels will greatly smooth your travels.

There are countless **guidebooks** on walks around Cape Town, hikes up Table Mountain, dive sites, fishing locations, surfing breaks and windsurfing spots. For the best-stocked shelves and nicest atmosphere, head to one of the Exclusive Books stores (see p.150). You'll also find useful books on all aspects of South Africa at the secondhand bookshops down Long Street.

If there's an office of **South African Tourism**, the official organization promoting the country, near you, it's worth visiting for its free map and information on hotels and organized tours. Alternatively, you can check out its website ⓦwww.southafrica.net, which includes content specific to users in South Africa, the UK, the USA, Canada, Germany, the Netherlands and France.

South African Tourism offices abroad

Australia Suite 301, Level 3, 117 York St, Sydney NSW 2000 ⓣ02/9261 5000.
Netherlands Jozef Isarëlskade 48A, NL-1072 SB, Amsterdam ⓣ0900/202 0433.
UK 6 Alt Grove, Wimbledon, London SW19 4DZ ⓣ0870/155 0044.
US 500 5th Ave, 20th Floor, Suite 2040, New York NY 10110 ⓣ1-800/593-1318.

Travellers with disabilities

Facilities for **disabled travellers** in South Africa are not as sophisticated as those found in the First World, but they're sufficient to ensure you have a satisfactory visit. By accident rather than design, you'll find pretty good accessibility to many buildings, as South Africans tend to build low (single-storey bungalows are the norm), with the result that you'll have to deal with fewer stairs than you may be accustomed to. As the car is king, you'll frequently find that you can drive to, and park right outside, your destination.

There are **organized tours** and holidays specifically for people with disabilities, and **activity-based packages** for disabled travellers to South Africa are increasingly available. These packages offer the possibility for wheelchair-bound visitors to take part in safaris, sport and a vast range of adventure activities, including whitewater rafting, horse-riding, parasailing and zip-lining. Tours can either be taken as self-drive trips or packages for large groups. The contacts below will be able to put you in touch with South Africa travel specialists.

If you want to be more independent on your travels, it's important to know where you can expect help and where you must be self-reliant, especially regarding transport and accommodation. It's also vital to know your limitations, and to make sure others know them. If you do not use a wheelchair all the time but your walking capabilities are limited, remember that you are likely to need to cover greater distances while travelling (often over rougher terrain and in hotter temperatures) than you are used to. If you use a wheelchair, have it serviced before you go and take a repair kit with you.

Titch Tours (26 Station Rd, Rondebosch 7700, Cape Town ⓣ021 689 4151, ⓦwww .titchtours.co.za) has a portfolio that includes programmes in South Africa for physically disabled and visually impaired people. You could also visit ⓦ**www.access-able.com**, a US-based website with resources for travellers with disabilities.

A growing number of popular tourist attractions are being designed to facilitate **disabled access**. For example, the Kirstenbosch Botanical Gardens has Braille and wheelchair trails. Cape Town's Waterfront, one of the city's top attractions, has specially designed parking bays as well as ramps and broad walkways around the development itself.

South Africa has a growing number of **hotels** with facilities for disabled people. South African Tourism publishes an accommodation guide, available from all its offices (see p.48), which includes up-to-date information about disability-friendly establishments.

Rental of cars with hand controls and automatic transmission can be arranged for no extra charge through Avis or Budget (see p.32), but a month's prior notice is recommended. A Special Parking Disc, which allows **parking** concessions to people with severe mobility impairment, can be obtained through Cape Town's traffic department in Plantation Road, Ottery (ⓣ021 799 5100). You should bring any appropriate disc or badge from your home country, which can be used to get a temporary disc.

The City

The City

1

The city centre

Cape Town's city centre has a stunning physical setting, dominated by the omnipresent Table Mountain to the southwest and the pounding Atlantic to the northeast. It is the most historically intense district in the country and the oldest urban area in South Africa, and while the prime attractions lie elsewhere, the city centre does have some interesting museums and its streets still pulse with the cultural fusion that has been Cape Town's hallmark since its founding in 1652.

Strand Street marks the edge of Cape Town's original beachfront (though you'd never guess it today), with the **Lower City Centre** to the northeast and the **Upper City Centre** to the southwest. The obvious orientation axis, however, is **Adderley Street**, which connects the main train station in the north with St George's Cathedral. Southwest of here is the symbolic heart of Cape Town (and arguably South Africa), with the **Houses of Parliament**, museums, historic buildings, archives and De Tuynhuys, the Western Cape office of the President, arranged around the **Gardens**.

Northwest of Adderley Street is the closest South Africa gets to a European quarter – a tight network of streets with cafés, buskers, bookstores, street stalls and antique shops congregating around the pedestrianized **St George's Mall** and **Greenmarket Square**. Parallel to St George's Mall, **Long Street**, the quintessential Cape Town thoroughfare, is lined with colonial Victorian buildings that house pubs, bistros, nightclubs, backpacker lodges, bookshops and antique dealers, whose wrought-iron balconies afford glimpses of Table Mountain and the sea. The **Bo-Kaap**, or Muslim quarter, three blocks further northwest across Buitengragt, exudes a piquant contrast to this, with its minarets, spice shops and cafés selling curried snacks.

Southeast of Adderley Street and close to one another lie three historically loaded sites. The **Castle of Good Hope** – the oldest building in South Africa – is an indelible symbol of Europe's colonization of South Africa, a process whose death knell was struck from nearby **City Hall**, the attractive Edwardian building from which Nelson Mandela made his first speech after being released. South of the castle lie the poignantly desolate remains of **District Six**, the coloured inner-city suburb that was razed in the name of apartheid.

The Upper City Centre

Once *the* place to shop in Cape Town, **Adderley Street**, lined with handsome buildings from several centuries, is still worth a stroll today. Its attractive streetscape

The language of colour

It's striking just how un-African Cape Town looks and sounds. Lying halfway between East and West, Cape Town drew its population from Africa, Asia and Europe, and traces of all three continents are found in the genes, language, culture, religion and cuisine of South Africa's coloured population. The dominant language of the city is **Afrikaans** (a close relative of Dutch), the only "European" language to evolve outside Europe. Although English is universally spoken and understood, Afrikaans is the mother tongue of a large proportion of the city's **coloured** residents, as well as a good number of whites.

The term "coloured" is fraught with confusion, but in South Africa doesn't have the same connotations as in Britain and the US; it refers to South Africans of mixed race. This comes as a surprise to most visitors, who assume that it's all black and white in South Africa, when in fact issues of ethnicity and language are extremely complex. Most brown-skinned people in Cape Town (over fifty percent of the population), and many others throughout the country, are coloureds, with slave and Khoikhoi ancestry going back to the seventeenth to early nineteenth centuries.

In the late nineteenth century, Afrikaans-speaking whites, fighting for an identity, sought to create a "racially pure" culture by driving a wedge between themselves and coloured Afrikaans-speakers. They reinvented Afrikaans as a "white man's language", eradicating the supposed stigma of its coloured ties by substituting Dutch words for those with Asian or African roots. In 1925, the white dialect of Afrikaans became an official language alongside English, and the dialects spoken by coloureds were treated as comical deviations from correct usage.

For Afrikaner nationalists this wasn't enough, and after the introduction of apartheid in 1948, they attempted to codify perceived racial differences. Under the **Population Registration Act**, all South Africans were classified as white, coloured or Bantu (the apartheid term for Africans). The underlying assumption was that these distinctions were based on objective criteria. For the apartheid authorities, it seemed fairly clear

has been wantonly blemished by a series of large 1960s shopping centres, but just minutes away from crowded malls, among the streets and alleys around Greenmarket Square, you can still find some human scale and historic texture.

Low-walled channels, ditches, bridges and sluices once ran through Cape Town, earning it the name Little Amsterdam. During the nineteenth century, the canals were buried underground, and in 1850 Heerengracht (Gentlemen's Canal), formerly a waterway that ran from the Company Gardens down to the sea, was renamed Adderley Street (see box, p.55). There's little evidence of the canals today, except in name – one section of the street is still called Heerengracht and a parallel street to its west is called Buitengragt (sometimes spelled Buitengracht after the Dutch style, and meaning the Outer Canal).

The destruction of old Cape Town continued well into the twentieth century, with the razing of many of the older buildings. One of the ugliest newcomers is the **Golden Acre shopping complex**, dominating the northeastern (harbour) end of Adderley Street. Built in the 1970s, it's Cape Town's unavoidable public transport hub today, employing an unfriendly network of subways and walkways to draw together all the major road and rail services into town. Inside sit the **Golden Acre Ruins**, the remains of southern Africa's oldest colonial structure – a reservoir built in 1663 by the Dutch. All that's left is a small bit of wall behind glass, and you might easily walk past and think that the builders who worked on the complex forgot to finish the plastering. Although the mall itself and its environs are anything but picturesque, here you do get an authentic taste of ordinary Capetonians doing their who was "Bantu" and who was white, but the coloureds posed particular problems. First, they weren't homogenous so, to accommodate this, the **Coloured Proclamation Act** of 1959 defined eight categories of coloured: Cape Coloured; Malay (Muslim); Griqua; Chinese; Indian; Other Indian; Other Asiatic; and Other Coloured. For reasons of expediency related to trade, Japanese people were defined as "honorary white".

The second difficulty surrounding coloureds was the fact that their appearance spans a range from those who are indistinguishable from whites to those who look like Africans. A number of coloureds managed successfully to reinvent themselves as whites, and apartheid legislation made provision for the racial reclassification of individuals. Between 1983 and 1990, nearly five thousand "Cape Coloureds" were reclassified as "white" and over two thousand Africans were reclassified as "Cape Coloured". Notorious tests were employed – one, for example, where a pencil would be placed in a person's hair and twirled; if the hair sprang back they would be regarded as coloured, but if it stayed twirled they were white.

Far more than mere semantics, these classifications became fundamental to what kind of life a person could expect. There are numerous cases of families in which one sibling was classified coloured, while another was termed white and could then live in comfortable white areas, enjoy good employment opportunities (many jobs were closed to coloureds), and have the right to send their children to better schools and universities. Many coloured professionals, on the other hand, were evicted from houses they owned in comfortable suburbs such as Claremont, which overnight were declared white.

With the demise of apartheid, the make-up of residential areas is shifting – and so is the thinking on ethnic terminology. Some people now reject the term "coloured" because of its apartheid associations, and refuse any racial definitions; others, however, proudly embrace the term, as a means of acknowledging their distinct culture, with its slave and Khoikhoi roots.

shopping, something you won't find at the sanitized Victoria and Alfred Waterfront. On Saturday mornings, if you exit onto Adderley Street, you'll often encounter the spirited sounds of busking brass bands or choirs. Among the sidewalks and pedestrianized sections outside, which run down to the station, there's a closely packed **flea market** offering curios, crafts and electronic goods (but watch your wallet). A little further south lies a **flower market**, run by members of the Bo-Kaap Muslim community.

Two grandiose bank buildings stand on opposite sides of Adderley Street; the fussier of the two is the erstwhile **Standard Bank**, fronted by Corinthian columns and covered with a tall dome – a temple to the partnership of empire and finance. Recently renovated, at a cost of around R25m, it is now a trendy, very upmarket 220-seater **restaurant**, complete with palm trees to the ceiling, and named *Riboville* after a horse that won the Durban July race in 1974. The **First National Bank**, completed in 1913, was the last South African building designed by Sir Herbert Baker (see box, p.112). If you pop in for a quick look, still in place inside the banking hall you'll find a solid timber circular writing desk with the original inkwells, resembling an altar.

The Groote Kerk

Sometimes described as "Cape Gothic" in style, the **Groote Kerk** (Great Church; daily 9.30am–4.30pm; free), diagonally opposite the First National

Bank, is essentially a Classical building with Gothic and Egyptian elements. Designed and built between 1836 and 1841 by Hermann Schutte (see p.97), a German who became one of the Cape's leading early nineteenth-century architects, the church replaced an earlier Baroque one that had become too small for the swelling ranks of the Dutch Reformed congregation at the Cape. The beautiful freestanding clock tower adjacent to the newer building is a remnant of the original church.

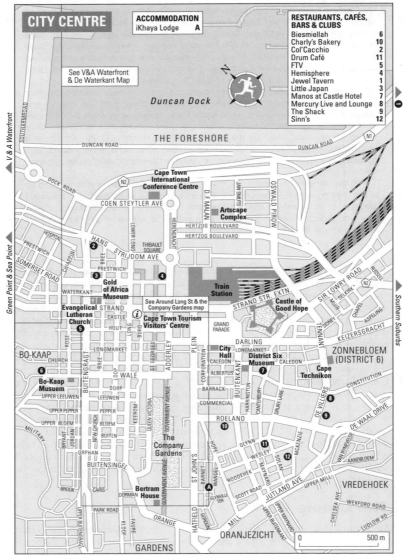

CITY CENTRE

ACCOMMODATION
iKhaya Lodge   A

RESTAURANTS, CAFÉS, BARS & CLUBS

Biesmiellah	6
Charly's Bakery	10
Col'Cacchio	2
Drum Café	11
FTV	5
Hemisphere	4
Jewel Tavern	1
Little Japan	3
Manos at Castle Hotel	7
Mercury Live and Lounge	8
The Shack	9
Sinn's	12

See V&A Waterfront & De Waterkant Map

Duncan Dock

THE FORESHORE

DUNCAN ROAD   DUNCAN ROAD

Cape Town International Conference Centre

COEN STEYTLER AVE

Artscape Complex

HERTZOG BOULEVARD
HERTZOG BOULEVARD

Gold of Africa Museum

Train Station

Castle of Good Hope

Evangelical Lutheran Church

Cape Town Tourism Visitors' Centre

See Around Long St & the Company Gardens map

GRAND PARADE

DARLING

BO-KAAP

City Hall

District Six Museum

ZONNEBLOEM (DISTRICT 6)

Bo-Kaap Museum

Cape Technikon

ROELAND

The Company Gardens

VREDEHOEK

Bertram House

ORANJEZICHT

0   500 m

GARDENS

V & A Waterfront

Green Point & Sea Point

Southern Suburbs

▼ *Cable Station, Camps Bay & Atlantic Seaboard*

The naming of Adderley Street

Although the Dutch used Robben Island (see p.77) as a political prison, the South African mainland only narrowly escaped becoming a second Australia, a **penal colony** where British felons and enemies of the state could be dumped. By the 1840s, "respectable Australians" were lobbying for a ban on the transportation of criminals to the Antipodes, and the British authorities responded by trying to divert convicts to the Cape.

In 1848, the British ship *Neptune* set sail from Bermuda for Cape Town with a cargo of 282 prisoners. There was outrage when news of its departure reached Cape Town; five thousand citizens gathered on the Grand Parade the following year to hear prominent liberals denounce the British government, an event depicted in *The Great Meeting of the People at the Commercial Exchange* by Johan Marthinus Carstens Schonegevel, which hangs in the Rust-en-Vreugd Museum (see p.67). When the ship docked in September 1849, governor Sir Harry Smith forbade any criminal from landing while, back in London, politician **Charles Adderley** successfully addressed the House of Commons in support of the Cape colonists. In February 1850, the *Neptune* set off for Tasmania with its full complement of convicts, and grateful Capetonians renamed the city's main thoroughfare **Adderley Street**.

The soaring space created by the vast vaulted ceiling and the magnificent pulpit, a masterpiece by sculptor Anton Anreith and carpenter Jan Jacob Graaff, are worth stepping inside for. The pulpit, supported on a pair of sculpted lions with gaping jaws, was carved by Anreith after his first proposal, featuring Faith, Hope and Charity, was rejected by the church council for being "too Popish".

Slave Lodge ✳ ✳ ✳ ·

At the top corner of Adderley Street, just as it veers sharply northwest into Wale Street, is **Slave Lodge** (Mon–Fri 10am–4.30pm, Sat 9am–1pm; R7, children R2), previously known as the Cultural History Museum. For nearly two centuries – more than half the city's existence as an urban settlement – Cape Town's economic and social structures were founded on slavery (see box, p.57), and Slave Lodge was built in 1679 for the Dutch East India Company (VOC) – the largest single slaveholder at the Cape – to house its human chattels. By the 1770s, almost a thousand slaves were held at the lodge. Under VOC administration, the lodge also became the Cape Colony's main brothel, its doors thrown open to all comers for an hour each night. Following the British takeover and the auctioning of the slaves, the lodge became the Supreme Court in 1810, and remained so until 1914, after which the building was used as government offices, though in 1966 it became a museum.

Slave Lodge houses an eclectic collection of antiquities and artefacts from around the world, as well as good displays on the Cape and an exhibition, still evolving, about slavery. A couple of small but interesting displays can be found on the ground floor, to the left of the entrance hall. The first deals with **Khoisan hunter-gatherers**, the original inhabitants of the Cape (and South Africa), focusing on their knowledge of plants and herbs, many of which are still in use today. An adjacent room houses "**186 Years of Slavery**", centred around a model of the lodge as it was three hundred years ago. A poignant memorial plaque on one wall lists, by first name only, the slaves who endured the appalling conditions of the fortress-like structure, and a map on another wall refers to sites in the city centre with slave connections: where they worked, worshipped, were sold, punished and executed.

▲ Slave Lodge

Behind Slave Lodge, on the traffic island in Spin Street, a simple and inconspicuous plinth marks the site of the **Old Slave Tree**, under which slaves were bought and sold.

Slavery at the Cape

Slavery was officially **abolished** at the Cape in 1838, but its legacy lives on in South Africa. The country's **coloured inhabitants**, who make up fifty percent of Cape Town's population, are largely descendants of slaves and indigenous Khoisan people, and some historians argue that apartheid was a natural successor to slavery. Certainly, domestic service, still widespread throughout South Africa, and certain labour practices such as the "*dop* system", in which workers on some wine farms are partially paid in rations of cheap plonk, can be traced directly back to slavery.

By the end of the eighteenth century, the almost 26,000-strong slave population of the Cape exceeded that of the free burghers. Despite the profound impact this had on the development of social relations in South Africa, it remained one of the most neglected topics of the country's history, until the publication in the 1980s of a number of studies on slavery. There's still a reluctance on the part of most coloureds to acknowledge their slave origins.

Few if any slaves were captured at the Cape for export, making the colony unique in the African trade. Paradoxically, while people were being captured elsewhere on the continent for export to the Americas, the Cape administration, forbidden by the VOC (see p.282) from enslaving the local indigenous population, had to look further afield. Of the 63,000 slaves imported to the Cape before 1808, most came from East Africa, Madagascar, India and Indonesia, representing one of the broadest cultural mixes of any slave society. This diversity initially worked against the establishment of a unified group identity, but eventually a **Creolized culture** emerged which, among other things, played a major role in the development of the **Afrikaans** language.

Long Street

Parallel to Adderley Street, buzzing Long Street is one of Cape Town's most diverse thoroughfares, a great place for leisurely exploration, with views of Table Mountain, Signal Hill and Lion's Head, as well as glimpses of the sea. When it was first settled by Muslims some three hundred years ago, Long Street marked Cape Town's boundary; by the 1960s, it had become a sleazy alley of drinking holes and whorehouses. Miraculously, it's all still here, but with a whiff of gentrification. Mosques still coexist with bars, brothels trade above old-fashioned locksmiths, pawnbrokers function alongside porn shops, while gun shops sit next to delicatessens, antique dealers, craft shops and cafés. Also here are a number of excellent secondhand and Africana bookshops.

A Cape Town institution, established in 1906, the **Long Street Baths** (Mon–Sat 7am–8pm, Sun 8am–6pm) occupy the top of the road, where it hits Buitensingel (Outer Crescent). The steam rooms are great for relaxing on a winter's day and are open separately to women (Tues 9am–1pm, Thurs & Sat 9am–6pm) and men (Tues 1–7pm, Wed & Fri 9am–1pm, Sun 8am–noon). A four-hour session (R105) gets you a private cubicle and towel, access to the dry or wet steam rooms, the plunge pool and a short massage. Use of the pool costs R12.

Further north, an unmistakable landmark at no. 185, the **Palm Tree Mosque** (not open to the public) is fronted by a lone palm tree, its fronds caressing the upper storey. Significant as the only surviving eighteenth-century house in the street, it was erected in 1780 by Carel Lodewijk Schot as a private dwelling. The house was bought in 1807 by Frans van Bengal, a member of the local Muslim community, and a freed slave, Jan van Boughies, who became its imam, turning the upper floor into a mosque and the lower into his living quarters.

Across Wale Street is one of Cape Town's most intriguing places for African crafts, and one of the easiest to miss. The inconspicuous frontage of the

▲ Long Street

Pan African Market (Mon–Fri 9am–5pm) at no. 76 belies the three-floor warren of passageways and rooms, which burst at the hinges with traders selling vast quantities of art and artefacts from all over the continent. Hidden among less inspiring offerings you'll find terrific masks from West Africa, brass leopards from Benin as well as contemporary South African art textiles. Also gathered here are leathersmiths, tailors, hair-braiders, a drum instructor and vendors selling CDs and musical instruments.

The South African Missionary Meeting-House Museum

Further towards the harbour end of Long Street at no. 40, the **South African Missionary Meeting-House Museum** (Mon–Fri 9am–4pm;

Gold of Africa Museum

Evangelical Lutheran Church Complex

Koopmans-De Wet House

Waterfront Buses

Train Station

STRAND

STRAND EXTN.

Cape Town Tourism Visitors' Centre (i)

CASTLE STREET

Golden Acre Shopping Mall

South African Missionary Meeting House Museum

HOUT STREET

BUITENGRAGT

LOOP STREET

BURG STREET

ADDERLEY STREET

PARLIAMENT STREET

PLEIN

GRAND PARADE

Flower Market

SHORTMARKET STREET

First National Bank

Waterfront Buses

Pan African Market

BREE

Greenmarket Square

LONGMARKET STREET

Groote Kerk

CORPORATION

Old Town House

ST GEORGE'S MALL

CHURCH STREET

LONG STREET

WALE STREET

SPIN STREET

Slave Lodge

St George's Cathedral

DORP STREET

Houses of Parliament

Palm Tree Mosque

LEEUWEN

South African Library

KEEROM STREET

QUEEN VICTORIA STREET

Tuynhuys

ROELAND

PEPPER STREET

LOOP

BREE

BLOEM

PLEIN

BUITEN STREET

CHURCH

NEW

Company Gardens

GOVERNMENT AVENUE

Long Street Baths

BUITENSINGEL

Long Street Baths

PADDOCK AVENUE

South African National Gallery

SA Jewish Museum

Holocaust Centre

ST JOHN'S

Great Synagogue

KLOOF STREET

ORANGE

GREY'S PASS

South African Museum

Bertram House

District Six Museum

Bo-Kaap

ACCOMMODATION

Cape Heritage Hotel	**B**
Cape Town Hollow Hotel	**H**
Cat & Moose	**G**
Long Street Backpackers	**D**
Metropole Hotel	**A**
St Paul's B&B Guest House	**F**
Travellers' Inn	**E**
Tudor Hotel	**C**

0   50 m

CITY CENTRE: AROUND LONG ST & THE COMPANY GARDENS

RESTAURANTS, PUBS & CLUBS

95 Keerom	19	Ginja	1	Masala Dosa	10	On Broadway	3
Addis in Cape	9	Ivy Garden	7	M-Bar and		The Purple Turtle	5
Africa Café	4	Jo'burg	18	Lounge	A	Rhodes House	17
Bukhara	8	Kennedy's	20	Mexican Kitchen		Royale	21
Chrome	13	The Lounge	15	Café	16	Savoy Cabbage	2
Five Flies	11	Mama Africa	14	Mr Pickwick's	12	Sutra	6

free) was the first missionary church in the country, where slaves were taught literacy and instructed in Christianity. This exceptional building, completed in 1804 by the South African Missionary Society, boasts one of the most beautiful frontages in Cape Town. Dominated by large windows, the facade is broken into three bays by four slender Corinthian pilasters surmounted by a gabled pediment. Inside, an impressive Neoclassical timber **pulpit** perches high above the congregation on a pair of columns, framing an inlaid image of an angel in flight.

The society itself was founded in 1799 by Reverend Vos, who was alarmed that many slaveholders neglected the religious education of their property. The owners believed that once their slaves were baptized, their emancipation became obligatory – a misunderstanding of the law, which merely stated that Christian slaves couldn't be sold. Vos, himself a slaveholder, saw proselytization to those in bondage as a Christian duty, and even successfully campaigned to end the prohibition against selling Christian slaves, which he believed was "a great obstacle in this country to the progress of Christianity", because it encouraged owners to avoid baptizing their human chattels.

Cape Heritage Square

From Long Street, if you head northwest down Shortmarket Street, you'll come to **Cape Heritage Square**, the largest restoration project ever undertaken in Cape Town. The square is home to the *Cape Heritage Hotel* as well as a conglomeration of restaurants, wine merchants, art galleries, jewellers and fashion shops, many of which are housed in a complex dating back to 1771. Set around a courtyard, in which the oldest known (and still fruit-bearing) vine in South Africa continues to flourish, the square is worth visiting for a glimpse of the superb restoration work.

The Bo-Kaap

Minutes from Parliament, on the slopes of Signal Hill, is the **Bo-Kaap**, one of Cape Town's oldest and most fascinating residential areas. Its streets are characterized by brightly coloured nineteenth-century Dutch and Georgian terraces, which conceal a network of alleyways that are the arteries of its **Muslim community**. The Bo-Kaap harbours its own strong identity, made all the more unique by the destruction of District Six, with which it had much in common. A particular dialect of Afrikaans is spoken here, although it is steadily being eroded by English.

Bo-Kaap residents are descended from dissidents and slaves imported by the Dutch in the sixteenth and seventeenth centuries. They became known collectively as "**Cape Malays**", a term you'll still hear, even though it's a complete misnomer: most originated from Africa, India, Madagascar and Sri Lanka, with fewer than one percent actually from what's now Malaysia.

The easiest way to get to the Bo-Kaap is by foot along Wale Street, which trails up from the south end of Adderley Street and across Buitengragt, to become the main drag of the Bo-Kaap. There's a deceptively quaint feel to the area: apart from Wale Street, this is not really a place to explore alone. It's better to join one of several **tours** that take in the museum and walk you around the district. The best (and cheapest, at R120 including the museum entrance fee) is run by Bo-Kaap Guided Tours (℡021 422 1554 or 082 423 6932, ℮shireen .narkedien@gmail.com); it lasts two hours and is operated by residents of the area, whose knowledge goes beyond the standard tour-guide script.

A good place to head for is the **Bo-Kaap Museum**, 71 Wale St (Mon–Sat 9am–4pm; R5, children R1; ⓦwww.iziko.org.za/bokaap), near the Buitengragt end. It consists mainly of the family house and possessions of Abu Bakr Effendi, a nineteenth-century religious leader brought out from Turkey by the British in 1862 as a mediator between feuding Muslim factions. He became an important member of the community, founded an Arabic school and wrote a book in the local vernacular – now regarded as possibly the first book to be published in what can be recognized as Afrikaans. The museum also has exhibits exploring the local brand of Islam, which has its own unique traditions and nearly two dozen *kramats* (shrines) dotted about the peninsula.

One block south of the museum, at Dorp Street, is the **Auwal**, South Africa's first official mosque, founded in 1797 by the highly influential Imam Abdullah ibn Qadi Abd al-Salam (commonly known as Tuan Guru or Master Teacher), a Moluccan prince and Muslim activist who was exiled to Robben Island in 1780 for opposing Dutch rule in the Indies. While on the island he transcribed the Koran from memory and wrote several important Islamic commentaries, which provided a basis for the religion at the Cape for almost a century. On being released in 1792, he began offering religious instruction from his house in Dorp Street, before founding the Auwal nearby. Ten more mosques, whose minarets give spice to the quarter's skyline, now serve the Bo-Kaap's ten thousand residents.

A small Muslim shantytown, tucked away next to the old quarry below the cemetery, brings the immediacy of South Africa's housing crisis right to the edge of the city centre. Modern, low-cost developments, looking down from the heights of Signal Hill onto the photogenic Bo-Kaap townscape, have helped alleviate the community's housing shortage, but have added nothing to the architectural charm of the protected historic core bounded by Dorp and Strand streets, and Buitengragt and Pentz streets. Furthermore, many Bo-Kaap residents, tempted by the high prices their cottages can fetch, have sold them to outsiders who value the central location and picturesque quality of the area, a process which is seen to be diluting the Muslim lifestyle in the area.

Greenmarket Square and around

Turning southeast from Long Street into Shortmarket Street, you'll skim the edge of **Greenmarket Square**, which is worth a little exploration to take in the cobbled streets, coffee shops and grand buildings. As its name implies, the square started as a vegetable market, though it spent many ignominious years as a car park. Human life has returned, and it's now home to a flea market, selling crafts, jewellery and hippie clobber. This is also one of the few places in Cape Town to buy from Congolese and Zimbabwean traders, selling masks and malachite carvings.

The Old Town House ✱✱ ✱

On the western side are the solid limewashed walls and small shuttered windows of the **Old Town House** (Feb–Dec daily 10am–5pm; free), entered from Longmarket Street. Built in the mid-1700s, this beautiful example of Cape Dutch architecture, with a fine interior, has seen duty as a guardhouse, a police station and Cape Town's city hall. Today it houses the **Michaelis collection** of minor but interesting seventeenth-century Dutch and Flemish landscape paintings.

The seventeenth century was one of great prosperity for the Netherlands and has been referred to as the Dutch "Golden Age", during which the Netherlands threw off the yoke of its Spanish colonizers and sailed forth to establish colonies of its own in the East Indies, and of course at the Cape. The wealth that trade brought to the Netherlands stimulated the development of the arts, with paintings reflecting the values and experience of Dutch Calvinists. A notable example is **Frans Hals'** *Portrait of a Woman*, hanging in the upstairs gallery. Executed in shades of brown, relieved only by the merest hint of red, it reflects the Calvinist aversion to ostentation. The sitter for the picture, completed in 1644, would have been a contemporary of the settlers who arrived at the Cape some eight years later. Less dour and showing off the wealth of a middle-class family is the beautiful *Couple with Two Children in a Park*, painted by **Dirck Dirckz Santvoort** in the late 1630s, in which the artist displays a remarkable facility for portraying sensuous fabrics, which glow with reflected light; you can almost feel the texture of the lace trimming.

Other paintings, most of them quite sombre, depict mythological scenes, church interiors, still lifes, landscapes and seascapes, the latter being very close to the seventeenth-century Dutch heart, often illustrating vessels belonging to the Dutch East India Company or the drama of rough seas encountered by trade ships. A tiny **print room** on the ground floor has a small selection of works by Daumier, Gillray and Cruikshank, as well as one of **Goya**'s most famous works, *El Sueño de la Razón Produce Monstruos* (The Sleep of Reason Produces Monsters).

Small visiting exhibitions also find space here, and good evening classical concerts are a regular thing. You can pick up the Town House's quarterly newsletter, which lists forthcoming events. Tickets are available on the door immediately prior to the event.

St George's Mall and Church Street

Heading southeast from the square, you come to **St George's Mall**, a pedestrianized road that runs northeast from Wale Street to Thibault Square, near the train station. Coffee shops, snack bars and lots of street traders and buskers make this a more pleasant route between the station and the Company Gardens than Adderley Street, while dancers, drummers, choirs and painters add a certain buzz to the place. At the southern end of the mall, at Queen Victoria and Wale streets, **St George's Cathedral** is interesting more for its history than for its Herbert Baker Victorian Gothic design; on September 7, 1986, **Desmond Tutu** hammered on its doors symbolically demanding to be enthroned as South Africa's first black archbishop. Three years later, he heralded the last days of apartheid by leading thirty thousand people from the cathedral to the City Hall, where he coined his now famous slogan for the new order: "We are the rainbow people!" he told the crowd, "We are the new people of South Africa!"

Church Street (which crosses the mall towards its southern end) and its surrounding area abound with antique dealers, and on the pedestrianized section (where it is crossed by Burg Street), you'll find an informal antique market. Prices are competitive and you may pick up unusual pieces of jewellery, bric-a-brac, Africana and even old sheet music.

Government Avenue and the Company Gardens

A stroll down **Government Avenue**, the southwest extension of Adderley Street, makes for one of the most serene walks in central Cape Town. This oak-lined, pedestrianized boulevard runs past the rear of Parliament through the Gardens, and its benches are frequently occupied by snoring *bergies* (tramps).

Looming on your right as you enter the northeastern end of the avenue, the **South African Library** (Mon–Fri 9am–6pm, Sat 9am–1pm; free) houses one of the country's best collections of antiquarian historical and natural history

Lord Charles Somerset and De Tuynhuys

Under the governorship of **Lord Charles Somerset** (1814–26), an official process of Anglicization at the Cape included the enforcement of English as the sole language in the courts, but equally important was his private obsession with architecture, which saw the demolition of the two Dutch wings of **De Tuynhuys** in Government Avenue. Imposing contemporary English taste, Somerset reinvented the entire garden frontage with a Colonial Regency facade, characterized by a veranda sheltering under an elegantly curving canopy, supported on slender iron columns.

books, covering southern Africa. Built with the revenue from a tax on wine, it opened in 1822 as one of the first free libraries in the world.

Stretching from here to the South African Museum, the **Company Gardens** were the initial *raison d'être* for the Dutch settlement at the Cape. Established in 1652 to supply fresh greens to Dutch East India Company ships travelling between the Netherlands and the East, the gardens were initially worked by imported slave labour. This proved too expensive, as the slaves had to be shipped in, fed and housed, so the Company opted for outsourcing: it phased out its farming and granted land to free burghers, from whom it bought fresh produce. At the end of the seventeenth century, the gardens were turned over to botanical horticulture for Cape Town's growing colonial elite. Ponds, lawns, landscaping and a crisscross web of oak-shaded walkways were introduced. It was during a stroll in these gardens that Cecil Rhodes (a statue of whom you'll find here) first plotted the invasion of Matabeleland and Mashonaland (which together became Rhodesia and subsequently Zimbabwe). He also introduced an army of small, furry colonizers to the gardens – North American grey squirrels. Today the gardens are full of local plants, the result of long-standing European interest in Cape botany; experts have been sailing out since the seventeenth century to classify and name specimens. The gardens are still a pleasant place to meander, and feature an outdoor café.

Continuing along Government Avenue from the South African Library, past the rear of Parliament, you can peer through an iron gate to see the grand buildings and tended flowerbeds of **De Tuynhuys**, the office (but not residence) of the president. During the presidency of Nelson Mandela, one party of tourists stood amazed as the great man, who is renowned for his common touch, strolled across the lawns for a friendly chat.

A little further along, the tree-lined walkway opens out into a formal gravel area with ponds and statues, around which are sited the National Gallery, the Jewish Museum and the Great Synagogue to the southeast, and the South African Museum and Planetarium to the northwest.

The South African National Gallery

Not far from the southern end of Government Avenue, where it's joined by the tiny Gallery Lane, the **South African National Gallery** (Tues–Sun 10am–5pm; R10, children R5, free on Sat) is an essential port of call for anyone interested in the local art scene, and includes a small but excellent permanent collection of contemporary South African art. Displays change every three months as the number of items far exceeds the capacity of the exhibition space, but one of the pieces that regularly makes an appearance is **Jane Alexander**'s powerfully ghoulish plaster, bone and horn sculpture, *The Butcher Boys* (1985–6), created at the height of apartheid repression. It features three life-size figures with distorted faces that exude a chilling passivity, expressing the artist's interest in the way violence is conveyed through the human figure. Alexander's work is representative of "**resistance art**", which exploded in the 1980s, broadly as a response to the growing repression of apartheid. Resistance art, produced by committed people from all ethnic groups, was inspired by the idea that artists had a responsibility to engage politically; it spanned a wide range of subject matter, styles and media. **Paul Stopforth**'s powerful graphite-and-wax triptych, *The Interrogators* (1979), featuring larger-than-life-size portraits of three notorious security policemen, is a work of monumental hyperrealism.

Many other artists, unsurprisingly for a culturally diverse country, aren't easily categorized; while works have tended to borrow from Western traditions, their themes and execution are uniquely South African. The late **John Muafangelo** employed Biblical imagery in works such as *The Pregnant Maria* (undated), producing highly stylized, almost naive black-and-white linocuts, while in *Challenges Facing the New South Africa* (1990), **Willie Bester** used paint and found shantytown objects to depict the melting pot of the Cape Town squatter camps.

Since the 1990s, and especially in the post-apartheid period, the gallery has engaged in a process of redefining what constitutes contemporary **indigenous art** and has embarked on an acquisitions policy that "acknowledges and celebrates the expressive cultures of the African continent, particularly its southern regions". Material that would previously have been treated as ethnographic, such as a major **bead collection** as well as carvings and **craft objects**, is now finding a place alongside oil paintings and sculptures.

The only permanent collection consists of minor works by British artists, including George Romney, Thomas Gainsborough, Joshua Reynolds and some Pre-Raphaelites. The gallery has a **café** serving light lunches, snacks, coffees and cakes, as well as an excellent shop, though the eatery in the Gardens, under shady oaks just five minutes' walk away, is a better bet for refreshments.

The South African Jewish Museum

Next to the National Gallery but accessed from 88 Hatfield St, the **South African Jewish Museum** (Mon–Thurs & Sun 10am–5pm, Fri 10am–2pm; R50; ⓦ www.sajewishmuseum.co.za) is partially housed in South Africa's first synagogue, built in 1863. One of Cape Town's most ambitious permanent exhibitions, it tells the story of South African Jewry from its beginnings over 150 years ago to the present – a narrative which starts in the Old Synagogue from which visitors cross, via a gangplank, to the upper level of a new two-storey building, symbolically re-enacting the arrival by boat of the first Jewish immigrants at Table Bay harbour in the 1840s. Employing multimedia interactive displays, models and Judaica artefacts, the exhibition follows three threads: "**Memories**", looking at the roots and experiences of the immigrants; "**Reality**", covering their integration into South Africa; and "**Dreams**", examining a diversity of views about the role of Jews in South Africa, their relationship to Israel and their position in the world. Other displays examine anti-Semitism, apartheid and the Jews who opposed it, as well as Nelson Mandela's relationship with the Jewish community.

Drawing parallels between Judaism and the ritual practices and beliefs of South Africa's other communities, the "**Culture among Cultures**" display covers topics such as birth, marriage, circumcision and death. The **basement** level houses a walk-through reconstruction of a Lithuanian *shtetl* or village (most South African Jews have their nineteenth-century roots in Lithuania),

Today there are around sixteen thousand Jews in Cape Town, the majority descended from **Eastern European refugees** who fled discrimination and pogroms during the late nineteenth and early twentieth centuries.

Since 1795, when the occupying British introduced freedom of worship at the Cape, Jews in South Africa have faced few legal impediments. However, there were instances of semi-official anti-Semitism during the twentieth century, the most notable being in the policy of the Nationalist Party while in opposition during the 1940s. Before World War II, elements in the party came under the influence of Nazi ideology, which was being poured into South Africa by the German foreign and propaganda offices, and began to attribute all the ills facing Afrikanerdom to a "British–Jewish capitalist" conspiracy. In 1941, the party adopted a policy of ending Jewish immigration and even repatriating "undesirable immigrants", as well as placing stronger controls over naturalization and the introduction of a "vocational permit" system to protect "the original white population against unfair competition".

Ironically, on the eve of taking power in 1947, the party of apartheid turned its back on anti-Semitism: one of its first acts after winning the 1948 election was to recognize the newly created state of Israel, with which South Africa maintained strong links until the National Party relinquished power in 1994. The ANC government is far more sympathetic to the Palestinian cause, and far more critical of Israel than its predecessors.

as well as the **Discovery Centre**, an interactive computer with a genealogy bank, a searchable database on Jewish life and culture and a "glimpse into Israel". A restaurant, shop and auditorium are also housed in the museum complex.

The Holocaust Exhibition and the Great Synagogue

Opened in 1999, the **Holocaust Exhibition** (Mon–Thurs & Sun 10am–5pm, Fri 10am–1pm; free) is one of the most moving and brilliantly executed museums in Cape Town. Housed upstairs in the Holocaust Centre (in the same complex as the Jewish Museum), it resonates sharply in a country that only recently emerged from an era of racial oppression – a connection that the exhibition makes explicitly. A densely layered narrative is related through text, photographs, artefacts (such as a concentration camp uniform), film clips, soundtracks, multimedia and interactive video, while the design uses modulated lighting, cobblestones reminiscent of the ghettos and pieces of barbed wire and railway track to evoke the death camps.

Exhibits trace the history of anti-Semitism in Europe, culminating with the Nazis' Final Solution; they also look at South Africa's Greyshirts, who were motivated by Nazi propaganda during the 1930s and were later absorbed into the National Party. There are accounts of heroism, often tragic, including acts of resistance by Jews, and a touch screen portrays many individuals in Europe who risked their lives to protect or rescue the victims of Nazism. To conclude, a twenty-minute video tells the story of survivors who eventually settled in Cape Town.

The **Great Synagogue** next door is one of Cape Town's outstanding religious buildings. Designed by the Scottish architects Parker & Forsyth and completed in 1905, it features an impressive dome and two soaring towers after the style of central European Baroque churches. To see the arched interior and the alcove decorated with gilt mosaics, you need to ask at the Holocaust Centre, and may be asked to provide some form of identification.

The South African Museum and Planetarium

The nation's premier museum of natural history and human sciences, the **South African Museum and Planetarium** (daily 10am–5pm; museum R8 for adults, free for children; planetarium adults R20, children R6; ⓦ www.museums .org.za/sam) stands at 25 Queen Victoria St, northwest of Government Avenue. The museum's **ethnographic galleries** contain some very good displays on the traditional arts and crafts of several African groups, some exceptional examples of rock art (entire chunks of caves sitting in the display cases), and casts of the stone birds found at the archeological site of Great Zimbabwe, in south-eastern Zimbabwe. Upstairs, the **natural history galleries** display mounted mammals, dioramas of prehistoric Karoo reptiles, and Table Mountain flora and fauna. The highlight is the four-storey "whale well", in which a collection of beautiful whale skeletons hang like massive mobiles, accompanied by the eerie strains of their song.

The attached **planetarium** (shows Mon & Wed–Fri 2pm, Tues 2pm & 8pm, Sat noon, 1pm & 2.30pm) is recommended if you want to see the constellations of the southern hemisphere, with an informed commentary. There's also a changing programme of shows covering topics such as San sky myths, with some programmes geared specially for kids. Leaflets at the museum provide a list of forthcoming attractions, and you can buy a monthly chart of the current night sky – especially worthwhile if you're staying in an area without streetlights and can actually see the stars.

Bertram House

At the southernmost end of Government Avenue you'll come upon **Bertram House** (Tues–Thurs 10am–4.30pm; R5, children R2), whose beautiful two-storey brick facade looks out across a fragrant herb garden. Built in the 1840s, the museum is significant as the only surviving brick Georgian-style house in Cape Town, and displays typical furniture and objects of a well-to-do colonial British family in the first half of the nineteenth century.

The site was bought in 1839 by John Barker, a Yorkshire attorney who came to the Cape in 1823. His wife, Ann Bertram Findlay, who died in 1838, was responsible for building it, and Barker bestowed her middle name on the house. Declared a National Monument in 1962, Bertram House was extensively restored in the 1980s: imported face brick and Welsh slate were used to re-create the original facade, while the interior walls were redecorated in their earlier dark green and ochre, based on the evidence of paint scrapings. The reception rooms are decorated in the Regency style, while the porcelain is predominantly nineteenth-century English, although there are also some very fine Chinese pieces.

Houses of Parliament

South Africa's **Houses of Parliament**, east of Government Avenue, on Parliament Street, are a complex of interlinking buildings, with labyrinthine

corridors connecting hundreds of offices, debat
miscellaneous other rooms. Many of these are relics of
phase of apartheid when, in the interests of racial segrega
distinct legislative complexes sited here to cater to diffe

The original wing, completed in 1885, is an imposing\
building which first served as the legislative assembly of th
the Boer republics and British colonies amalgamated in
parliament of the Union of South Africa. This is the old p
seven decades of repressive legislation, including aparth
It's also where **Hendrik Verwoerd**, the arch-theorist of apartheid, met his
bloody end at the hand of Dimitri Tsafendas, a parliamentary messenger who
inexplicably went off the rails, committing the act because, as he told police, "a
tapeworm ordered me to do it". Due to his mental state, the assassin escaped
the gallows to outlive apartheid – albeit in an institution. Verwoerd's portrait,
depicting him as a man of vision and *gravitas*, used to hang over the main
entrance to the dining room. In 1996 it was removed "for cleaning", along
with paintings of generations of white parliamentarians.

The new chamber was built in 1983 as part of the **tricameral parliament**,
P.W. Botha's attempt to avert majority rule by trying to co-opt Indians and
coloureds – but in their own separate debating chambers. The "tricameral"
chamber, where the three non-African "races" on occasions met together, is
now the **National Assembly**, where you can watch sessions of parliament.
One-hour **tours** (Mon–Fri 9am–noon on the hour; free) take in the old and
new debating chambers, the library and museum, and should be booked in
advance through the Tours Section (☎021 403 2201). This is also the place to
contact for day tickets to the **debating sessions** – the most interesting of
which is question time (Wed from 3pm), when you can hear ministers being
quizzed by MPs. To join a tour, head to the Plein Street entrance to Parliament,
opposite the Receiver of Revenue (it's the more southerly of the two entrances
in this street); go through a security check, where you should ask for directions
to the Poorthuis entrance. From there you'll see arrows indicating the starting
point for tours.

Rust-en-Vreugd

The most beautiful of Cape Town's house museums, **Rust-en-Vreugd**
(Tues–Thurs 8.30am–4.30pm; R5), a couple of blocks east of the Gardens at 78
Buitenkant St, was built in 1778 for Willem Cornelis Boers, the colony's Fiscal
(a powerful position akin to the police chief, public prosecutor and collector of
taxes rolled into one), who was forced to resign in the 1780s following allegations
of wheeler-dealing and extortion. Under the British occupation, it was the
residence of Lord Charles Somerset during his governorship (1814–26).

The house was once surrounded by countryside, but now stands along a
congested route that brushes past the edge of the central business district.
Designed by architect Louis Michel Thibault and sculptor Anton Anreith, the
two-storey facade features a pair of stacked balconies, the lower one forming a
stunning portico fronted by four Corinthian columns carved from teak. The
front door, framed by teak pilasters, is a real work of art, rated by architectural
historian de Bosdari as "certainly the finest door at the Cape". Above the door,
the fanlight is executed in elaborate Baroque style.

Inside, the William Fehr Collection of artworks on paper occupies two
ground-floor rooms and includes illustrations by important documentarists such
as **Thomas Baines**, who is represented by hand-coloured lithographs and a

ercolours recording a nineteenth-century expedition up Table
Thomas Bowler, another prolific recorder of Cape scenes, painted
ing landscape of Cape Point from the sea in 1864, showing dolphins
ing in the foreground.

ne property is defined by a boundary of bay trees. A tranquil escape from the
busy street, the **garden** is a reconstruction of the original eighteenth-century
semiformal one, laid out with herbaceous hedges and gravel walkways, and
features a lawn with a gazebo.

Castle of Good Hope

From the outside, South Africa's oldest building looks somewhat miserable, and
its position on Darling Street, behind the train station and city-bus terminal,
does nothing to dispel this. Nevertheless the **Castle of Good Hope** (daily
9am–4pm; R20; ⓦ www.castleofgoodhope.co.za) is well worth the entrance fee;
inside, a meticulous ten-year restoration has returned the decor to the British
Regency style introduced in 1798. **Free tours** (daily 11am, noon & 2pm) are
useful for orientation and cover the main features, including the prison cells and
dungeons, with their centuries-old graffiti painstakingly carved by prisoners. In
the elegant courtyard there is a very pleasant **tea shop**, with Table Mountain
looming over the west wall. The Castle is also home to the Defence Force's
Western Province Command; you may see armed soldiers marching through
the courtyard.

The Castle

Finished in 1679, complete with the essentials of a moat and torture chamber,
the Castle replaced Van Riebeeck's earlier mud and timber fort, which stood
on the site of the Grand Parade. The Castle was built in accordance with
seventeenth-century European principles of fortification, comprising strong
bastions from which the outside walls could be protected by crossfire. There's
a strong sense of order in the pentagonal plan, though ironically there was
nothing orderly about the Castle's construction, which lasted over thirteeen
years, with work constantly coming to a standstill because of shortages of
labour or materials, and being revived by the outbreak of various wars in
Europe. For 150 years, the Castle remained the symbolic heart of the Cape
administration, and the centre of social and economic life, but in the late
nineteenth century – when the colony had expanded far beyond its walls –
there were at least three attempts by the authorities to demolish it, as it was
regarded as a white elephant.

The original, seaward entrance had to be moved to its present position
facing landward, because the spring tide sometimes came crashing in – a
remarkable thought given how far aground it is now thanks to land reclama-
tion. The **entrance gate** displays the coat of arms of the United Netherlands
and those of the six Dutch cities in which the VOC chambers were situated.
Still hanging from its original wooden beams in the tower above the
entrance is the **bell**, cast in 1697 by Claude Fremy in Amsterdam; it was used
variously as an alarm signal and as a summons to residents to receive
pronouncements.

Inside the walls, the courtyard is sliced in half by a defensive twelve-metre
high structure, or *kat*, from which cannons could be fired. The exquisite
ceremonial **kat balcony** provides entry to the *kat* and was where ordinances
were pronounced; it's flanked by two shallow curving staircases, and has a
portico supported on six fluted Ionic columns carved out of solid teak.

The William Fehr Collection

Elaborately carved double doors at the rear of the *kat* balcony open onto four interleading rooms that were the heart of VOC government at the Cape and which now house the bulk of the **William Fehr Collection**, one of the country's most important exhibits of decorative arts. The contents, acquired by businessman William Fehr from the 1920s, were sold and donated to the government in the 1950s and 1960s and continue to be displayed informally as Fehr preferred. The galleries are filled with items found in middle-class Cape households from the seventeenth to nineteenth centuries, with some fine examples of elegantly simple Cape furniture from the eighteenth century. Early colonial views of Table Bay appear in a number of paintings, including one by Aernot Smit that shows the Castle in the seventeenth century, right on the shoreline. Among the fascinating items of antique oriental ceramics are a blue-and-white Japanese porcelain plate from around 1660, displaying the VOC monogram, and a beautiful polychrome plate from China dating to about 1750, which depicts a fleet of Company ships in Table Bay against the backdrop of a very oriental-looking Table Mountain.

The Grand Parade and the City Hall

To the northwest of the Castle, the **Grand Parade** is a large open area where the residents of District Six used to come to trade. On Wednesdays and Saturdays it still transforms itself into a **market**, where you can buy a whole array of bargains ranging from used clothes to spicy food.

The Grand Parade appeared on TV screens throughout the world on February 11, 1990, when 100,000 people gathered to hear **Nelson Mandela** make his first speech after being released from prison, from the balcony of **City Hall**. A slightly fussy Edwardian building dressed in Bath stone, City Hall manages, despite its drab surroundings, to look impressive against Table Mountain.

District Six

South of the Castle, in the shadow of Devil's Peak, is a vacant lot shown on maps as the suburb of **Zonnebloem**. Before being demolished by the apartheid

▲ City Hall

authorities, it was an inner-city slum known as **District Six**, an impoverished but lively community of 55,000 predominantly coloured people. Once regarded as the soul of Cape Town, the district harboured a rich cultural life in its narrow alleys and crowded tenements: along the cobbled streets, hawkers rubbed shoulders with prostitutes, gangsters, drunks and gamblers, while craftsmen plied their trade in small workshops. This was a fertile place of the South African imagination, inspiring novels, poems, jazz and the blockbuster *District Six: The Musical*, by David Kramer, which in the late 1980s played to packed houses and spawned a series of hits.

In 1966, apartheid ideologues declared District Six a **White Group Area** and the bulldozers moved in, taking fifteen years to drive its presence from the skyline, leaving only the mosques and churches. But, in the wake of the demolition gangs, international and domestic outcry was so great that the area was never developed apart from a few luxury town houses on its fringes and the hefty Cape Technikon, a college that now occupies nearly a quarter of the former suburb. After years of negotiation, the original residents are moving back under a scheme to develop low-cost housing in the district.

The District Six Museum

Few places in Cape Town speak more eloquently of the effect of apartheid on the day-to-day lives of ordinary people than the compelling **District Six Museum** (Mon 9am–3pm, Tues–Sat 9am–4pm; R10; Ⓦwww.districtsix .co.za). On the northern boundary of District Six, on the corner of Buitenkant and Albertus streets, the museum occupies the former **Central Methodist Mission Church**, which offered solidarity and ministry to the victims of forced removals right up to the 1980s, and became a venue for anti-apartheid gatherings. Today, it houses a series of fascinating displays that include everyday household items and tools of trades, such as hairdressing implements, as well as documentary photographs, which evoke the lives of the individuals who once lived here. Occupying most of the floor is a huge map of District Six as it was, annotated by former residents, who describe their memories, reflections and incidents associated with places and buildings that no longer exist. There's also an almost complete collection of original street signs, secretly retrieved at the time of demolition by the man entrusted with dumping them into Table Bay.

Strand Street

A major artery from the N2 freeway to the central business district, **Strand Street** neatly separates the Upper from the Lower city centre. Between the mid-eighteenth and mid-nineteenth centuries, Strand Street was one of the most fashionable streets in Cape Town because of its proximity to the shore. Its former cachet is now only discernible from the handful of quietly elegant National Monuments left standing amid the roar of traffic: **Martin Melck House** (accommodating the **Gold of Africa Museum**), the **Evangelical Lutheran Church** and **Koopmans-De Wet House**.

Gold of Africa Museum

Since the discovery of gold near Johannesburg in the late nineteenth century, South Africa has been closely associated in the Western mind with the precious

metal and the riches it represents. However, the outsta
Museum at 96 Strand Str (Mon–Sat 9.30am–5pm
Ⓦ www.goldofafrica.com), just off Buitengragt, foct
different side to gold – the exquisite **artworks** crafte
twentieth-century **African goldsmiths** from Mali, S
Côte d'Ivoire. Arguably the most important such co
acquired in 2001 from the Barbier-Mueller Museum in G
ancient gold routes, and includes several hundred beau
masks, crocodiles, birds, a gold crown and human figure
sculpted **Golden Lion** from Ghana that is the symbol o

also a small auditorium with a continuous **film show**; a w… cenar where you
can have a snack, a coffee and quaff a glass of Cape wine; a **studio** where
goldsmiths practise their art; and a **shop** selling postcards, gold leaf and beautiful
little souvenirs.

Evangelical Lutheran Church

Next door to the Gold of Africa Museum, at the corner of Buitengragt and
Strand Street, stands the **Evangelical Lutheran Church** (Mon, Wed & Fri
9am–noon; free), converted by Anton Anreith (see box, p.92) in 1785 from a
barn. The establishment of a Lutheran church in Cape Town struck a significant
blow against the extreme **religious intolerance** that pervaded under VOC rule.
Before 1771, when permission was granted to Lutherans to establish their own
congregation, Protestantism was the only form of worship allowed and the
Dutch Reformed Church held an absolute monopoly over saving people's souls.
The Lutheran Church's congregation was dominated by Germans, who at the
time constituted 28 percent of the colony's free burgher population.

The facade of the Evangelical Lutheran Church includes Classical details such
as a broken pediment perforated by the clock tower, as well as Gothic features
such as arched windows. Inside, the magnificent **pulpit**, supported on two
life-size Herculean figures, is one of Anton Anreith's masterpieces; the white
swan perched on the canopy is a symbol of Lutheranism.

Koopmans-De Wet House

Sandwiched between two office blocks close to Cape Town Tourism,
Koopmans-De Wet House at 35 Strand St (Tues–Thurs 9.30am–4.30pm;
R5) is an outstanding eighteenth-century pedimented Neoclassical town house
and museum, accommodating a very fine collection of antique furniture and
rare porcelain. An inexpensive guide booklet gives interesting contextual
background to the house and its history, while a separate brochure describes
items in the collection: both are available at the entrance.

The earliest sections of the house were built in 1701 by **Reyner Smedinga**,
a well-to-do goldsmith who imported the building materials from Holland. The
house changed hands more than a dozen times over the following two centuries,
with minor additions made in the 1760s and a second storey added between
1774 and 1790. In 1806, it came into the hands of the De Wet family, eventually
becoming the home of **Marie Koopmans-De Wet** (1834–1906), a prominent
figure on the Cape social and political circuit.

The building's **facade** has been attributed to Louis Thibault and Anton
Anreith (see box, p.97), but there's no proof of this. Whoever was responsible,
the house represents a fine synthesis of Dutch elements (sash windows and large
entrance doors) with the demands of local conditions; the huge rooms, lofty

...tered windows reflect the high summer temperatures, while the ...s plastered masonry seats at each end. The **lantern** in the fanlight ...rance to the house was a feature of all Cape Town houses in the ...nth and early nineteenth centuries, its purpose to shine light onto the ...t and thus hinder slaves from gathering at night to plot.

The Lower City Centre

In the mid-nineteenth century, the city's middle classes viewed the **Lower City Centre** and its low-life activities with a mixture of alarm and excitement – a tension that remains today. **Lower Long Street** divides the area just inland from the docklands into two. To the east is the **Foreshore**, an ugly post-World War II wasteland of grey corporate architecture, among which is the **Artscape Centre**, Cape Town's prestige arts complex. The Foreshore is at last being redeveloped, its centrepiece being the **Cape Town International Convention Centre**, completed in 2003 and linked by a canal and pedestrian routes with the Waterfront.

The Foreshore

The Foreshore, an area of reclaimed land northeast of Strand Street, stretching to the docks, and east of Lower Long Street, was developed in the late 1940s in a spirit of modernism – large highly planned urban spaces – that was sweeping the world. It was intended to turn Cape Town's harbour into a symbolic gateway to Africa; instead, it turned out as a series of large concrete boxes surrounded by acres of windswept tarmac parking lots. The opening in 2004 of the prestigious International Convention Centre (and its proximity to some high-rise hotels and parking garages) has opened up the area, but there is no street life at all, and no reason to explore.

Heerengracht, a truncated two-lane carriageway running from Adderley Street to the harbour, has massive roundabouts at each end solemnly guarded by statues of Jan van Riebeeck and Bartholomeu Dias. It was meant to be the ceremonial axis through this grand scheme, joining the city to the sea, but it never quite makes it to the water, coming to a disappointing standstill at the dock perimeter fence, before bearing east under the dismal shadow of the N1 and N2 flyovers.

The only building worth visiting here – when there's something on – is the **Artscape Complex** (previously known as the Nico Theatre Complex), Cape Town's major performance venue, in D.F. Malan Street just east of Heerengracht. Incorporating the large Main Theatre, it also houses the small Arena Theatre, the opera house and a decent coffee shop; for more on events staged here, see Chapter 10.

Duncan Dock

North of the Foreshore, **Duncan Dock** is Cape Town's working harbour. Work started on the dock in 1938, swallowing the city beachfronts at Woodstock and Paarden Island to cater for the growing supertanker traffic that was outstripping the capacity of the Victoria and Alfred Docks. The dock today is a forbidding industrial landscape of large ships and towering cranes cut off from the city by an enormous perimeter fence.

V&A Waterfront, De Waterkant and Robben Island

The **Victoria and Alfred Waterfront**, usually known simply as the Waterfront, adjoins the west of Duncan Dock and is Cape Town's original Victorian harbour. After two decades of stagnation, it was redeveloped in the 1990s and is now the most popular attraction on the peninsula, incorporating the city's central shopping area, its most fashionable eating and drinking venues, the site of an excellent **aquarium** – one of Cape Town's highlights – and the Nelson Mandela Gateway – the embarkation point for trips to **Robben Island**. Authentic nineteenth-century buildings, imitation Victorian shopping malls, piers with waterside walkways and a functioning harbour complement the wide range of restaurants, outdoor cafés, pubs, clubs, cinemas, museums and outdoor entertainment, with magnificent Table Mountain rising beyond.

West of the Foreshore and rubbing up against the west side of the city centre and the V&A Waterfront to its north is Cape Town's thriving clubland, incorporating **De Waterkant** and **Somerset Road**, the city's self-proclaimed "gay village". With its high density of **nightclubs** and **pubs**, the area around Somerset Road, which heads from the city centre into Green Point, has become the best place in Cape Town to club-crawl, one of the few places you're guaranteed action seven nights a week. For coverage of the coast from Green Point onwards, see Chapter 5.

The V&A Waterfront

Throughout the first half of the nineteenth century, arguments raged in Cape Town over the need for a proper dock. The Cape was often known as the **Cape of Storms** because of its vicious weather, which left Table Bay littered with wrecks. Many makeshift attempts were made to ameliorate the situation,

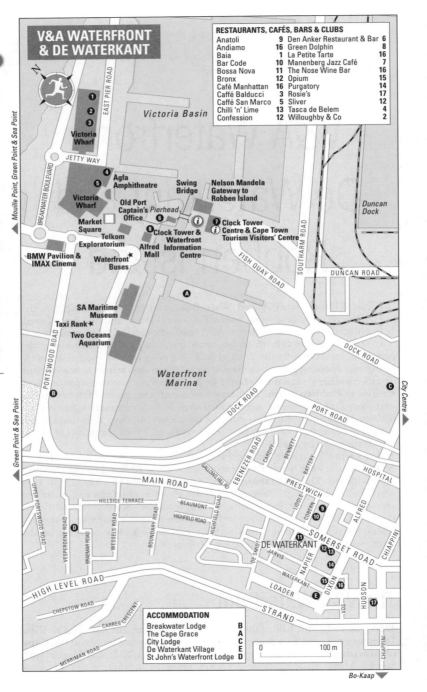

V&A WATERFRONT & DE WATERKANT

RESTAURANTS, CAFÉS, BARS & CLUBS

Anatoli	9	Den Anker Restaurant & Bar	6
Andiamo	16	Green Dolphin	8
Baia	1	La Petite Tarte	16
Bar Code	10	Manenberg Jazz Café	7
Bossa Nova	11	The Nose Wine Bar	16
Bronx	12	Opium	15
Café Manhattan	16	Purgatory	14
Caffé Balducci	3	Rosie's	17
Caffé San Marco	5	Sliver	12
Chilli 'n' Lime	13	Tasca de Belem	4
Confession	12	Willoughby & Co	2

Victoria Basin

Victoria Wharf

Mouille Point, Green Point & Sea Point

EAST PIER ROAD

JETTY WAY

BREAKWATER BOULEVARD

Agfa Amphitheatre

Victoria Wharf

Swing Bridge

Nelson Mandela Gateway to Robben Island

Old Port Captain's Office

Pierhead

Clock Tower Centre & Cape Town Tourism Visitors' Centre

Clock Tower & Waterfront Information Centre

Market Square

Telkom Exploratorium

Alfred Mall

BMW Pavilion & IMAX Cinema

Waterfront Buses

Duncan Dock

SOUTHARM ROAD

FISH QUAY ROAD

DUNCAN ROAD

SA Maritime Museum

Taxi Rank

Two Oceans Aquarium

PORTSWOOD ROAD

Green Point & Sea Point

Waterfront Marina

DOCK ROAD

City Centre

DOCK ROAD

PORT ROAD

CARDIFF

BENNETT

BATTERY

HOSPITAL

MAIN ROAD

GALLOWS HILL RD

EBENEZER ROAD

PRESTWICH

ALFRED

CHIAPPINI

UPPER PORTSWOOD ROAD

HILLSIDE TERRACE

BEAUMONT

HIGHFIELD ROAD

BOUNDARY ROAD

HIGHFIELD ROAD

WESSELS ROAD

BRAEMAR ROAD

VESPERDENE ROAD

LIDDLE

COBERN

SOMERSET ROAD

DE WATERKANT

DE SMIDT

JARVIS

NAPIER

WATERKANT

DIXON

HUDSON

HIGH LEVEL ROAD

LOADER

STRAND

VOS

CHEPSTOW ROAD

CARRES CRESCENT

CHIAPPINI

MERRIMAN ROAD

Bo-Kaap

ACCOMMODATION

Breakwater Lodge	B
The Cape Grace	A
City Lodge	C
De Waterkant Village	E
St John's Waterfront Lodge	D

0   100 m

including the construction of a lighthouse in 1823, and work was begun on a jetty at the bottom of Bree Street in 1832. Clamour for a harbour grew in the 1850s, with the increase in sea traffic arriving at the Cape, reaching its peak in 1860, when the Lloyds insurance company refused the risk of covering ships dropping anchor in Table Bay.

The British colonial government dragged its heels due to the costs involved, but eventually conceded; on a suitably stormy September day in 1860, at a huge ceremony, the teenage Prince Alfred tipped the first batch of stones into Table Bay to begin the **breakwater**, the westernmost arm of the harbour, which was subsequently completed with convict labour. In 1869, the dock – consisting of two main basins – was completed, and the sea was allowed to pour in.

The Waterfront is one of the easiest points in Cape Town to reach by **public transport**. Golden Arrow municipal buses leave for here from Adderley Street, from outside the train station and from Beach Road in Sea Point. The open-topped City Sightseeing Bus also stops at the Waterfront. Arriving by **car**, you'll find yourself well catered for, with several car parks and garages. If you want to leave by taxi, head for the rank on Breakwater Boulevard.

The Marina and the Victoria and Alfred basins

Victoria Basin, the smaller **Alfred Basin** to its west, and the **Marina** beyond, create the northern half of the Waterfront's geography of piers and quays. The shopping focus of the Waterfront is **Victoria Wharf**, an enormous flashy mall on two levels, extending along Quays Five and Six. It's here that most visitors to the Waterfront arrive. The restaurants and cafés on the mall's east side, with their outdoor seating, have fabulous views of Table Mountain across the busy harbour. On the west side of Victoria Wharf and physically linked to it, the rather contrived **Red Shed Craft Workshop** (Mon–Sat 9am–9pm, Sun 10am–9pm) brings together craft workers such as glass-blowers, leatherworkers, township artists and jewellery-makers under one huge roof. The outdoor action centres around **Market Square** and the **Agfa Amphitheatre**, where you can sometimes catch free rock, jazz or traditional African musical performances and occasionally hear the Cape Town Symphony Orchestra (details from the information centre in the Clock Tower Precinct).

South of here along the Alfred Basin's North Quay, **Alfred Mall Shopping Centre** is a complex of fifteen touristy curio shops, boutiques and restaurants. East of the Alfred Shopping Mall, the Pierhead is dominated by the **Old Port Captain's Office**, a gabled Arts and Crafts building erected in 1904, with an imposing presence that reflected its status as the nerve centre of the harbour in the early twentieth century. It's now the headquarters of the Victoria and Alfred Waterfront Company, which manages the Waterfront area.

Two Oceans Aquarium

At the Marina's North Wharf, the **Two Oceans Aquarium** on Dock Road (daily 9.30am–6pm; adults R75, children R35; Ⓦ www.aquarium.co.za) showcases the Cape's unique marine environment, where the warm Indian Ocean mingles with the cold Atlantic. A designated route (which you're not obliged to follow) takes in the nine major galleries in sequence, starting on the **ground floor** with the **Indian Ocean**, where you'll see tank after tank of psychedelic fish. One of the most beautiful displays features scores of small gossamer jellyfish floating gently in their ultraviolet-lit cylindrical tank like parachutists. To the rear of the

▲ The Clock Tower

ground floor, the **Diversity Hall**, as its name implies, contains an astonishing variety of strange marine creatures, including giant spider crabs, octopuses, sea horses and the deadly devil firefish, whose lacy beauty disguises lethal spines. Also on the ground floor, the **Agfa Auditorium** shows videos on South Africa's marine life and related topics (such as underwater photography).

The **basement** houses the **Alpha Activity Centre**, a good place to keep kids occupied, with free organized activities such as puppet shows and face painting, and computers which allow youngsters to explore marine ecology. The centre is combined with the **Diving Animals** display, where you can watch a group of resident Cape fur seals frolicking underwater.

The **top floor**, reached via a ramp, accommodates the **Story of Water**, which, in glorious reconstruction, traces the course of a river from its mouth to its source, via a salt marsh and lagoon. Not to everyone's taste, it features a small colony of African penguins (which you can see in their natural state at Boulders Beach; see p.117), while captive sea birds fly about the rafters. In the **Kelp Forest** in an adjacent gallery, a dense jungle of giant seaweed sways hypnotically with the rhythmic surge of the water; you can sit in the small amphitheatre and gaze at beautiful shoals of silvery fish shimmering through sunlit sea. From here, a ramp takes you in a gentle downward spiral through the **Predators** exhibit, for many visitors the most compelling attraction of all. A massive tank, open to the ocean, houses some large resident ragged-tooth sharks, which glide past as you walk through a glass underwater tunnel; other species confined here include rays and giant turtles.

Among the highlights of the aquarium is the **shark feeding** every Sunday at 3.30pm, when you can watch *raggies* – ragged-tooth sharks – being hand-fed by divers. Smaller sharks, stingrays and turtles get their turn on Monday, Wednesday and Friday at 3.30pm, and penguins are fed daily at noon and 3pm. If you have an Open Water 1 diving qualification, you can actually **dive** in the predators tank (book a day before on ℡021 418 3823; R450).

Fish Quay

From the Pierhead you can use the **swing bridge** to cross to **Fish Quay**, the **Clock Tower Precinct** and the **Nelson Mandela Gateway to Robben Island** (daily 7.30am–5.30pm; free). The embarkation point for ferries to Robben Island, this two-storey building also incorporates a restaurant with a great view and a small museum with hi-tech interactive displays, featuring a history of Robben Island, the voices of prisoners and resistance songs.

Rising up from Fish Quay, the **Clock Tower**, which houses the Waterfront Information Centre, is Cape Town's finest architectural folly. Built as the original Port Captain's office in 1882, this strange-looking octagonal structure with Gothic windows consists of three stacked rooms with a stairwell running through its core. The mirror room on the second floor enabled the Port Captain to survey all the activities of the harbour without leaving his office. Adjacent to the Clock Tower, the **Clock Tower Centre** is a compact two-storey shopping mall, with a substantial Cape Tourism visitor centre.

Robben Island

Lying only a few kilometres from the commerce of the Waterfront, flat and windswept **Robben Island** is suffused by a meditative, otherworldly silence. This key site of South Africa's liberation struggle was intended to silence apartheid's domestic critics, but instead became an international focus for opposition to the regime. Measuring six square kilometres and sparsely vegetated by low scrub, it was Nelson Mandela's "home" for nearly two decades.

The catamaran from the Waterfront (see overleaf) takes about half an hour to reach this potent symbol of apartheid, where ex-prisoners and ex-warders work as guides, sharing their experiences. After arrival at the tiny Murray's

②

A number of vendors at the Waterfront sell tickets for cruises, which may go close to Robben island, but only the official ones sold at the **Nelson Mandela Gateway** will get you onto it (R150, including catamaran fare, island entry and 3hr 30min tour). Bookings must be made in advance (☎021 419 1300, ⊕www.robben-island.org .za) as the boats are often full, especially in December and January. Be sure to present your booking reference number and arrive at least half an hour before departure to collect your ticket. The boats operate hourly every day, except at noon and 4pm; in summer they run between 8am and 6pm, in winter between 9am and 3pm. All trips are dependent on the weather.

Bay harbour, you are taken on a **bus tour** around the island and a **tour of the prison**.

The bus tour stops off at several historical landmarks, the first of which is the **kramat**, a beautiful shrine built in memory of Tuan Guru, a Muslim cleric from present-day Indonesia who was imprisoned here by the Dutch in the eighteenth century. On his release, he helped to establish Islam among slaves in Cape Town, where it has flourished ever since. The tour also passes a **leper graveyard** and **church** designed by Sir Herbert Baker, both of which are quiet reminders that the island was a place of exile for leprosy sufferers in the early twentieth century.

Robert Sobukwe's house seems to echo with loneliness, and is perhaps the most affecting relic of incarceration on the island. It was here that Sobukwe, leader of the Pan Africanist Congress (a radical offshoot of the ANC), was held in solitary confinement for nine years. He was initially sentenced to three years, but was regarded as so dangerous by the authorities that they passed a special law – the "Sobukwe Clause" – to keep him on Robben Island for a further six years. No other political prisoners were allowed to speak to him, but he would sometimes gesture his solidarity with other sons of the African soil by letting sand trickle through his fingers as they walked past. After his release in 1969, Sobukwe was restricted to Kimberley under house arrest, until his death from cancer in 1978.

Another stopoff is the **lime quarry** where Nelson Mandela and his fellow inmates spent countless hours of hard labour. The soft, pale stone is extremely bright under the summer sun, as a result of which Mandela and others have in later years suffered eye disorders. As the years passed, the lime quarry became a place of furtive study among the prisoners, with the help of sympathetic warders.

The bus tour also takes in a stretch of coast dotted with shipwrecks and abundant sea birds and waterfowl, including the elegant **sacred ibis**. You may also spot some of a recently expanded population of **antelope**: springbok, eland and bontebok.

The Maximum Security Prison

The **Maximum Security Prison**, a forbidding complex of unadorned H-blocks on the edge of the island, is introduced with a tour through the famous **B-Section**; you'll be guided by a former inmate, after which you're free to wander. B-Section is a small compound full of tiny rooms that has become legendary in South African history; initially a place of defeat for the resistance movement, it ironically came to incubate and concentrate the energies of liberation. **Mandela's cell** has been left exactly as it was, without embellishments or display, but the rest have been left locked and empty.

In the nearby **A-Section**, the "Cell Stories" exhibition skilfully suggests the sparseness of prison life. The tiny isolation cells feature personal artefacts loaned by former prisoners (including a functional saxophone made of found objects), plus boards bearing quotations, recordings and photographs.

Towards the end of the 1980s, cameras were sneaked onto the island, and inmates took snapshots of each other, which have been enlarged to almost life size and mounted as the **Smuggled Camera Exhibition** in the **D-Section** communal cells. The jovial demeanour of the prisoners indicates their realization that the end was within sight; moreover, the warm camaraderie that

▲ Maximum Security Prison, Robben Island

The history of Robben Island

Nelson Mandela may have been the most famous Robben Island prisoner, but he certainly wasn't the first. In the seventeenth century the island became a place of banishment for those who offended the political order (initially the Dutch, later the British and the Afrikaner Nationalists). The island's first prisoner was the indigenous Khoikhoi leader **Autshumato**, who learnt English in the early seventeenth century and became an emissary of the British. After the Dutch settlement was established, he was jailed on the island by Jan van Riebeeck in 1658. The rest of the seventeenth century saw a succession of East Indies political prisoners and Muslim holy men exiled here for opposing Dutch colonial rule.

During the nineteenth century, the **British** used Robben Island as a dumping ground for deserters, criminals and political prisoners, in much the same way as they used Australia. Captured **Xhosa leaders** who defied the British Empire during the Frontier Wars of the early to mid-nineteenth century were transported by sea from the Eastern to the Western Cape to be imprisoned, and many ended up on Robben Island. In 1846, the island's brief was extended to include a whole range of the **socially marginalized**: criminals and political detainees were now joined by vagrants, prostitutes, lunatics and the chronically ill. All were victim to a regime of brutality and maltreatment, even in hospital. In the 1890s, a leper colony existed alongside the social outcasts. Lunatics were removed in 1921 and the lepers in 1930. During World War II, the **Defence Force** took over the island to set up defensive guns against a feared Axis invasion, which never came.

Robben Island's greatest era of notoriety began in 1961, when it was taken over by the **Prisons Department**. Prisoners arriving at the island prison were greeted by a slogan on the gate that read: "Welcome to Robben Island: We Serve with Pride." By 1963, when Nelson Mandela arrived, it had become a maximum security prison. All the warders – but none of the prisoners – were white. Prisoners were only allowed to send and receive one letter every six months, and common-law criminals and political prisoners were housed together until 1971, when they were separated in an attempt to further isolate the politicals. Harsh conditions, including routine beatings and forced hard labour, were exacerbated by geographical location. There's nothing but sea between the island and the South Pole, so icy winds routinely blow in from across the Atlantic – and inmates were made to wear shorts and flimsy jerseys. Like every other prisoner, Mandela slept on a thin mat on the floor (until 1973, when he was given a bed because he was ill) and was kept in a solitary confinement cell, measuring two metres square, for sixteen hours a day.

Amazingly, the prisoners found ways of **protesting**, through hunger strikes, publicizing conditions when possible (by using visits from the International Committee of the Red Cross, for example) and, remarkably, by taking legal action against the prison authority to stop arbitrary punishments. They won improved conditions over the years, and the island also became a university behind bars, where people of different political views and generations met; it was not unknown for prisoners to give academic help to their warders.

The last political prisoners were released from Robben Island in 1991 and the remaining common-law prisoners were transferred to the mainland in 1996. On January 1, 1997, control of Robben Island was transferred from the Department of Correctional Services to the Department of the Arts, Culture, Science and Technology, which established it as a museum. In December 1999 the entire island was declared a **UN World Heritage Site**.

evidently connects them suggests how people endured so many years of captivity. Another good option during the prison visit is the **Living Legacy** tour in **F-Section**, in which ex-political prisoner guides describe their lives here and answer your questions.

Going wild in Cape Town

There aren't many cities where you can walk in the mountains, chill on the beach, go clubbing and watch wildlife – all in the same day. Then, not many cities have a national park on their doorstep. In Cape Town you're never far from the Table Mountain National Park, the craggy wilderness that curls around the city centre in the north and extends to Cape Point in the south. And although this is no longer lion country (the last one was shot in the 1720s), you can still see countless varieties of animals, birds and reptiles here, including the biggest mammals of all – whales.

Baboon ▲

African penguins ▼

All creatures great and small

There's a lot more to the Table Mountain National Park than Cape Town's iconic flat-topped peak and the cable car. The vegetation of the park, known as **fynbos** (see box), sustains a complex web of life that in turn sustains it: mammals, birds and insects all play their part in pollinating *fynbos* plants. The denizens of the National Park range from tiny ants to prehistoric-looking lizards, iridescent birds and large mammals, which you stand a chance of seeing if you visit.

Commonest of the peninsula's large mammals are **baboons**, which number between 300 and 400 and are commonly seen in the Cape of Good Hope section of the Park. Another common species are **dassies**, or rock hyraxes, the fluffy beasts which resemble large guinea pigs and routinely sun themselves around the Upper Cable Station on Table Mountain. Of the scores of other mammals present, including **caracals, genets, polecats, Cape foxes** and some twenty species of **mice**, among the ones you'll most likely see are **Cape Mountain zebras, bontebok** (a large antelope) and **mongooses**.

Pack a pair of binoculars to get a better look at any of the 250 **bird** species supported by the *fynbos*. Of these three are endemic to the Table Mountain National Park, where a classic sight is a brightly coloured sunbird using its long curved beak to coax nectar from a bell-like erica flower. The Cape Peninsula is also extremely rewarding for spotting sea birds from the land, but the marine creatures that attract more curious visitors than any other are the

Black girdled lizard ▼

African **penguins** that have made their colony at Boulders Beach.

Look out also for the innumerable small creatures such as the black **lizards** that hang around on rocks like tiny dinosaurs and **tortoises** with beautifully decorated shells as well as **insects**, including dung beetles, bees and damselflies.

▲ Dung beetle

▲ Bontebok

▼ Protea

Fynbos

Early Dutch settlers were alarmed by the lack of good timber on the Cape Peninsula's hillsides, which were covered by nondescript, scrubby bush they described as *fijn bosch* (literally "fine bush") and which is now known by its Afrikaans name **fynbos** (pronounced "fayn-bos"). The settlers planted exotics, like the oaks that now shade central Cape Town, and over the ensuing centuries their descendants established pine forests on the sides of Table Mountain in an effort to create a landscape that fulfilled their European idea of the picturesque. It's only relatively recently that Capetonians have come to proudly claim *fynbos* as part of the peninsula's heritage. You'll encounter *fynbos* all over Cape Town, especially on the mountainsides; despite their rather unpromising grey-green appearance from afar, if you get into the *fynbos* at any time of year (spring and summer are best), you'll encounter countless beautiful little flowering shrubs.

Fynbos is remarkable for its astonishing variety of plants, its 8500 species making it one of the world's biodiversity hot spots. The Cape Peninsula alone, measuring less than 500 square kilometres, has 2256 plant species (nearly twice as many as Britain, which is 5000 times bigger). The four basic types of *fynbos* plants are **proteas** (South Africa's national flower); **ericas**, amounting to 600 species of heather; **restios** (reeds); and **geophytes**, including ground orchids and the startling, flaming red disas, which can be seen in flower on Table Mountain in late summer.

Common dolphins ▲

Seals ▲

Whale's tail ▼

Ocean's eleven: denizens of the deep

That the breaking waves of Cape Town are one of the city's major drawcards isn't exactly news. But there's a whole lot more to the city's shoreline than beaches, sun and surf. Cape Town's biggest animal attractions are the **southern right whales** which come into False Bay during their calving season (peak period between mid-Aug and mid-Oct). There are some superb vantage points between Muizenberg and Cape Point and it's not unknown to step out of a seafront café in St James or Kalk Bay to be confronted by the hulking forty-ton form of a whale breaching just off the shore.

Dolphins are also commonly spotted off the coast, but of the ten or so species recorded in Western Cape waters the three you're most likely to see are Common, Bottlenosed and Dusky. **Seals** can be seen hanging around the harbours at Hout Bay and Kalk Bay, and most famously at the V&A Waterfront where they duck and dive and sun themselves along the harbour walls.

If you kit up with scuba gear you can explore the coast's swaying **kelp forests** that harbour crayfish, sea urchins and scores of other species. Even if you're not a diver you can get a taste of all this at the Two Oceans Aquarium at the V&A Waterfront, which has one of the world's finest kelp forest displays as well as **sharks** and other denizens of the southern deep.

And if all this sounds somewhat sedate, a more energetic option is to get onto the water on a guided kayaking trip. A standard excursion takes you to the penguin colony at Boulders Beach, while a longer and more adventurous outing rounds Cape Point. On either of these trips there is a chance of encountering whales, dolphins, seals and who-knows-what, in their own element.

③

Table Mountain and the City Bowl suburbs

T he icon that for hundreds of years and from hundreds of kilometres announced Cape Town to seafarers, **Table Mountain**, a 1087-metre flat-topped massif with dramatic cliffs and eroded gorges, dominates the northern end of the Peninsula. Indigenous Khoikhoi pastoralists knew it as Hoerikwaggo (The Mountain of the Sea), a name which aptly characterizes the drama of this monumental hunk of landscape rising out of the oceans. For visitors today, Table Mountain is one of the world's great physical symbols, representing a shorthand for the Mother City itself, in much the same way that the opera house represents Sydney or Big Ben stands for London.

Between the mountain and the CBD lie the **City Bowl suburbs**, the very desirable residential districts favoured by those well-to-do Capetonians who prefer the urbanity of the district to the leafier southern suburbs. Given the City Bowl suburbs' proximity to the city centre and the Atlantic seaboard, as well as to restaurants and entertainment, and the great views across the centre to the harbour, the area is unsurprisingly popular with visitors, with numerous B&Bs and guesthouses to choose from, and Cape Town's top two backpacker lodges: *Ashanti* and *The Backpack* (see p.126).

Table Mountain

Table Mountain is a compelling feature in the middle of the city. The north face of the mountain overlooks the city centre, with the distinct formations of **Lion's Head** and **Signal Hill** to the west and **Devil's Peak** to the east. A series of gable-like formations known as the **Twelve Apostles** make up the mountain's west face. The southwest face towers over Hout Bay, the east face over the southern suburbs.

The mountain is a wilderness where you'll find wildlife and 1400 species of flora. Indigenous mammals include baboons, dassies (see box, p.84) and porcupines. The animals that resemble mountain goats are Himalayan **tahrs**, descended from specimens introduced by Cecil Rhodes onto his estate, and which escaped to flourish on the mountain. A number of tahrs were controversially shot in 2004, in an attempt to allow native antelope species to flourish instead.

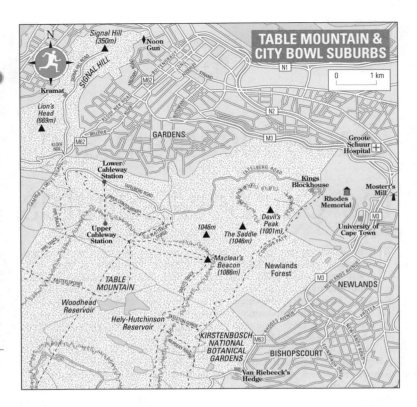

The least challenging – but certainly not least interesting – way up and down the mountain is via the highly popular **cable car** at the western table. **Climbing** the mountain will give you a greater sense of achievement than being ferried up by the cable car, but proceed with extreme caution: the weather is subject to rapid changes, both in general and in localized areas.

The cable car

Installed in 1997, Table Mountain's state-of-the-art Swiss cable-car system offers dizzying views across Table Bay and the Atlantic; the floor of the fishbowl-shaped cars is designed to complete a 360-degree rotation on the way, giving passengers a full panorama. To make a real outing of it, go up for breakfast at the upper station's restaurant or take a picnic and a bottle of Cape bubbly to enjoy on the tabletop, an incomparable spot to watch the sun go down.

Cars leave from the **lower cableway station** on Tafelberg Road (daily every 10–15 min: Jan & Dec 8am–9pm; Feb & March 8.30am–7.30pm; April 8.30am–5.30pm; May–Oct 8am–5pm; Nov 8am–7pm), with return **tickets** costing R130 for adults and R68 for children, while under-4s ride for free. Note that operations can be disrupted by bad weather or maintenance work; for information on current schedules call ☎021 424 8181, or check ⓦwww.tablemountain.net.

You can get to the lower cableway station by Rikki, metered taxi, or in one of the minibus taxis that ply the route here from Adderley Street. The open-topped

City Sightseeing Bus also serves the cableway. If you're driving, you'll find parking along Tafelberg Road, but you may be in for a bit of a walk in peak season – the stretch of parked cars can extend several hundred metres.

Climbs and walks

Reckoned the most-climbed massif in the world, Table Mountain has suffered under the constant pounding of hikers and wanton vandalism – footpaths have been eroded, indigenous vegetation degraded and litter scattered around – although the damage isn't always obvious, certainly not from the dizzying vista at the top. Unless you're going with a knowledgeable guide, attempt only the **routes** outlined here, which are the simplest. Every year the mountain strikes back, taking its toll of lives; it may look sunny and clear when you leave, but conditions at the top could be very different. One of the commonest causes of difficulties is people losing the track (often because of mist suddenly descending) and becoming trapped; other hazards include the strength of the sun and violent winds. If you plan on tackling one of the hundreds of walks and climbs on its slopes, go properly prepared (see box, p.85).

There are also **full-day guided hikes** which are thoroughly recommended, the hikes tailored to your level of fitness and with some rock climbing possible; prices include transport and packed lunches. You may choose to come back the easy way by cable car, or partially abseil. See the entries on abseiling, rock climbing and walking in Chapter 12 for more details.

Signal Hill and Lion's Head

From the roundabout at the top of **Kloof Nek** – the saddle between Table Mountain and Lion's Head, over which Kloof Nek Road runs to reach the Atlantic seaboard – a road leads all the way along **Signal Hill** to a car park and lookout, with good views over Table Bay, the docks and the city. A cannon was formerly used for sending signals to ships at anchor in the bay, and the **Noon Gun**, still fired from its slopes daily, sends a thunderous rumble through the

Dassies

The outsized fluffy guinea pigs you'll encounter at the top of Table Mountain are **dassies** or hyraxes (*Procavia capensis*) which, despite their appearance, aren't rodents at all, but the closest living relatives of elephants. Their name (pronounced like "dusty" without the "t") is the Afrikaans version of *dasje*, meaning "little badger", given to them by the first Dutch settlers. Dassies have poor body temperature control and, like reptiles, rely on shelter against both hot sunlight and the cold. They wake up sluggish and seek out rocks where they can catch the sun in the early morning – this is one of the best times to look out for them. One adult stands sentry against predators and issues a low-pitched warning cry in response to a threat.

Dassies are very widely distributed, having thrived in South Africa with the elimination of predators, and can be found in suitably rocky habitats all over the country. They live in colonies consisting of a dominant male and eight or more related females and their offspring.

Bo-Kaap and city centre below. Halfway along the road is a sacred Islamic *kramat* (shrine), one of several dotted around the peninsula which "protect" the city. You can also walk up **Lion's Head**, an unstrenuous hike that seems to bring out half the population of Cape Town every full moon.

Platteklip Gorge and Maclear's Beacon

The first recorded ascent to the summit of Table Mountain was by the Portuguese captain Antonio de Saldanha, in 1503. He wisely chose **Platteklip Gorge**, the gap visible from the front table (the north side) which, as it turned out, is the most accessible way up. A short and easy extension will get you to Maclear's Beacon which, at 1086m, is the highest point on the mountain. The Platteklip route starts out at the lower cableway station and has the added advantage of ending at the upper station, so you can descend in a car.

From the lower station, walk east along Tafelberg Road until you see a high embankment built from stone and maintained with wire netting. Just beyond and to the left of a small dam is a sign pointing to Platteklip Gorge. A steep fifteen-minute climb brings you onto the **Upper Contour Path**. About 25m east along this, take the path indicated by a sign reading "Contour Path/ Platteklip Gorge". The path zigzags from here onwards and is very clear. The gorge is the biggest cleavage on the whole mountain, leading directly and safely to the top, but it's a very steep slog which will take two to three hours in total if you're reasonably fit. Once on top, turn right and ascend the last short section onto the **front table** for a breathtaking view of the city. A sign points the way to the upper cableway station – a fifteen-minute walk along a concrete path thronging with visitors.

Maclear's Beacon is about 35 minutes from the top of the Platteklip Gorge on a path leading eastward, with white squares on little yellow footsteps guiding you all the way. The path crosses the front table with Maclear's Beacon visible at all times. From the top you'll get views of False Bay and the Hottentots Holland Mountains to the east.

The Pipe Track

One of the most rewarding and easiest walks along the mountainside takes the **Pipe Track**, a service road which follows water pipes from the mountain reservoirs to Kloof Nek. The track runs on the level for roughly 7km, on the west flank of Table Mountain, beneath the Twelve Apostles, following the mountain's contours and offering fantastic views of the Atlantic. The Pipe Track isn't a circular route, so you can turn back at any point; the whole walk can take up to three hours each way.

The route begins at some stone steps at Kloof Nek opposite the bus terminus for the cable car, just to the west of the Tafelberg Road turn-off (if you're driving, park on Tafelberg Road). Steps lead up alongside forestry staff houses before the road levels off under some pines. The path intersects several climbs up the mountain, useful indicators as to how far you've come. The first, after about 45 minutes, is indicated by a sign to Blinkwater Ravine (closed to the public due to rockfalls). A further ten to fifteen minutes brings you to the Kasteelspoort ascent (signposted under gum trees) followed by Woody Ravine and finally the signpost at Slangolie Ravine, roughly 25 minutes after Kasteelspoort, where the path ends. The rock bed on Slangolie is steep, unstable and to be avoided. Turn back when you see the first of the Woodhead Tunnel danger signs.

Skeleton Gorge and Nursery Ravine

You can combine a visit to the gardens at Kirstenbosch (see p.93) with an ascent up Table Mountain via one route and a descent down another, ending at the Kirstenbosch National Botanical Gardens' **restaurant** for tea. Starting at the restaurant, follow the **Skeleton Gorge** signs, which lead you onto the **Contour Path**. At the Contour Path, a plaque indicates that this is **Smuts' Track**, the route favoured by Jan Smuts, the Boer leader and South African prime minister (see box, p.86). The plaque marks the start of a broad-stepped climb up Skeleton Gorge, involving wooden steps, stone steps, wooden ladders

Table Mountain safety

Make sure you:

- Don't climb alone. As well as general mountain-safety issues, there have been a number of tourist muggings recently, so it's recommended you walk with a guide; one reliable recommendation is Ross Suter (☏082 437 5145).
- Inform someone you're going up the mountain; tell them your route, when you're leaving and when you expect to be back.
- Leave early enough to give yourself time to complete your route during daylight.
- Don't try to descend via an unknown route. If you get lost in poor weather, seek shelter, keep warm and wait for help.
- Never leave even the tiniest scrap of litter on the mountain.
- Never make fires. No cooking is allowed, even on portable stoves.

Wear:

- Good footwear. Boots or running shoes are recommended.
- A broad-rimmed hat.

Take:

- A backpack.
- A water bottle. Allow two litres per person.
- Enough food.
- A warm jersey.
- A windbreaker.
- A raincoat.
- Sunglasses.
- High-factor sunscreen.
- Plasters for blisters.
- A map (available from Cape Union Mart at the Waterfront, or Cavendish Square Shopping Centre in Claremont).

Jan Smuts

The life of Jan **Christiaan Smuts**, one of South Africa's greatest figures, perhaps embodies more than any other this country's strained relationship with itself in the first half of the twentieth century. Born to an Afrikaner farming family, Smuts spoke English with the distinctive linguistic burr of Swartland and excelled as a scholar at Stellenbosch and then Cambridge universities. During the Anglo-Boer War he waged a wideranging and ultimately undefeated guerrilla campaign as the leader of a Boer commando. However, he came to believe in a unified South Africa under a British flag, and was appointed commander-in-chief of imperial forces in East Africa during World War I, attending meetings of the British War Cabinet in the final phases of the war.

Smuts served as prime minister of South Africa between 1919 and 1924, and again between 1939 and 1948, when he led South Africa into World War II on the British side. Like his fellow leader and statesman Winston Churchill, he failed to hold together support at home and in 1948 lost the postwar general election to the hardline Afrikaner D.F. Malan.

Smuts spent much of his career in domestic politics trying to hold together disparate political and social moralities among English and moderate Afrikaans-speaking whites. He is remembered by white South Africans as a wily, tainted politician rather than as a great humanitarian. Yet he was, like very few South Africans before or since, a man of global vision and influence who as a 76-year-old played an important role in drafting the United Nations charter in 1946. He also published a philosophical treatise and was known for his love of nature and the outdoors, in particular Table Mountain.

and loose boulders. Be prepared for steep ravines and difficult rock climbs – and under no circumstances stray off the path. It requires reasonable fitness, but can take as little as an hour. Skeleton Gorge can be an unpleasant way down, especially in the wet season when it gets slippery.

Nursery Ravine is recommended for the descent. At the top of Skeleton Gorge, walk a few metres to your right to a sign indicating **Kasteelspoort**. It's just 35 minutes from the top of Skeleton along the Kasteelsport path to the head of Nursery Ravine. The descent returns you to the 310-metre Contour Path, which leads back to Kirstenbosch. This entire walk lasts about five hours.

The City Bowl suburbs

The City Bowl suburbs, the residential area south of Orange Street and the Company Gardens, gently climbing the lower slopes of Table Mountain, is not so much a district to explore as one in which to consume. That there are so many good restaurants, pubs and coffee bars along the throbbing artery of **Kloof Street** – the continuation of Long Street – is indicative of the affluence of the area. Along Kloof you'll also find the **Labia**, an arthouse cinema complex that attracts movie buffs from all over the peninsula.

The most obvious landmark of the district is the **Mount Nelson Hotel** (see p.127), on the south side of Orange Street in the suburb of **Gardens**, an area which takes its name from the historic gardens on the opposite side of the road. Harking back to the heyday of British colonialism, the grand hotel is announced by a gigantic white pedimented gateway supported on nearly two dozen Corithinthian columns, and is guarded day and night by a pith-helmeted sentinel.

CITY BOWL SUBURBS

RESTAURANTS, CAFÉS, BARS & CLUBS

Café Paradiso	7
Kauai Juice	2
Lazari	4
Limoncello	5
Melissa's	6
Mount Nelson Hotel Garden Room	0
Raith Gourmet	3
Sawaddee	1

ACCOMMODATION

African Sun	J
Ashanti Lodge and Guest House	K
The Backpack	A
Belmont House	M
Bergzicht	E
Blencathra	O
Cape Milner Hotel	C
Leeuwenvoet House	H
Lezard Bleu	P
Mount Nelson Hotel	D
Oak Lodge	I
Saasveld Lodge	G
Underberg Guest House	F
Villa Belmonte Hotel	N
Welgelegen Guest House	L
Zebra Crossing	B

Long Street

Gardens Shopping Centre

Bertram House

Reservoir

Molteno Reservoir

GARDENS

0   200 m

▲ Kloof Street

Behind the hotel, the suburbs on either side of Kloof Street are characterized by a jumpy urbanity – and urbanness – found in few other parts of Cape Town, where sleazy but fast-gentrifying flatland rubs up against airy Victorian villas, modern cottages and stylish pieds-à-terre. The most elevated residential areas, close to Kloof Nek, among them **Higgovale**, **Oranjezicht** and **Tamboerskloof**, are packed with properties that carry suitably elevated price tags.

4

The southern suburbs

A way from Table Mountain and the city centre, the bulk of Cape Town's residential sprawl extends east into South Africa's interior. It's here that the **southern suburbs**, the formerly whites-only residential areas, stretch out down the east side of Table Mountain, ending just before Muizenberg on the False Bay coast. All the main suburban attractions are concentrated in this area and, not surprisingly, the best shopping areas and cinemas.

From anywhere in the southern suburbs you can see Table Mountain rising above Cape Town. The area offers some quick and highly rewarding escapes from the city heat, all of which hug the eastern slopes of the mountain and its extension, the **Constantiaberg**. Closest to the centre and most sublime of these is **Kirstenbosch National Botanical Gardens**, a meticulously maintained parkland of indigenous foliage. Further afield, in the **Constantia Winelands**, lie South Africa's oldest wineries, at Klein Constantia, Groot Constantia, Buitenverwachting and Steenberg, each centred on its own historic eighteenth-century Cape-Dutch homestead; and in the same vicinity is the dappled **Tokai Forest**, a relaxing refuge from the midsummer sun – and the howling southeaster.

The quickest way of reaching the southern suburbs from the city centre, Waterfront or City Bowl suburbs is the **M3 highway**; indeed taking the car is the only convenient way to get to Constantia, Kirstenbosch and Tokai. Outside rush hour, it takes about thirty minutes to get from the centre to Tokai, where the highway ends. Travelling by **train**, you can reach Woodstock, Salt River, Observatory, Mowbray, Rosebank and Rondebosch.

East of the **M5 highway**, which skirts through the margins of the southern suburbs, lie the **Cape Flats** – the windswept flatlands that splay out towards South Africa's interior which became the apartheid dumping ground for Africans and coloureds.

Woodstock to Rosebank

First and oldest of the suburbs as you take an easterly exit from town is **Woodstock**, unleafy and windblown, but redeemed by some nice Victorian buildings, originally occupied by working-class coloureds, and now yuppifying. To its east, **Salt River** is a harsh, industrial, mainly coloured area, built initially for workers and artisans, while **Observatory**, abutting its southern end, is generally regarded as Cape Town's bohemian hub, a reputation fuelled by its proximity to the University of Cape Town in Rondebosch and its large student population. Many of the houses here are student digs, but the narrow Victorian

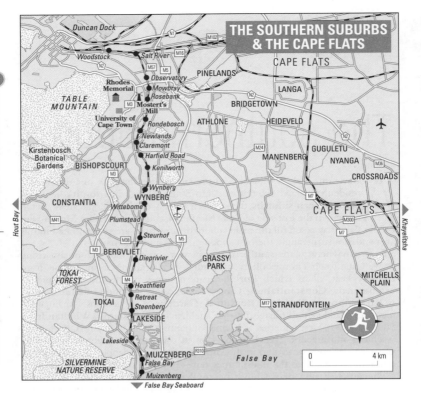

THE SOUTHERN SUBURBS
& THE CAPE FLATS

False Bay Seaboard

streets are also home to young professionals, hippies and arty types. The refreshingly unrestored peeling arcades on Observatory's Lower Main Road, and the streets off it, have some nice cafés and lively bars, as well as a wholefood shop, an African fabrics shop, and a couple of antiques emporiums. The huge Groote Schuur Hospital, which overlooks the freeway that sweeps through Observatory, was the site of the world's first heart transplant in 1967.

Along Station Road, away from the mountain and south of Observatory, is **Mowbray**, originally called Drie Koppen (Three Heads), after the heads of three slaves impaled there in 1724, but its name was changed in the 1840s. In the nineteenth century, this was the home of philologist Willem Bleek, who lived with a group of San convicts given up by the colonial authorities so that he could study their languages and attitudes. Bleek's pioneering work still forms the basis of much of what we know about traditional Khoisan life.

Rosebank, to Mowbray's south, has a substantial student community, some staying in the so-called Tampax Towers, the unmistakable circular residential blocks on Main Road. Just beyond them is the brown-bricked **Baxter Theatre**, one of Cape Town's premier arts complexes (see Chapter 10).

Irma Stern Museum

Irma Stern is acknowledged as one of South Africa's pioneering artists of the twentieth century, more for the fact that she brought modern European ideas to the colonies than for any huge contribution she made to world art. The **UCT Irma Stern Museum**, Cecil Road, Rosebank (Tues–Sat 10am–5pm; R10), was the artist's home for 38 years until her death in 1966. The museum is definitely worth visiting to see Stern's collection of Iberian, African, Oriental and ancient artefacts. The whole house, in fact, reflects the artist's fascination with exoticism, starting with her own Gauguinesque paintings of "native types", the fantastic carved doors she brought back from Zanzibar, and the very untypical garden that brings a touch of the tropics to Cape Town with its exuberant bamboo thickets and palm trees.

Born in a backwater town in South Africa in 1894 to German Jewish parents, Stern studied at Germany's Weimar Academy. In reaction to the academy's conservatism, she adopted **expressionist distortion** in her paintings, some of which were included in the Neue Sezession Exhibition in Berlin in 1918. Stern went on several expeditions into Zanzibar and the Congo in the 1940s and 1950s, where she found the source for her intensely sensuous paintings, which shocked South Africa at the time.

Although Stern's work was appreciated in Europe, when she returned to South Africa after World War II critics claimed that her style was simply a cover for technical incompetence. South African art historians now regard her as the towering figure of her generation. One of her most famous works is the much reproduced *The Eternal Child* (1916), a simple but vibrant portrait of a young girl, while *The Wood Carriers* (1951) uses raw ochres, browns and oranges to create an exoticized portrayal of a pair of African women.

Rondebosch and the Rhodes Memorial

South of Rosebank, neighbouring **Rondebosch** is home to the **University of Cape Town** (UCT), whose nineteenth-century buildings are handsomely festooned with creepers and sit grandly on the mountainside, overlooking Main Road and the M3 highway. Of passing interest on the campus is the **Woolsack**. This "cottage in the woods for poets and artists", just off Woolsack Road, was designed in 1900 by Sir Herbert Baker for **Cecil John Rhodes**. Rhodes invited **Rudyard Kipling** to "hang up his hat there" whenever he visited the Cape. Taking his friend at his word, Kipling fled the English winter every year from 1900 to 1907, bringing his family to Cape Town and spending five to six months at the Woolsack, where he is said to have written his famous poem *If*. The house is now occupied by the university's architecture faculty.

Rhodes features big in this neck of the woods: if you continue south from the Woolsack down the M3 (here known as Rhodes Drive), you'll pass **Groote Schuur**, another house built for him. Bordering on Main Road, Groote Schuur is one of Herbert Baker's most celebrated South African buildings, exemplifying the Cape Dutch Revival style. Rhodes' large estate here became the official prime ministerial residence of the Cape, then of South Africa, and when the country switched to a presidential system it became the home of the president – though Nelson Mandela preferred to use a nearby residence named Genadendal. Neither building is open to the public.

Rhodes Memorial

Next to the UCT campus, north towards the city, is the **Rhodes Memorial**, grandiosely conspicuous against the slopes of Devil's Peak. On a site chosen by Herbert Baker and Rudyard Kipling, the monument is reached via a signposted road that spurs northwest off the M3, just as Rhodes Drive becomes the Princess Anne Interchange. Herds of wildebeest and zebra nonchalantly graze on the slopes nearby as cars fly past on the M3.

Built to resemble a Greek temple, the memorial celebrates Rhodes' energy with a sculpture of a wildly rearing horse. The empire-builder's bust is planted at the top of a towering set of stairs, lined with reclining lions inspired by the Avenue of the Sphinxes at Karnak in Egypt. Carved in stone beneath the bust is a ponderous inscription by Kipling: "The immense and brooding spirit still shall order and control." Also on site is a **tea garden** with terrific views of Cape Town.

Below the memorial, alongside the M3, is the incongruous **Mostert's Mill**, a windmill built two centuries ago when there were wheat fields here instead of highways. From the memorial you can walk to the King's Blockhouse, formerly a signalling station to Muizenberg, and onto the Contour Path which follows the eastern side of the mountain, way above the southern suburbs to Constantia Nek.

Newlands, Claremont, Bishopscourt and Wynberg

Continuing south from Rondebosch along the Van der Stel Freeway (the M3) or along the more congested Main Road, you pass some of Cape Town's most prestigious suburbs. **Newlands**, almost merging with Rondebosch, is home to

▲ Mostert's Mill

the city's famous rugby and cricket stadiums. Worth a stop-off here at 31 Newlands Ave is **Montebello Craft and Design Centre** (Mon–Fri 9am–4.45pm, Sat & Sun 9.30am–3pm), a complex of exceptionally good craft shops and craftworkers' studios, with a restaurant under shady oaks.

The well-heeled suburb of **Claremont**, south of Newlands, is an alternative focus to the city centre for shopping and entertainment, with two cinema complexes and plenty of shops at **Cavendish Square Mall**. Alongside the high-quality shops, hawkers sell clothes, vegetables and herbs; closer to Claremont station, you can buy tasty *boerewors* from women cooking them outdoors on *skottel braais* (braziers).

A little further south, beyond the signpost to Kirstenbosch Gardens, is **Bishopscourt**. As the name suggests, it's home to the Anglican bishop of Cape Town, and it was in a mansion here that Archbishop Desmond Tutu lived even in the years when blacks weren't supposed to live in whites-only suburbs. Partly because of its prime siting – some plots have views of both Newlands Forest and the sea – this is one of the poshest areas in Cape Town; a number of consuls live here in huge properties behind high walls, which are about all you see as you pass through the area.

Further down the line, **Wynberg** is known for its Maynardville Shakespearean open-air theatre (see p.146) and its quaint row of shops and restaurants in Wolfe Street. By contrast Wynberg's Main Road offers a distinctly less genteel shopping experience, an interesting stroll past street vendors and fabric shops, as well as food outlets catering to the large number of workers travelling between Wynberg and Khayelitsha in the Cape Flats.

Kirstenbosch National Botanical Gardens

Five kilometres south of Rondebosch, in Rhodes Avenue, are the **Kirstenbosch National Botanical Gardens** (daily: April–Aug 8am–6pm; Sept–March 8am–7pm; R30, children R5; ☎021 799 8783), the third most popular tourist attraction in Cape Town (surpassed only by the Waterfront and the cable-car trip up Table Mountain). Kirstenbosch is the oldest and largest botanical garden in South Africa, created in 1895 by Cecil Rhodes, whose camphor and fig trees are still here. Today, over 22,000 indigenous plants – and a research unit and library – attract researchers and botanists from all over the world. There's a nursery selling local plants, while characteristic Cape plants, found nowhere else in the world, are cultivated on the slopes. In 2004 the gardens became part of South Africa's sixth UNESCO World Heritage site – the first botanical garden in the world to achieve this status, which in this instance recognizes the international significance of the *fynbos* plant kingdom (see *Going wild in Cape Town* colour section) that predominates at Kirstenbosch.

The gardens are magnificent, glorying in lush shrubs and exuberant blooms. Little signboards and paved paths guide you through the highlights of the gardens, with trees and plants identified to enhance the rambling. The most interesting route is the one created for blind visitors, with labels in Braille and an abundance of aromatic and textured plants. There is a free **walking tour** daily at 10am, and **golf-car tours** (R25) every hour on the hour.

If you're visiting the gardens in summer, one of the undoubted delights is to bring a picnic for a Sunday evening **open-air concert** (Dec–March 4.30–6.30pm;

see p.38), where you can lie back on the lawn, sip Cape wine and savour the mountain air and sunsets. Otherwise, there's an outdoor coffee shop, open daily for breakfast, lunch and teas, plus a restaurant with a fire going for winter days, though eating out in the gardens is more about the fabulous location than the food or service.

The gardens trail off into wild vegetation, covering a huge expanse of the rugged eastern slopes and wooded ravines of Table Mountain. The setting is quite breathtaking – this is a great place to have tea and stroll around gazing up the mountain, or to wander onto the paths, which meander steeply to the top with no fences cutting off the way. Two popular paths, starting from the Contour Path above Kirstenbosch, are **Nursery Ravine** and **Skeleton Gorge** (see p.85). Note that women should *not* walk alone in the isolated upper reaches of Kirstenbosch.

If you don't have a car and don't want to take an organized tour, the best way to get to Kirstenbosch is by Rikki or one of the local taxi services, a couple of which usually rank outside the gardens. Additionally, the City Sightseeing Bus (see box, p.28) stops at the gardens six times a day. There are municipal **bus** services (℡080 1212 111) from Cape Town's Golden Acre terminus (Mon–Fri 7.30am, 12.35pm & 3.35pm, except public holidays) and Mowbray terminus (also Mon–Fri except holidays 7am, 8am, 9am, 1pm, 2.35pm & 4pm) aimed at Kirstenbosch or Bishopscourt workers. If you're driving, take the M3 and leave it at the signposted Rhodes Drive turn-off (M63), close to Newlands.

Constantia and its winelands

South of Kirstenbosch lie the elegant suburbs of **Constantia** and the Cape's oldest **winelands**. Luxuriating on the lower slopes of Table Mountain and the Constantiaberg, with tantalizing views of False Bay, the winelands are an easy drive from town, not more than ten minutes off the Van der Stel Freeway (the M3), which runs between the centre and Muizenberg.

The winelands started cultivated life in 1685 as the farm of **Simon van der Stel**, the governor charged with opening up the fledgling Dutch colony to the interior. Thrusting himself wholeheartedly into the task, he selected for his own use an enormous tract of the choicest land set against the Constantiaberg. He named the estate after his daughter Constancia, and this is now (with a minor change of spelling) the name of Cape Town's oldest and most prestigious residential area. Exuding the easy ambience of landed wealth, Constantia is a green and pleasant place, shaded by oak forests and punctuated with farm stalls, stables, the Cape Dutch-style Constantia Mall and shops and, of course, the vineyards.

Constantia grapes have been making wine since Van der Stel's first output in 1705. After his death in 1712, the estate was divided up and sold off as the modern **Groot Constantia**, **Klein Constantia** and **Buitenverwachting**. In 1990, the nearby Steenberg Estate was bought up by a large Johannesburg mining conglomerate. All four estates are open to the public and offer tastings; they're definitely worth visiting if you aren't heading further afield to the Winelands proper.

There is no public **transport** to Constantia, but Groot Constantia features on most organized tours of Cape Town or the peninsula. To get to Groot Constantia

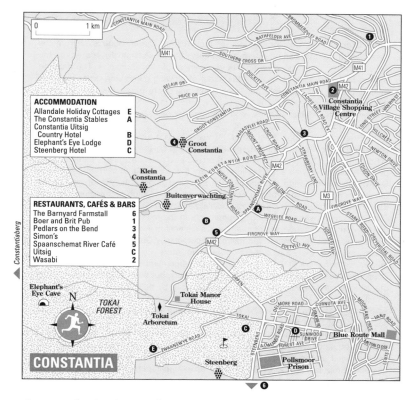

ACCOMMODATION
Allandale Holiday Cottages E
The Constantia Stables A
Constantia Uitsig
  Country Hotel B
Elephant's Eye Lodge D
Steenberg Hotel C

RESTAURANTS, CAFÉS & BARS
The Barnyard Farmstall 6
Boer and Brit Pub 1
Pedlars on the Bend 3
Simon's 4
Spaanschemat River Café 5
Uitsig C
Wasabi 2

CONSTANTIA

by car, take the signposted Groot Constantia exit from the M3 onto Ladies Mile Extension, and follow the signs to Groot Constantia. Buitenverwachting and Klein Constantia are on Klein Constantia Road, just off Ladies Mile Extension, and are clearly signposted.

Groot Constantia

The largest estate and the one most geared to tourists is **Groot Constantia** (ⓦ www.museums.org.za/grootcon), Cape Town's fourth most-visited attraction. Its big pull is that it retains the rump of Van der Stel's original estate, as well as the original buildings, though its portrayal of life in a seventeenth-century colonial chateau makes scant reference to the slave labour that underpinned its operations.

The **manor house**, a quintessential Cape Dutch building, was Van der Stel's original home, modified at the end of the eighteenth century by the French architect Thibault. It's thought that the magnificent gables were added in the eighteenth or early nineteenth centuries, with an allegorical figure representing Abundance recessed into a niche in the central gable. The interior forms part of the **museum** and is decorated in a style typical of eighteenth- and nineteenth-century Cape landowners, containing interesting Neoclassical as well as Louis XV and XVI furniture and Delft and Chinese ceramics.

Cape Dutch architecture

Cape Dutch style, which developed in the Western Cape countryside from the seventeenth to the early nineteenth century, is so distinctively rooted in the Winelands that it has become an integral element of the landscape. The dazzling limewashed walls look stunning in the midst of glowing green vineyards, while the thatched roofs and elaborate curvilinear gables seem to mirror the undulations of the surrounding mountains. The style was embraced in the twentieth century as part of white South African identity, and elements appear on the facades of many **suburban homes**.

The **Posthuys** (1673) in Main Road, Muizenberg, is a rude thatch-roofed cottage consisting of a single rectangular space. Thought to be the oldest colonial dwelling in South Africa, it has tiny windows which served as a defence against feared attacks by the Khoikho, as well as protection from the fierce winds that lash the peninsula. One of the few surviving examples of the so-called "longhouse", it represents the primitive language from which a rich vernacular Cape Dutch architecture evolved during the first two hundred years of colonial settlement.

Although there were important developments in the internal organization of Cape houses during this period, their most obvious element is the **gable**. End-gables were common in medieval northern European and particularly Dutch buildings, but central gables set into the long side of roofs were more unusual, and became the quintessential feature of the Cape Dutch style. Large numbers of buildings in central Cape Town had gables during the eighteenth century, but they had disappeared from the urban streetscape by the 1830s, to be replaced by buildings with flush facades and flat roofs.

Arson appears to be a major reason for these developments. There was a succession of town fires believed to have been started by slaves, including one that razed Stellenbosch in 1710 and Cape Town's **great fires** of 1736 and 1798. The consequence was a series of measures that shaped the layout of central Cape Town as well as the design of its houses. Flat roofs, clad in fireproof materials, became compulsory on all VOC buildings, as exemplified by the **Old Town House** (1755) off Greenmarket Square. After the 1798 conflagration, alarmed officials studied reports from London's Great Fire of 1666 and introduced legislation based on the lessons learned. To retard the spread of flames, narrow alleys were provided between houses, there was a total ban on thatched roofs, and any protrusions on building exteriors – including shutters – were banned. This led to the flush facades and internal shutters that typify early nineteenth-century Cape town houses. With the disappearance of pitched roofs, the urban gable withered away, surviving symbolically in some instances as minimal roof decoration, one example being the **Bo-Kaap Museum** (1763–68) in Wale Street, which sports a wavy parapet.

If you walk straight through the house and down the ceremonial axis, you'll come to the so-called **cellar** (actually a two-storey building above ground), fronted by a brilliant relief pediment. Attributed to the sculptor Anton Anreith, it depicts a riotous bacchanalia, featuring Ganymede, a young man so handsome that Zeus, in the form of an eagle, carried him off to be the cup-bearer of the gods. Inside, you can see a collection of wine-related objects dating from antiquity – such as amphoras – to the present.

Otherwise, there's a pretty average **museum** full of period furniture (daily 10am–5pm; R10), a gift shop, art gallery and two **restaurants**. **Cellar tours** start every hour on the hour (daily 10am–4pm; R27 including five wines to taste; booking essential on ☎021 794 5128) and there's **wine tasting** (daily: May–Nov 10am–4.30pm; Dec–April 9am–5.30pm; R22).

Rural homesteads developed from the plain longhouse to become increasingly elaborate over time. As landowners became more wealthy, the size of homesteads grew, and the house plan became more complex. The spread of fire from one building to another wasn't a major consideration in the countryside, where VOC building regulations carried little weight. Consequently, the pitched roof survived here. Gables, similarly, became the hallmark of country manors, being an important element of the facade, positioned above the front door to provide a window admitting light into the loft. Because they were just above the front door, they could also provide protection for the entrance against burning thatch. From these functional origins gables evolved into important symbols of wealth, with landowners vying to erect the biggest, most elaborate and most fashionable examples.

Cape Dutch architects

Between 1750 and 1850 – the golden century of Cape architecture – three men were associated with some of the most highly regarded buildings in the colony. So elevated is their status that numerous apocryphal attributions exist, claiming their hand in various projects.

Anton Anreith (1754–1822) was born near Freiburg in Germany, where it is believed he was apprenticed to a Rococo master-sculptor. He joined the Dutch East India Company's army as a private in 1776, but quickly gained employment as a carpenter, later earning the commission to reconstruct the facade of the Lutheran Church in Strand Street. In 1786 he became the VOC's master-sculptor and was probably responsible for the Kat balcony at the Castle of Good Hope.

Hermann Schutte (1761–1844), born in Bremen, was apprenticed to an architect in Germany for seven years. After joining the Dutch East India Company as a stone-mason, he came to the Cape in 1790 and worked on the Robben Island quarries, where he lost an eye and a hand in a blasting accident. He was discharged from the VOC and became a private building contractor, benefiting from numerous commissions from the influential Louis Michel Thibault. Schutte designed the Groote Kerk in Adderley Street and is also believed to have been responsible for the Green Point Lighthouse, the first lighthouse erected along the South African coast.

Louis Michel Thibault (1750–1815), a highly trained architect, was born near Amiens in France. Having held the honour of premier student at l'Academie Royale d'Architecture in Paris, he joined the Dutch East India Company as Lieutenant of Engineers, effectively making him the colony's principal military engineer and government architect, in which capacity he designed most of the major public buildings in Cape Town. Examples of his work include the Good Hope Masonic Lodge, which served as the parliamentary debating chamber prior to 1884, the current facade of the Slave Lodge, and the imposing gables at Groot Constantia.

Klein Constantia and Buitenverwachting

Smaller in scale than Groot Constantia, Klein Constantia and Buitenverwachting both offer free wine tasting in less regimented conditions than at the bigger estate, and although the buildings are far humbler, the settings are equally beautiful. **Klein Constantia**, Klein Constantia Road (free wine tasting and sales Mon–Fri 9am–5pm, Sat 9am–1pm; Ⓦ www.kleinconstantia.com), has a friendly atmosphere and produces some fine wines, such as its Cabernet Sauvignon Reserve and a number of excellent whites, among which its Semillon really stands out. Something of a curiosity is its **Vin de Constance**, the re-creation of an eighteenth-century Constantia wine that was a favourite of Napoleon, Frederick the Great and Bismarck. It's a delicious dessert wine,

▲ Buitenverwachting

packaged in a replica of the original bottle, and makes an original souvenir. There's also wildlife here: look out for the guinea fowls that roam the estate munching on beetles that attack young vine leaves; in summer, migrant steppe buzzards prey on unsuspecting starlings, which eat the grapes.

Buitenverwachting (roughly pronounced "bay-tin-fur-vuch-ting", with the "ch" as in the Scottish rendition of loch), also on Klein Constantia Road (Mon–Fri 9am–5pm, Sat 9am–1pm; free; ⓦ www.buitenverwachting.co.za), is a bucolic place in the middle of the suburbs, with sheep and cattle grazing in the fields as you approach the main buildings. Despite deep historic roots, the estate is mould-breaking and has for many years provided its workers with some of the best living conditions of any South African farm. Unusual labour practices include the provision of two social workers, weekly visits by a doctor to the farm clinic, and worker involvement in the selection of new staff. Ducks, part of the environmentally friendly approach, are used for pest control, feeding on snails that prey on vines.

The architecture and setting at the foot of the Constantiaberg are as good reasons to come here as are the top-ranking wines, among them the classy Christine – a claret-style blend – and some excellent whites, including the Sauvignon Blanc and Chardonnay. Overlooking the vineyards and backing onto the garden, the **homestead** was built in 1794 (the 1769 on the gable appears to be wrong) by Arend Brink, and features an unusual gabled pediment broken with an urn motif.

Buitenverwachting's expensive **restaurant** of the same name (Tues–Sat lunch & dinner; ☎021 794 3522) is regularly voted one of South Africa's ten best. For a day out on the farm (they have cattle and horses, too), they also do luxury **picnic lunches** (Nov–April Mon–Sat 12.30–2.30pm; R100; booking essential – contact Adrienne on ☎021 794 1012 or 082 973 8543), which you can enjoy under the oaks in the fabulous gardens.

Tokai

Effectively the southern extension of Constantia, forested **Tokai** is an excellent area for leafy recreation away from the centre, with some relaxed and child-friendly places for eating and drinking, and sheltered from the southeaster. Here you can also take in some wine tasting at the nearby **Steenberg Vineyards**, which incorporates a luxury golfing resort.

To drive to Tokai from the centre of Cape Town, head south along the M3 and exit north onto Ladies Mile Road; continue for 100m before turning south into Spaanschemat River Road (M42), signposted Tokai, which runs through the suburb. You can easily combine Tokai with a trip to the seaside, as the suburb is fifteen minutes' drive from the False Bay seaboard. Along the M42 before Steenberg is an outstanding, if slightly pricey, lunch stop at the *River Café* (closed Sun), part of the Constantia Uitsig Wine Estate. The food is fresh and imaginative, and you can eat alfresco looking out at the vineyards.

Tokai Forest

Most people come out to Tokai for the well-marked hiking paths and mountain-biking trails in the pine plantations of the **Tokai Forest**. You can get here from Spaanschemat River Road, turning west into Tokai Road, which heads straight to the forest. About 500m from Spaanschemat River Road, the road passes through pine forests which are equipped with picnic tables, though this isn't the nicest part of the forest or the best place to picnic. Instead, keep on till you reach the arboretum. A little further along the road from the picnic sites, you can't fail to see the imposing **Tokai Manor House** (not open to the public). Designed by Louis Michel Thibault (see box, p.971) and built around 1795, this National Monument is an elegant gem of Cape Dutch architecture combined with the understated elegance of French Neoclassicism.

A hundred metres to its west lies the entrance to another National Monument, the historic tree plantation that constitutes the **Tokai Arboretum** (daily dusk to dawn; R10 donation). It's the work of Joseph Storr Lister, who was a nineteenth-century Conservator of Forests for the Cape Colony. In 1885 he experimented with planting 150 species of trees from temperate countries, with oaks and eucalyptus featuring extensively as well as some beautiful California redwoods. Storr discovered that conifers were best suited to the Cape, which is why the plantation to the west of the arboretum, owned by the Safcol timber company, consists mainly of pines. The arboretum is the best place to begin rambling and an ideal place to bring **children**, with outdoor seating, plenty of shade and logs to jump on and over. There's also a car park and a thatched **café** (closed Mon) close to the entrance gate for tea and scones.

Several tracks and trails crisscross the arboretum and plantation, providing easy walks and mountain-biking trails (bring your own bike). Longer hikes include the walk from the entrance gate to **Elephant's Eye Cave** (6km there and back), which can easily be completed in well under three hours. The route passes through pine forests before opening into montane *fynbos* that covers the slopes of the Constantiaberg, eventually leading to the cave, which offers terrific panoramas. Ask for a map and directions at the entrance gate or at the adjacent café.

Steenberg Vineyards

In a fabulous location at the foot of Steenberg mountain, the **Steenberg Vineyards** (Mon–Fri 8.30am–4.30pm; Sept–Feb also Sat 9am–1pm; free;

The Cape Flats and the townships

East of the northern and southern suburbs, among the industrial smokestacks and the windswept **Cape Flats**, and reaching well beyond the airport, is Cape Town's largest residential quarter, taking in the **coloured districts**, **African townships** and shantytown **squatter camps**. The Cape Flats are exactly that: flat, as well as barren and windswept, with the M5 acting as a dividing line between them and the southern suburbs.

The Flats can be both shocking and heartening, their abject poverty coexisting with a spirit of enterprise and stoicism. The African townships were set up as dormitories to provide labour for white Cape Town, not as places to build a life, which is why they had no facilities and no real hub. The **men-only hostels**, another apartheid relic, are at the root of many of the area's social problems. During the 1950s, the government set out a blueprint to turn the tide of Africans flooding into Cape Town. No African was permitted to settle permanently in the Cape west of a line near the Fish River, the old frontier over 1000km from Cape Town; women were entirely banned from seeking work in Cape Town and men prohibited from bringing their wives to join them. By 1970 there were ten men for every woman in Langa.

In the end, apartheid failed to prevent the influx of work-seekers desperate to come to Cape Town. Where people couldn't find legal accommodation they set up the squatter camps of makeshift iron, cardboard and plastic sheeting. During the 1970s and 1980s, the government attempted to demolish these and destroy anything left inside – but no sooner had the police left than the camps reappeared, and they are now a permanent feature of the Cape Flats. One of the best known of all South Africa's squatter camps is **Crossroads**, whose inhabitants suffered campaigns of harassment that included killings by apartheid collaborators and police, and continuous attempts to bulldoze it out of existence. Through sheer determination and desperation its residents hung on, eventually winning the right to stay. Today, the government is making attempts to improve conditions in the shanty-towns by introducing running water and sanitation; families and ad hoc traders are now moving in.

Ⓦwww.steenberg-vineyards.com) comprise a fine Cape Dutch manor house and three other farm buildings, set around a large formal garden dating from 1695. This is South Africa's oldest wine estate: the lands were granted by Governor Simon van der Stel to the five-times widowed Catherina Michelse in 1682 and sold on in 1695 to Frederik Roussouw. That year, Roussouw erected the first buildings, and produced the first wine here. After his death, his widow Christina Diemer turned the estate into a highly profitable business,

Langa is the oldest and most central township, lying just east of the former whites-only suburb of Pinelands and north of the N2. In this relentlessly grey place, without the tiniest patch of green relief, you'll find women selling sheep and goats' heads, alongside state-of-the-art public phone bureaus run by enterprising township businessmen from inside recycled cargo containers. Nuclear families live in smart suburban houses while, not far away, there are former men-only hostels where as many as three families share one room.

South of the African ghettos is **Mitchell's Plain**, a coloured area stretching down to the False Bay coast (you'll skirt Mitchell's Plain if you take the M5 to Muizenberg). More salubrious than any of the African townships, Mitchell's Plain reflects how under apartheid lighter skins meant better conditions, even if you weren't quite white. But for coloureds the forced removals were no less tragic, many being summarily forced to vacate family homes because their suburb had been declared a White Group Area. Many families were relocated here when District Six was razed (see p.69), and their communities never fully recovered – one of the symptoms of dislocation are the violent gangs which have become an everyday part of Mitchell's Plain youth culture.

Township tours and homestays

Several projects are under way to encourage tourists into the townships but, as a high proportion of Cape Town's nearly two thousand annual murders take place here, the recommended way to visit is on a **tour**. A few of the firms listed on pp.21–22 offering township tours, all of which are operated by residents of the Cape Flats or in cooperation with local communities, emphasize face-to-face encounters with ordinary people. They include visits to *shebeens*, nightclubs and a township restaurant, chats with residents of squatter camps and the Langa hostels, and meetings with traditional healers and music makers, township artists and craftworkers. Some tours also take in "sites of political struggle", where significant events in the fight against apartheid occurred. If you want to really get under the skin of the townships, there's no better way than to stay in one of the **township B&Bs** listed on p.132.

providing hospitality to travellers and provisions to the fleet (the VOC declared Simon's Town its winter port in 1741). Steenberg now boasts a luxury country hotel, using the refurbished buildings that were declared a National Monument in 1996. Of its wines, the Merlot, Sauvignon Blanc and Semillon stand out.

Across the road from Steenberg is **Pollsmoor Prison**, where numerous political prisoners did time during the apartheid era, including Nelson Mandela towards the end of his period of incarceration.

The Atlantic seaboard

able Mountain's steep drop into the ocean along much of the western
Peninsula forces the suburbs along the **Atlantic seaboard** into a ribbon
of developments clinging dramatically to the slopes. The sea washing the
west side of the Peninsula can be very chilly, far colder than on the False
Bay seaboard. Although not ideal for bathing, the Atlantic seaboard offers mind-
blowing views from some of the most incredible coastal roads in the world,
particularly beyond **Sea Point**, and there are opportunities for **whale-spotting**
– try your luck at Chapman's Peak towards Hout Bay, and between Llandudno
and Sea Point, where the road curves along the ocean. The coast itself consists
of a series of bays and white-sanded beaches edged with smoothly sculpted
bleached rocks; inland, the Twelve Apostles, a series of rocky buttresses, gaze
down onto the surf. The beaches are ideal for sunbathing, or sunset picnics – it's
from this side of the peninsula that you can watch the sun sink into the ocean,
creating fiery reflections on the sea and mountains behind as it slips away.

Mouille Point to Clifton

Just to the west of the V&A Waterfront, Mouille Point and its close neighbour,
Green Point, are among the suburbs closest to the city centre. **Mouille**
("moo-lee") **Point** is known principally for its squat rectangular Victorian
lighthouse, commissioned in the 1820s, and painted with diagonal red and
white stripes.

Mouille Point merges with the far larger suburb of **Green Point**, which
continues both inland from it and west along the ragged Atlantic shore. Over
the last couple of years Green Point's proximity to the Waterfront – an easy
ten-or-so minutes' walk away – and its position along the coast has turned it
from a sleazy district into a humming area of excellent accommodation, eating
places and clubs.

West along Main Road, Green Point merges with **Sea Point**, a long-established
place for great restaurants. Middle-class couples, pram-pushing mothers, street kids,
hookers and drunks create an uneasy blend of respectability and seediness that
disappears as you move into Bantry Bay and the wealthier suburbs down the
Atlantic seaboard. The closest seaside to the city centre is a block down from Main
Road, although it's too rocky for swimming. Halfway along the kilometre-long
beach promenade, alongside Beach Road, you'll catch views of **Graaff's Pool**, an
institutionalized and exclusively male nudist spot. At the westernmost end is the
only place in the vicinity to swim, at Sea Point Pavilion's unheated Olympic-sized

THE ATLANTIC SEABOARD

GREEN POINT

Three Anchor Bay

BEACH ROAD

Signal Hill (350m)

Sunset Beach

SEA POINT

Queen's Beach

KLOOF NEK ROAD

Bantry Bay

TABLE MOUNTAIN NATIONAL PARK

ATLANTIC

OCEAN

Lion's Head (669m)

CLIFTON

Clifton Bay

KLOOF NEK

TAFELBERG ROAD

Camps Bay

CAMPS BAY

CAMPS BAY DRIVE

Bakoven Bay

BAKOVEN

Koeëlbaai

TABLE MOUNTAIN NATIONAL PARK

VICTORIA AVE

Lui Bay

T W E L V E   A P O S T L E S

Logie's Bay

CECILIA STATE FOREST

RHODES DRIVE

Llandudno

CONSTANTIA MAIN ROAD

Kirstenbosch Gardens & Bishopscourt

Sunset Rocks

M6

World of Birds

Sandy Bay

HOUT BAY ROAD

M63

CONSTANTIA

Klein Constantia

TABLE MOUNTAIN NATIONAL PARK

TABLE MOUNTAIN NATIONAL PARK

TOKAI FOREST

Hout Bay

N

Hout Bay Harbour

Constantiaberg (928m)

The Sentinel (331m)

CHAPMAN'S PEAK DRIVE

Hout Bay

TOKAI ROAD

Duiker Island

0   2 km

Chapman's Peak & Scarborough

▲ Mouille Point lighthouse

saltwater pool (May–Nov 8.30am–4.30pm; Dec–April 7am–6pm; R20), alongside the crashing surf, with lawns for sunbathing.

At the westernmost edge of Sea Point lies **Bantry Bay**, combining the density of Sea Point with the wealth of the Atlantic suburbs; here mansions are raked up on steep slopes above the Atlantic, guarded by the granite boulders of Lion's Head. The upmarket resort hotels and self-catering apartment blocks are just far enough for comfort from the sleaze of Sea Point, but close enough should you want to walk to a restaurant.

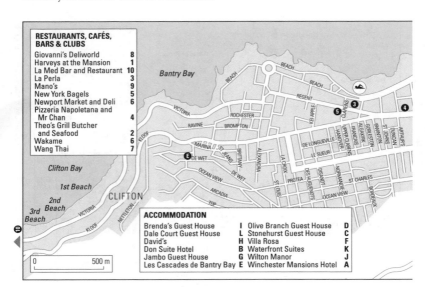

RESTAURANTS, CAFÉS, BARS & CLUBS

Giovanni's Deliworld	8
Harveys at the Mansion	1
La Med Bar and Restaurant	10
La Perla	3
Mano's	9
New York Bagels	5
Newport Market and Deli	6
Pizzeria Napoletana and Mr Chan	4
Theo's Grill Butcher and Seafood	2
Wakame	6
Wang Thai	7

ACCOMMODATION

Brenda's Guest House	I	Olive Branch Guest House	D
Dale Court Guest House	L	Stonehurst Guest House	C
David's	H	Villa Rosa	F
Don Suite Hotel	B	Waterfront Suites	K
Jambo Guest House	G	Wilton Manor	J
Les Cascades de Bantry Bay	E	Winchester Mansions Hotel	A

Clifton

Fashionable **Clifton**, on the next cove, along Victoria Road (the M6), sits on the most expensive real estate in Africa, studded with fabulous seaside apartments and with four sandy **beaches**, reached via steep stairways. The sea here is good for surfing and safe for swimming, but bone-chillingly cold. First Beach (they're all numbered) is frequented by muscular ball-players, surfers and their female counterparts, but is usually the least crowded of the four beaches. Second and Third beaches are split between the teenies and 30-somethings, with beautiful men and some cruising on Third; if in doubt, head for Fourth, which is suitable for families because it has the fewest steps. Hout Bay **buses** go to Clifton from the city centre several times a day (a 30min journey). Parking can be impossible along the M6 in summer, so you may be best off parking up in the residential area. Bring your own refreshments, as there's only one overpriced café on Fourth Beach and hardly any shops.

Camps Bay to Sandy Bay

A little to the south of Clifton, the suburb of **Camps Bay** climbs the slopes of Table Mountain and is scooped into a small amphitheatre, bounded by the Lion's Head and the Twelve Apostles sections of the Table Mountain range. This, and the airborne views across the Atlantic, makes Camps Bay one of the most desirable places to live in Cape Town. The main drag, Victoria Road, skirts the coast and is packed with trendy restaurants, while the wide sandy beach is accessible by bus and is consequently enjoyed by families of all shapes and colours. Lined by a row of palms and some grassy verges with welcome shade for picnics, Camps Bay beach is very busy around the Christmas and Easter

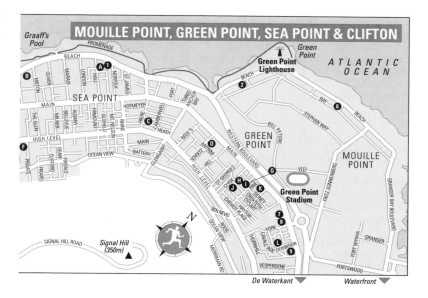

MOUILLE POINT, GREEN POINT, SEA POINT & CLIFTON

New Year, New Year – so good they do it twice

A longstanding tradition in Cape Town is **Tweede Nuwe Jaar** (second new year), on January 2 – until recently an official public holiday. Historically this was the only day of the year when slaves were allowed off, and the day has persisted as a holiday of epic proportions. If you're in Cape Town over this period, Tweede Nuwe Jaar is the time to party, when **Cape minstrels** from the coloured community dance through the streets of the city centre. Expect each troupe to be dressed up in matching outfits, often featuring outrageous colour combinations. Some roads in the centre are blocked off during the day for the festivities, which process through the city and end up at **Green Point Stadium**.

The style of minstrelsy that characterizes the carnival dates back to the 1880s, when minstrel entertainers from visiting US ocean liners joined in the city's New Year revelry. One good reason to come is to hear the locally evolved style of singing known as *ghommaliedjies* (drum songs), accompanied by banjos, which began as slave songs performed at New Year and evolved in the twentieth century into a part of working-class coloured culture.

Up to the 1970s, an important part of the carnival was a parade from District Six through the streets of Cape Town. Sadly this died out when District Six was razed, and with it some of the spontaneity and vigour of the event. Many coloureds were moved out to the Cape Flats, and now have to be bussed to the stadium.

breaks. However, it's exposed to the southeaster, and there's the usual Atlantic chill and an occasional dangerous backwash.

There's little development between Camps Bay and the wonderful cove of **Llandudno**, 20km from Cape Town along Victoria Road (not served by public transport). Here a steep and narrow road winds down past smart homes to the shore, where the sandy beach is punctuated at either end by magnificent granite boulders and rock formations. This is a good sunbathing spot and a choice one for bring-your-own sundowners. The small car park frequently spills over into the suburban streets at peak periods.

Isolated **Sandy Bay**, Cape Town's main nudist beach, can only be reached via a twenty-minute walk from Llandudno. In the apartheid days, the South African police went to ingenious lengths to trap nudists, but nowadays the beach is relaxed, so feel free to come as undressed as feels comfortable. There are no facilities whatsoever – bring whatever supplies you may need. A path leads from the south end of the Llandudno car park, through *fynbos* vegetation and across some rocks, to the beach; it's a fairly easy walk, but watch out for broken glass if you're barefoot.

Hout Bay

Although no longer the quaint fishing village it once was, **Hout Bay** still has a functioning fishing harbour and is the centre of the local crayfish industry. Despite ugly modern development and a growing shantytown, the natural setting is awesome, with the twin heads of the Sentinel and Chapman's Peak defining entry to the bay. Leopards no longer stalk its *kranse* and *koppies*, but their former presence is recalled by a bronze statue looking down from Chapman's Peak Drive to the east. The best way to take in the landscape is on one of the short cruises just out of the bay, from the harbour to **Duiker Island**, home to a large seal colony. Drumbeat (☎021 790 5859) and Nauticat (☎021 790 7278) are reliable operators with departures at 9.45am, 11am, noon, 2pm and 3pm, the trip costing R50 there and back.

The sea off the long slender **beach** is no good for swimming – not only is it too cold, it's also too close to the harbour and too prone to have fish scales floating in the surf – but the beach itself is perfect for walks. Away from the harbour, the village is just managing to hang onto its historic ambience, with the **Hout Bay Museum**, 4 St Andrews Rd (Tues–Fri 9am–4pm, Sat 8am–2pm; R5), offering good exhibits on the Strandlopers – Khoisan who hunted and gathered along the shore – and the local fishing industry. The nearby **World of Birds**, Valley Road (daily 9am–5pm; R55, children R35, under-3s free), requires at least two hours to see the more than three thousand birds and small animals housed in surprisingly pleasant and peaceful walk-through aviaries. From Tuesday to Thursday, and at weekends, you can watch penguins being fed at 11.30am and 3.30pm, pelicans at 12.30pm and birds of prey at 4.10pm. A large

▲ Hout Bay harbour

walk-in monkey jungle (daily 11.30am–1pm & 2–3.30pm) includes among its inhabitants cute squirrel monkeys; visitors can handle and play with them. There's a café serving light lunches, or you can picnic at the Flamingo Terrace. Young children are well catered for with a couple of on-site playground areas.

Hout Bay is at a convenient junction for the rest of the peninsula. From Cape Town, it's 20km away along either the coast or inland via Constantia; at a push you can get there by bus (see p.27) or use a minibus taxi. From Simon's Town across the peninsula spine, Hout Bay is 26km away via the Glencairn Expressway. The bay has the highest concentration of **places to stay** south of Sea Point, including hotels and bed and breakfasts. **Hout Bay Tourism** (Mon–Fri 9am–5pm, Sat 9am–1pm; ☎021 791 8380), adjacent to the museum, can book accommodation. Next to the harbour and car park, the little **Mariner's waterfront** development shelters the Seafood Emporium, selling fresh fish, including the Cape speciality of *snoek*, a bony but delicious fish. There's a decent fish **restaurant** upstairs with outdoor seating overlooking the beach. For straightforward fish and chips, use their downstairs takeaway facility.

Chapman's Peak Drive to Scarborough

East of Hout Bay, **Chapman's Peak Drive** is a thrilling journey. For 10km the road carves into the mountainside on the one side, dropping precipitously hundreds of metres to the ocean on the other; unceasingly spectacular views take in the breadth of Hout Bay, west to the Sentinel on a curved outcrop. Viewpoints are provided along the route, but take care in high winds as there are occasional rockfalls – mostly contained in nets on the mountain side. Scores of cyclists sweat their way round, making considerate driving a necessity. Chapman's Peak Drive is a toll road (R23 per vehicle) with a single toll booth at the northern (Hout Bay) end of the road.

Noordhoek, a fast-developing settlement at the southern end of the descent from Chapman's Peak Drive, consists of smallholdings and riding stables in a gentle valley planted with oaks. The Noordhoek Farm Village as you come off Chapman's Peak is a centre of sorts, with delicious fare and some decent craft shops and a children's play area. From here, a long white untamed beach stretches 6km across Chapman's Bay to Kommetjie. The sands are fantastic for walking and **horse-riding**, but can resemble a sandblaster when the southeaster blows. Swimming is hazardous, though surfers relish the rough waters around the rocks to the north. Signposted on the left if you're heading south is the excellent *Red Herring* restaurant and pub (see p.139), which has views of the beach; it's set back from the sea, about ten minutes' walk from the car park. Also signposted in the vicinity is *Monkey Valley Resort* (see p.130), which welcomes non-guests for reasonably priced meals with great views.

Although only a few kilometres south of Noordhoek along the beach, getting to **Kommetjie** by road involves a fifteen-kilometre detour inland. The beach's small inlet (*kommetjie*), which is always a few degrees above the surrounding sea temperature, is perfect for swimming. Just to the north, **Long Beach** is a favourite surfing spot, used by devotees even during the chilly winter months.

Almost 10km by road from Kommetjie, the developing village of **Scarborough** is the most far-flung suburb along the peninsula. A long wide beach edges temptingly to its south just beyond Schusters River Lagoon – resist its potentially treacherous sea and stick to the lagoon.

6

The False Bay seaboard to Cape Point

n summer, the waters of **False Bay** are several degrees warmer than those on the Atlantic seaboard, which is why Cape Town's oldest and most popular seaside development is along this flank of the peninsula. A series of village-like suburbs, backing onto the mountains, each served by a Metrorail station, is dotted all the way south from **Muizenberg**, through **St James**, **Kalk Bay**, **Fish Hoek** and down to **Simon's Town**. Each has its own character, and restaurants, shops and places to stay, while Simon's Town, one of South Africa's oldest settlements, is worth taking in as a day-trip and makes a useful base for visiting the Cape of Good Hope section of the **Table Mountain National Park** (ⓦ www.sanparks.org/parks/table_mountain) and **Cape Point**.

Driving here from Cape Town, you can take the M3 south, or the M5 via the less salubrious Cape Flats. From Muizenberg, Main Road and the railway line spectacularly hug the shore all the way to Simon's Town. **Boyes Drive**, a high-level alternative to Main Road, runs for about 5km between the suburbs of Lakeside and Kalk Bay, and offers spectacular views across to the Hottentots Holland Mountains on the east side of False Bay. The road is also one of several spots on the Cape Peninsula where, at the right time of year, you just might spot whales (see box, p.110).

The **train ride** to Simon's Town, taking an hour from Cape Town, is reason enough to visit, and most stations are situated close to the surf.

Muizenberg and the Historical Mile

Once boasting South Africa's most fashionable beachfront, **Muizenberg** is now rather run-down, but is attempting to re-create itself with a new beachfront housing development and a splurge of good coffee shops – and nothing can detract from its long, safe and fabulous beach (though don't take anything

Whale spotting on the False Bay seaboard

The commonest whales around Cape Town are southern rights, and the best **whale-watching spots** are on the warmer **False Bay** side of the peninsula, with the season running roughly from August to November, though there are possibilities on the **Atlantic seaboard** too (see p.102). Whichever seaboard you're visiting, remember to have **binoculars** handy.

Along the False Bay seaboard, look out for whale signboards, indicating good places for sightings. **Boyes Drive**, running along the mountainside behind Muizenberg and Kalk Bay, provides an outstanding vantage point. To get there by car, head out on the M3 from the city centre to Muizenberg, taking a sharp right into Boyes Drive, at Lakeside, from where the road begins to climb, descending finally to join Main Road between Kalk Bay and Fish Hoek.

Alternatively, sticking close to the shore along Main Road, the stretch between **Fish Hoek** and **Simon's Town** is recommended, with a particularly nice spot above the rocks at the south end of Fish Hoek Beach, as you walk south towards Glencairn. **Boulders Beach** at the southern end of Simon's Town has a whale signboard, and smooth rocky outcrops above the sea to sit on and gaze out over the water. Even better vantage points are further down the coast between Simon's Town and **Smitswinkelbaai**, where the road goes higher along the mountainside. Without a car, you can get the train to Fish Hoek or Simon's Town and whale-spot from the Jager's Walk beach path that runs along the coast from Fish Hoek to Sunny Cove, just below the railway line.

It's worth noting that there are more spectacular spotting opportunities further east, especially around Hermanus and Walker Bay (see p.187). Information on the locations of whale sightings in the past 24 hours is available from the MTN **Whale Route Hotline** (☏083 910 1028).

valuable onto it and don't leave anything unguarded). Brightly coloured bathing boxes are reminders of a more elegant heyday, when it was visited by the likes of Agatha Christie, who enjoyed riding its waves while holidaying here in the 1920s: "Whenever we could steal time off," she wrote, "we got out our surf boards and went surfing."

Muizenberg's gently shelving, sandy beach is the most popular along the peninsula for swimming, the water tending to be flat and warm. There's good

▲ The coastal train to Simon's Town

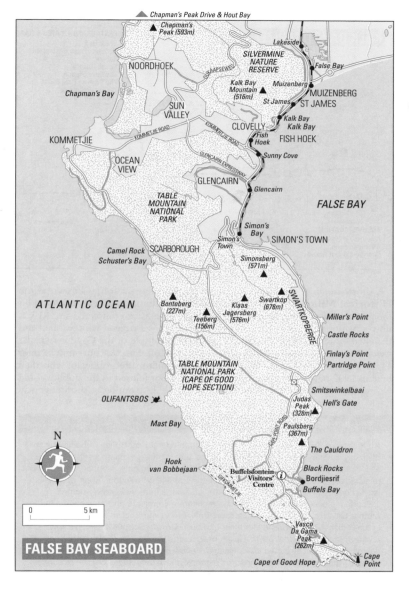

Chapman's Peak Drive & Hout Bay

FALSE BAY SEABOARD

surfing in its breakers, and grown-ups and children can take **surfing lessons** from Gary's Surf School on the beachfront (☏021 788 9839; R450 for 2hr including gear rental). A waterslide and minigolf at the northern end of the beach also help keep kids well occupied. Away from the beach, there is a thriving Congolese community as well as pale-skinned alternative types who get their organic veggie boxes from the *Olive Station* café and deli (see p.139) off Main Road.

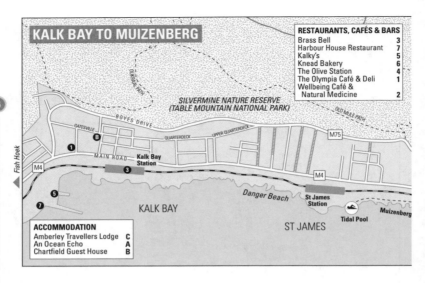

RESTAURANTS, CAFÉS & BARS

Brass Bell	3
Harbour House Restaurant	7
Kalky's	5
Knead Bakery	6
The Olive Station	4
The Olympia Café & Deli	1
Wellbeing Café & Natural Medicine	2

ACCOMMODATION

Amberley Travellers Lodge	C
An Ocean Echo	A
Chartfield Guest House	B

A short stretch of the shore, starting at Muizenberg station, is known as the **Historical Mile**, dotted with a run of notable buildings and easily explored on foot. **Muizenberg station**, an Edwardian-style edifice completed in 1913, is now a National Monument, while the **Posthuys** is a rugged whitewashed and thatched building dating from 1673 and a fine example of the Cape vernacular style. **Rhodes' Cottage Museum** (summer Mon–Sun 9.30am–4pm; winter 11am–2pm; free) was bought in 1899 by the millionaire politician, who died here in 1902 before his grander dwelling next door (closed to the public) could be completed. The cottage contains memorabilia painting a distinctly rosy

The Cape Dutch Revival

A process of defining Cape Town's architectural identity as British Imperial but still distinctly African reached its climax at the turn of the twentieth century. Closely associated with Cecil John Rhodes, the diamond magnate who became prime minister of the Cape in 1890, this architecture projected a feudal vision of a British landed gentry in Africa, lording it over the landscape from their stately homes.

Rhodes is connected with numerous architectural projects and monuments in the Mother City. He commissioned **Herbert Baker**, a young English architect schooled in the British Arts and Crafts Movement, to build **Groote Schuur** (1898), his home on Klipper Road in Rondebosch. Baker used recognizable Cape elements such as gables, curving multi-paned windows and steeply pitched roofs, while other aspects relate to quite different traditions: for example the barley-sugar chimneys suggest Tudor prototypes and the gargoyles are replicas of totemic bird figures taken by Rhodes from Great Zimbabwe.

The style synthesized by Baker became known as the **Cape Dutch Revival**, and was again used by the architect at **Rust en Vrede** (1902), Rhodes' seaside residence in Main Road, Muizenberg. The Cape Dutch Revival has become well established in South African architectural parlance: it became popular in the twentieth century to use Cape Dutch elements, particularly gables, in suburban houses, no matter how inappropriate their scale or context.

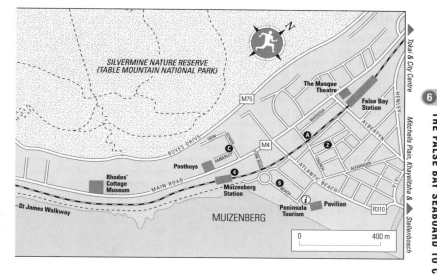

portrait of the man, with photographs, a model of the Big Hole in Kimberley in the Northern Cape (where Rhodes made his fortune at the diamond diggings), and a curious diorama of World's View in Zimbabwe's Matopos Hills, where he lies buried.

Plans are in the pipeline to upgrade and restore Muizenberg's neglected beachfront, which is one of the closest beaches to the populous Cape Flats. Several decent restaurants and cafés are leading the way, though there's a dearth of beachfront hotels; to book accommodation in the area, contact **Peninsula Tourism** (Mon–Fri 8.30am–5.30pm, Sat 9am–noon; ℡021 787 9140), housed in the pavilion on Beach Road.

St James, Danger Beach and Kalk Bay

St James, 2km south of Muizenberg, is more upmarket, its mountainside homes accessed mostly up long stairways between Main Road and Boyes Drive. The best reason to hop off the train here is for the **sheltered tidal pool** and the twenty-minute walk along the **paved coastal path** that runs along the rocky shore to Muizenberg – one of the peninsula's easiest and most rewarding walks, with panoramas of the full sweep of False Bay. Look out for the occasional seal that makes an appearance and, in season, whales.

The compact St James beach draws considerable character from its much-photographed Victorian-style bathing boxes, whose bright, primary colours catch your eye as you pass by road or rail. The beach tends to be overcrowded at weekends and during school holidays; far fewer visitors take the trouble to stroll along the short footpath that leads south along the lawned shore from St James to the adjacent sandy stretch of **Danger Beach**, an excellent spot for sunbathing and building sand castles. As the name suggests, its surf should be treated with respect as there is a powerful undertow here.

Kalk Bay

One of the most southerly and smallest of Cape Town's suburbs, **Kalk Bay** centres around a lively working harbour with wooden fishing vessels, mountain views and a tiny strip of shops packed with trendy coffee shops and antique dealers, plus a couple of places where you might catch some nightlife. Kalk Bay somehow managed to slip through the net of the Group Areas Act, making it one of the few places on the peninsula with an intact coloured community, and Kalk Bay and the larger Hout Bay (see p.106) are the only harbour settlements still worked by coloured fishermen.

The settlement is arranged around the small docks, where you can watch the boats come in; you can also buy fresh fish, which are flung onto the quayside and sold in spirited and noisy auctions. The harbour is busiest on Saturdays and Sundays when Capetonians descend to pick up something for a weekend braai or to have lunch at *Kalky's*, an informal fish-and-chips **restaurant**. Other places to wine and dine here include *Harbour House*, the popular *Brass Bell* pub and restaurant and the *Olympia Deli* (see p.139).

Fish Hoek

Fish Hoek, south of Kalk Bay, boasts one of the peninsula's finest family **beaches** along the False Bay coast. The best and safest swimming is at its southern end, where the surf is moderately warm, tame and much enjoyed by boogie boarders. Thanks to the beach, there's a fair amount of accommodation (see p.131), but this is otherwise one of the dreariest suburbs along the entire False Bay coast. An obscure by-law banning the sale of alcohol in supermarkets or bottle stores boosts the town's image as the Mother Grundy capital of the peninsula.

Facilities include a playground, changing rooms, toilets, fresh water, and the *Fish Hoek Galley Seafood Restaurant* right on the beach. From behind the restaurant, a picturesque concrete pathway called **Jager's Walk** provides a good vantage point for seeing whales. It skirts the rocky shoreline above the sea for 1km to Sunny Cove, from where it continues for 6km as an unpaved track to Simon's Town.

If you're driving, Fish Hoek is well placed for access to the Atlantic seaboard or for heading into the Constantia winelands. Just south of the suburb, you can strike west on the Glencairn Expressway (M6), or alternatively take the equally scenic Kommetjie Road (M65) about 4km further south (more convenient than the M6 if you're coming from Simon's Town). The two intersect halfway across the peninsula at Sun Valley, where Kommetjie Road continues west, veering slightly south to the coastal suburban village of Noordhoek. At Sun Valley, the M6 strikes north and splits about a kilometre after the intersection.

Silvermine Nature Reserve

Rising up behind Boyes Drive is the **Silvermine Nature Reserve** (dawn–dusk; R20, children R10), which runs across the peninsula's spine, almost stretching to the west side at Chapman's Peak. Comprising part of the Table Mountain chain of peaks, it offers walks and drives with fabulous views of False Bay, the mountains, indigenous forest and montane *fynbos*. It's most easily reached via the **Oukaapseweg** (Old Cape Road, the M64), which runs through Tokai to Noordhoek and Simon's Town.

The northwesterly branch hits the coast at Chapman's Point, and continues along the precipitously beautiful Chapman's Peak Drive (see p.108), which eventually reaches the City Bowl along the Atlantic shore. The northeasterly branch heads along the winding treelined Ou Kaapseweg (M64, becoming the M42), passing through the Silvermine Nature Reserve and the winelands.

Simon's Town

The country's third-oldest European settlement, and also South Africa's principal naval base, **Simon's Town** isn't the hard-drinking, raucous place you might expect. It's exceptionally pretty, with a near-perfectly preserved street-scape, slightly marred on the ocean side by the domineering **naval dockyard**, but this, and glimpses of naval squaddies square-bashing behind the high walls or strolling to the station in their crisp white uniforms, are what give the place its distinct character. Just 40km from Cape Town, roughly halfway down the coast to Cape Point, Simon's Town makes the perfect base for a mellow break along the peninsula, offering easy day-trips by train to Cape Town. A few kilometres to the south is the rock-strewn **Boulders Beach**, with its colony of nonchalant **African penguins** – reason in themselves to venture here.

Founded in 1687 as the winter anchorage of the Dutch East India Company, Simon's Town was one of several places in and around Cape Town modestly named by **Governor Simon van der Stel** after himself. Its most celebrated visitor was Lord Nelson, who convalesced here as a midshipman while returning home from the East in 1776. Nineteen years later, the British sailed into Simon's Town and occupied it as a bridgehead for their first invasion and occupation of the Cape. After just seven years they left, only to return in 1806. Simon's Town remained a British base until 1957, when it was handed over to South Africa.

There are fleeting hints, such as the occasional mosque, that the town's predominantly white appearance isn't the whole story. In fact, the first **Muslims** arrived from the East Indies in the early eighteenth century, imported as slaves to build the Dutch naval base. After the British banning of the slave trade in 1807, ships were compelled to disgorge their human cargo at Simon's Town, where one district became known as Black Town. In 1967, when Simon's Town was declared a White Group Area, there were 1200 well-established coloured families descended from these slaves. By the early 1970s, the majority had been forcibly removed under the Group Areas Act to the township of Ocean View, whose inspiring name belies its desolation. After their departure their dwellings were destroyed or allowed to rot, depriving the town of significant historic buildings. In 1973, town clerk Charles Chevalier complained that "the loss of the non-white population has had a depressing effect on the commercial life of the town".

The Town

Trains are met at Simon's Town by Rikkis (☎021 786 2136), which you can book for excursions to Boulders and on to Cape Point. A short way south of the station along St George's Street (the main drag), a signposted road to the left points to the museums. The building now housing the **Simon's Town Museum**, Court Road (Mon–Fri 9am–4pm, Sat 10am–4pm, Sun 11am–4pm;

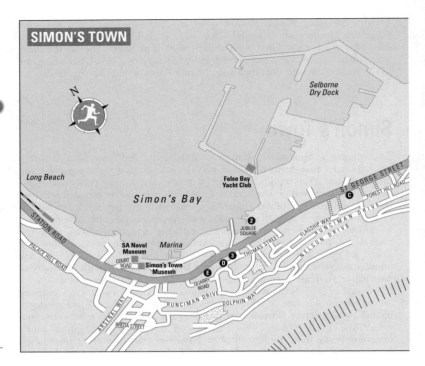

R10), was once the Old Residency built in 1772 for the Governor of the Dutch East India Company, and has also served as the slave quarters (the dungeons are in the basement) and town brothel. The museum's motley collection includes maritime material and an inordinate amount of information and exhibits on Able Seaman Just Nuisance, a much-celebrated seafaring Great Dane. He enjoyed drinking beer with the sailors he accompanied into Cape Town, and was adopted as a mascot by the Royal Navy in World War II. The building also reputedly still houses the ghost of Eleanor, the 14-year-old daughter of Earl McCartney, who lived here in the closing years of the eighteenth century. Forbidden by her parents from playing on the sands with the children of coloured fishermen, Eleanor would escape to the beach through a secret tunnel she had discovered. The dankness of the tunnel supposedly gave her pneumonia, from which she tragically died.

At the **South African Naval Museum** (daily 10am–4pm; free) next door, lively displays include the inside of a submarine, a ship's bridge that simulates rocking, and a lot of official portraits of South African naval commanders from 1922 to the present.

In the centre of Simon's Town, a little over a kilometre south of the station, lies **Jubilee Square**, a palm-shaded car park just off St George's Street. Flanked by some good cafés, shops and a great fish-and-chips restaurant, the street has on its harbour-facing side a broad walkway featuring a statue of the ubiquitous Able Seaman Just Nuisance. A couple of sets of stairs lead down to the **Marina**, a modest development of shops and a couple of good restaurants set right on the waterfront.

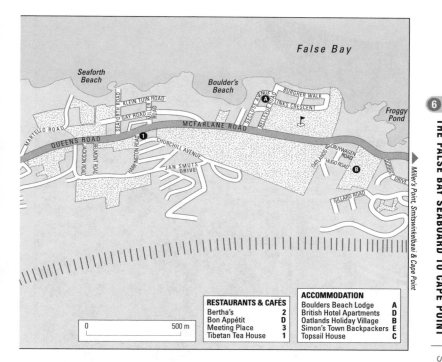

Seaforth
Beach

False Bay

*Boulder's
Beach*

BURGHER WALK

LINKS CRESCENT

Froggy
Pond

A

KLEIN TUIN ROAD

GAY ROAD

SEAFORTH ROAD

MILLER ROAD

SECURE AVENUE

BELLEVUE ROAD

MCFARLANE ROAD

MARTELLO ROAD

QUEENS ROAD

JACKSON ROAD

BELMONT ROAD

CHURCHILL AVENUE

HARRINGTON ROAD

JAN SMUTS
DRIVE

CRUYWAGEN
ROAD

OATLANDS RD

HUGO ROAD

B

DOBBIE'S DRIVE

GILLARD ROAD

6

◄ Miller's Point, Smitswinkelbaai & Cape Point

0 ──────── 500 m

RESTAURANTS & CAFÉS	
Bertha's	2
Bon Appétit	D
Meeting Place	3
Tibetan Tea House	1

ACCOMMODATION	
Boulders Beach Lodge	A
British Hotel Apartments	D
Oatlands Holiday Village	B
Simon's Town Backpackers	E
Topsail House	C

THE FALSE BAY SEABOARD TO CAPE POINT | Simon's Town

Long and Seaforth beaches

Nearest to the station, **Long Beach** offers no shade and is, therefore, little used. However, on windless days it can be pleasant for long walks, with views of the Hottentots Holland Mountains, and its tidal pool is safe for bathing. Access is by a number of gaps in a brick wall alongside the main road and about midway along the beach (opposite Hopkirk Way), by a flight of steps. There are changing rooms and toilets nearby, and fresh water.

One of the best beaches for swimming is 2km east of Jubilee Square at **Seaforth**, where clear, deep waters lap around rocks. It's calm, protected and safe, but not pretty (it's bounded on one side by the looming grey mass of the naval base), though it does have plenty of lawn shaded by palm trees, and a restaurant with outdoor seating and fresh fish on the menu.

Boulders

Two kilometres from the station towards Cape Point lies **Boulders**, the most popular local beach (R15, children R5), with a number of places to stay. The area takes its name from the huge rounded rocks that create a cluster of little coves with sandy beaches and clear sea pools which are gorgeous for swimming. However, the main reason people come to Boulders is for the **African penguins** (formerly known as jackass penguins), in the Boulders section of the Table Mountain National Park (open 24hr; April–Sept daily 8am–5pm; Oct–March daily 7am–7pm; R15, children R5), a fenced reserve on Boulders Beach.

▲ Fisherman, Simon's Town

Passing sailors used to prey on the quirky birds and their eggs, and more recently they have fallen victim to vandals, and some locals who consider them pests; they're now protected by a guard. African penguins usually live on islands off the west side of the South African coast, the Boulders birds forming one of only two mainland colonies in the world. This is also the only place where the endangered species are actually increasing in numbers, and provides a rare opportunity to get a close look at them.

Miller's Point and Smitswinkelbaai

Almost 5km to the south is the popular **Miller's Point** resort, which has a number of small sandy beaches and a tidal pool protected from the southeaster. A **campsite** at the caravan park offers great sea views. Along Main Road, the notable *Black Marlin* seafood **restaurant** attracts busloads of tourists, while the boulders around the point attract rock agama and black zonure lizards and dassies.

The last place before you get to the Cape of Good Hope Nature Reserve is **Smitswinkelbaai** (pronounced "smits-vin-cull-buy"). This little cove has a small beach safe for swimming, but feels the full blast of the southeaster. It's not accessible by car, as local property-owners fiercely guard their privacy; to get there, you must park next to the road and walk down a seemingly endless succession of stairs.

Table Mountain National Park – Cape of Good Hope

Most people who visit the **Cape of Good Hope section** of Table Mountain National Park (daily: April–Sept 7am–5pm; Oct–March 6am–6pm; R55, children R10; ℡021 780 9100) come to see the southernmost tip of Africa and the place where the Indian and Atlantic oceans meet at **Cape Point**. In fact, this is the site of neither: the continent's real tip is at Cape Agulhas, some 300km southeast of here (see p.198), but Cape Point is a lot easier to get to and an awesomely dramatic spot, which should on no account be missed. The reserve sits atop massive sea cliffs with huge views, strong seas, and an even wilder wind, which whips off caps and sunglasses as visitors gaze southwards from the old lighthouse buttress.

Most visitors see the Point as part of a circular trip, returning via Kommetjie and the especially scenic Chapman's Peak Drive (see p.108). Numerous **tours** spend a day stopping off at the peninsula highlights; Day Trippers (℡021 511 4766) runs fun tours for R425 (including a picnic lunch), some of which give you the option of cycling part of the way. For general tours that take in the reserve, see p.33. There's no public transport to the reserve, although you can charter a Simon's Town **Rikki** (℡021 786 2136) there and back. To **drive** there, take the M3 to Muizenberg, continuing on the M4 via Simon's Town to the reserve gates, where you'll be given a good **map** that marks the main driving and walking routes, as well as the tidal pools and other facilities. Go as early as you can in the day to avoid tour buses and the likelihood of the wind gusting more strongly as the day progresses. The **Buffelsfontein Visitors' Centre** (daily 7.30am–5pm; ℡021 780 9204), 8km from the entrance gate, is worth a look, boasting attractive displays about the local fauna and flora as well as video screenings on the ecology of the area.

The reserve

From the car park, it's a short, steep walk – one crawling with tourists – up to the famous viewpoint, the original lighthouse. A **funicular** (R45 return) runs the less energetic to the top of the first lighthouse, where there's a curio shop. There's also a rather good **restaurant**, the *Two Oceans*, at the car park, which has outdoor seating (but it's usually too windy to be pleasant) and huge picture windows taking in the drop to the sea below. Built in 1860, the lighthouse was too often dangerously shrouded in cloud, and failed to keep ships off the rocks, so in 1914 another was built lower down and closer to the Point. This second lighthouse isn't always successful in averting disasters, but is still the most powerful light beaming onto the sea from South Africa.

Most visitors make a beeline for Cape Point, seeing the rest of the reserve through a vehicle window, but walking is the best way to appreciate indigenous Cape **flora**. At first glance the landscape appears rocky and bleak, with short, wind-cropped plants, but the vegetation is surprisingly rich. Amazingly, many bright blooms in Britain and the US, including varieties of geraniums, freesias, gladioli, daisies, lilies and irises, are hybrids grown from indigenous Cape plants.

Along with indigenous plants and flowers, you may well spot some of the animals living in the reserve's **fynbos** habitat (see *Going wild in Cape Town* colour section for more). **Ostriches** stride through the low fynbos, and occasionally **African penguins** come ashore. A distinctive bird on the rocky shores is the **black oystercatcher** with a bright red beak, jabbing limpets off the rocks. You'll also see **Cape cormorants** in large flocks on the beach or rocks, often drying their outstretched wings. Running up and down the water's edge (where, as on any other beach walk in the Cape, you'll see piles of shiny brown *Ecklonia* kelp) are **white-fronted plovers** and **sanderlings**, probing for food left by the receding waves. As for mammals, **baboons** lope along the rocky shoreline and can be a menace; keep your car windows closed, as it's not unknown for them to invade vehicles, and they're adept at slyly swiping picnics. Feeding them is provocative and can incur a fine. Grazing on the heathery slopes are **bontebok**, **eland** and **red hartebeest**, as well as **Cape rhebok** and **grysbok**. If you're very lucky, you may even see some of the extremely rare **Cape mountain zebras**.

You'll find the **beaches** along signposted side roads branching out from the Cape Point road through the reserve. The sea here is too dangerous for swimming, but there are safe tidal pools at the adjacent **Buffels Bay** and **Bordjiesrif**, midway along the east shore. Both have braai stands, but more southerly Buffels Bay is the nicer, with big lawned areas and some sheltered spots to have a picnic.

Walks

There are several waymarked **walks** in the Cape of Good Hope Nature Reserve. If you're planning a big hike it's best to set out early, as shade is rare and the wind can be foul, especially during summer, often increasing in intensity as the day goes on. One of the most straightforward **hiking routes** is the signposted forty-minute trek from the car park at Cape Point to the more westerly **Cape of Good Hope**. For exploring the shoreline, a clear path runs down the Atlantic side which you can join at **Gifkommetjie**, signposted off Cape Point Road. From the car park, several sandy tracks drop quite steeply down the slope across rocks, and through bushes and milkwood trees to the shore, along which you can walk in either direction. Alternatively, take a copy of the Government Printer's 1:50,000 map *3318 C.D. Cape Town* for some more intrepid exploration. Take water on any walk in the reserve, as there are no reliable fresh sources.

Navigators have been braving the rocks, winds and swells of Cape Point since the Portuguese first "rounded the Cape" in the fifteenth century. Plenty of wrecks lie submerged off its coast, and at **Olifantsbos** on the west side you can walk to a US ship sunk in 1942, and a South African coaster which ran aground in 1965.

Listings

Listings

Accommodation

Standards of accommodation in Cape Town (and, for that matter, along the Garden Route) are very high. There are some outstanding boutique hotels, luxury guesthouses and country retreats in beautiful settings – at prices which would only get you a good B&B back home. Other than in the cheapest rooms, you'll always get a private bath or shower, and you'll often have use of a garden and pool, or your own private patio.

The downside of all this comfort is that there are few, if any, inexpensive hotels. If you're on a modest budget, you have two main options. **Backpacker lodges** offer basic hostel accommodation in a dormitory, usually for around R100 per person, and many have double rooms too. Backpacker places are independently run, and listed in the free *Coast to Coast* booklet which covers the whole country and is widely available in tourist information offices and hostels countrywide. Alternatively, you can make use of **self-catering** apartments and cottages, with prices starting at R500 for two people in Cape Town, less out of town. You can expect the kitchen to come with crockery and cutlery, and for linen and towels to be provided. One of the best things about self-catering is the wide choice of location: there are self-catering places on farms, near beaches, in forests and in wilderness areas.

Family accommodation is plentiful, and hotels often have rooms with extra beds or interconnecting rooms. Kids usually stay for half price. Note, however, that some of the posher B&Bs do not accept children as guests.

One unusual prospect – and one of very few ways to experience black South Africa – is to stay in one of the African **townships** in Cape Town. Accommodation is generally in comfortable middle-class places with good security, and you'll have a fantastic time, with great hospitality. They are also inexpensive compared with the high prices you'll pay in central Cape Town.

In this book, accommodation **prices** are, unless stated otherwise, quoted **per double room**, though for backpacker hostels the rate is per person. Note, however, that on the ground many rates are quoted per person rather than per room – make doubly sure which it is when you phone to book. Except in backpacker lodges, a full English **breakfast** (which can be a lavish buffets that will set you up for the day) is almost always included in the rate, and even where it's not it is usually available to order. Some cottages are priced for the whole cottage, as they can often sleep a group or family.

The rates given in this book are for **high season** – basically, the South African summer – though note that within this period, prices rise sharply over the Christmas and New Year period, and also over Easter. **Booking ahead** for the high season is strongly recommended. There's a lull in the midwinter **low season** (June–Aug), during which time you should have no problem finding plenty of good-value places to stay, often with hefty discounts.

In Cape Town, the greatest concentration of accommodation is in the City Bowl and the Atlantic seaside strip as far as Sea Point. Cape Town Tourism has efficient accommodation-booking desks for all budgets, while if you're stuck, A–Z Holiday Accommodation, 15 Winton Crescent, Woodbridge Island 7441 (☎021 551 2785, ⓦ www.a-zholidayhomes.co.za), can provide self-catering accommodation during December and January, ranging from a two-person apartment for R800 a day to a R18,000 superluxury house. As for **online** accommodation booking, some of the best websites are ⓦ www.cape-venues.co.za, ⓦ www.capestay.co.za and ⓦ www.safarinow.com.

City centre

The city centre's accommodation is highly concentrated along **Long Street**, featuring more backpacker lodges per square metre than on any other street in Cape Town and, in their wake, a growing number of student travel agencies, cheap car-rental outfits and adventure-activity outlets. Long Street is also the lively focus for restaurants, clubs and pubs. The heart of the city centre extends four blocks east of here, taking in the **Company Gardens**. Accommodation in and around this whole area is marked on the map on p.59, except for the *iKhaya Lodge*, shown on the map on p.54.

Cape Heritage Hotel 90 Bree St ☎021 424 4646, ⓦ www.capeheritage.co.za. An elegant and tastefully restored hotel located in a row of houses dating back to 1771, in Cape Heritage Square, just below the Bo-Kaap. The rooms are spacious and each is furnished according to a theme – African, Japanese and Dutch, to name three. Although there's no garden, the hotel does feature a pleasant courtyard. Doubles R1375.

Cape Town Hollow Hotel 88 Queen Victoria St ☎021 423 1260, ⓦ www.capetownhollow.co.za. A smart multistorey hotel with a/c rooms, cable TV, baths and showers. It's two minutes from the South African Museum and National Gallery, an easy and pleasant walk away via the Company Gardens. Doubles R1260.

Cat & Moose 305 Long St ☎021 423 7638, ⓦ www.catandmoose.co.za. The most stylish of the Long St backpacker lodges, housed in an eighteenth-century building a couple of doors from the steam baths at the south end of the city centre. Timber floors with Turkish-style rugs, exposed beams, earthy reds and ochres as well as some African masks imbue it with a warm ethnic feel. The dorms, triples and double rooms are arranged around a small leafy courtyard, with a waterfall cascading into a plunge pool. Dorms R85, doubles R250.

iKhaya Lodge Wandel St, Dunkley Square ☎021 461 8880, ⓦ www.ikhayalodge.co.za.

A guesthouse three short blocks away from the Company Gardens and museums. Its eleven standard rooms in the main guesthouse, five luxury loft suites and two self-catering apartments, done out in ethnically inspired decor, have mountain or (cheaper) city views. The lodge's patio overlooks the outdoor eateries of trendy Dunkley Square. Doubles from R950.

Long Street Backpackers 209 Long St ☎021 423 0615, ⓦ www.longstreetbackpackers.co.za. The oldest Long St backpacker lodge, on the top two floors of an unexceptional three-storey former apartment block arranged around a courtyard, with dorms, doubles and singles. Quieter than some of the other lodges in the vicinity, it's a well-organized place, with a laundry, Internet facilities and a travel desk; there's also a lively bar and a kitchen. Dorms R100, doubles R250.

Metropole Hotel 38 Long St ☎021 424 7247, ⓦ www.metropolehotel.co.za. A well-situated hotel that makes for a thoroughly urban stay. Done out in subtly contrasting oatmeal and beige shades, the rooms are comfortable if functional. The best parts are the public areas, bar and restaurant. Gay-friendly. Doubles R1000.

St Paul's B&B Guest House 182 Bree St ☎021 423 4420, ℻021 423 1580. A charming, well-managed and inexpensive guesthouse in a Georgian building (formerly a maternity hospital) in a calm street on the city-centre fringes, within easy striking distance of the sights. The rooms are large, comfortable and light with huge windows, and sharing bathroom and kitchen facilities. Doubles from R500.

Travellers' Inn 208 Long St ☎021 424 9272, ⓦwww.travellers-inn.co.za. Pleasant budget accommodation in an early twentieth-century building above a cybercafé. With no bar and no backpacker scene, this is a good bet for travellers wanting to avoid the hectic social atmosphere of the city-centre hostels. Apart from the light and spacious family rooms with twin beds and a double bunk, the rooms are small and sparely furnished; all rooms share bathroom facilities. Weekly and monthly discounts are available. Doubles from R500.

🏃 **Tudor Hotel 153 Longmarket St ☎021 424 1335, ⓦwww.tudorhotel.co.za.** En-suite B&B rooms in a very central and reasonably priced hotel overlooking cobbled Greenmarket Square, and handy for taxis. Doubles from R740.

V&A Waterfront and De Waterkant

In keeping with the gentrified ambience of the **V&A Waterfront** (usually referred to simply as the Waterfront), accommodation here tends to be upmarket; there are, however, a couple of reasonably priced places to stay, especially in the area just south of the Waterfront and **De Waterkant**. Accommodation here is marked on the map on p.74.

🏃 **Breakwater Lodge Portswood Rd, Waterfront ☎021 406 1911 (ask for Lodge Reservations), ⓦwww.breakwaterlodge.co.za.** The most affordable place to stay on the doorstep of the Waterfront, this is a sparkling white hotel linked to Cape Town University's Graduate School of Business, and partially housed in a nineteenth-century prison building. Although the lodge lacks personality, it does have thoroughly decent en-suite rooms with TV and phone, and there are also over a hundred budget rooms with one bathroom per two rooms. Doubles from R845.

The Cape Grace West Quay, Waterfront ☎021 410 7100, ⓦwww.capegrace.com. One of South Africa's most expensive and most exclusive hotels, this was Bill and Hillary Clinton's choice when they visited Cape Town in 1998. Spectacularly sited on a slender spit overlooking the Waterfront's small vessel marina to one side and the Alfred Basin to the other, the hotel's rooms have either harbour or Table Mountain views and are furnished in pared-back French period style. Doubles from R4400.

City Lodge On the corner of Alfred and Dock rds, Waterfront ☎021 419 9450, ⓦwww .citylodge.co.za. A perfectly adequate if rather austere hotel, part of a national chain, less than 1km from both the Waterfront and the city centre. The rooms have TV and there's a small swimming pool. Rates are cheaper Fri–Sun nights, and you can also pick up discounts using the hotel's room-auction site ⓦwww.bid2stay.co.za. Doubles from R1000.

De Waterkant Village and De Waterkant House Reception at 1 Loader St, De Waterkant ☎021 409 2500, ⓦwww.dewaterkant.com. Attractively restored historic cottages adjacent to the Bo-Kaap and less than 1km from the Waterfront and city centre. The luxury cottages in Waterkant, Loader, Dixon and Napier sts have up to three bedrooms; some have garages, swimming pools and roof gardens with harbour or mountain views. Also part of the district is De Waterkant House, which has nine rooms sharing a pool and terrace with views over the Waterfront. Doubles R880–990.

St John's Waterfront Lodge 6 Braemar Rd ☎021 439 1404, ⓦwww.stjohns.co.za. The closest hostel to the Waterfront (a 15-min walk away), well run by friendly and helpful staff. Accommodation is in four dorms sleeping eight to nine people, as well as some doubles, one of which is en suite. There are two swimming pools, a great garden and a bar, and the restaurant serves reasonably priced light meals till midnight. There's also Internet access, a coin-operated washing machine and a travel centre. Dorms R100, doubles R280, en-suite flatlet R350.

City Bowl suburbs

The **City Bowl suburbs** are popular for accommodation, and the most northerly sections are just five to ten minutes' walk from the Company Gardens and the museums. A few backpacker lodges can be found along **Kloof Street**, the continuation of trendy Long Street. The further up you go, the leafier the suburbs become, and you'll find the pricier and more comfortable B&Bs, guesthouses and hotels along the lower slopes of Table Mountain, overlooking the city centre and Duncan Dock. There's no public transport to the City Bowl suburbs, but most of the accommodation listed here is under 3km from Cape Town station. For locations, see the map on p.87.

Inexpensive

African Sun 3 Florida Rd, Vredehoek ☎021 461 1601, ✉afpress@iafrica.com. A small self-catering apartment, attached to a family house a little over 1km from the city centre. Furnished with pared-back ethnic decor, it's run by friendly, well-informed owners. A five-percent discount is offered if you produce this book. Good value. Doubles from R450.

Ashanti Lodge and Guest House 11 Hof St, Gardens ☎021 423 8721, 🌐www.ashanti.com. King of the Cape Town lodges, this is a massive, superbly refurbished two-storey Victorian mansion. Details such as stripped timber, chic marbling, soaring ceilings, a beautifully kept front garden, a cosy TV lounge and a swimming pool with sun terrace give it the edge. The private rooms (with twin or double beds) and dorms (sleeping six to eight) are furnished with custom-made wrought-iron bunks and beds. They also have a quieter guesthouse around the corner in Union St, containing keenly priced en-suite double/twin rooms with TVs and a communal kitchen. Dorms R120, doubles R320–450.

The Backpack 74 New Church St, Tamboerskloof ☎021 423 4530, 🌐www.backpackers.co.za. An excellent lodge in three interconnected houses, on the cusp of the City Bowl suburbs and the city centre, and easily walkable to both. Well run and with excellent service, it's furnished with bold colours and ethnic fabrics, with plenty of outdoor space, including a pool terrace in its own garden. Accommodation is in dorms (sleeping six to ten) and private rooms (several of which are en suite); some rooms are suitable for families. Dorms R130, doubles R285.

Belmont House 10 Belmont Ave, Oranjezicht ☎021 461 5417, 🌐www.capeguest.com. A tastefully restored 1920s house with seven, fresh rooms, each with its own shower or bath. Either take the B&B option, or self-cater in the communal kitchen. There's a five-percent discount if you produce this book. Doubles from R600.

Blencathra On the corner of De Hoop and Cambridge aves, Tamboerskloof ☎021 424 9571, 🌐www.blencathra.co.za. A large relaxed family house with stunning views on the slopes of Lion's Head, 2km from the city centre and 4km from the Atlantic seaboard beaches. They offer peaceful, spacious self-catering rooms, four of which are en suite, attracting a young crowd who want to avoid the backpacker scene. The garden has seating and a swimming pool. Doubles from R500.

Oak Lodge 21 Breda St, Gardens ☎021 465 6182, 🌐www.oaklodge.co.za. More an event than a lodge, this highly recommended hostel in an 1860s Victorian house has dramatic dungeons, dragon murals, and a lively atmosphere; it's also spacious and well serviced, and has an immaculate kitchen. There are four dorms and sixteen rooms, one of which is en suite. Dorms R80, doubles from R280.

Saasveld Lodge 73 Kloof St, Tamboerskloof ☎021 424 6169, ✉saasveld@icon.co.za. A rather impersonal 1950s-style, four-storey guesthouse on a buzzing thoroughfare lined with good eating places, less than 1km from the centre. The rooms are en suite and have TV and phone. The rate excludes breakfast. Doubles R485.

Zebra Crossing 82 New Church St ☎021 422 1265, 🌐www.zebra-crossing.co.za. Cape Town's only backpacker lodge that actually boasts about being quiet. On the northern edge of the City Bowl suburbs, it's an easy walk to the Kloof St restaurants and pubs as well as those in the city centre. The café-bar serves full meals and decent coffee, and there are two pleasant terraces under vines. Accommodation is in three spacious dorms (sleeping eight), eleven doubles and three singles; the best rooms are the three doubles in the annexe, from whose balcony you can take in views of the mountain. Child-friendly. Dorms R80, doubles R240.

Moderate to expensive

Bergzicht 5 Devonport Rd, Tamboerskloof ℡021 423 8513, ⊛www.bergzicht.co.za. Friendly and informal guesthouse with good views, caring hosts and a pool. Rooms are simply furnished with wicker furniture. Doubles from R800.

Cape Milner Hotel 2a Milner Rd, Tamboerskloof ℡021 426 1101, ⊛www.capemilner.com. A smart, reasonably priced hotel, partly incorporating an early eighteenth-century building, at the foot of Signal Hill. The airy rooms all boast views of Table Mountain and minimalist decor, and the service is excellent. There's also a swimming pool, restaurant and bar on the premises. Doubles from R1600.

Leeuwenvoet House 93 New Church St, Tamboerskloof ℡021 424 1133, ⊛www .leeuwenvoet.co.za. A tranquil restored Victorian guesthouse, with twelve en-suite rooms kitted out with pine and wicker and equipped with TV, phone and fan. Situated on a major thoroughfare with secure parking, it's a 15-min walk from the city centre, with airport transfers available. Doubles from around R970.

Lezard Bleu 30 Upper Orange St, Oranjezicht ℡021 461 4601, ⊛www.lezardbleu.co.za. Seven luxurious en-suite rooms, furnished with maple beds and cupboards in a spacious open-plan 1960s house. Each room has sliding doors opening onto a garden. Located in a pleasant part of town, it's 1km from the centre and about half that distance to a nature reserve on the lower slopes of Table Mountain. Doubles from R1020.

Mount Nelson Hotel 76 Orange St, Gardens ℡021 483 1000, ⊛www.mountnelson.co.za. Cape Town's *grande dame*: a fine and famous high-colonial Victorian hotel, built in 1899 (and extended in the late 1990s). Set in extensive established gardens, with arrival along a palm-lined colonnade, it takes itself terribly seriously and charges accordingly: doubles from around R5875.

Underberg Guest House 6 Tamboerskloof Rd, Tamboerskloof ℡021 426 2262, ⊛www .underbergguesthouse.co.za. Located on the doorstep of the city centre, this Victorian guesthouse offers excellent value. Its high ceilings and compact size – there are only eleven rooms – create an atmosphere that is both intimate and airy. Doubles from R875.

Villa Belmonte Hotel 33 Belmont Ave, Oranjezicht ℡021 462 1576, ⊛www .villabelmontehotel.co.za. The Western Cape's smallest five-star hotel, on the lower slopes of Table Mountain and 1km from the city centre, feels like an elegant Italian country villa. The rooms, some of which lead onto a lovely garden, are individually decorated and rates vary according to size. Good value, given the level of comfort and style. Doubles from R1690.

Welgelegen Guest House 6 Stephen St, Gardens ℡021 426 2373, ⊛www.welgelegen.co.za. A Victorian guesthouse with mountain views, furnished with considerable style. Doubles R1450–1750.

Southern suburbs

Cape Town's **southern suburbs** are the formerly whites–only areas closest to the mountain. **Rosebank**, **Claremont**, **Newlands** and **Rondebosch** are leafy, quiet and convenient for the Simon's Town train line, providing easy access to both the city centre and the False Bay seaboard.

Lush **Constantia** is one of Cape Town's poshest suburbs, only twenty minutes' drive from either coast as well as the V&A Waterfront. Sharing the same valley is the adjoining suburb of **Tokai**, worth considering if you want to be well out of the centre; it's close to forest walks and ten minutes from the beach. Inexpensive accommodation is rare in Tokai, but if money's no object and you're looking for somewhere exceptional and romantic, you might just find it here in a Cape Dutch manor house. A car is essential if you're staying in Tokai or Constantia, as they're not served by public transport.

Carmichael House 11 Wolmunster Rd, Rosebank ☏ 021 689 8350, ⓦ www.carmichaelhouse .co.za. A two-storey guesthouse, close to the University of Cape Town, in a building dating from the turn of the last century, with six big rooms equipped with phone, safe and hairdryer. There's a peaceful garden, a swimming pool and secure parking, plus fax and email facilities. Doubles R680.

The Courtyard Liesbeek Ave, Mowbray ☏ 021 448 3929, ⓦ www.citylodge.co.za. Exceptional value, considering the high level of luxury. A beautiful early nineteenth-century Cape Dutch homestead under thatch, with terracotta floors, brass chandeliers and large lawns in a semi-rural setting. There's a hotel minibus which you can pay to use. Breakfast is extra. Doubles from R980.

Gloucester House Bed & Breakfast 54 Weltevreden Ave, Rondebosch ☏ & ⓕ 021 689 3894. A private house with two bedrooms, and a lounge/dining room for self-catering. Guests may use the large garden, swimming pool and barbecue area. Doubles from R500.

🏃 **Houtkapperspoort** Hout Bay Main Rd, around 5km from Hout Bay and 15km from the city centre ☏ 021 794 5216, ⓦ www .houtkapperspoort.co.za. Rustic one- and two-bedroom stone-and-brick self-catering cottages set up against the Table Mountain Nature Reserve, close to Constantia Nek. You can take paths straight from the estate up the mountain slopes, play tennis or take a dip in the solar-heated pool. Highly recommended. Cottages from R960.

Ivydene Off Glebe Rd, Rondebosch ☏ 021 685 1747, ⓔ ivydene@mweb.co.za. Five flats in a delightful old house near the university, with a garden, swimming pool and friendly atmosphere. There are discounts for stays over a week or more. R400–600 per flat.

Kinloch Garden Apartment 3 Palm St, Newlands ☏ 021 683 5199, ⓔ marinella@mweb.co.za. Attached to a family home, this comfortably furnished self-catering apartment has a separate entrance and private garden with stunning views of Table Mountain. It's a 20-min walk to Kirstenbosch and Claremont shops. Doubles R400.

The Vineyard On the corner of Colinton and Protea rds, Newlands ☏ 021 657 4500,

ⓦ www.vineyard.co.za. An excellent, classy hotel in a restored country villa built for Lady Anne Barnard in 1799. The public spaces are decorated in elegant Cape Dutch style, with an outstanding panorama of Table Mountain from the extensive garden. Great choice for a luxury stay. Doubles R1300–4760.

Constantia and Tokai

Accommodation in these areas is shown on the map on p.95.

Allandale Holiday Cottages 72 Zwaanswyk Rd, Tokai ☏ 021 715 3320, ⓦ www.allandale.co.za. One-, two- and three-bedroom self-catering brick cottages on a smallholding adjoining Tokai Forest, on the slopes of Constantiaberg, 2min from the motorway and 20min from Cape Town. Each cottage has a garden area with a braai and outdoor seating, and the site boasts a pool and tennis courts. Four-person cottages from R830.

The Constantia Stables Chantecler Lane, Constantia ☏ & ⓕ 021 794 3653. Six en-suite doubles, each with its own entrance and patio, in converted stables. The six-course breakfasts are excellent, and you can relax around the pool in a large garden. Doubles from R900.

Constantia Uitsig Country Hotel Spaanschemat River Rd, Constantia ☏ 021 794 6500, ⓦ www .constantiauitsig.co.za. Sixteen custom-built and upmarket Cape Dutch-style cottages, in a garden setting on Constantia Uitsig wine estate, next door to Steenberg. There are a couple of excellent restaurants on site, including the *Uitsig* (see p.137). Doubles from R2850.

🏃 **Elephant's Eye Lodge** 9 Sunwood Drive, Tokai ☏ 021 715 2432, ⓦ www .elephantseyelodge.co.za. Half a dozen rooms at a friendly B&B family home in a converted Cape Dutch farmhouse, in its own large grounds with a pool, minutes from Tokai Forest. Two of the rooms have basic self-catering facilities. Doubles from R550.

Steenberg Hotel Corner Steenberg and Tokai rds, Tokai ☏ 021 713 2222, ⓦ www.steenberghotel .com. A luxurious place on South Africa's oldest wine estate at the foot of the

Steenberg Mountain. Accommodation is in the original manor house and three other farm buildings (now national monuments), which are perfect examples of Cape Dutch architecture, dating back to 1682. Arranged around a large formal garden, the buildings have whitewashed walls, thatched roofs, ornate gables and are furnished with seventeenth- and eighteenth-century Cape antiques. Doubles from R2750.

Atlantic seaboard

Down the **Atlantic seaboard** lie the seaside suburbs of Mouille (pronounced "moo-lee") Point, Green Point, Three Anchor Bay and Sea Point and Bantry Bay. Historically Cape Town's hotel and high-rise land, this is now packed with a range of accommodation, making it a good alternative to the City Bowl if you want to be close to the city centre.

South from Bantry Bay along Victoria Drive, the well-heeled mountainside suburb of **Camps Bay** has soaring views over the Atlantic, with the advantage of being close to the city centre, and with its own restaurants and shops. Though nearby **Llandudno** lacks shops or restaurants, it can boast similar vistas and a supremely beautiful beach with clusters of granite boulders at either end. **Hout Bay** is the main urban concentration along the lower half of the peninsula, with a harbour, pleasant waterfront development and the only public transport beyond Camps Bay. Beyond Hout Bay is the semi-rural settlement of **Noordhoek**, close to the Table Mountain National Park, with good horse-riding, beach walks and surfing.

Green Point

The places reviewed in this section are shown on the map on pp.104–105.

Brenda's Guest House 14 Pine Rd ☏021 434 0902 or 083 627 5583, ⓦ www.brendas .co.za. Four rooms inside and another in the garden of a 1900s house, all brightly decorated, with wicker furniture. There's poolside seating on a bricked terrace. Doubles from R840.

Dale Court Guest House 1 Exhibition Terrace Rd ☏021 439 8774, ⓦ www.dalecourt.co.za. Conveniently located, reasonable if unremarkable B&B that accommodates children. The guesthouse manages the eight-storey block opposite, comprising functional self-catering apartments for families. B&B doubles from R850.

David's 12 Croxteth Rd ☏021 439 4649, ⓦ www.davids.co.za. An elegant and airy B&B in a quiet residential street just off the main road. Separate from the guesthouse are a selection of self-catering apartments which it manages. Gay-friendly. Doubles from R600.

Jambo Guest House 1 Grove Rd ☏021 439 4219, ⓦ www.jambo.co.za. Small, atmospheric establishment with four double rooms in a quiet cul-de-sac off Main Rd, just over 1km from the V&A Waterfront. The lush leafy exterior and enclosed garden with pond are delightfully relaxing, and the service is excellent. A luxury suite has a large sitting area, Jacuzzi and French doors opening onto the garden. Doubles from R1040.

Olive Branch Guest House 9 Richmond Rd ☏021 434 9198, ⓦ www.olivebranch.co.za. Nine adequate en-suite rooms, reasonably priced for Green Point with easy access to the Waterfront. Doubles from R850.

Waterfront Suites 153 Main Rd ☏021 439 5020, ⓦ www.waterfront-suites.co.za. Small four-storey block quite close to the waterfront, with modern, impersonal but extremely comfortable self-catering apartments offering brilliant value. The kitchens are well equipped, and the rooms are serviced daily. Apartments from R650.

Wilton Manor 15 Croxteth Rd ☏021 434 7869, ⓦ www.wiltonmanor.co.za. A quiet and friendly guesthouse with a homely atmosphere in a Victorian house close to the city centre. The service is good, and there's also a small garden. Doubles from R850.

Sea Point and Bantry Bay

The places reviewed in this section are shown on the map on pp.104–105.

Don Suite Hotel 249 Beach Rd, Sea Point ☎021 434 1083, ⓦwww.don.co.za. A five-storey block of 27 self-catering apartments across the road from the beachfront promenade and 300m from the lively Main Rd restaurant strip. All the flats, studio apartments and one- and two-bedroom units are modern and well equipped; rates vary depending on whether or not you get a view. Doubles from R1000.

🏃 **Les Cascades de Bantry Bay** 48 De Wet Rd, Bantry Bay ☎021 434 5209, ⓦwww.lescascades.co.za. One of the most beautiful guesthouses in the country, in a prime location perched above the Atlantic. There are luxurious lounges, verandas and swimming pools, and every room has a full sea view and deck or balcony, and features Balinese-influenced decor in warm earthy tones. The Belgian owners cook up a storm. Unusually for such an upmarket place, they do take children. Doubles R1650–2650.

Stonehurst Guest House 3 Frere Rd, Sea Point ☎021 434 9670, ⓦwww.stonehurst.co.za. An airy tin-roofed Victorian residence with original fittings and Cape furniture. There's also a pleasant front garden, a kitchen and guest lounge. Most rooms are en suite, and some rooms have balconies. Doubles from R1300.

Villa Rosa 277 High Level Rd, Sea Point ☎021 434 2768, ⓦwww.villa-rosa.com. A friendly eight-room guesthouse in a salmon-pink two-storey Victorian house on the lower slopes of Signal Hill, two blocks from the beachfront promenade. Decorated with simplicity and style, all rooms have TVs, phones and safes, but only some, on the upper floor, have sea views. Doubles from R1300.

Winchester Mansions Hotel 221 Beach Rd, Sea Point ☎021 434 2351, ⓦwww.winchester .co.za. A self-consciously colonial-style 1920s hotel, in a prime spot across the road from the seashore, with an atmosphere straight from the pages of Agatha Christie. Palm trees at the front of the three-storey Cape Dutch Revival building hint at the interior: rooms have ceiling fans, and a cool Italianate courtyard restaurant is overlooked by balconies draped in luxuriant creepers. There's a good restaurant, too. Doubles from R1785.

Camps Bay and points south

Bay Hotel Victoria Road, Camps Bay ☎021 438 4444, ⓦwww.thebay.co.za. Luxurious, glitzy five-star hotel on the fashionable beach-front strip. Its late-1980s construction blends neo-Cape Dutch with Mediterranean styles and cane furniture, to conjure up a laidback colonial fantasy. Doubles from R2700.

🏃 **Ekogaia Farm Cottages** 2 Nthombeni Way, Noordhoek ☎021 789 1751 or 083 403 2623, ⓦwww.ekogaia.co.za.co.za. Two thatched self-catering cottages on an attractive organic smallholding, each built with a "low ecological footprint" design, with outdoor patios, mountain and sea views, plenty of privacy and picnic and play areas for children. Doubles from R500.

Leeukop 25 Sedgemoor Rd, Camps Bay ☎021 438 1361, Ⓔleeukopbb@hotmail.com. The most reasonably priced B&B accommodation in Camps Bay, near the beach and cafés, in two stylishly arty and comfortable apartments adjoining the cheerful proprietor's home. The flats are fully equipped, and you can either self-cater or stay on a B&B basis. Doubles from R1000.

Monkey Valley Resort Mountain Rd, Noordhoek ☎021 789 1391, ⓦwww.monkeyvalleyresort .com. An attractive group of mainly wooden and thatched two-storey chalets spread over several acres of Chapman's Peak 40km south of the city centre. Overlooking the 7km of Noordhoek Beach, the site is surrounded by indigenous vegetation, with no other houses in sight, though no monkeys either. You can eat in the restaurant, self-cater or stay on a B&B basis, in a variety of accommodation options, depending on the size of the group. Double sea-facing suites from R1790.

Sunbird Mountain Retreat Boskykloof Rd, Hout Bay ☎021 790 7758, ⓦwww.sunbirdlodge .co.za. Three pleasant, spacious self-catering apartments and a guesthouse that includes a family unit, all nestling in a forest high up on the mountainside. All the rooms have great views and there's a secluded swimming pool. Doubles from R650, self-catering from R580.

False Bay seaboard

The Metrorail line to the handsome, historic village of Simon's Town reaches the coast at **Muizenberg**, the oldest of Cape Town's seaside suburbs. To its south, en route to Simon's Town, are a series of settlements, including salubrious **St James**, **Kalk Bay** with its working harbour and great cafés, and **Fish Hoek**, which is known for the best swimming beach along the False Bay seaboard. **Simon's Town** is regarded by most Capetonians as a separate village, which it originally was, although it's now quite definitely part of the metropolis. During the day, trains arriving in Simon's Town are met by Rikkis taxis, which will take you anywhere in the vicinity.

Muizenberg, St James and Kalk Bay

The places reviewed in this section are shown on the map on pp.112–113.

Amberley Travellers Lodge 15 Amberley Rd, Muizenberg ☎021 788 7032, ⊛www .amberleylodge.com. A restored two-storey house with gleaming wooden floors, and spacious rooms and kitchen. Doubles from R250 excluding breakfast.

An Ocean Echo 3 Church Rd, Muizenberg ☎021 788 7966 or 083 309 1283, ⊛anoceanecho .co.za. A busy backpacker lodge in a two-storey Victorian house, on the railway line. Upstairs are three double rooms with their own kitchen, bathroom, and sharing a wraparound wooden deck. Dorms R65, doubles R240.

Chartfield Guest House 30 Gatesville Rd, Kalk Bay ☎021 788 3793, ⊛www .chartfield.co.za. Unpretentious, accommodation, 100m from Kalk Bay station restaurants and shops, in a well-kept rambling house halfway up the hill overlooking the harbour, with terrific sea views. The best rooms are the one in the loft with its own balcony, and the two semicircular corner ones with 180-degree views. Doubles from R400.

Fish Hoek

Sunny Cove Manor 72 Simon's Town Rd, Fish Hoek ☎021 782 2274, ⊛www.sunnycovemanor .com. Near Sunny Cove station, this cheerful B&B has four suites, three of them two-bedrooms affairs; all bar the back room have outstanding sea views, and there's secure on-site parking. If you cross the road and the railway line, you're on Jager's walkway, which leads after a short walk to Fish Hoek Beach. Doubles R600.

Tranquility Guest House 25 Peak Rd, Fish Hoek ☎021 782 2060, ⊛www.tranquil.co.za. Warm and welcoming, with panoramic views of the mountainside and ocean (the beach is within walking distance). There are four cosy B&B en-suite rooms, plus a self-catering apartment with its own entrance. Guests can soak in the outdoor Jacuzzi. Doubles R900.

Simon's Town and around

For the locations of the establishments reviewed here, see the map on pp.116–117.

Boulders Beach Lodge 4 Boulders Place, Boulders Beach ☎021 786 1758, ⊛www .bouldersbeach.co.za. Twelve B&B rooms and two self-catering flats above the Boulders Beach car park, a 2min walk from Boulders Coastal Park and the African penguin colony, and just over 1km from Simon's Town. The self-catering units sleep two to six people. Meals are available at the adjacent restaurant (daily 8am–9.30pm). Doubles R950.

British Hotel Apartments 90 St George's St ☎021 786 2214, ⊛www.british-hotel.co.za. Three-bedroom self-catering apartments in a grand 1898 Victorian hotel, that once had Cecil Rhodes and the nineteenth-century explorer, Mary Kingsley, as guests; there are also more modest doubles with baths. Part of a picturesque main street, this is an experience rather than just somewhere to stay, with Victorian colonial decor, high ceilings and huge balconies overlooking the street and the docks. Doubles R900.

Oatlands Holiday Village Froggy Pond, 3km from Simon's Town and 1km from the Boulders Beach penguin colony ☎021 786 1410, ⊛www .oatlands.co.za. Across the road from the beach and near a golf course, this family resort is set in large grounds with its own pool and playground. There are over twenty self-catering chalets of various sizes, sleeping two to six people; there's also a pub and restaurant on the premises. Doubles from R500.

Simon's Town Backpackers 66 St Georges St ☎ **021 786 1964,** 🌐 **www.capepax.co.za.** Conveniently located in the heart of Simon's Town, within walking distance of the station. The double rooms are fairly spacious and there's a large balcony with a view of the waterfront. You can rent one of the bicycles and ride to Cape Point or

paddle in a kayak past the penguin colony. Doubles R220.

Topsail House 176 St Georges St ☎ **021 786 5537.** An old convent converted into a backpacker lodge, with more space than average, though a tad staid. There are various accommodation options including an extraordinary bedroom in a chapel, though it's the en-suite doubles upstairs that are the nicest. Doubles from R240.

African township homestays

One of the best ways of getting a taste of the African townships is spending a night there. The number of township residents offering ⚡ **B&B accommodation** in their homes is still small, but growing. You'll have a chance to experience the warmth of *ubuntu* – traditional African hospitality – by staying with a family with whom you'll generally eat breakfast and dinner; they can also usually take you around their area to *shebeens*, music venues or just to meet the neighbours.

A number of the township B&Bs will send someone to meet you at the airport, while many people are dropped off at their accommodation by tour operators. If you're driving, your accommodation will give you detailed directions or arrange to meet you at a convenient landmark, such as a garage or police station.

For information about township B&Bs other than the ones listed below, contact the **Cape Tourism Centre** in Guguletu (Mon–Fri 8am–5pm, Sat 8.30am–2pm; ☎021 637 8449 or 082 476 1278, 🌐www.tourismcapetown.co.za).

Kopanong Khayelitsha ☎ **021 361 2084 or 082 476 1278.** One of the most dynamic B&B operations in the township, run by the tireless Thope Lekau, who has a mission to replace gawping tourists in their buses with guests who engage with township life. This former NGO worker will treat you to a history of the township, introduce you to local music and dish up a traditional family breakfast. A traditional dinner is available on request, as is a guided tour. Doubles R500.

Majoro's Khayelitsha ☎ **021 361 3412 or 082 537 6882.** Hosted by the charming Maria Maile in her family home, which has two rooms, sharing a bath and toilet. Dinner includes traditional fare such as *mielie pap*, and you'll be treated to an English breakfast with a difference, which may include bacon and egg with fish cakes, sausage and home-made steamed bread. Doubles R380.

Malebo's Khayeletisha ☎ **021 361 2391.** Three rooms sharing bath and toilet facilities in the welcoming home of Lydea Masoleng and her husband. In the morning you'll be served a continental breakfast; dinners, which combine Western fare with traditional African food, are available on request. You're welcome to join your hosts on outings to a *shebeen* or, on Sun, to church. Doubles R400.

Maneo Langa ☎ **021 694 2504.** Friendly hostess Thandiwe Peter has two outside rooms and one inside the family house, in Cape Town's oldest township, and the closest to the city centre, so most guests drive here. She will take guests to some of the township highlights, including a local *shebeen* where you may see singing and dancing. Doubles R380.

8

Eating

E
ating out is one of the highlights of visiting Cape Town. The city has a large number of relaxed and convivial **restaurants**, which generally serve imaginative and healthy food of a high standard, with international cuisines readily available. Prices are inexpensive compared with much of the developed world, and foreign visitors can eat innovative food by outstanding chefs in upmarket restaurants, for the kind of money they'd spend on a pizza back home. Another plus has been the rise of continental-style **cafés**, easy-going places all over the city where you can eat just as well as you would in a regular restaurant, or drink coffee all night without feeling obliged to order food.

One element which seems to unite the country is a love of **meat**: this is an ideal place to try out all kinds of interesting types of meat, from ostrich to springbok, and good quality steaks are inexpensive and freely available. As for **seafood**, you can expect fresh fish at every good restaurant. Cape Town itself offers cold-water fish such as kingklip, hake and *snoek*; the cold waters further up the country's west coast yield quantities of crayfish and mussels, while fresh fish, oysters and prawns are flown in from warmer waters, including Mozambique.

As a visitor you might struggle to keep in check the locals' assumption that meat – and lots of it – is the ideal choice for your meals, but **vegetarians** need not despair, as there's usually at least one concession to meatless food on menus. Even steakhouses will have something on offer and generally feature reasonable salad bars.

Cape cuisine (see box below) is worth sampling at least once, here in the city where it developed. It's the exclusive focus of a couple of restaurants, though many restaurants pay some homage to the style, and in fact most of the dishes considered as Cape cuisine have actually crept into the South African diet.

Cape cuisine

Styles of cooking brought by Asian and Madagascan slaves have evolved into **Cape cuisine** (sometimes known as **Cape Malay** food – a misnomer given that few slaves came from Malaysia). Associated with Cape Town's Muslim community, the cuisine is characterized by mild, semi-sweet curries with a strong Indonesian influence, and though it doesn't offer that much variety, it can be delicious. Dishes include **bredie** (stew), of which **waterblommetjiebredie**, made using water hyacinths, is a speciality; **bobotie**, a spicy minced dish served under a savoury custard; and **sosaties**, a local version of kebab using minced meat. For dessert, dates stuffed with almonds make a light and delicious end to a meal, while **malva** pudding is a rich combination of milk, sugar, cream and apricot jam.

The obvious accompaniment to your meals are **Cape wines**, costing R50 and up for a bottle of something quaffable (for more on locally produced wines, see p.167), though **beer** is definitely the national drink (see p.141). As a rule, restaurants are licensed, but Muslim establishments serving Cape cuisine don't allow alcohol at all.

As regards **prices**, a restaurant described as inexpensive in our reviews can be expected to have main courses priced below R60, while a moderate establishment will charge R60–80 for a main course, and an expensive place more than this. For details of where to buy seafood, wines and other provisions to **self-cater**, see p.151.

City centre

Cape Town's once down-at-heel city centre is enjoying a renaissance, and its **restaurants** are being joined by plenty of continental-style **cafés**, most of which stay open till around 11pm.

Around Long Street

The places reviewed below are shown on the map on p.59.

95 Keerom 95 Keerom St ☏021 422 0765. Flashy and fabulous for the very flush. Clean, light Italian nouvelle cuisine. Expensive. Mon–Fri lunch & dinner, Sat dinner only.

Addis in Cape 41 Church St ☏021 424 5722. Delicious traditional Ethiopian dishes and yummy *injera* (flat bread) to soak up the flavours. Bring your own cutlery if required. Friendly and casual. Moderate. Mon–Sat lunch & dinner.

Africa Café 108 Shortmarket St, Cape Heritage Square ☏021 422 0221. Probably the best restaurant in Cape Town for African cuisine, with a fantastic selection from around the continent. Given that you're served a communal feast of sixteen dishes, and can have as many extra helpings as you like, its R170 per head price tag is pretty reasonable. Booking essential. Inexpensive–moderate. Dinner daily from 6.30pm, except Sun in winter.

Bukhara 33 Church St ☏021 424 0000. A popular upmarket North Indian restaurant, with green marble floors and a show kitchen where you can watch the chefs at work. The food is superb. Booking is essential to get into one of the two evening sittings (7pm & 9pm). Expensive. Mon–Sat lunch & dinner, Sun dinner only.

Five Flies 14–16 Keerom St ☏021 424 4442. Wonderfully imaginative food, with a sophisticated blend of world cuisines which really

works. The presentation delights, while the feel is elegant without being formal. Expensive. Mon–Fri lunch, dinner daily.

Ginja 121 Castle St ☏021 426 2368. Situated in a stylishly renovated, 160-year-old grain warehouse, this restaurant offers quality international fusion cuisine. The house specialty is the slow-roasted duck breast. Expensive. Mon–Sat dinner only.

Ivy Garden Restaurant Old Town House, Greenmarket Square. Tucked away in the sheltered courtyard of the museum, this casual place is good for salads, *bobotie*, pickled fish, *potjiekos*, or just a beer. Inexpensive. Mon–Fri 8.30am–4pm, Sat 8.30am–1pm.

Mama Africa 178 Long St ☏021 424 8634. Food from around the continent, including a mixed grill of springbok, impala, kudu, ostrich, even crocodile. You can also sit at the 12-metre bar – in the form of a green mamba – and listen to live African music. Moderate. Mon–Sat dinner only.

Masala Dosa 167 Long St ☏021 424 6772. Inexpensive and fast South Indian cuisine with a taste of Bollywood. Worth visiting just for the ginger and apple lassi. Daily noon–10pm.

Mexican Kitchen Café 13 Bloem St ☏021 423 1541. A casual restaurant serving good-value burritos, enchiladas, nachos and calamari fajitas, with some fine vegetarian options and deli-style takeaways. Fun atmosphere, though service is slow. Inexpensive. Daily until midnight.

Mr Pickwick's 158 Long St. The place to go for midnight munchies. Hearty and cheap "tin-plate" meals, including a challenging range of hot and cold "foot-long" sandwiches. Inexpensive. Mon & Tues 8am–2am, Wed–Sat 8am–4am.

Royale 273 Long St ☎021 422 4536. Gourmet burgers that pack a surprise, with unusual combinations, such as brie and roasted vegetables in the bun. Choose from lamb, beef, chicken and seven vegetarian patties including tofu. Inexpensive. Mon–Sat noon till late.

Savoy Cabbage 101 Hout St ☎021 424 2626. Sophisticated and innovative European-style peasant food, madly expensive but absolutely worthwhile for the best gourmet food in town. Menu changes daily. Mon–Fri lunch & dinner. Sat dinner only.

Elsewhere in the centre

The places reviewed in this section are marked on the map on p.54.

Biesmiellah In the Bo-Kaap, on the corner of Upper Wales and Pentz sts ☎021 423 0850. One of the oldest and best-known restaurants for traditional Cape cuisine; especially recommended are the spicy stews and wickedly rich *malva* pudding. No alcohol. Moderate. Mon–Sat from 11am.

🏃 **Charly's Bakery** 20 Roeland St. The most spectacular cakes and pastries in Cape Town, with fun and funky toppings, plus breakfasts and light lunches but don't expect anything from the decor. The moist, rich chocolate cakes are recommended, or try the gingerbread men and colourful cup

cakes designed to delight the child within. Inexpensive. Mon–Fri 7.30am–4pm.

Col'Cacchio Seeff House, 42 Hans Strijdom Ave. An offbeat pizza restaurant, which also serves pasta and salads, and bills itself as low-fat and heart-friendly. Has over forty different designer pizza toppings, such as smoked salmon, sour cream and caviar. No bookings. Inexpensive. Lunch Mon–Fri, dinner daily.

🏃 **Jewel Tavern** Off Vanguard Rd, Duncan Docks ☎021 448 1977. An unpretentious Taiwanese sailors' eating house, now "discovered" by Cape Town's *bons viveurs*. Located in the middle of the docks, it serves superb food, including great hot and sour soup and spring rolls, sometimes made while you watch. Moderate–expensive. Daily mid-morning till 10pm.

Little Japan 48 Riebeeck St ☎021 421 4360. A hole in the wall with a brilliant selection of reasonably priced Japanese food, and not just sushi. Mon–Fri lunch, dinner daily except Sun.

Manos at Castle Hotel On the corner of Canterbury and Constitution sts ☎021 461 4946. Mozambican–Portuguese soul food. Good for steaks, seafood and *peri-peri* chicken. The *Castle Bar* downstairs serves light meals. Mon–Sat lunch & dinner.

Sinn's Wembley Square, McKenzie Rd ☎021 465 0967. Fine dining and busy all-day cocktail bar for the hip, young Wembley Square crowd. Moderate–expensive. Daily 9am–11pm.

V&A Waterfront and De Waterkant

The **Waterfront** offers a lot if you want to eat well and your budget is fairly generous, though like all shopping malls in South Africa, it is full of chain eateries and unimpressive quick eats. **De Waterkant** has some hip places in a gentrified historic quarter with several gay-friendly places; see the map on p.74 for locations.

The Waterfront

Baia Upper Level, Quay 6 ☎021 421 0935. Sit on the terraced balcony and take in the views of Table Mountain while dining on masterfully cooked fresh fish and seafood. The spicy seafood bouillabaisse is worth a try. Expensive. Daily lunch & dinner.

🏃 **Caffé Balducci** Quay 6 ☎021 421 6002. An upmarket café-restaurant with a fresh feel, lovely views, and interesting

Californian–Italian food with South African overtones. Expensive, but worth it. Daily 9am–midnight.

Caffé San Marco Piazza level, Victoria Wharf ☎021 418 5434. A coffee shop and bar on the piazza, offering an all-day breakfast menu, good sandwiches on Italian breads and fresh salads. The grilled calamari with garlic and chilli is delicious. There are eighteen flavours of ice cream and sorbet. Moderate. Daily 8.30am–11.30pm.

Tasca de Belem Shop 154, Piazza level, Victoria Wharf ☏021 419 3009. Portuguese specialities, with funky outdoor seating in summer. The flame-grilled Mozambican chicken is good, as are the *peri-peri* chicken livers. Moderate. Daily 11am–11pm.

🏃 **Willoughby & Co Shop 6182, Lower Level, Victoria Wharf ☏021 418 6115.** Best fish restaurant at the waterfront. Sushi and seafood, lively atmosphere. Daily lunch & dinner.

De Waterkant

🏃 **Anatoli 24 Napier St ☏021 419 2501.** A Turkish restaurant in an early twentieth-century warehouse buzzing with atmosphere. The excellent *meze* include exceptionally delicious *dolmades*, and there are superb desserts such as pressed dates topped with cream. Great for vegetarians. Moderate. Dinner Mon–Sat until 11pm.

Andiamo Cape Quarter piazza, Dixon St ☏021 421 3688. Italian deli with a courtyard restaurant serving salads, pastas and sandwiches. The deli itself does a great selection of meats, cheeses, salads, dips and fresh breads – phone ahead and they'll put a picnic together for you. Moderate. Daily 9am–11pm.

La Petite Tarte Cape Quarter, Dixon St ☏021 425 9077. Tiny, authentically French café whose menu includes sweet and savoury tarts, the latter coming in mushroom, and ham and blue cheese varieties. They also blend flavoured Ceylon and herbal teas to create unusual flavours. Inexpensive. Daily 7.30am–5pm, Wed–Fri till 8pm.

The Nose Wine Bar and Restaurant Cape Quarter, Dixon St ☏021 425 2200. Tastings from a wide selection of the Cape's finest wines (there's a nominal charge for the privilege), as well as light meals, stews, fish and steaks. Moderate. Mon–Sat 11am–late.

City Bowl suburbs

The vast majority of eating places in the City Bowl suburbs lie in a continuous strip along Kloof Street – or just off it – in Gardens. See the map on p.87 for the locations of the places reviewed here.

Café Paradiso 110 Kloof St, Gardens ☏021 423 8653. Good Greek and Mediterranean dishes, including a weigh-your-plate *meze* bar. The outside terrace has views up to the mountain and down over the city and docks. Moderate. Daily lunch & dinner.

Kauai Juice 50 Kloof St, Gardens. If you're in need of something healthy, this is the place to go. It's famous for its smoothies imbued with such exotics as ginseng, wheat grass and echinacea, and it also does low-fat Thai-influenced beef, chicken and veggie sandwiches, plus delicious salads. Inexpensive. Daily 8am–10pm.

🏃 **Lazari Corner of Upper Maynard St and Vredehoek Ave ☏021 461 9865.** A meeting place for City Bowl habituees. Fresh, interesting breakfasts and lunches, home-baked cakes and biscuits. Moderate. Daily breakfast, lunch & dinner.

🏃 **Limoncello 8 Breda St, Gardens ☏021 461 5100.** Small Italian trattoria serving unfailingly excellent pastas and pizzas. Does the best calamari in Cape Town and a great risotto of the day. Moderate. Mon–Fri lunch & dinner, Sat & Sun dinner only.

Melissa's 94 Kloof St, Gardens. Breakfasts, light meals and fine desserts in the small café, while the food emporium sells freshly made Mediterranean fare. Moderate. Mon–Fri 7.30am–9pm, Sat & Sun 8am–9pm.

Mount Nelson Hotel Garden Room 76 Orange St, Gardens. Colonial-style high tea in Cape Town's oldest and most gracious hotel is a definite culinary highlight of the city, the large tea table piled with hot and cold pastries, classic savouries like smoked salmon sandwiches, and cakes. You can skip lunch and dinner after the R135 feast you get here. Moderate. Daily 1.30–5.30pm.

Raith Gourmet Gardens Centre, Mill St, Gardens. Meat-focused deli and café with an exceptional selection of foods and some marvellous sandwiches; German specialities include sauerkraut fried with strips of bacon. Inexpensive. Mon–Fri 8.30am–6pm, Sat 8.30am–1pm.

Sawaddee Orange St ☏021 422 1633. Casual, quick Thai food, close to the Labia cinema. The calamari with pepper and garlic sauce is recommended. Moderate. Closed Sun.

Southern suburbs

Woodstock to Constantia

Chandani 85 Roodebloem Rd, Woodstock ☎ 021 447 7887. Great north Indian food, with a large vegetarian menu in a tastefully restored Victorian house. Quite posh, but prices are very reasonable. Mon–Sat lunch & dinner.

Don Pedros 113 Roodebloem Rd, Woodstock ☎ 021 447 4493. Since the 1980s, when it was a regular haunt for anti-apartheid activists, *Don Pedros* has been a place for good, cheap food – curries, stews, pasta, salads – and a scruffy Capetonian ambience, somewhere to linger all evening over a beer or coffee without feeling hassled. There are smoking and non-smoking rooms; it's also a gay-friendly place where people tend to hang out after shows. Inexpensive. Daily 10am–late.

Gardener's Cottage 31 Newlands Ave, Montebello Estate, Newlands. Serves hearty English breakfasts and light lunches – quiches, salads and lasagnes – as well as tea and coffee. It's set in a complex of old farm buildings under ancient pine trees, with neighbouring arts and crafts workshops at which to browse. Moderate. Tues–Fri 8am–4.30pm, Sat & Sun 8.30am–4.30pm.

Kirstenbosch Tea Room Rhodes Drive, Newlands. The venue rather than the food is the draw here, with outdoor eating to make the most of the mountain views. There's a large self-service place, close to the main entrance, ideal for the children to romp around in while you have a coffee under the trees by the river, or another tea room under thatch and umbrellas, close to the upper entrance to the Gardens. Moderate. Daily 8.30am–5pm.

Organic Living Cafe Deli 39 Constantia Rd, Wynberg ☎ 021 797 1123. Delicious organic health-food buffet charged by weight, with fresh juices and cakes too. Sit inside or in the leafy courtyard. Good for kids. Moderate. Mon–Fri 8.30am–5pm, Sat until 3pm.

Spaanschemat River Café Constantia Uitsig Wine Estate, Spaanschemat River Rd ☎ 021 794 3010. This delightful venue, situated in the farm's old schoolhouse, serves sumptuous breakfasts, lunches and teas. Try the extravagant eggs benedict. Booking essential in high season. Moderate–expensive. Closed Sun.

Uitsig Constantia Uitsig Country Hotel, Spaanschemat River Rd ☎ 021 794 4480. Considered one of the finest restaurants (and one of the priciest) in South Africa for its Mediterranean-influenced cuisine. Expensive. Daily lunch & dinner. Closed July.

Wasabi Old Village Centre, Constantia Village ☎ 021 794 6546. Quality sushi bar in a stylish modern setting. The crab salad, *ramen* soups and Japanese noodles come up tops on the menu. Inexpensive–moderate. Daily lunch & dinner.

Atlantic seaboard

Green Point, Mouille Point and Sea Point establishments reviewed below appear on the map on pp.104–105.

Green Point

Giovanni's Deliworld 103 Main Rd. With indoor and pavement seating, this friendly buzzing Italian deli and coffee shop is handy for coffee, excellent made-to-order sandwiches, salads and dips, as well as good pre-packaged meals. Moderate. Daily 8am–9pm.

Mano's 39 Main Rd ☎ 021 434 1090. Italian food, with exciting salads and one of the best crème brûlées in town. Popular with models and other beautiful people. Moderate. Mon–Fri lunch & dinner, Sat dinner only.

Theo's Grill Butcher and Seafood Beach Rd ☎ 021 439 3494. Upmarket, and right on the beachfront, *Theo's* offers superb Greek-style meat and seafood dishes. Moderate. Mon–Fri lunch & dinner, Sat dinner only.

Wang Thai 105 Main Rd ☎ 021 439 6164. Cape Town's best Thai restaurant, serving such delights as hot and spicy prawn soup, steamed fish with lemon juice and chilli, and its special – thinly sliced, seared sirloin. Moderate. Daily lunch & dinner.

▲ Beachfront dining at Camps Bay

Mouille Point

Newport Market and Deli 47 Beach Rd. A light, airy deli with views onto Table Bay, offering coffee, excellent sandwiches, salads and some hot dishes. Inexpensive. Mon–Fri 7.30am–8pm, Sat & Sun from 8am.

Wakame 47 Beach Rd ☎021 433 2377. Asian fusion food with killer desserts – try the chocolate and banana spring rolls. Every table has a view of the ocean. Booking essential. Moderate–expensive. Daily lunch & dinner.

Sea Point

Harveys at the Mansion Winchester Mansion Hotel, 221 Beach Rd ☎021 434 2351. The *nouvelle cuisine* menu includes combinations such as puréed peas with bone marrow, and there are great views of the sun setting over the Atlantic from the cool courtyard garden. Moderate–expensive. Daily breakfast, lunch & dinner.

La Perla On the corner of Beach and Church sts ☎021 434 2471. Classic Italian-run restaurant which has been a favourite forever, with good seafood, soup, pasta, but no pizza, at its beachfront setting. Moderate–expensive. Daily lunch & dinner.

Mr Chan 178a Main Rd ☎021 434 2239. Worthwhile Chinese restaurant with excellent Hong Kong-style beef. Moderate. Mon–Sat lunch & dinner.

New York Bagels 51 Regent Rd. A fantastic deli with a sit-down section. Choose from a dizzying array of bagels and hom-emade fillings, from chopped liver to herring, plus stir-fries, pasta and pastries. Inexpensive. Daily till late.

Pizzeria Napoletana 178 Main Rd ☎021 434 5386. Family-style Italian restaurant with hearty, good-value cooking. Moderate. Mon–Sat lunch & dinner.

Camps Bay and points south

Café Caprice 37 Victoria Rd, Camps Bay ☎021 438 8315. Directly opposite Camps Bay beach, this lively Mediterranean-style restaurant is a great place to soak up street life and sunshine. Inexpensive–moderate. Daily 9am till late.

La Cuccina Food Store Victoria Mall, Victoria Rd, Hout Bay. High-quality deli and café food in pleasant surrounds, the delicious food amply compensating for the lack of sea views. At lunchtime it has buffets of quiches, salads and lasagne. Moderate. Daily 8am–7pm.

Marika's 38 Victoria Rd, Bakoven ☎021 438 2727. Good summer venue serving fresh Greek food. Though there are no sea views, you're close enough to the beach to explore the rocks and sand on a satisfied belly. Moderate. Tues–Sat dinner, Sun lunch only.

Mariners Wharf Bistro The harbour, Hout Bay. A relaxed, well-run place with terrace seating overlooking the harbour. Good for seafood to eat in or take away. Moderate. Daily 10am–6pm.

Paranga's Shop 1, The Promenade, Victoria Rd, Camps Bay ☏021 438 0404. Young people's hang-out at the beach, a place to see and be seen while you munch on salads, seafood, pasta or sushi. Tues–Sun 9am till late, Mon from noon.

Red Herring On the corner of Beach and Pine rds, Noordhoek ☏021 789 1783. A country restaurant that does grilled meats including springbok and kudu, plus a good choice of vegetarian options or fresh fish. Moderate. Tues–Sun dinner only.

🏃 **Theo's Grill Butcher and Seafood Promenade Building, Victoria Rd, Camps Bay ☏021 438 0410.** Brilliant steaks sold by weight, plus seafood; the atmosphere is buzzy, and there's some outdoor seating. Moderate. Daily lunch & dinner.

False Bay seaboard

Muizenberg

See the map on pp.112–113 for the locations of places reviewed here.

Knead Bakery Muizenberg beachfront. Unbeatable seaside location for bustling café breakfasts and light lunches with contemporary chrome and mirrored decor, and an excellent bakery counter. Moderate. Daily 8am–5pm.

The Olive Station Muizenberg Station, Main Rd. Bright and friendly place where you can snack on Levantine-influenced food. The olive bread, desserts and Lebanese cheese or lamb and pine-nut pies are especially good. There's a warehouse for curing olives on site, with other tasty bits on sale. Some seats overlook the station and beach. Inexpensive. Mon & Wed–Sun breakfast & lunch, Thurs only dinner till 9pm.

Wellbeing Café & Natural Medicine 37 Palmer Rd ☏021 788 9489. This Sufi-run organic food store, green-tea café and natural medicine clinic is the jewel in the crown of shabby chic Muizenberg village high street. Light meals, freshly squeezed organic juices and home-baked bread, Inexpensive. Tues–Thurs & Sat–Sun 10am–6pm, Fri 10am–noon & 4–6pm.

Kalk Bay

See the map on pp.112–113 for the locations of places reviewed here.

Brass Bell Kalk Bay station, Main Rd. Primarily an unpretentious drinking spot, *Brass Bell* has arguably the best location on the peninsula, with False Bay's waves breaking against the wall of its outdoor terrace. The views of both the peninsula mountains and the Hottentots Holland peaks are unbeat-able, but the disappointing seafood meals can't match the magnificent setting. Moderate. Daily until late.

🏃 **Harbour House Restaurant At the harbour ☏021 788 4133.** Freshly caught seafood and Mediterranean fare, at a venue situated spectacularly on the breakwater of Kalk Bay harbour; book a table with bay views or enjoy sundowners on the deck. There's a fireplace and comfortable sofas for winter. Moderate–expensive. Daily lunch & dinner.

Kalky's At the harbour. For years, this totally unpretentious eating place has been serving the fishing community the best traditional fish and chips on the peninsula, and great-value seafood platters; fish is hauled off the boats and straight into the frying pan. You sit at benches to eat, though takeaway is available. Inexpensive. Daily.

🏃 **The Olympia Café & Deli Main Rd.** One of the few places that draws parochial uptown Capetonians down the False Bay seaboard, and a regular meeting spot for locals. Always buzzing, with views of the harbour, for breakfast *Olympia* offers great coffee or freshly squeezed orange juice, accompanied by freshly baked Danish pastries, filled croissants or delicious home-made biscuits. Gourmet lunch menus are chalked up on a board, with local fish often featured. Its bakery around the corner produces excellent breads and pastries every day. Moderate. Daily 7am–9pm.

Simon's Town and around

See the map on pp.116–117 for the locations of the places reviewed here.

Bertha's 1 Wharf Rd ☏021 786 2138. Relax with views of False Bay and the harbour while enjoying a middle-of-the-road, child-friendly menu, with meat, chicken, fish and

vegetarian dishes. Moderate. Daily from
7.30am until evening.

Bon Appétit 90 St George's St ☏ **021 786
2412.** In the old *British Hotel*, *Bon
Appétit* offers classic, beautifully presented
French cuisine. Emmanuel, owner and chef,
is Michelin-trained, so expect the best.
Expensive. Tues–Sat lunch & dinner.

The Meeting Place 98 St George's St ☏ **021 786
1986.** Enjoy Mediterranean café food while
surveying harbour goings-on from the
upstairs balcony. Vegetarians are well
catered for, and there's a deli downstairs.
Moderate. Tues–Sun lunch & dinner.

**Tibetan Tea House 2 Harrington Rd,
Seaforth Beach** ☏ **021 786 1544.** Traditional Tibetan recipes, served up in a venue
signalled by its prayer flags. It's completely
vegetarian, so don't expect yak meat in the
lentil Sherpa Stew. Inexpensive. Daily
10am–5pm.

Drinking, nightlife and live music

White South Africans tend to do their drinking at home, so for them pubs and bars are not the centres of social activity they are in the US or the UK, though in the African townships *shebeens* – informal bars – occupy this role. That said, the city is well populated with **bars**, ranging from the hip to the eccentric to the seedy. Traditional pubs are not a big feature, and where they do exist, they're generally depressingly empty dives or cod-Irish franchises. Most liquor licences stipulate that the last round is served at 2am, but this is far from strictly followed.

South Africans tend to be fiercely loyal to their brand of **beer**, though they all taste pretty much the same, given that virtually all beer in the country is produced by the huge South African Breweries monopoly, one of the world's largest beer makers. It's given a good run for its money by Namibian Breweries, whose Windhoek Lager is rated by cognoscenti as better than SAB's offerings. **Lager** is the predominant style, likely to taste a bit thin and bland to a British palate, though it can be wonderfully refreshing drunk ice-cold on a sweltering day. One or two **microbreweries** have sprung up, best known of which are Mitchell's in Knysna, which produces some distinctive ales, and Birkenhead in Stanford; their beers can be found at some bottle stores and bars between Cape Town and Port Elizabeth. Imported beers are expensive compared with the local product, with the exception of the great Czech Pilsner Urquell, which has been bought by SAB as part of its global expansion.

As for **nightlife**, Cape Town has finally shaken off its reputation as a place where the word was synonymous with hitting the sack. Things have become much more cosmopolitan in recent years, the scene spiced up by African and European visitors and immigrants. Mainstream house is very popular in the city's **clubs**, but there are also strong followings for drum 'n' bass, trance, hip-hop, dub and Latin grooves, as well as **kwaito**, the dance style of young black Jo'burg. Though *kwaito* is still predominantly a black scene, coloured and white youth are gradually getting into it.

Many clubs have a short lifespan – and many of the best regular parties hop from venue to venue. Some of the more enduring clubs are listed here, but watch the press for up-to-the-minute information. The daily *Cape Argus* newspaper runs a club column on Tuesdays, and the monthly listings magazine *Cape Review* is also useful. Backpacker hostels are often the most up-to-date sources of party information. Cover charges vary from R40 to over R200 for big events with international DJs. And if you find yourself wandering about at

▲ A musician playing in the International Jazz Festival

night in search of a party, head for the strip of clubs along **Somerset Road** in Green Point, where there's always something going on well into the early hours. It's worth remembering that all drugs are illegal in South Africa, and aggressive police raids on clubs are by no means unknown.

Some of the township-tour operators (see p.101) offer **township club outings**, so you can hear authentic sounds in the clubs without the hassle of negotiating badly-lit areas at night. In addition, Our Pride Tours (℡021 531 4291) does Sunday-morning gospel excursions to the townships, calling at various churches. **Live music** is something of a hit-and-miss affair in Cape Town, with bands tending to flit from one bar or club to another. African bands tend to be scarce, as the best-known black South African groups get bigger audiences in Johannesburg and abroad. Some live African sounds can be heard at two restaurants, *Marco's* (15 Rose Lane, Bo-Kaap ℡021 423 5412) and *Mama Africa* (see p.134), but otherwise you'll need to watch for concert posters wrapped on street lamps and scan the local press to find out who might be playing, and where. At least there are a couple of stalwart venues for **jazz**, notably the *Green Dolphin* and *Mannenberg's*, both at the Waterfront, with the bonus of the annual Cape Town International Jazz Festival in late March (see p.38). For information on **classical concerts** and **opera**, see p.146.

City centre

Around Long Street

See the map on p.59 for the locations of the places reviewed in this section.
Chrome 6 Pepper St ℡083 700 6079. The Main Dance Arena caters for a younger crowd of party animals, with its own VIP area available only by reservation. The Platinum VIP Lounge offers a relaxed party vibe for the more mature punter.
Jo'burg 218 Long St ℡021 422 0142. A good place to schmooze to a funky soundtrack, in the company of a hip art-school and media crowd. There's a range of live music on Sun nights. Daily 5pm–4am.

Kennedy's Restaurant and Cigar Lounge 251 Long St ☎ **021 424 1212.** A swanky bar offering cigars from all over the world, with brilliant martinis and margueritas, good food, an older crowd, and live jazz every evening. Mon–Fri noon till late, Sat 7pm till late.

The Lounge 194 Long St ☎ **021 424 7636.** A longstanding, trendy refuge for Cape Town's smart and glamorous. Upstairs, make for the superb balcony and grab a table overlooking vibrant Long St. House and jungle dominate the turntables. Mon–Sat 8pm–2am.

Mama Africa 178 Long St ☎ **021 424 8634.** A relaxed and spacious bar-restaurant in the heart of Long St clubland, *Mama Africa* boasts a 12-metre bar in the form of a green mamba. Traditional percussion groups perform regularly, and it's popular with European and North American visitors. Music Mon–Sat 8.30pm–late.

The Purple Turtle On the corner of Shortmarket and Long sts. A cavernous, vaguely seedy bar frequented by goths, metalheads and other creatures, with bands on Sat nights. Daily 11am–late.

Rhodes House 60 Queen Victoria St ☎ **021 424 8844.** A relaxed and fashion-conscious place, with a range of house sounds. Themed parties with designated dress codes also happen – call before turning up. Wed–Sat 10pm till late.

Sutra 86 Loop St ☎ **021 422 4219.** Deep house and R&B sounds. Wed, Fri & Sat 9pm till late.

Elsewhere in the centre

The places here appear on the map on p.54.

Drum Café 84 Harrington St ☎ **021 462 1064.** Every Monday and Wednesday at 9pm there's a facilitated drum circle lead by a South African or West African drum teacher,

suitable for all levels of experience; the smaller Mon groups are better if you're a complete novice, while the Sat-afternoon sessions at 3pm are for families. For those who prefer to leave things to the professionals, there are often parties at the weekends; ring for the current schedule. Light meals are available, and the café is fully licensed. Mon, Wed, Fri & Sat 9pm–late.

FTV 114 Hout St ☎ **021 426 6000.** *Fashiontv-cafe* is a chic hang-out open for coffees, lunches, cocktails and dinner. Mon–Fri open from 10am until very late, Wed, Fri & Sat open in the evenings.

Hemisphere 31st Floor, Absa Centre, 2 Riebeeck St ☎ **021 462 1064.** One of the most stylish bar/lounges in a city full of style, set at the top of one of the city's tallest buildings and with awe-inspiring views of the city below. It's smart but relaxed and the stylish decor caters to comfort. Tues–Fri 4.30pm till late, Sat open from 9pm.

Marimbas Cape Town International Conference Centre, corner of Coen Steytler Ave and Heeren-gracht ☎ **021 418 3366.** There's live music – afro-jazz or marimba – on Thurs, Fri & Sat nights. There's no charge, as long as you are dining there or drinking at the bar.

Mercury Live and Lounge 43 De Villiers St, District Six ☎ **021 465 2106.** Live music and underground hip-hop parties at a spacious venue with minimalist decor. Mon–Sat 8pm till late.

The Shack 45b De Villiers St, District Six ☎ **021 465 2106.** Comprising a restaurant, bar and pool hall, with sounds from the 1960s up to the 1980s. Under the same management is the adjoining *Blue Lizard*, which plays acid jazz, house and trip-hop. Open till late: Mon–Sat from 1pm, Sun from 6pm.

V&A Waterfront and De Waterkant

As well as upmarket restaurants, the **Waterfront** and **De Waterkant** also offer reasonable nightlife. De Waterkant is where you'll find gay bars and clubs while the Waterfront is rather squeaky clean. For the locations of the venues below, see the map on p.74.

Bossa Nova 43 Somerset Rd, De Waterkant ☎ **021 425 0295.** Upmarket lounge and dance club, where evenings start off with commercial music and gradually shift into the rhythmic sounds of Latin America.

Tues–Sat; drinks and light music from 5pm and DJs from around 9.30pm.

Chilli 'n' Lime 23 Somerset Rd, De Waterkant ☎ **021 426 4469.** Painfully stylish upmarket club with two dance floors and four bars, which hosts pulsing house and hip-hop parties. Frequented by a 20-something left-field student crowd. Tues–Sat 8am–4am.

Den Anker Restaurant and Bar Pierhead. One of the livelier Waterfront venues, a busy pub and Continental-style bistro, patronized by tourists and well-heeled locals. *Den Anker* specializes in imported Belgian beers, both on tap and bottled. Daily 11am–midnight.

Green Dolphin Pierhead ⌖021 421 7471. A top-notch jazz venue (though a tad chilly in winter), hosting quality jazz bands nightly at 8.30pm. Dinner – there's excellent seafood – is served from 6pm. Daily noon–midnight.

Opium 6 Dixon St ⌖021 425 4010. An über trendy club featuring acid jazz and funky house music. Wed–Sat 10pm–2am.

Purgatory 8b Dixon St ⌖021 421 7464. The place to hang out with waiflike models and other good-looking people swaying to house music. Wed–Sat 11pm till late.

Southern suburbs

The southern suburbs offer some sedate and less than exciting drinking spots. Best place for some action is Lower Main Road in Observatory where there are a few cafés, restaurants and nightspots – cruise about and wander into wherever takes your fancy.

Boer and Brit Pub Alphen Hotel, Alphen Drive, off the M41, Constantia. A cosy English-style pub at a historic Cape Dutch hotel. It's gracious yet relaxed, with tables under oak trees, a warm hearth on cold nights and bar meals. Daily 10am–11pm.

Foresters' Arms 52 Newlands Ave, Newlands. Preppie students and professionals gather to quaff draught beer at the very popular and busy "Forries", in the heart of leafy Newlands. A big wood-panelled pub, it boasts a beautiful hedged-in courtyard where you can grab a bench for a drowsy afternoon pint. Mon–Sat 10am–11pm, Sun 9am–4pm.

Pedlars on the Bend Spaanschemat River Rd, Constantia. An upmarket bar at one of the posher restaurants in this ritzy suburb, with a delightful outdoor area shaded by oaks. Daily 11am–11pm.

The Cape Flats

West End and Club Galaxy College Rd, Rylands ⌖021 637 9132. Definitely the most happening place on the Flats are these two nightclubs in one building, the former a top jazz venue with live and recorded sounds, the latter a straight-up dance club playing R&B and mainstream house to a smart young crowd. Thurs–Sat 8pm–late.

Atlantic seaboard

Café Caprice 37 Victoria Rd, Camps Bay ⌖021 438 8315. A lively restaurant by day, where the pace increases come evening when DJs play anything from Ella Fitzgerald to *kwaito*. Open morning till late; DJs feature nightly in summer, Fri–Sun the rest of the year.

Dizzy Jazz Café 41 Camps Bay Drive, Camps Bay ⌖021 438 2686. A crowded and lively nightspot with a big veranda and sea views, featuring a variety of live music nightly and serving draught beer and quality seafood. R20 cover charge. Daily noon–4am (music from 8.30pm).

La Med Bar and Restaurant Glen Country Club, Victoria Rd, Clifton ⌖021 438 5600. A great sundowner venue overlooking the rocks at Clifton Beach, drawing a sporty, mainstream crowd; it's a favourite spot for hang-gliders from Lion's Head to visit, after they've landed in the adjacent field. There's live music Wed, Fri & Sat. Daily noon till late.

Red Herring On the corner of Pine and Beach rds, Noordhoek. A pub above a smart restaurant with an outdoor deck overlooking the panoramic Noordhoek valley. Busy on warm weekend afternoons, when a clean-cut 20-something crowd gathers. Tues–Sun 11am–midnight.

Cape colonial

Cape Town's quirky mix of historical buildings reflects the city's erstwhile status as the halfway stop on the old maritime trade route between Europe and the East, and its subsequent colonization first by the Dutch and then by the English. The city's most popular tourist destination, the V&A Waterfront, is a late-twentieth-century development superimposed on the remnants of the Victorian docks and the eighteenth-century Chavonnes Battery. In the city itself, hunkering down between the contemporary bungalows and office blocks, you'll find Cape Dutch houses, Moravian churches, Georgian mosques and Victorian terraces.

Koopmans-De Wet House ▲

Europe in Africa

Cape Town is South Africa's least African city – something clear from its architecture. Don't look for traditional African huts here (or anywhere else in the Western Cape): there aren't any. The city you see is entirely the product of the last 350 years – a result of European colonization. Three-and-a-half centuries may not seem long by European standards, but by South African ones it makes Cape Town the *grande dame* of the subcontinent.

The **Castle**, a Dutch Renaissance fortress built in the 1660s, and now a museum, marks Europe's first tenuous toehold in southern Africa. But the real signature architecture of the southwestern Cape is the **Cape Dutch** style that developed in its wake – Northern Europe's response to Africa. The plethora of thatch and gabled Cape Dutch manor houses, surrounded by vineyards, are a defining component of the Winelands' landscape, while in Cape Town, urban Cape Dutch manifests itself in the outstanding **Koopmans-De Wet House** and **Rust-en-Vreugd** in the city centre, or the more modest terraces of the **Bo-Kaap**, built by freed Muslim slaves in the mid-nineteenth century.

But that's far from the whole story. On occupying the Cape, the British introduced their own building styles, with the result that no place in the country has the architectural variety and historic range you'll find on the Cape Peninsula. Stroll down Cape Town's **Long Street** and you'll be greeted by a collage of frontages that span Dutch and British architectural influences: at the top end, the eighteenth-century Palm Tree Mosque rubs shoulders with some half-dozen backpacker lodges housed in two- and three-storey **Victorian** buildings, while

The Bo-Kaap ▲

Simon's Town ▼

near the harbour end the magnificent early-nineteenth-century Dutch Mission Church abuts an **Art Nouveau** office, just a stone's throw from the city centre's modest skyscrapers. Nearby, the Baroque-style **Old Town House**, built in the 1750s, looks across Greenmarket Square at a collection of multistorey **Art Deco** buildings from the 1920s and 1930s.

In the **suburbs** close to the city centre, the town houses of Observatory, Woodstock, Sea Point and Green Point, built in the 1880s and 1890s, have a uniquely local flavour. While still recognizably Victorian, they sport local adaptations that include verandas and balconies edged with intricate ironwork to shelter their facades from the elements.

Along the coast, the two seaboards present two entirely different faces. Take the train down the **False Bay** seaboard and you can get off at Muizenberg's Edwardian railway station, while all the way to St James a mixture of Victorian, Edwardian, Arts and Crafts and twentieth-century houses cling implausibly to the steep mountainside. Further south, at the end of the line, **Simon's Town**'s intact main street retains its distinctive colonial character with its two-storey balconied streetscape.

On the **Atlantic** side is Africa's wannabe Malibu – Clifton, Bakoven and Camps Bay – where a cut-and-paste of **twentieth-century** styles jostle for their place in *House and Garden*, from cool modernist boxes-with-a-view to kitsch, multimillion-rand status symbols.

Miles away in all senses, on the Cape Flats, South Africa's most ubiquitous modern architecture comes in the form of the rust and polychrome corrugated-iron **shacks** occupying any piece of vacant land – the modern urban equivalent of the traditional African hut.

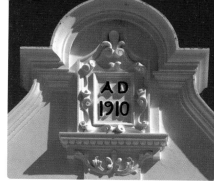

▲ Edwardian detail

▼ Township building

▼ Long Street verandas

Backcountry buildings

Some of South Africa's most rewarding historical architecture is off the beaten track, along backroads and in the *dorps*. Just outside Cape Town the Winelands region is awash with old buildings. Dorp Street in **Stellenbosch** is ranked by one architectural historian as "one of the most beautiful streets in the whole of South Africa" for its intact oak-lined streetscape, some of its buildings dating back to the early 1700s.

All over the **Western Cape** countryside you'll encounter simple, limewashed dwellings that were – and often still are – farmworkers' homes. In a similar vein the coastal village of **Arniston** is built around a settlement of some eighty stark white thatch, stone and mud-plastered fishermen's cottages.

Much of the historic architecture of the **Garden Route** has been swamped by recent beachfront development, but you'll still find gems such as the nineteenth-century Dutch Reformed Church in **George**, which combines the Cape vernacular with Classical and Regency elements. Parts of **Knysna** still cling to their architectural past, with timber Victorian cottages, the Georgian Old Magistrate's Court and several country churches.

If you're looking for **country vernacular**, one of the most rewarding journeys is along the inland Route 62, the back road that passes through the mountains of the Little Karoo parallel to the Garden Route. You'll encounter *dorp* after *dorp* with historic streetscapes – one of the prettiest is **Montagu**, founded in the 1850s and lined with Cape Dutch dwellings, shops and churches. Along the same route, **Barrydale** is a pleasingly unpretentious Victorian farming village, while **Calitzdorp** has a wonderful Byzantine-style Dutch Reformed Church and **Oudtshoorn** is striking for its unique sandstone Victorian Gothic "feather palaces", built during the ostrich-feather boom.

Dutch Reformed Church, Calitzdorp ▲

Ladysmith, a hamlet along the R62 ▲

Oudtshoorn feather palace ▼

Theatre, comedy, classical music and cinema

D espite scarce resources (state funds have been redirected to more pressing areas), **theatre** in South Africa is making a valiant attempt to lift itself out of its post-democracy doldrums. Protest theatre, a fertile genre in the oppressive 1970s and 1980s, is now obsolete, and it's no longer seen as self-indulgent for plays to deal with personal rather than political issues. As yet there is no real successor to the world-renowned playwright Athol Fugard, several of whose works were first staged here, though a steady trickle of new **plays** are being written and performed in Cape Town, some of them innovative and hard-hitting. Writers and directors to look out for include the brilliant Brett Bailey, Marthinus Basson, Reza de Wet, Fiona Coyne (who also hosts the South African version of *The Weakest Link*), Roy Sargeant and the duo of Heinrich Rosehofer and Oscar Petersen. As regards **musicals**, David Kramer and the late Taliep Petersen have produced several hit shows celebrating the history and culture of Cape Town. Their *Kat and the Kings* took Broadway and London's West End by storm a few years back, bagging the 1999 Olivier Award for the best new musical.

Comedy, too, is starting to shape up well with the annual **Smirnoff International Comedy Festival**, held at the Baxter Theatre around October, showcasing global and local talent. South Africa's best-known stage satirist is Pieter Dirk Uys, whose character Evita Bezuidenhout, South Africa's answer to Dame Edna Everage, has relentlessly roasted South African society since apartheid days. The best way to experience him is to head out at the weekend to **Darling**, Uys's country home town, and something of an artists' colony, an hour's drive north of Cape Town on the R27, where you can take in one of his hilariously camp shows over lunch in the converted local train station, *Evita se Perron* (☎022 492 2831, ⓦwww.evita.co.za), filled with Afrikaner kitsch and tat.

Home-grown comedians to look out for include Marc Lottering and Kurt Schoonraad, coloured Capetonians who replaced the hammy old sets dominated by white men. In a similar vein, but with roots in the black community, David Kau is as caustic about Jo'burg township dwellers as he is about white South Africans. Funniest of the lot is Nik Rabinowitz, a Jewish comedian who is fluent in Xhosa and sails close to the wind with jokes about every racial and cultural grouping in South Africa.

Classical music has a small but faithful following, with concerts tending to take place on Tuesdays and Thursdays. There are free lunchtime concerts, often showcasing the work of students from Cape Town University's South African College of Music, on Thursdays at 1pm during term time, and sometimes on Wednesday 2pm; these take place at the Baxter Theatre (see below) or at the college itself (℡021 650 2640) just behind. The Baxter is often also the venue for recitals by visiting soloists and chamber ensembles, put on by the Cape Town Concert Series organization (W www.ctconcerts.co.za).

It's always a treat to catch one of the performances by **Cape Town Opera** (W www.capetownopera.co.za), to hear black South Africans – who dominate opera in South Africa – injecting some African spice into a programme that still predominantly features European works, with many young singers appearing here before they hit the international scene. Performances are mainly held at the Baxter or Artscape, with additional shows at the Waterfront in February and open-air performances at the Spier winery (see p.172) near Stellenbosch in February and March.

Tickets for most of the venues and performances listed in this chapter are available from Computicket (see p.164).

Venues

Artscape D.F. Malan St ℡021 410 9838, W www .artscape.co.za. Once the Camelot of state-funded white performing arts, Artscape has reinvented itself as a less elitist theatre, though high-quality ballet and opera are still produced, while adventurous new dramas appear periodically. Don't be intimidated by the monumental 1970s architecture.

Baxter Theatre Centre Main Rd, Rondebosch ℡021 685 7880, W www.baxter.co.za. This mammoth brick theatre complex, its design inspired by Soviet Moscow's central train station, mounts an eclectic programme – innovative plays, comedy festivals, jazz and classical concerts and kids' theatre.

Little Theatre University of Cape Town, Orange St ℡021 480 7128, W www.uct.ac.za/about /arts/littletheatre. A showcase for innovative work from the University of Cape Town drama school; the productions range from self-indulgent to breathtaking. The drama school has a long tradition of producing fine actors, and counts Richard E. Grant among its graduates.

Manenberg's Jazz Café Clock Tower Precinct, Waterfront ℡021 421 5639, W www.manen-bergsjazzcafe.com. One of Cape Town's premier venues for live music, specializing in Cape and African jazz and attracting some of the hottest names in South African music. Open till late: Mon & Thurs–Sun from 8.30pm, Fri & Sat from 9.30pm.

Maynardville Open Air Theatre On the corner of Church and Wolfe sts, Wynberg W www .maynardville.co.za. Under the summer stars in Maynardville Park, every year in Jan & Feb, an imaginative production of a Shakespeare play is staged by the cream of Cape Town's actors and designers. Book through Computicket (see p.164).

▼ Maynardville Open Air Theatre

MAYNARDVILLE
OPEN AIR THEATRE

On Broadway 88 Shortmarket St, city centre ℡021 424 1194. One of the few venues committed to the city's small cabaret scene is this bar-restaurant with live performances for an ethnically mixed crowd every night. Drag shows on Tues & Sun, cabaret Wed–Sat, and satirist Pieter Dirk Uys performs Mon evening. Daily 7pm–late.

Theatre On The Bay Link St, Camps Bay ℡021 438 3300, Ⓦwww.theatreonthebay.co.za. An upmarket theatre catering to a mature audience, and staging accomplished – if rather predictable – productions of mainstream contemporary plays and farces, plus musical tributes and revues.

Cinemas

Despite the fact that Cape Town is booming as a film-production centre, local feature films are scarce. For an intelligent mix of art films, cult classics and new releases, try the Labia, 69 Orange St, or the Labia on Kloof, at the Lifestyles on Kloof Centre, Kloof Street Gardens (both on ℡021 424 5927, Ⓦwww .labia.co.za).

Mainstream cinemas most convenient for visitors are the Nu-Metro (℡021 419 9700, Ⓦwww.numetro.co.za) and Ster-Kinekor Cinema Nouveau (℡021 425 8222, Ⓦwww.sterkinekor.com) at the V&A Waterfront; the Ster-Kinekor Cavendish Commercial (℡0860 300 222) at Cavendish Square Shopping Centre, Claremont; and, at the same shopping centre, the Ster-Kinekor Cinema Nouveau (℡021 683 4063). The Ster-Kinekor complex at the Blue Route Mall in Tokai (℡021 713 1280, Ⓦwww .sterkinekor.com) is convenient if you're staying along the False Bay seaboard. All the above cinemas advertise daily in the *Cape Times* and *Cape Argus*.

Shopping

The **V&A Waterfront** is the city's most popular shopping venue, with good reason: it has a vast range of shops, the setting on the harbour is lovely and there's a huge choice of places to eat and drink when you want to rest your feet – but expect to pay above the odds for everything. The city centre also offers variety and, for some people's taste, a grittier and more interesting venue for browsing, especially if you're looking for collectables, antiques and secondhand books. Cape Town's suburbanites tend to do their shopping at the upmarket Cavendish Square Mall in **Claremont** or one of many other shopping centres. If you're staying in the inner-city suburbs of Green Point and Sea Point, adjacent to the V&A Waterfront, you'll find supermarkets and other functional shops along Main Road, while the City Bowl suburbs are served by the Gardens Shopping Centre. There are other smaller shopping areas dotted about the other suburbs.

Shopping hours have traditionally been Monday to Friday 8.30am to 5pm, and Saturday until 1pm, though lots of supermarkets, bookshops and other specialist outlets are now open beyond 5pm and also on Sundays, though don't expect much to be open on Sunday afternoons, except at the Waterfront or Cavendish Square.

Malls and shopping centres

South African shopping tends to follow the American model, with **malls** where you can browse in a bookshop as well as bank, buy clothes and groceries and go to the movies. Malls always have several coffee shops and restaurants.

Blue Route Mall Tokai Rd, Tokai. A functional single-storey centre with branches of Checkers Hyper and Woolworths, handy if you're staying in Constantia or along the False Bay. Mon–Fri 9am–5.30pm, Sat & Sun 9am–3pm.

Cavendish Square Claremont station, Vineyard Rd, Claremont. An upmarket multistorey complex, the major shopping focus for the southern suburbs. Mon–Thurs & Sat 9am–6pm, Fri 9am–9pm, Sun 10am–4pm.

Constantia Village Shopping Centre Main Rd, Constantia. A small exclusive mall including two large supermarkets. Mon–Fri 9am–5pm, Sat 9am–2pm.

Gardens Shopping Centre Mill St, Gardens. Small shopping mall in the City Bowl, very close to the Company's Gardens and city centre, with a large supermarket, excellent deli and most of the shops you'll need. Mon–Fri 9am–6pm, Sat 9am–3pm; some shops also Sun 10am–2pm.

Victoria Wharf Shopping Centre V&A Waterfront. It would be possible to visit Cape Town and never leave the Waterfront complex, which has a vast range of upmarket shops packed into the Victoria Wharf Shopping Centre, including outlets of all the major South African chains, selling books, clothes, food and crafts. Mon–Sat 9am–9pm, Sun 10am–9pm.

Arts, crafts and jewellery

Cape Town is not known for its indigenous **arts and crafts**, and many of the goods you'll buy here are from elsewhere in Africa, especially Zimbabwe and Zambia. There are several crafts outlets in the city centre and the V&A Waterfront, but you'll often pick up the same wares for a lot less money at the pavement **markets** scattered around town. Don't expect exotic West African-style affairs, however: Cape Town's markets are more like European or North American flea markets. Two of the most browsable streets for crafts and gifts are Long Street in the city centre, and Main Road in Kalk Bay. If you're after South African **gold** and **jewellery**, you'll find the Victoria Wharf Shopping Centre one of the best places to browse.

Craft shops

Africa Nova Cape Quarter, Dixon St, De Waterkant ☎021 425 5123. A better-than-average selection of ethnic crafts and curios as well as contemporary African textiles and artwork, with an emphasis on the individual and handmade. Mon–Fri 9am–5pm, Sat & Sun 10am–2pm.

African Image Branches at the corner of Church and Burg sts (☎021 423 8385); and Shop 6228, Victoria Wharf, V&A Waterfront (☎021 419 0382). One of the best places for authentic traditional and contemporary African arts and crafts, from fabrics and antique sculpture to beadwork, but goods are a little overpriced. Church & Burg branch Mon–Fri 9am–5pm, Sat 9am–1.30pm; Waterfront branch daily 9am–9pm.

Carrol Boyes Victoria Wharf ☎021 424 8263, ⓦ www.carrolboyes.co.za. Designer cutlery, tableware and other household items, distinctively embellished with sinuous curves and patterns. Daily 9am–9pm.

Clementina Ceramics 20 Main Rd, Kalk Bay ☎021 788 8718. Unique, colourful contemporary South African ceramics, guaranteed to brighten up your kitchen back home. Tues–Sun 10am–5pm.

Ethno Bongo Mainstream Shopping Centre, Main Rd, Hout Bay ☎021 790 0802. A charming shop in the main shopping centre in Hout Bay, selling wonderful and well-priced crafts, jewellery and accessories made from recycled metal and wood, and also quirky kaftans and ethnic clothing – highly recommended for unique gifts and souvenirs. Mon–Fri 9.30am–5.30pm, Sat 9.30am–4pm, Sun 10am–2pm.

Kalk Bay Gallery 62 Main Rd, Kalk Bay ☎021 788 1674. Graphics, engravings as well as African art and artefacts – good value, with

the chance of picking up something very collectable. Mon–Fri 9am–5pm, Sat & Sun 9.30am–5pm.

▼ Kalk Bay antiques shops

Mike Cope Jewellery 5 St Helier Rd, Muizenberg ☎021 788 2083. Call before visiting the home studio, just off the main road, of one of Cape Town's master jewellers. He'll be able to show you a small selection of bold, eye-catching work, often nature-inspired.

Montebello Craft & Design Centre 31 Newlands Ave, Newlands ☎021 685 6445. A great selection of crafts, jewellery, beadwork, ceramics, woven goods, even musical instruments and garden items, in a centre where people from townships are trained to become artisans. Besides watching the craftsmen at work, you can eat here at the excellent restaurant. Mon–Sat 9am–5pm, shorter hours on Sun.

Rose Korber Art Consultancy 48 Sedgemoor Rd, Camps Bay ☎021 438 9152. This should be the first stop for the serious collector, with an exceptional selection of contemporary art and crafts, including ceramics and beadwork from around the continent. Mon–Fri 9am–5pm.

Yellow Door Upper floor, Gardens Centre, Gardens ☎ 021 465 4702. One of the largest and best selections of local crafts and design, including ceramics, fabrics, jewellery, basketry, metalwork and interior decor. Mon–Fri 9am–6pm, Sat 9am–4pm, Sun 10am–2pm.

Craft markets

Cape Town Station Forecourt, Adderley St. Thronging ranks of market traders selling African crafts, as well as radios and leather goods. Not principally aimed at tourists, so it's pretty authentic. Mon–Fri 8am–5pm, Sat 8am–2pm.

Constantia Craft Market Alphen Common, corner of Spaanschemat River and Ladies Mile rds, Constantia. Sizeable outdoor flea market where you can pick up good local crafts and items from around the continent, ride a camel or a pony and have a cup of tea. First & last Sat & first Sun of the month.

Green Point Market Western Blvd, Green Point. A massive open-air market displaying everything from African arts and crafts to plants, car parts, and anything home-made. Sun 9am–4pm.

Greenmarket Square Burg St. City-centre open-air market where you can pick up knick-knacks. It's also the best place in town for colourful handmade Cape Town beachwear, and good for T-shirts, shorts and sandals. Mon–Fri 8am–5pm, Sat 8am–2pm.

Pan African Market 76 Long St. A multicultural hothouse of township and contemporary art, artefacts, curios and crafts. There's also a café specializing in African cuisine, a bookshop, a Cameroonian hairbraider and a West African tailor. Mon–Fri 9am–5pm, Sat 9am–3pm.

Red Shed Craft Workshop Victoria Wharf, V&A Waterfront. A market where some two dozen craftworkers make and sell ceramics, textiles, candles and jewellery, and where you can see glass-blowers at work. Mon–Sat 9am–9pm, Sun 10am–9pm.

Sivuyile Craft Centre On the corner of NY1 and NY4, Guguletu, Cape Flats. Township market attached to an information centre close to the N2 freeway, where bead-workers, wire-workers and other artists make traditional and modern crafts. Mon–Fri 8am–5pm, Sat 9am–2pm.

Victoria Rd Market Camps Bay. Carvings, beads, fabrics and baskets sold from a market spectacularly sited on a clifftop overlooking the Atlantic. Daily.

Books

South Africa produces a lot of **books** given the size of its reading population: you'll find good locally published novels and endless volumes on history, politics and natural history. For new books there are some pleasant places in the suburbs or at the Waterfront to browse for half an hour, while Upper Long Street has over half a dozen secondhand book and specialist comic shops in close proximity, interspersed with congenial cafés.

Clarke's Bookshop 211 Long St ☎ 021 423 5739. The best place in Cape Town for South African books, with a huge selection of local titles covering literature, history, politics, natural history and the arts, plus very well-informed staff. They also deal in collectors' editions of South African books. Mon–Fri 9am–5pm, Sat 9am–1pm.

Exclusive Books Branches at Victoria Wharf, V&A Waterfront (☎ 021 419 0905; Mon–Fri 9am–10.30pm, Sat 9am–11pm, Sun 10am–9pm); Lower Mall, Cavendish Square, Claremont (☎ 021 674 3030; Mon–Thurs 9am–9pm, Fri & Sat 9am–10.30pm, Sun 9.30am–9pm); **Constantia Village Shopping Centre, Main Rd, Constantia (☎ 021 794 7800; Mon–Sat 9am–8pm, Sun 9am–5pm).** A friendly bookshop, ideal for browsing; the reasonably well-stocked shelves include magazines and a wide choice of coffee-table books on Cape Town and South African topics.

Kirstenbosch Shop Kirstenbosch National Botanical Gardens ☎ 021 762 2510. A good selection of natural-history books, field guides and travel guides covering southern Africa, as well as a range of titles for kids.

You don't need a gardens ticket to browse. Daily 9am–7pm.

The Travellers Bookshop King's Warehouse, Victoria Wharf, V&A Waterfront ☎ **021 425 6880.** Cape Town's only specialist travel bookshop

stocks a decent range of titles, mainly about South Africa and especially the Cape, covering history, politics, natural history and the arts. Daily 9am–9pm.

CDs and records

For pretty standard selections of mainly British and American sounds, try the ubiquitous chains such as CNA (🌐 www.cna.co.za) and Musica (🌐 www .musica.co.za).

African Music Store 90a Long St ☎ **021 426 0867.** Very small, centrally located shop specializing in African music. It also has a modest collection of instruments, such as shakers and thumb pianos. Mon–Fri 9am–5pm, Sat 9am–2pm.

CD Warehouse V&A Waterfront (next to the V&A Hotel) ☎ **021 425 6300.** One of the best ranges of African music in the city. Daily

9am–9pm, with slightly longer hours possible on Sat & Sun.

Look & Listen Shop F14, Upper level, Cavendish Square, Claremont ☎ **021 683 1810.** Cape Town's largest music store, with a selection of all kinds of sounds, including good local jazz and a respectable selection from all over the African continent. Daily 9am–10.30pm.

Food and provisions

Self-catering is the cheapest way to eat in Cape Town, and can also be good fun. **Braais** – as South Africans call barbecues – can happen anywhere with any excuse, and there are countless places on beaches, in the forests or up Table Mountain where you can enjoy a terrific **picnic**. There are some excellent (if pricey) **delicatessens**, several of which are strung along Main Road, Green Point and Sea Point. You'll also find delicious food and some unusual fruit and vegetables at the more sophisticated **farm stalls**. A great way to spend a Saturday morning is to head for the **Woodstock Market**, Old Biscuit Mill, 373–375 Albert Rd off Lower Main Road (Sat 9am–2.30pm), which sells locally produced cheeses, wood-fired bread and olive oil, with a good selection of organic stuff, which you can sample on-site with excellent coffee or fresh juices, or take home. In a similar vein, though smaller and less sophisticated, and in a rural setting, is the **Tokai Market** (Sat 9am–1pm), signposted off the Spaanschemacht Road. If you're heading south from the centre of town, take the Ladies Mile exit from the M3 onto Spaanschemacht, head south again, and turn right into the forest at a signboard marked "The Range", which is just beyond Constantia Uitsig Wine Estate.

The larger branches of the better **supermarkets** have fishmonger counters where you can buy fresh fish, though by far the most atmospheric places to buy seafood are the Hout Bay and Kalk Bay harbours (see p.106 & p.114 respectively). Cape Town also has a sprinkling of stores specializing in **health foods** (see p.153) and modest selections of organic fruit and vegetables, the best choice being at the large branches of Woolworths.

Supermarkets tend to have decent **wine** at competitive prices, but for more interesting labels, there are some first-rate specialist wine merchants. Otherwise, you can buy alcoholic beverages at **bottle stores** (the equivalent of the British off-licence), which generally keep normal shopping hours, although some stay open until 6.30pm. Note that retail outlets do not sell alcohol on a Sunday.

Supermarkets

Pick 'n Pay **V&A Waterfront; Gardens Shopping Centre, Mill St, Gardens; Main Rd, Camps Bay; Main Rd, Observatory; Corner of Main and Campground rds, Claremont; Blue Route Mall, Tokai; Constantia Village, Main Rd, Constantia.** Larger and cheaper than Woolworths, this is one of the best places for groceries, with a good deli counter and a choice of prepared meals, including excellent-value ready-grilled whole chickens. Mon–Sat generally 8.30am–6pm, though the Waterfront and Observatory branches stay open later; on Sun all branches close at 2.30pm.

Woolworths **Adderley St; V&A Waterfront; Cavendish Square Mall, Claremont; Blue Route Mall, Tokai; Constantia Village, Main Rd, Constantia.** Excellent for quality fast-cook meals, fresh produce and cold foods, such as olives, hummus and various Mediterranean dips, but it can be pricey. Generally daily 9am–6pm, or until 9pm at the Waterfront.

Delis and farm stalls

Andiamo **Cape Quarter, Dixon St, De Waterkant.** Italian deli where you can select from meats, cheeses, salads, dips, meze and fresh breads to take on your mountain walk. Phone ahead and they'll put the picnic together for you. Daily 9am–11pm.

The Barnyard Farm Stall **Steenberg Rd (adjacent to the well-signposted Steenberg Wine Estate), Tokai** ☎021 712 6934. One of Cape Town's nicest farm stalls, with a selection of high-class cheeses, breads, home-baked cakes, wines, patés, coffee beans and many other delights. There's also the major attraction of a very worthwhile outdoor café. A good stop if you're doing the Constantia winelands. Daily 8.30am–5.30pm.

Giovanni's **103 Main Rd, Green Point.** Excellent breads and delicious Italian foods to take away and – if temptation overcomes you – there's always the option of sitting down for a coffee and a snack. Daily 8.30am–9pm.

Melissa's **94 Kloof St, Gardens; and Constantia Village.** Highly delectable imported and local specialities, with the option of eating in. Gardens Mon–Fri 7.30am–8pm, Sat & Sun 8am–9pm; Constantia 7.30am–7pm, Sat & Sun 8am–6pm.

New York Bagel Deli **51 Regent Rd, Sea Point.** A great array of bagels with a selection of Eastern European Jewish fillings – salt beef, gherkins, chopped liver and pickled herring – and an array of delicious pastries. Daily 7am–9pm.

Fresh fish

Fish Market **Mariner's Wharf, Hout Bay Harbour.** Fresh seafood from South Africa's original waterfront emporium, but slicker and less atmospheric than Kalk Bay Harbour. Mon–Fri 9am–5.30pm, Sat & Sun 9am–6pm.

Kalk Bay Harbour **Harbourside, Kalk Bay.** Buy fresh fish directly from the fishermen and have it gutted and scaled on the spot. Your best bet is lunchtime, especially at weekends, though catches are dependent on several factors including the weather and rough seas.

Pick 'n Pay Supermarkets There are good fish counters at this supermarket chain's larger branches in upmarket areas, such as the Waterfront, Constantia Village and Gardens Centre.

Wine

Caroline's Fine Wines **15 Long St** ☎021 419 8984; **and King's Warehouse, V&A Waterfront** ☎021 425 5701. Caroline Rillema has been in the wine business since 1979 and offers daily tastings of the Cape's finest and most exclusive wines. Mon–Fri 9am–5pm, Waterfront also Sat 9am–5pm.

Vaughan Johnson's **Dock Rd, V&A Waterfront** ☎021 419 2121. One of Cape Town's best-known wine shops, which has a huge range of labels from all over the country, though it can be a bit pricey. Mon–Fri 9am–6pm, Sat 9am–5pm, Sun 10am–5pm.

Wine Concepts **50 Kloof St; and Castle Building, on the corner of Kildare Rd and Main Rd, Newlands.** An excellent selection of South African and foreign wines from a knowledgeable and helpful outfit. Mon–Thurs 9am–7pm, Fri 9am–8pm, Sat 9am–5pm.

Woolworths **See above.** The own-label wines of South Africa's upmarket supermarket chain have come a long way since the days when you'd sneakily decant them so no one would know their source. Cognoscenti now happily flaunt these competitively priced wines.

Health foods and alternative therapies

For additional information on Cape Town's thriving health food/alternative therapies scene, look out for *Link-Up*, a free listings magazine, and the glossier *Odyssey* (R30). The latter is the place to track down sources of Southern African healing crystals and essential oils (disappointingly though, there are few oils from Cape plants except for geraniums), and locate practitioners of various therapies. Both publications are available from health-food shops and alternative health venues. A useful website for the city's organic scene is ⑩ www.mothercityliving.co.za.

Health Connections 151 Main Rd, Diep River, Tokai ☎ 021 715 6697. Wheat-free, sugar-free and dairy-free goods. You don't have to visit to buy its products, as Pick 'n Pay supermarkets and other health-food stores stock them. Martin's Bakery, close by at 43 Main Rd, Diep River has a great selection of wheat-free and sugar-free baked goods.
Natural Remedies Pearce St, Claremont ☎ 021 674 1692. The best place in the southern suburbs for homeopathic and herbal remedies, aromatherapy oils, beauty products and a range of health foods. Mon–Fri 9am–5.15pm, Sat 8.30am–1pm.

Organic Living 39 Constantia Rd, Wynberg ☎ 021 797 1123. Beautiful, spacious premises with shaded outdoor seating, and tempting allergy-free, organic food at its lunchtime buffets, with a few products and organic veggies for sale inside the shop. Massage and facials on offer. Mon–Sat 9am–5pm.
White's Chemist 77 Plein Park, Plein St ☎ 021 465 3332. A long-established manufacturer and supplier of homeopathic remedies, powders, tinctures and books. Also sells homeopathic first-aid kits and herbal products. Mon–Fri 7.30am–5pm, Sat 8am–12.30pm.

12

Sports and outdoor activities

One of Cape Town's most remarkable features is the fact that it melds with the Table Mountain National Park, a patchwork of mountains, forests and coastline – all on the city's doorstep. There are few, if any, cities in the world where outdoor pursuits are so easily available and affordable, and every second person hikes or cycles at the weekend. You can try activities such as sea kayaking, abseiling, rock climbing and scuba diving for little more than the price of a night out back home. A notable activity locally is **kloofing**, which basically entails jumping into a deep river from a cliff above. Alternatively, just let everyone else get on with it while you sink a few beers and watch the cricket, rugby or soccer.

Participation sports and outdoor activities

Abseiling and kloofing You can abseil off Table Mountain with Abseil Africa (℡021 424 4760) for around R395 for a half-day trip (excluding cable-car fee). It also does full-day trips (minimum group of 4) that include kloofing, hiking, abseiling, breakfast, lunch and a light supper, for R595 or a summit walk on Table Mountain for R120, which you can combine with abseiling for R495.

Bird-watching The peninsula's varied habitats attract nearly four hundred different species of birds. Good places for bird-watching include Lion's Head, Kirstenbosch Gardens and the Cape of Good Hope section of Table Mountain National Park, as well as at Kommetjie and Hout Bay; you can find out about knowledgeable guides through the Cape Bird Club (℡021 559 0726). For a more institutionalized experience, try the World of Birds in Hout Bay.

Cycling Cycling (for rental outlets see p.32) is popular all over the peninsula, and is a great way to take in the scenery. For information about the Cape Argus Pick 'n Pay Cycle Tour, the largest individually timed bike race in the world (see p.38), contact Pedal Power Associates (℡021 689 8420, ⓦwww .cycletour.co.za), which also organizes fun rides from September to May.

Golf The Milnerton golf course, Bridge Rd, Milnerton (℡021 552 1047), is tucked in between a lagoon and Table Bay north of the city, and boasts classic views of Table Mountain. Other popular local courses include the Rondebosch Golf Club, Klipfontein Rd, Rondebosch (℡021 689 4176), and the Westlake Golf Club, Westlake Ave, Lakeside (℡021 788 2020). Prices are around R190/400 for 9/18 holes; clubs can be rented for R150 and caddy fees are R130. Booking is essential.

Gyms Virgin Active clubs are upmarket, well-appointed gyms dotted around the peninsula. Their call centre (℡0860 200 911) or website (ⓦwww.virginactive.co.za) can tell you where the nearest gym to you is and the cost of day or short-term membership.

Horse-riding Horse Trail Safaris, Indicator Lodge, Skaapskraal Rd, Ottery (east of Wynberg across the M5; ☎082 575 5669), offers riding through the dunes to Strandfontein and the False Bay coast as well as overnight trips; Sleepy Hollow Horse Riding, Sleepy Hollow Lane, Noordhoek (☎021 789 2341), covers the spectacular Noordhoek Beach. Both charge around R300 for 1hr 30min.

Kayaking Real Cape Adventures (☎021 790 5611 or 082 556 2520, ⊛www.seakayak .co.za) offers a range of half- or full-day sea-kayaking packages that include trips around Cape Point, to the penguin colony at Boulders Beach and around Hout Bay. It also does trips of several days' duration around the peninsula, on which you spend the nights at guesthouses. The cheapest trip costs R200 per person for two hours' kayaking.

Kite-flying The Kite Shop, Shop 110, Ground Floor, Victoria Wharf (☎021 421 6231), sells kites of all shapes, colours and sizes.

Mountain biking Day Trippers (☎021 511 4766, ⊛www.daytrippers.co.za) offers expert mountain-bike tours, including one from Scarborough to Cape Point. In the city centre, Downhill Adventures, on the corner of Kloof and Orange sts (☎021 422 0388), offers similar tours starting from its shop; for experienced mountain bikers it has a Tokai forest tour (R450 half day, minimum of 4 people).

Paragliding Cape Town has great air thermals for paragliding. If you're tempted to leap off any of the surrounding mountains then contact Para-Pax (☎082 881 4724), which offers tandem flights for R850. A picture of your horrified face will cost R130. Dress warmly.

Rock climbing High Adventure (☎021 689 1234 or 082 437 5145) will take you to unusual and unique locations depending on your ability. Packages are tailor-made, with a minimum of two people. You can learn how to clamber up Table Mountain's famous facade with the Cape Town School of Mountaineering (☎021 531 4290), which charges R750 for a two-day rock-climbing course, usually over weekends; it also guides experienced climbers.

Sandboarding Downhill Adventures (see under "Mountain biking") is the pioneer of this latest adventure sport, which is much the same as snowboarding except that the slopes are sand dunes and you're wearing shorts. Boards, boots and bindings are provided, as well as expert instruction for beginners. Half-day (R450) and full-day (R595) trips take you to the finest slopes in the area.

Scuba diving While the Cape waters are cold, they're good for seeing wrecks, reefs and magnificent kelp forests. False Bay is invariably warmer than the Atlantic seaboard and thus preferred in winter. Short dives cost R200 from the shore, up to around R300 from a boat; expect to pay R400 to rent all the gear. An internationally recognized PADI open-water diving qualification can be completed for around R2500. To arrange scuba-diving courses and equipment rental, contact Orca Industries, on the corner of Herschel and Bowwood rds, Claremont (☎021 671 9673), or the Scuba Shack, Shop 3, Glen Cairn Shopping Centre, Glencairn (☎021 782 6279).

Skydiving The ultimate way to see Table Mountain and Robben Island is from a tandem jump 3000m up; contact Skydive Cape Town (☎082 800 6290, ⊛www .skydivecapetown.za.net; R1250).

Steam baths The steam rooms at the Long Street Baths are great for relaxing on a winter's day. They're open separately to women (Mon 9am–6pm, Tues 9am–1pm, Thurs & Sat 9am–6pm) and men (Tues 1– 7pm, Wed & Fri 9am–1pm, Sun 8am–noon). A four-hour session (R92) gets you a private cubicle and towel, access to the dry and wet steam rooms, the plunge pool and a short massage.

Surfing Top surfing spots include Big Bay at Bloubergstrand north of the city (competitions are held here every summer), plus Llandudno, Muizenberg, Kalk Bay and Long Beach (near Kommetjie and Noordhoek). For information on competitions, contact Surfing South Africa (☎021 674 2972) or check out ⊛www.wavescape.co.za, the best place on the Web for everything you want to know about surfing in SA, including what the waves are up to. To learn to surf, contact Downhill Adventures (see under "Mountain biking"; half day R350, full day R500, with all equipment provided) or Gary's Surf School on Muizenberg beachfront

(☎021 788 9839). Muizenberg is the best beach for beginner surfers, with warmer waters and long, regular waves.

▼ Learning to surf, Muizenberg

Swimming In the summer there are surf lifesaver patrols on duty at Milnerton, Camps Bay, Llandudno, Muizenberg and Fish Hoek beaches, though the only beaches where the water is really warm enough to swim in are on the False Bay coast at Muizenberg, Fish Hoek and Simon's Town. For pools, try Long St Baths, Long St (☎021 400 3302; daily 7am–7pm; R13), Cape Town's only public heated indoor pool; or Newlands Swimming Pool, on the corner of Main and San Souci rds, Newlands (☎021 467 4197; daily: April–Sept 9am–5pm; Oct–March 7am–6.30pm; R13, children R7), an Olympic-sized chlorinated pool, which isn't heated but has nice lawned areas for children and a lovely mountain view. The appealing Sea Point Swimming Pool at Beach Rd, Sea Point (☎021 434 3341; adults R13, children R7), is an Olympic-sized chlorinated seawater pool, right on the edge of the ocean with grassed areas for sunbathing. If you're a lap swimmer, consider joining one of the Virgin Active gyms (see p.154) which have excellent pools.

Walking The best places for gentle strolls are Newlands Forest, up from Rhodes Memorial, and the beaches. For hiking, head for anywhere on Table Mountain, Tokai Forest, Silvermine Nature Reserve or Cape Point Nature Reserve. Note, though, that it's best not to hike alone on Table Mountain. As well as general mountain-safety issues, there have been several tourist muggings recently, so you're advised to walk with a guide. See p.85 for further advice and information. High Adventure (see under "Rock climbing") does guided hikes up Table Mountain, geared to your level of fitness and with experienced guides (half day R350, full day R500 including a packed lunch). If you want to go further afield, they'll arrange multi-day trips where you can opt to have your bags carried or have food prepared for you.

Windsurfing and kitesurfing While most Capetonians moan about the howling southeaster in summer, it's handy if you're into windsurfing; not much happens in the winter, as the winds just aren't as good. Langebaan, a 75min drive north of town, is one of the best spots. For further help, contact Cape Sport Centre, Langebaan (☎022 772 1114, ⊛www.capesport.co.za), which also does kitesurfing, in which the sail on your board lifts you above the waves. Prices for windsurfing start at R220 for 2hr for rigs, while instruction for beginners starts at R200; a 10-hour kitesurfing package costs R1650 including gear and instruction. Otherwise, the place to go in Cape Town is Bloubergstrand in the northern suburbs. Blouberg Windsurf and Leisure ☎021 554 1663 or 082 420 2990, ⊜blouwind@mweb .co.za) here rentsout equipment, cars with racks and has long-term accommodation at Bloubergstrand, as well as being able to offer general advice to its clients, such as information on which airlines offer free carriage of windsurfing equipment.

Spectator sports

Cricket This is keenly followed by a wide range of Capetonians. The city's cricketing heart is at Newlands Cricket Ground (also known after its sponsors as Sahara Park), 61 Campground Rd, Newlands (☎021 657 2003). One of the most beautiful grounds in the world, Newlands nestles beneath venerable oaks and the elegant profile of Devil's Peak, and plays host to provincial, test and one-day international matches. **Rugby** The Western Cape is one of the world's rugby heartlands, and the game is followed religiously here. Provincial, international and Super 12 contests are fought on the hallowed turf of Newlands Rugby Stadium, Boundary Rd, Newlands (☎021 659 4600).

Soccer Though soccer matches aren't as well attended as cricket or rugby, Cape Town soccer is burgeoning with talent and is likely to get a huge boost now that South Africa is hosting the 2010 World Cup. The dusty streets of the Cape Flats have produced superb young footballers such as Benni McCarthy (Porto, Ajax Amsterdam, Celta Vigo) and Quinton Fortune (Atletico Madrid, Manchester United). The most ambitious and professional club in the city is Ajax (pronounced "I-axe") Cape Town (🕸www.ajaxct.org), jointly owned by its Amsterdam namesake. The most exciting games to attend are those between a local outfit and one of the Soweto glamour teams, Orlando Pirates and Kaizer Chiefs. Matches take place at Green Point Stadium, off Beach Rd; Athlone Stadium, off Klipfontein Rd, Athlone; and Newlands Rugby Stadium (see opposite).

SPORTS AND OUTDOOR ACTIVITIES | Spectator sports

Gay and lesbian Cape Town

South Africa has the continent's most developed and diverse gay and lesbian scene – and Cape Town is its gay capital, on its way to becoming an African Sydney, attracting gay travellers from across the country and the globe. Furthermore, the country has the world's first gay-and-lesbian-friendly **constitution**: not only is homosexuality legal in South Africa between consenting adults of 18 or over, but the constitution outlaws any discrimination on the grounds of sexual orientation. Outside the big cities, however, South Africa remains a pretty conservative place where open displays of public affection by gays and lesbians are unlikely to go down well; many whites will find it un-Christian, while blacks will think it un-African. It's still especially hard for African and coloured gay men and women to come out, and this is reflected in Cape Town's scene, which remains largely white.

Cape Town's **gay village**, with B&Bs, guesthouses, pubs, clubs, cruise bars and saunas, is concentrated along the entertainment strips of Somerset Road and Main Road in the interconnected inner-city suburbs of Green Point, Sea Point and De Waterkant, adjacent to the centre. The *Pink Map*, published by A&C Maps (☏021 685 4260, ⓦwww.capeinfo.com), lists gay-friendly and gay-owned places in Cape Town and is distributed at the visitor centre in town, the one in the Clock Tower at the V&A Waterfront, as well as the airport and hotels; the publishers will send a copy anywhere in the world on request.

Cape Town hosts a hugely popular annual **gay party**, organized by Mother City Queer Projects (ⓦwww.mcqp.co.za), which has turned into a ten-day festival held each December (6–16). People dress as outrageously as possible according to the official yearly theme (past ones have included "Kitchen Kitsch", "The Twinkly Sea Project" and "Farm Fresh") and the event seeks to rival Sydney's Mardi Gras. There's also an annual **gay pride festival** in February (ⓦwww.capetownpride .co.za) and a gay and lesbian **film festival** in April (see p.38).

For information on what's on, you can check the gay section of the Western Cape listings magazine *Cape Review*, or the gay supplement published on the last Thursday of the month in the *Cape Argus*, Cape Town's daily afternoon newspaper. While in town, be sure to tune into Bush Radio's gay programme "In the Pink" (Thurs 8–9pm, 89.5FM).

As you'd expect in a city where the great outdoors figures so prominently, there are a number of **beaches** popular with gay men, including Third Beach at Clifton, which is great for body-ogling, Graaff's Pool at Sea Point (beware hustlers and litter here) and the cruisey, nudist Sandy Bay, accessed from Llandudno beach.

Resources and contacts

capetown.tv ⓦ www.capetown.tv. Comprehensive site for gay travellers, covering everything from arts and theatre to cruising spots and travel information.

Gay Cape Town ⓦ www.gaynetcapetown.co.za. Aimed specifically at the gay traveller to Cape Town, with practical info on sights, events and accommodation.

Gay, Lesbian and Bisexual Helpline ☎ 021 422 2500. Helpline of the Cape Town-based Triangle Project (see opposite). Daily 1–9pm.

Gay South Africa ⓦ www.gaysouthafrica.org.za. A slick, well-organized portal with links covering all topics of gay interest.

Q ⓦ www.q.co.za. Excellent gay spin-off site of the *Mail & Guardian*, with news and coverage of a variety of topics, including a good travel section.

Triangle Project ☎ 021 448 3812, ⓦ www.triangle.org.za. The longest-established gay organization in South Africa, based in Cape Town, is a good first port of call for all types of information.

Wanderwomen ⓦ www.wanderwomen.co.za Travel website for gay or straight women, where you can plan and book your entire South African itinerary.

Clubs and bars

Bar Code 18 Cobern St, De Waterkant. A leather uniform and jeans bar that attracts an older crowd, *Bar Code* has a darkroom and hosts monthly underwear and fetish parties. Daily 9pm till late.

Bronx 35 Somerset Rd, Green Point. Attracting a mixed crowd, this is a hugely popular bar with a dance floor and loads of energy. Daily 8pm till late.

▼ Café Manhattan

Café Manhattan 74 Waterkant St, De Waterkant. A restaurant-bar which serves affordable food on an outside terrace beneath oak trees. There's live music Thurs and Sun evenings. Straight-friendly. Daily 10am–late.

Evita se Perron Darling Station, Arcadia Rd, Darling ☎ 022 492 2831, ⓦ www.evita.co.za. An hour's drive north of Cape Town, on the R27, the town of Darling is well worth getting to for its campily converted train station, which plays host to the satirical shows of Pieter Dirk Uys (see p.145). A great day out.

M-Bar and Lounge Metropole Hotel, 38 Long St. A sophisticated lounge and bar in a stylishly appointed hotel, and an upmarket gay hangout par excellence. Cocktails served from noon until late. Straight-friendly.

On Broadway 21 Somerset Rd, De Waterkant ☎ 021 424 1194, ⓦ www.onbroadway.co.za. One of the few venues committed to the city's small cabaret scene is this bar-restaurant with live performances for an ethnically mixed crowd. Booking is essential. Shows nightly 7pm–late, with drag shows on Sun.

Rosie's 125a Waterkant St, De Waterkant, opposite Café Manhattan. A small intimate pool bar attracting bears and leather boys, with a restaurant that's a popular after-work drinking spot. Open till late: Tues–Fri from 4pm, Sat & Sun from 2pm.

Sauna

The Hothouse 18 Jarvis St, Green Point ⓦ www.hothouse.co.za. A luxurious pleasure complex featuring Jacuzzis, sauna, a sundeck with a superb view, a full bar with a limited food menu, video room, fireplace and satellite TV. Entrance R60–80 depending on days and times; luxury cabins R120. Mon–Fri noon–2am, Sat & Sun 24hr.

Cape Town for kids

Cape Town is an excellent place to travel with children. The city enjoys fine weather, and activities in its many nature reserves, gardens and historic estates let under-10s work off some energy in a safe environment. Older children can take advantage of a range of outdoor activities on offer, for details of which, see Chapter 12.

Many activities for kids are either free or inexpensive. Children's prices in this chapter apply to under-16s, unless otherwise stated.

Museums and sights

MTN Science Centre Century City, Entrance 5, Canal Walk Mall (reached via the Sable St exit off the N1) ☏ 021 529 8100, ⊛ www .mtnsciencentre.org.za. Interactive exhibits which make science fun and accessible. The shop here is the best place for presents for children with an interest in experiments. R25. Mon–Thurs 9.30am–6pm, Fri & Sat 9.30am–8pm, Sun 10am–6pm.

Ratanga Junction Century City, signposted off N1 ☏ 0861 200 300, ⊛ www.ratanga.co.za. Popular and safe theme park with thrilling rides such as the Cobra, Crocodile Gorge and Monkey Falls. An easy and fun day out for parents as well as kids. Don't bring your own food – everything must be purchased on site. It's only open seasonally, so call beforehand. The R110 entry price gives you unlimited rides.

Scratch Patch and Mineral World Dido Valley Rd, off Main Rd, Simon's Town ☏ 021 786 2020, and **V&A Waterfront** ☏ 021 419 9429. Over-3s can fill a bag here with the reject polished gemstones which literally cover the floor. At the Simon's Town venue you can also see one of the world's biggest gemstone tumbling

plants in operation (Mon–Fri only). Mon–Fri 8.30am–4.45pm, Sat & Sun 9am–5pm; R12–75, depending on size of container.

South African Museum and Planetarium See p.66. Great for rainy days, especially for 5- to 12-year-olds, who'll enjoy the four-storey whale well and African animal dioramas, as well as the dinosaur displays. The Discovery Room (Mon–Fri 10am–3pm, Sat & Sun 11am–4.30pm) features live ants, massive spiders and a crocodile display. The planetarium has special children's shows over weekends and in school holidays.

Two Oceans Aquarium See p.75. Not only one of Cape Town's most rewarding museums, but also features loads of interest to children. Apart from the excitement of just looking at the weird and wonderful sea creatures, kids can actually handle a few species in the touch pool – sometimes this includes a small shark or sea urchins – while the Alpha Activity Centre usually has puppet shows or face painting, as well as computer terminals where older kids can learn about marine ecology.

Beaches and swimming pools

Cape Town's **beaches** are a classic and easy summer weekend family destination outing. This selection is particularly suitable for toddlers and smaller kids and generally also offers something for parents. Most beaches are pretty undeveloped, so it's best to take what you need in the way of food and drinks with you. Sea water and swimming pool temperatures are published each day in the weather section of the *Cape Times*. Get to the beach as early as possible so you can leave by 10–11am before the sun gets too strong, and to avoid the wind which often gusts up in the late morning.

On the False Bay seaboard, **Boulders Beach** (see p.117) is one of the few beaches to visit when the southeaster is blowing. It has safe, flat water, making it ideal for kids – and its resident penguin-breeding colony is an added attraction. **Fish Hoek** (see p.114) is one of the best Peninsula beaches, with gentle waves that are warm in summer, a long stretch of sand and a playground. The paved Jager's Walk which runs along the rocky coast here is suitable for pushchairs and offers beautiful views of the Hottentots Holland Mountains. **St James** (see p.113) boasts a safe tidal pool with a small sandy beach and photogenic bathing boxes. From here you can walk to Muizenberg along a pushchair-friendly coastal pathway, with more views of distant mountains across the water.

The **Atlantic seaboard** is too cold for serious swimming, but does have some lovely stretches of sand, boulders and rock pools – and astonishing scenery. The beaches here are excellent for picnics, and on calm summer evenings idyllic for sundowners and sunsets. In the summer they're less windy than the False Bay beaches, but the afternoons are often baking hot. The closest stretch of coast to the centre ideal for prams – and roller-blading – is the paved **Sea Point promenade**, stretching 3km from the lighthouse in Mouille Point to Sea Point Pavilion, with the draw of playgrounds and ice-cream sellers en route. The tidal pool and small rock pools of **Camps Bay** (see p.105) make this popular beach very child-friendly, and it's easily reachable from the centre by car or bus. Finally, the six-kilometre stretch of white sand from **Noordhoek** to **Kommetjie** (see p.108) provides fine walking, kite-flying and horse-riding opportunities, with stupendous views of Chapman's Peak. If you're heading for Kommetjie, consider a spot of camel-riding at Imhoff Farm Village (see below).

As regards child-friendly swimming pools, **Newlands Pool** (see p.156) has a toddlers' pool and little playground in the large grounds, while the marvellous **Sea Point Pool** at Sea Point Pavilion (see p.156) has two paddling pools for children and lawns to laze on.

Outdoor and picnic spots

The Barnyard Farmstall Steenberg Rd (M42), next to Steenberg Estate, between Tokai Rd and the Ou Kaapse Weg. An excellent place for an outdoor snack or cup of coffee at a small farmyard, with ducks and chickens wandering around, and an unusually good kids' playground. For more on the farmstall, see p.152.

Imhoff Farm Village Kommetjie Rd, opposite the Ocean View turn-off ☎021 783 4545 or 083 735 5227. Great for camel rides (daily 11.30am–4.30pm; R25); toddlers can ride with a parent in the same saddle, while kids aged 4 and up can ride on their own. Tues–Sun 10am–5pm.

Kirstenbosch National Botanical Gardens See p.93. Top of the list for a family outing, with extensive lawns for running about, trees and rocks to climb and streams to paddle in. There's no litter, no dogs, it's extremely safe and you can push a pram all over the walkways; it's also great for picnics or to have tea outdoors at the café. For older kids there are short waymarked walks.

Newlands Forest 9km south of the centre, off the M3 to Muizenberg. Gentle walks in and around pine forests and streams on the wooded southern slopes of Table Mountain, with a flattish pathway suitable for pushchairs. It's good for picnics if you want to get out of the city and don't have time to go further afield. Safest at weekends and in the afternoons when the joggers and dog walkers are out. Use the access point off the M3 signposted "Forestry Office", where there's ample parking. Dawn–dusk; free.

Silvermine Nature Reserve See p.114. A good place to see *fynbos* vegetation at close quarters, stroll around the lake and picnic with small children; however, it is exposed, and not recommended in heavy winds or mist. For older children there are some mountain-top walks with relatively gentle gradients, which give spectacular views over both sides of the peninsula. Especially recommended is the hike to Elephant's Eye cave on Constantiaberg.

Tokai Forest Arboretum See p.99. Walks and mountain biking, as well as a thatched tea shop with outdoor seating. It's also a great place for young children to explore, with logs to jump off and a gentle walk to a stream.

⑮

Directory

Airlines 1Time ☏0861 345 345; British Airways ☏021 936 9000; KLM Royal Dutch Airlines ☏021 935 8500; Kulula.com ☏0861 585 852; Lufthansa ☏021 415 3535; Mango ☏0861 162 646; Nationwide ☏021 936 2050; Olympic Airways ☏021 419 2502; Qantas ☏011 441 8550; South African Airways ☏021 936 1111; Virgin Atlantic ☏011 340 3400.

Banks and exchange Main branches with ATMs are easy to find in the shopping areas of the city centre, the middle-class suburbs and at the Waterfront. For foreign-exchange transactions outside normal banking hours, try one of the following: American Express, Shop 11a, Alfred Mall, Waterfront (Mon–Fri 9am–7pm, Sat 9am–5pm, Sun 9am–5pm); Rennies Foreign Exchange, Victoria Wharf, V&A Waterfront (Mon–Sat 9am–9pm, Sun 10am–9pm); or Master Currencies, Cape Town International Airport (Mon–Sun 6.30am–10pm).

Consulates Canada, 60 St George's Mall ☏021 423 5240; Germany, 22 Riebeek St ☏021 405 3000; UK, Southern Life Centre, 8 Riebeek St ☏021 405 2400; USA, 11625 Reddam Ave, Tokai ☏021 702 7300. The embassies for most countries are in Pretoria.

Couriers Contact DHL (☏0860 345000, ⓦwww.dhl.co.za) or Fedex (☏021 380 5777, ⓦwww.fedex.com) for details of their services and rates.

Credit card representatives American Express ☏080 011 0929 (lost/stolen), Mastercard ☏0800 990 418, Visa ☏0800 990 475.

Emergencies Police ☏10111, ambulance ☏10177, Table Mountain rescue ☏021 948 9900, general emergencies (including fires) ☏107.

Flight information Call the airport on ☏021 937 1200.

Hospitals and clinics The largest state hospital is Groote Schuur, Hospital Drive, Observatory (☏021 404 9111), just off the M3. Nearer the centre and convenient for the City Bowl and Atlantic seaboard is Somerset Hospital, Beach Rd, Mouille Point (☏021 402 6911); it has outpatient and emergency departments, although it's generally overcrowded, under-staffed and seemingly under-equipped. It's far preferable to go to one of the well-staffed, efficient and well-equipped private hospitals listed in the phone directory. The two largest hospital groups are the Netcare (emergency response ☏082 911) and Medi-Clinic chains, with hospitals all over the Cape Peninsula. Most central of Netcare's hospitals is the Christiaan Barnard Memorial Hospital, 181 Longmarket St (☏021 480 6111); you'll get to see a doctor quickly here and costs are not excessive unless you require major surgery, in which case health insurance is a must.

Laundry Most backpacker hostels have coin-operated washing machines, while guesthouses, hotels and B&Bs will usually offer a laundry service for a charge. There are laundries offering service washes in the city centre and most suburban areas.

Left luggage Virtually every backpacker hostel provides luggage storage facilities, and most other accommodation will be happy to take care of your luggage for a day or two.

Mobile phone rental Available from Cellucity, Shop 6193, V&A Waterfront (☏021 418 1306), for around R35 per day for the handset, with calls charged at R2.40/min. You'll need to provide your credit-card details. Rentals can also be done at the airport when you arrive.

Pharmacies Chemists with extended opening hours include: Hypermed Pharmacy, corner York and Main rds, Green Point (☏021 434 1414; Mon–Fri 8.30am–9pm, Sat & Sun 9am–9pm); Sunset Pharmacy, Sea Point

Medical Centre, Kloof Rd, Sea Point (☎021 434 3333; daily 8.30am–9pm); and Tamboerskloof Pharmacy, 16 Kloof Nek Rd, Tamboerskloof (☎021 424 4450; daily 9am–9pm).

Police The central station is on Caledon Square, Buitenkant St ☎021 467 8000.

Post office The main branch, on Parliament St in the city centre (Mon, Tues, Thurs & Fri 8am–4.30pm, Wed 8.30am–4.30pm, Sat 8am–noon), has a poste restante and enquiry desk.

Taxis There are a number of reliable companies, including Marine Taxi Hire (☎021 434 0434), Sea Point Radio Taxis (☎021 434 4444) and Unicab (☎021 448 1720).

Ticket agencies Computicket (☎083 915 8000, ☻www.computicket.co.za) books most theatre, cinema and sporting events, as well as airline and bus tickets. There are Computicket offices in the major shopping malls.

Travel agents The largest travel franchise in the country is Sure Travel, which has about two dozen offices across Cape Town (call ☎0800 221 656 for the nearest); try also One World Travel Centre, 309 Long St (☎021 423 0777). Cape Town Tourism can also book trips.

Weights and measures South Africa is fully metricated, and kilometres, grammes, kilogrammes, litres and degrees Celsius are the norm. Shoe sizes follow the British system.

Beyond
the City

Beyond the City

⑯

The Winelands

ess than an hour from Cape Town, the **Winelands** give full reign to the sybaritic pleasures of eating, drinking and visual feasting. Dutch colonial heritage reaches its peak in this region of white, gabled homesteads sitting among vineyards against a backdrop of slatey crags. The district – mapped in the colour section at the back of this book – takes in Cape Town's earliest European settlements, at Stellenbosch, Paarl, Franschhoek and Somerset West, each with its own established **wine route**, on which you travel from one wine estate to the next to sample the wines. As well as wine sampling and the chance to take in mountain and farmland scenery, the area boasts some of South Africa's best restaurants.

Franschhoek is the smallest of the towns, with a cultivated Provençal character and a centre of culinary excellence. It also has the best setting, at the head of a narrow valley, and is the place to head for if you're principally after a

South African wines

South Africa's **wine industry** has emerged out of years of sanction-enforced doldrums, casting aside a 350-year-old tradition of trying to make French wine, and nailed its colours to the fresh and fruity New World mast. Production is rising all the time to meet the demands of the ever-growing export market, and a number of South African winemakers are achieving international recognition. With the vast bulk of wines costing less than R100 a bottle (and the very best for double this), anyone with an adventurous streak can indulge in a bacchanalia of sampling without breaking the bank.

In general, South Africa's **white** wines such as Sauvignon Blanc and Riesling are a slightly better quality overall than its red wines. Among the **reds**, you should look out for wines made from the **Pinotage** grape, unique to South Africa. **Port** is also made, though connoisseurs of the Portuguese equivalent will struggle to recognize the over-sweet, over-sticky South African style. On the other hand, a handful of excellent **sparkling wines** are produced, including Champagne-style, fermented-in-the-bottle bubbly, known locally as Methode Cap.

The best way to sample wines is by visiting wineries. The oldest and most rewarding wine-producing regions are the Constantia estates in Cape Town (see p.94) and the Winelands; other wine-producing areas covered by this book include Walker Bay around Hermanus (see p.191) and the Little Karoo along the R62 (see p.261). If you plan on anything more than the briefest of tours, think about buying the annually updated *John Platter's South African Wine Guide* (⊛www.platteronline.com), which provides ratings of the produce of every winery in the country. *Wine* magazine, published every month and available from all newsagents, has useful features on wineries, places to eat, wine reviews, information on latest bottlings and a diary of events.

good lunch and beautiful drive out of Cape Town. **Stellenbosch**, by contrast, has some attractive historical streetscapes, a university and a couple of decent museums, cafes and shops.

One of the region's scenic highlights is the drive along the **R310** through the heady **Helshoogte Pass** between Stellenbosch and the R45 Franschhoek–Paarl road. **Paarl**, also a pretty drive from Stellenbosch, is a workaday farming town strung out along an extraordinarily long main road which cuts through a fertile valley with stunning granite rock formations above the town. By contrast, the sprawling town of **Somerset West** has only one drawcard, but it's an outstanding one – **Vergelegen**, by far the most stunning of all the Wineland estates, which can be tacked onto the Stellenbosch wine route.

Any of the Winelands towns is an easy **drive** from Cape Town, with time to visit three or four wineries on a day-trip, and the option of **overnighting**. You can get to Stellenbosch and Paarl using the **Metrorail** service from Cape Town (see p.28), though be aware that trains pass through rough areas of the Cape Flats and aren't recommended for that reason. There are a handful of buses to Stellenbosch and Paarl, but without your own transport, it's best to do a day-tour taking in the highlights of the area – several Cape Town companies offers these (see p.33).

When **planning** your trip, choose an area to explore and don't try to visit too many wineries in a day unless you want to return home in a dizzy haze. Bear in mind that many wineries offer a lot more than wine-tasting – for example, horse-riding, meals or picnics in their grounds; a picnic is a great idea if you're travelling with children or simply want to drink in the mountainous views in a bucolic haze. Summer is the best time to visit, when days are longer (as are opening hours), the vines are in leaf and there's activity at the wineries. In winter the wine has been made and there are fewer cellar tours, though the landscape is still gorgeous, and many of the region's upmarket guesthouses let their rooms at half-price.

Wine tasting and buying are supposed to be fun, so don't take them too seriously. If you aren't a wine buff, you'll often find staff at tasting rooms are happy to talk you through a wine, which can be especially interesting once you begin to pick up the characteristics of different wines. Most estates charge a **fee** for a wine-tasting session (anywhere up to R25) and some only have tastings at specific times; see the individual accounts for more details. Note also that some wineries are **closed on Sundays**.

Stellenbosch

Dappled avenues of three-century-old oaks are the defining feature of **STELLENBOSCH**, 46km east of Cape Town – a fact reflected in its Afrikaans nickname Die Eikestad (the oak city). Street frontages of the same vintage, pavement cafés, water furrows and a European town layout centred on the Braak, a large village green, add up to a well-rooted urban texture that invites casual exploration.

One of the first actions of **Simon van der Stel** after arriving at the Cape in November 1679 to take over as VOC commander was to explore the area along the Eerste River (first river), where he came upon an enchanting little valley. Less than a month later it appeared on maps as Stellenbosch (Stel's bush), the first of several places dotted around the Cape which the governor

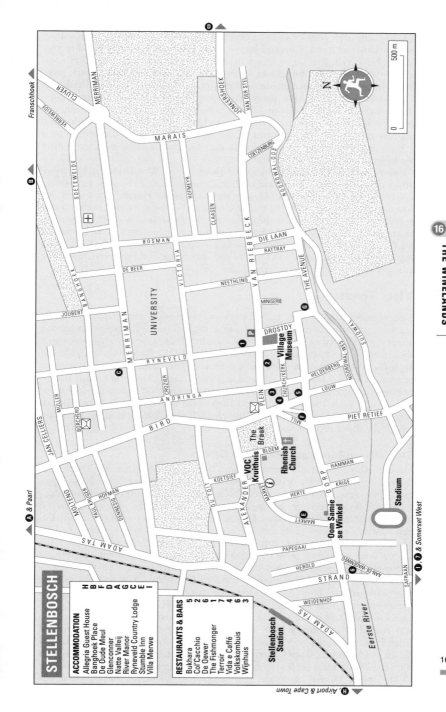

STELLENBOSCH

ACCOMMODATION
Allegria Guest House	H
Banghoek Place	B
De Oude Meul	F
Glenconner	D
Natte Valleij	A
River Manor	G
Ryneveld Country Lodge	C
Stumble Inn	E
Villa Merwe	I

RESTAURANTS & BARS
Bukhara	5
Col'Cacchio	2
De Oewer	6
The Fishmonger	1
Terroir	7
Vida e Caffè	4
Volkskombuis	6
Wijnhuis	3

was to name after himself or members of his family; another was Simonsberg overlooking the town. Charged by the Dutch East India Company directors in the Netherlands with opening up the Cape interior, van der Stel soon settled the first **free burghers** in Stellenbosch. Within eight years, sixty freehold grants had been made; within the next two decades, Stellenbosch had established itself as a prosperous, semi-feudal society dominated by landowners, and in 1702 the Danish traveller, Abraham Bogaert, admired how it had "grown with fine dwellings, and how great a treasure of wine and grain is grown here". By the end of the eighteenth century there were over a thousand houses and some substantial burgher estates in and around Stellenbosch, many of which still exist.

Stellenbosch today is the undisputed heart of the Winelands, having more urban attractions than either Paarl or Franschhoek, while at the same time being at the hub of the largest and oldest of the Cape **wine routes**. The city is also home to Stellenbosch University, Afrikanerdom's most prestigious educational institution, which does something to enliven the atmosphere. But even the heady promise of plentiful alcohol and thousands of students haven't changed the fact that at heart this is a conservative place, which was once the intellectual engine room of apartheid, and fostered the likes of Dr H.F. Verwoerd, the prime minister who dreamed up apartheid (see p.67).

The Town

Stellenbosch's attractions lie principally in its setting and streetscape; it's a lovely place to simply wander around, and safe at night. The tourist office on Market Street is a good place to start your explorations. Heading east up this road, you'll soon reach a whitewashed block that was the **VOC Kruithuis** (Jan–May & Sept–Dec Mon–Fri 9am–2pm) – the Dutch East India Company's powder magazine – which houses a small and unprepossessing collection of four British uniforms, assorted rifles, some intriguing but unexplained laptop-sized cannons and powder kegs. From here, a right turn south down the side of the **Braak** will take you past the **Rhenish Church** in Bloem Street, built in 1823 as a school for slaves and coloured people.

The Village Museum and Dorp Street

Head north up Ryneveld Street and you'll encounter Stellenbosch's highlight, the extremely enjoyable **Village Museum** at no. 18 (Mon–Sat 9.30am–5pm, Sun 10am–5pm; R15), which cuts a cross-section through the town's architectural and social heritage by means of four fortuitously adjacent historical dwellings from different periods. They're beautifully conserved and furnished in period style, and you'll meet the odd worker dressed in period costume. Earliest of the houses is the homely **Shreuderhuis**, a vernacular cottage built in 1709, with a small courtyard garden filled with aromatic herbs, pomegranate bushes and vine-draped pergolas – bearing more resemblance to the early Cape settlement's European aesthetics than to modern South Africa. Across the garden, **Blettermanhuis**, built in 1789 for the last Dutch East India Company-appointed magistrate of Stellenbosch, is an archetypal eighteenth-century Cape Dutch house, built on an H-plan with six gables. **Grosvenor House**, opposite, was altered to its current form in 1803, reflecting the growing influence of English taste after the 1795 British occupation of the Cape. The Neoclassical facade, with fluted pilasters supporting a pedimented entrance, borrows from high fashion then current at the heart of the growing Empire. The more modest **O.M. Bergh House**, across the road, is a typical Victorian dwelling that was once similar to Blettermanhuis, but was "modernized" in the mid-nineteenth century on a rectangular plan, with a simplified facade without gables.

From the Village Museum, head back south into **Dorp Street**, Stellenbosch's best-preserved historic axis, well worth a slow stroll just to soak in the ambience of buildings, gables, oaks and roadside irrigation furrows. Look out for **Krige's Cottages**, an unusual terrace of historic town houses at nos. 37–51, between Aan-de-Wagenweg and Krige Street. The houses were built as Cape Dutch cottages in the first half of the nineteenth century; Victorian features were added subsequently, resulting in an interesting hybrid, with gables housing Victorian attic windows and decorative Victorian verandas with filigree ironwork fronting the elegantly simple Cape Dutch facades.

Practicalities

Metrorail **trains** travel between Cape Town and Stellenbosch roughly every two hours during the day, and take about an hour. Infrequent (and expensive) intercity buses from Cape Town and Port Elizabeth pass through Stellenbosch, calling at the train station.

About 1km from the station, the busy **tourist office** at 36 Market St (May–Aug Mon–Fri 9am–5pm, Sat 9.30am–2pm, Sun 10am–2pm; Sept–April Mon–Fri 8am–6pm, Sat 9am–5pm, Sun 10am–4pm; ☎021 883 3584, ⓦwww.stellenboschtourism.co.za) provides basic information on local attractions, and can supply the *Discover Stellenbosch on Foot* leaflet (R5), which describes a walking tour covering a daunting 62 sites, or direct you to a walking tour. Easy Rider Wine Tours, based at *Stumble Inn* backpacker lodge (see p.172), offers daytime package tours to four wineries (R300), with cheese tasting at Fairview Estate and lunch thrown in.

Accommodation

Stellenbosch has no shortage of **places to stay**, from backpacker lodges to total luxury. Apart from a handful of out-of-town farmstays, all the accommodation is within easy walking distance of the town centre.

Allegria Guest House Cairngorm Rd, Stellenbosch ☎021 881 3389, ⓦwww.allegria.co.za. Small, well-run establishment on a country estate 8km west of Stellenbosch between two wine farms. Under the warm proprietorship of hospitable Dutch couple Jan and Annemarie, the guesthouse offers six rooms with three levels of luxury, a swimming pool and great views. Doubles from R890.

Banghoek Place 193 Banghoek Rd ☎021 887 0048. Slightly more upmarket sister hostel to *Stumble Inn* (see below), with mostly en-suite double, twin and triple rooms that offer terrific value, and also three small dorms. Discount packages available that include two nights' accommodation plus a wine tour. Dorms R100 per person, en-suite doubles R350, en-suite triples R450.

De Oude Meul 10a Mill St (off Dorp St) ☎021 887 7085, ⓦwww.deoudemeul.snowball.co.za. Located in the middle of town on a fairly busy street, above an antique shop, these pleasing rooms are good value. Doubles R700.

Glenconner Jonkershoek Rd, 4km from centre ☎021 886 5120, ⓦwww.glenconner.co.za. Pretty cottages on a farm in a spectacular valley, tranquil and close to the walks in the Jonkershoek Nature Reserve. Breakfast can be taken under an old oak tree. Self-catering doubles R590, B&B doubles R750.

Natte Valleij On the R44, 12km north of town ☎021 875 5171, ⓦwww.nattevalleij.co.za. Guests have a choice of a large cottage sleeping six, or a smaller unit attached to an old wine cellar. There's a swimming pool, and breakfast is served on the veranda. Doubles from R560.

River Manor 6–8 The Ave ☎021 887 9944, ⓦwww.rivermanor.com. Enjoy a totally romantic, if formal, stay in two historic houses with rose-petal-strewn beds, oil lamps, plush dressing gowns and wicker chairs to laze on in the sun around the pool, with spa facilities on site for extra pampering. Doubles from R1040.

Ryneveld Country Lodge 67 Ryneveld St ☏ 021 887 4469, ⓦ www.ryneveldlodge.co.za. Gracious late-nineteenth-century building, now a National Monument and furnished with Victorian antiques. The rooms are spotless, with the two best rooms upstairs leading onto a wooden deck. There are also three family cottages which sleep up to four, and a pool. Doubles from R900.

Stumble Inn 12 Market St ☏ 021 887 4049, ⓦ www.stumbleinnstellenbosch.hostel.com. The town's best and oldest established hostel in

two houses from the turn of the last century, with friendly, switched-on staff and a relaxed atmosphere. Just down the road from the tourist office, the hostel offers doubles, dorms and camping, and is also noted for its good-value tours (see p.171). Dorms R70 per person, doubles R200 per room.

Villa Merwe 6 Cynaroides Rd, Paradyskloof ☏ 021 880 1185, ⓦ www.villamerwe.co.za. Three immaculate and comfortable rooms in the owner's modern house, each with its own entrance and bathroom, with a lounge, pool and garden. It's a 5min drive from the centre. Doubles from R600 May–Sept, R740 Oct–April.

Eating and drinking

You'll be spoilt for choices of good places to eat in Stellenbosch, both in the centre and on some of the surrounding estates. Many places have outdoor seating, and in the evenings, the student presence ensures a relaxed and sometimes raucous drinking culture.

Bukhara Dorp and Bird sts ☏ 021 882 9133. Succulent North Indian dishes prepared in a kitchen behind a glass wall, in full view of diners. Prices are moderate or even steep, though portions are large. Favourites include butter chicken and tandoori lamb chops. Service is excellent and the ambience relaxed. Daily noon–3pm & 6–10.30pm.

Col'Cacchio Shop 8, Simonsplein Centre, Plein St. Better than average pizzeria, popular with students. Try the Morituri topped with bacon, chicken, feta, red pepper and avocado. Daily noon–11pm. Inexpensive.

The Fishmonger Sanlam Building, Ryneveld St ☏ 021 887 7835. A superb mid-priced seafood restaurant, reasonable value and with outdoor seating, though lacking in ambience. Mon–Tues & Thurs–Sat noon–10pm, Wed noon–3.30pm & 6–10pm, Sun noon–9pm.

Moyo Spier Lynedoch Rd (R310) ☏ 021 809 1133. An extravaganza of an eatery (one of four restaurants at Spier) in the gardens of one of the Western Cape's largest and most tourist-friendly wine estates. It's made to feel like a cross between an African village and a bedouin encampment, with seating for 1200 in gazebos, tents and tree houses, and the vast all-you-can-eat buffet brings together a dazzling array of flavours and dishes from across Africa. With live performance and optional face-painting thrown in, you can't help but enjoy yourself. Daily noon–4pm & 6pm till late.

Terroir Kleine Zalze Wine Estate, Strand Rd (R44) ☏ 021 880 8167. The culinary talk of the town, *Terroir* is some 12.5km from Stellenbosch on a wine and golf estate, with a formal but relaxed dining room and tables outside under shady oaks. The expensive French-inspired menu is based as far as possible on local organic produce, with a signature dish of belly of pork braised in ginger, soy and juniper berries served with smoked mash. Mon–Sat 12.30–2.30pm & 7–9.30pm, Sun lunch only.

Vida e Caffé On the corner of Bird and Kerk sts. Vibey Portuguese-style coffee shop in the middle of town. Part of a national chain, it boasts excellent service and coffee, while the clincher is the little slab of Lindt dark chocolate perched on the side of your saucer. Mon–Sat 8am–5pm & Sun 9am–4pm.

Volkskombuis/De Oewer Aan-de-Wagenweg, off Dorp St ☏ 021 887 2121. Two popular eateries on the banks of the Eerste River, these venues have the same management. There's an eclectic range of dishes from North Africa and the Mediterranean at *De Oewer*, while platters of mid-priced contemporary Cape Cuisine are the speciality of *Volkskombuis*. Mon–Sat noon–3pm & 6.30–10pm, Sun lunch only.

Wijnhuis On the corner of Church and Andringa sts ☏ 021 887 5844. At a mid-priced place whose name translates as "wine house", it's no surprise that the wine list is longer than the menu. Regulars come to enjoy their tipple with Mediterranean seafood dishes, grilled meat or pastas, served in an old

building with a light, contemporary feel. Wine tasting and buying wines is all part of the experience. Daily 8am–11pm.

The Stellenbosch wine estates

Stellenbosch was the first locality in the country to wake up to the marketing potential of a **wine route**. It launched its wine route in 1971, a tactic which has been hugely successful; today tens of thousands of visitors from all over the world are drawn here annually, making this the most toured area in the Winelands. Although the region accounts for only a fraction of South Africa's land under vine, its wine route is the most extensive in the country, comprising some two hundred establishments; apart from the tiny selection below (all of which are along a series of roads that radiate out from Stellenbosch) there are scores of other excellent places, which taken together would occupy months of exploration. All the wineries are clearly signposted off the main arteries.

Delaire On the Helshoogte Pass, 6km east of Stellenbosch along the R310 to Franschhoek ⓦ www.delairewinery.co.za. The restaurant here has the best views in the Winelands, looking through oaks across the Groot Drakenstein and Simonsig mountains and down into craggy valleys; the winery produces a couple of first-rate reds and whites. Mon–Fri 9am–5pm, Sat & Sun 10am–5pm; R15.

Jordan Vineyards 11.5km west of Stellenbosch off the R310 ⓦ www.jordanwines.com. A pioneer among the new-wave Cape wineries, Jordan's hi-tech cellar and modern tasting room is complemented by its friendly service. The drive there is half the fun, taking you into a *kloof* bounded by vineyards that get a whiff of the sea from both False Bay and Table Bay, which has clearly done something for its output – it has a long list of outstanding reds and whites. Mon–Fri 10am–4.30pm, Sat 9.30am–2.30pm & Sun 1am–2.30pm; R15, refundable with purchases.

Morgenhof 4km north of Stellenbosch on the R44 ⓦ www.morgenhof.com. French-owned château-style complex on the slopes of the vine-covered Simonsberg, under the energetic proprietorship of Anne Cointreau-Huchon (granddaughter of the founder of Remy Martin cognac). Morgenhof has a light and airy tasting room with a bar; among the numerous top-ranking wines worth sampling are the Merlot, Cabernet Sauvignon, Pinotage, Sauvignon Blanc, Chardonnay and Chenin Blanc. Delicious light lunches are served

outside, topped off with ice cream on the lawns. May–Oct Mon–Fri 9am–4.30pm, Sat & Sun 10am–3pm; Nov–April Mon–Fri 9.30am–5pm, Sat & Sun 10am–5pm; R10.

Neethlingshof 6.5km west of Stellenbosch on Polkadraai Rd (the R306) ⓦ www.neethlingshof .co.za. Centred around a beautifully restored Cape Dutch manor dating back to 1814, reached down a kilometre-long avenue of pines, Neethlingshof's first vines were planted in 1692. The estate produces very good wines, consistently hitting the high notes with its stunning Weisser Riesling Noble Late Harvest sweet dessert wines, a fine Chardonnay and several excellent reds. Daily 9am–5pm; tasting R25.

Overgaauw 6.5km west of Stellenbosch, off the M12. Notable for its elegant Victorian tasting room, this pioneering estate produces reds of excellent quality, among them Tria Corda, a claret-like wine, and a high-flying Cabernet Sauvignon. Overgaauw was the first winery in the country to produce Merlots, and it's still the only one to make Sylvaner, a well-priced, easy-drinking dry white. Mon–Fri 9am–5pm, Sat 10am–12.30pm; R10.

Rustenberg Wines Rustenberg Rd, 5km north of Stellenbosch ⓦ www.rustenberg.co.za. One of the closest estates to Stellenbosch, Rustenberg is also one of the most alluring, reached after a drive through orchards, sheep pastures and tree-lined avenues. An unassuming working farm, it has a romantic pastoral atmosphere, in contrast to its architecturally stunning, hi-tech tasting room in the former stables. The first vines were planted here in 1692, but the viniculture looks to the future. Most of its wines under the Rustenberg label are worth tasting, but also look out for highly drinkable and less expensive reds and whites under the Brampton brand – its second label. Mon–Fri 9am–4.30pm, Sat 10am–1.30pm; free.

Simonsig Estate 9.5km north of Stellenbosch, off Kromme Rhee Rd, which runs between the R44 and the R304 ⓦ www.simonsig.co.za. The winery has a relaxed outdoor tasting area under vine-covered pergolas, offering majestic views back to Stellenbosch of hazy stone-blue mountains and vineyards. Its vast range of first-class wines include its cutting-edge Red Hill Pinotage, Kaapse Vonkel sparkling wine (this was the first estate in the country to produce a bottle-fermented bubbly some three decades back), and the Merindol Syrah, which was

awarded 4.5 stars by the prestigious 2007 *Platter* guide. Mon–Fri 8.30am–5pm, Sat 8.30am–4pm; R15.

🏃 **Uva Mira About 8km south of Stellenbosch, off Annandale Rd, which spurs off the R44 ⓦ www.uvamira.co.za.** Enchanting boutique winery, worth visiting just for the winding drive halfway up the Helderberg. The highly original tasting room, despite being newly built, gives the appearance of a gently decaying historic structure, and there are unsurpassed views from the deck across mountainside vineyards to False Bay some 50km away – on a clear day you can even see Robben Island. The flagship wine is a highly rated red blend, but it's the single-vineyard Chardonnay that earned Uva Mira 4.5 stars in the 2007 *Platter* guide. Mon–Fri 8am–5pm & Sat 10am–4pm; R20.

Somerset West, Vergelegen and Morgenster

The only compelling reasons to trawl out to the unpromising town of **SOMERSET WEST**, 50km east of Cape Town along the N2, are for **Vergelegen** on Lourensford Road, and its immediate neighbour **Morgenster**, which are officially part of the Helderberg wine route, but can easily be included as an extension to a visit to Stellenbosch, just 14km to the north.

Vergelegen and Morgenster

An absolute architectural treasure as well as an estate producing a stunning range of wines, **Vergelegen** (daily 9.30am–4pm; entrance R10; wine tasting R2–10 per glass; ⓦ www.vergelegen.co.za) represents a notorious episode of corruption and the arbitrary abuse of power at the Cape in the early years of Dutch East India Company rule. Built by Willem Adriaan van der Stel, who became governor in 1699 after the retirement of his father Simon, the estate formed a grand Renaissance complex in the middle of the wild backwater that was the Cape at the beginning of the eighteenth century. Van der Stel acquired the land illegally and used Dutch East India Company slaves to build Vergelegen, as well as company resources to farm vast tracts of land in the surrounding areas. At the same time he abused his power as governor to corner most of the significant markets at the Cape. When this was brought to the notice of the Dutch East India Company in the Netherlands, Van der Stel was sacked and Vergelegen was ordered to be destroyed to discourage future miscreant governors. It's believed that the destruction was never fully carried out and the current building is thought to stand on the foundations of the original.

Vergelegen was the only wine estate visited by the British queen during her 1995 state visit to South Africa – a good choice, as there's enough here to

▲ Vergelegen

occupy even a monarch for an easy couple of hours. The **interpretive centre**, just across the courtyard from the shop at the building entrance, provides a useful history and background to the estate. Next door, the **wine-tasting centre** (open Nov–April) offers a professionally run sampling with a brief talk through each label. The **homestead**, which was restored in 1917 to its current state by Lady Florence Phillips, wife of a Johannesburg mining magnate, can also be visited. Its pale facade, reached along an axis through an octagonal garden that dances with butterflies in summer, has a classical triangular gable and pilaster-decorated doorways. Massive grounds planted with chestnuts and camphor trees and ponds around every corner make this one of the most serene places in the Cape.

Morgenster

Apart from its exquisite rustic setting, the tasting room at **Morgenster, Vergelegen**'s immediate neighbour (Mon–Fri 10am–5pm, Sat & Sun 10am–4pm; R10 for wine tasting, R10 for olive tasting; Ⓦ www.morgenster.co.za), has a veranda that looks onto a lovely lake with hazy mountains in the distance. Its two stellar blended reds aside, the estate offers the unusual addition of olive tasting, with three types of olive, three types of oil (including an award-winning cold-pressed extra virgin olive oil) and some delicious olive paste.

Paarl and around

Although **PAARL** is attractively ensconced in a fertile valley brimming with historical monuments, at heart it's a parochial *dorp*, lacking either the sophistication

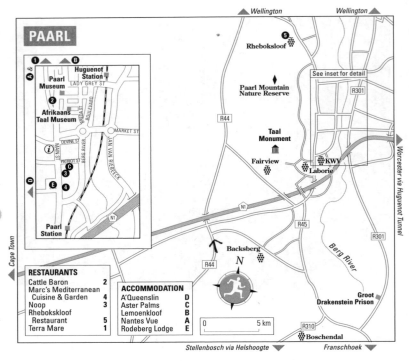

PAARL

Rheboksloof ❺ ❀

See inset for detail

Paarl Mountain
Nature Reserve

R301

❶ ▲   ▲ ❶
Huguenot
Station
Paarl
Museum   LADY GREY ST
❷
Afrikaans
Taal Museum
MARKET ST
DEVINE ST
ⓘ
❸ Ⓒ
Ⓔ ❹ Ⓓ
Paarl
Station
N1

R44

Taal
Monument
🏛

Fairview ❀   ❀ KWV
❀ Laborie

Worcester via Huguenot Tunnel

Cape Town ◀

N1

R45

R301

Berg River

Backsberg
❀
R44
N

Groot
Drakenstein Prison

RESTAURANTS
Cattle Baron   2
Marc's Mediterranean
 Cuisine & Garden   4
Noop   3
Rheboksloof
 Restaurant   5
Terra Mare   1

ACCOMMODATION
A'Queenslin   D
Aster Palms   C
Lemoenkloof   B
Nantes Vue   A
Rodeberg Lodge   E

0   5 km

R310

❀ Boschendal

16

THE WINELANDS | Paarl and around

of Stellenbosch or the striking setting and trendiness of Franschhoek. It is, however, a prosperous farming centre that earns its keep from the agricultural light industries – grain silos, canneries and flour mills – on the north side of town, and the cornucopia of grapes, guavas, olives, oranges and maize grown on the surrounding farms. Despite its small-town feel, Paarl has the largest municipality in the Winelands, with its most exclusive areas on the vined slopes of **Paarl Mountain** overlooking the town.

In 1657, just five years after the establishment of the Dutch East India Company refreshment station on the Cape Peninsula, a party under Abraham Gabbema arrived in the Berg River Valley to look for trading opportunities with the Khoikhoi, and search for the legendary gold of Monomotapa. They obviously had treasure on the brain, because on waking after a rainy night to the sight of the silvery dome of granite dominating the valley, they dubbed it **Peerlbergh** (pearl mountain), which in its modified form, Paarl, became the name of the town. Thirty years later, the commander of the Cape, Simon van der Stel, granted strips of the Khoikhoi lands on the slopes of Paarl Mountain to French Huguenot and Dutch settlers. By the time Paarl was officially granted town status in 1840, it was still an outpost at the edge of the Drakenstein Mountains, a flourishing wagon-making and last-stop provisioning centre. This status was enhanced when the first **rail line** in the Cape connected it to the Peninsula in 1863. Following in the spirit of the first Dutch adventurers of 1657, thousands of treasure-seekers brought custom to Paarl as the gateway to the interior during the diamond rush of the 1870s and the gold fever of the 1880s.

The town holds deep historical significance for the two competing political forces that forged modern South Africa. **Afrikanerdom** regards Paarl as the hallowed ground on which their language movement was born in 1875 (see box below), while for the **ANC** (and the international community), Paarl will be remembered as the place from which Nelson Mandela made the final steps of his long walk to freedom, when he walked out of **Groot Drakenstein Prison** (then called Victor Verster) in 1990.

The history of Afrikaans

Afrikaans is South Africa's third mother tongue, spoken by fifteen percent of the population and outstripped only by Zulu and Xhosa. English, by contrast, is the mother tongue of only nine percent of South Africans, and ranks fifth in the league of the eleven official languages.

Signs of the emergence of a new southern African dialect appeared as early as 1685, when H.A. van Rheede, a Dutch East India Company official from the Netherlands, complained about a "distorted and incomprehensible" version of Dutch being spoken in the Drakenstein Valley around modern-day Paarl. By absorbing English, French, German, Malay and indigenous words and expressions, the language continued to diverge from mainstream Dutch, and by the nineteenth century was widely used in the Cape by both white and coloured speakers, but was regarded by the elite as an inferior creole, unsuitable for literary or official communication. Even the first attempts by dominee **Stephanus du Toit** and the Genootskap van Regte Afrikaners (League of True Afrikaners) to have Afrikaans recognized as a separate language from Dutch, and their launching in 1875 of *Die Patriot*, the first white Afrikaans **newspaper**, made little impact outside Paarl.

Ironically, it was the British defeat of the Afrikaner republics in the second Anglo-Boer War at the turn of the twentieth century that provided the catalyst for a mass white Afrikaans movement. The scorched-earth policy of the British had driven many Boers from the lands and produced a demoralized and semi-literate Boer underclass, while the official British policy of anglicizing South Africa helped to unite the white Afrikaner proletariat and elite against the common English enemy.

In 1905, **Gustav Preller**, a young journalist from a working-class Boer background, set about reinventing Afrikaans as a "white man's language". He aimed to eradicate the stigma of its "coloured" ties by substituting Dutch words for those with non-European origins. Preller began publishing the first of a series of populist magazines written in Afrikaans and glorifying Boer history and culture. Through this **Second Language Movement**, whites took spiritual control over Afrikaans and the pressure grew for its recognition as an official language, which came in 1925.

When the National Party took power in 1948, its apartheid policy went hand in hand with promoting the interests of its Afrikaans-speaking supporters and a concerted programme of the **upliftment of poor whites** began. Afrikaners were installed throughout the civil service and filled most posts in the public utilities. Despite the fact that there were more coloured than white Afrikaans speakers, the language quickly became associated with the **apartheid** establishment. This had electrifying consequences in the 1970s, when the government attempted to enforce Afrikaans as the sole medium of instruction in African schools, leading directly to the **Soweto uprising** in 1976, which marked the beginning of the end for Afrikaner hegemony in South Africa. The repressive period throughout the 1970s and 1980s and the forced removals under the Group Areas Act led many coloured Afrikaans speakers to adopt English in preference to their mother tongue, which they felt was tainted by apartheid.

There are few signs that Afrikaans will die out. Under the new constitution, existing language rights can't be diminished, which effectively means that Afrikaans will continue to be almost as widely used as before. It is now as much with coloured as white people that the future of the *taal* (language) rests.

The town and around

Unlike Stellenbosch and Franschhoek, which are ideal for wandering, the best preserved and oldest historical frontage in Paarl stretches for some 2km down oak-lined **Main Street**. It's here you'll find the **Paarl Museum** at no. 303 (Mon–Fri 9am–5pm, Sat 9am–1pm; R5), in a handsome, thatched Cape Dutch building with one of the earliest surviving gables (1787) in the "new style", characterized by triangular caps. The contents don't quite match up to the exterior, but include some reasonably enlightening panels on the architecture of the town, and several eccentric glass display cases of Victorian bric-a-brac. Post-apartheid transformation has introduced some coverage of the indigenous Khoisan populations of the area and the changes that came with European colonization, including slavery.

South down Main Street away from the museum, a left turn into Van der Lingen Street and then a right into Pastorie Street brings you to the **Afrikaans Taal Museum** (Mon–Fri 9am–4pm; R10), which chronicles the development of the Afrikaans language. Located in the house of Gideon Malherbe (1833–1921), one of the founders of the League of True Afrikaners, the museum's displays are in Afrikaans, and a leaflet available from the reception desk gives an English summary of exhibits. Some brief material gives an alternative history of Afrikaans, placing new emphasis on the role of slaves and coloured South Africans in its evolution.

The only other sight of any interest in Paarl itself is the grandiose **Taal Monument** (daily 9am–5pm), the controversial memorial to the Afrikaans language, standing just outside the centre on the top of Paarl Mountain. To get there, drive south along Main Street past the head office of the KWV, and follow the signs to your right up the slope of the mountain. The monument used to be as important a place of pilgrimage for Afrikaners as the Voortrekker Monument in Pretoria, although when it was erected in 1973 critics joked that monuments were usually erected to the dead. From the coffee and curio shop you can admire a truly magnificent panorama across to the Cape Peninsula and False Bay in one direction and the Winelands ranges in the other.

Groot Drakenstein (Victor Verster) Prison

Roughly 9km south of the N1 as it cuts through Paarl, along the R301 (the southern extension of Jan van Riebeeck Street), stands the **Victor Verster Prison**. Renamed **Groot Drakenstein** in 2000, this was Nelson Mandela's last place of incarceration. It was through the gates at Victor Verster that Mandela walked to his freedom on February 11, 1990, and it was here that the first images of him in 27 years were bounced around the world (under the Prisons Act, not even old pictures of him could be published during his incarceration). The working jail looks rather like a boys' school fronted by rugby fields beneath hazy mountains, and there's something bizarre about seeing a prison sign nonchalantly slipped in among all the vineyard and wine-route pointers.

The wineries

There are a couple of notable wineries in Paarl itself, but most are on farms in the surrounding countryside. Boschendal, one of the most popular of these, is officially on the Franschhoek wine route, but is in easy striking distance of Paarl.

Backsberg Estate 22km south of Paarl on Simondium Rd (WR1) ₩ www.backsberg.co.za. Notable as the first carbon-neutral wine estate in South Africa, Backsberg, which has been owned and run by the Back family for generations, hasn't sacrificed quality for environmental friendliness – it produces some top-ranking red blends, and a delicious

Chardonnay, in its Babylons Toren and Black Label ranges. Outdoor seating, with views of the rose garden and vineyard on the slopes of the Simonsberg, makes this busy estate a nice place to while away some time. There's also a restaurant and a maze to get lost in. Mon–Fri 8am–5pm, Sat 9.30am–4.30pm, Sun 10.30am–4.30pm; R10.

Fairview Suid Agter Paarl Rd, on the southern fringes of town Ⓦ www.fairview.co.za. One of the most fun of all the Paarl estates (especially for families), with a resident population of goats who clamber up the spiral tower, featured in the estate's emblem, at the entrance. A deli sells sausages and cold meats for picnics on the lawn, and you can also sample and buy the goats', sheep's and cows' cheeses made on the estate. As far as wine tasting goes, Fairview is an innovative, family-run place, but it can get a bit hectic when the tour buses roll in. The vast array of wines includes a range of first-class Shirazes and a top-ranking Pinotage. Mon–Fri 8.30am–5pm, Sat 8.30am–4pm, Sun 9.30am–4pm; R10.

Laborie Taillefert St Ⓦ www.laborie.co.za. One of the most impressive Paarl wineries, all the more remarkable for being right in town.

The beautiful manor is fronted by a rose garden, acres of close-cropped lawns, historic buildings and oak trees – all towered over by the Taal Monument. There's a truly wonderful tasting room with a balcony that jetties out over the vineyards trailing up Paarl Mountain. Apart from a top-drawer Shiraz, it also produces a marvellous dry Methode Cap Classique (Champagne-style) sparkler made exclusively from Chardonnay grapes, and Pineau de Laborie, a wickedly delicious Pinotage-based dessert wine. May–Sept Mon–Sat 9am–5pm; Oct–April Mon–Sun 9am–5pm; R10 for five wines.

Rhebokskloof Signposted off the R45, 11.5km northwest of Paarl, Ⓦ www.rhebokskloof.co.za. A highly photogenic wine estate, and popular wedding venue, Rhebokskloof sits at the foot of sculptural granite *koppies* overlooking a shallow **kloof** that borders on the mountain nature reserve. The estate's renowned restaurant (see p.180) overlooks an artificial lake with swans. Top of its extensive range are a Cabernet Sauvignon and a Chardonnay. Horse and quad-bike trails are also operated from here. Daily 9am–5pm; tasting R25 which includes snacks.

Practicalities

Metrorail and Spoornet **trains** from Cape Town pull in at Huguenot Station in Lady Grey Street at the north end of town, near to the central shops. Greyhound and Intercape intercity **buses** stop at the Shell Garage, on the main road at the south end of town. The garage is about 2km from the **tourist office**, 216 Main St (Mon–Fri 8am–5pm, Sat 9am–4pm & Sun 10am–2pm; ℡021 863 4937, Ⓦwww.paarlonline.com), which has a selection of good **maps** and can help with finding a place to stay.

Accommodation

Most places to stay in town are either along or just off Main Street, many in historic buildings, with camping and chalets just outside of town for the cheapest stay.

A'Queenslin 2 Queen St ℡082 577 0635, Ⓔ aqueenslin@telkomsa.net. Two en-suite rooms with their own entrances and garden spaces, and three double rooms that share a bathroom, in a split-level family home set in a quiet part of town, bounded on one side by vineyards and towered over by Paarl Rock. Limited self-catering is possible – there's a fridge and microwave. Doubles from R350, en suites from R400.

Aster Palms 3 Patriot St ℡021 872 0895, Ⓦwww.asterpalms.co.za. Hospitable B&B in a 1920s house a couple of blocks from the tourist office, with four airy double rooms and a lovely back garden with a solar-heated swimming pool. Doubles from R740 (including a bottle of wine).

Lemoenkloof 396a Main St ℡021 872 3782, Ⓦwww.lemoenkloof.co.za. A comfortable and tranquil owner-run guesthouse in a National Monument, with 1820s Cape Dutch and

Victorian features, a TV and fridge in each room, and a secluded swimming pool. Doubles from R780.

Nantes Vue 56 Mill St ☎021 872 7311, ⓦwww .nantes-paarl.co.za. En-suite doubles and a cottage that sleeps three, decorated with artistic flair in a friendly Cape Dutch guest-house, also a National Monument. Breakfast

is served on the veranda overlooking a small garden. Doubles from R760.

Rodeberg Lodge 74 Main St ☎021 863 3202, ⓦwww.rodeberglodge.co.za. Plain period furnishing gives the six en-suite rooms in this huge, centrally located Victorian town house a cool, spacious atmosphere. Ask for a room at the back if traffic noise bothers you. Doubles from R600.

Eating and drinking

A working town, Paarl has none of the Winelands foodie pretensions of Franschhoek, but you'll find a number of places along the main street for a decent snack and coffee or a meal, as well as a couple of outstanding places in the surrounding countryside, with great views of the vineyards and mountains.

Cattle Baron Gymnasium St ☎021 872 2000. Reliable family-oriented steakhouse that specializes in inexpensive to mid-priced beef, chicken and fish. Mon–Fri noon–3.30pm & 6–11.30pm, Sat 6–midnight, Sun noon–3.30pm, & 6–10.30pm.

Marc's Mediterranean Cuisine & Garden 129 Main St ☎021 863 3980. One of Paarl's most popular casual eateries, *Marc's* dishes up a moderately priced, simple but tasty menu that includes paella, meze, couscous, seafood and lamb, served in a converted historic house with a large outdoor area dotted with sun umbrellas and lemon trees. Daily noon–2.30pm & Mon–Sat 6.30–9.30pm.

Noop 217 Main St. Supercool pavement wine bar with an impressively long list of wines by the glass and some great takes on simple favourites such as burgers, biryanis and pies, inspired, says the owner, by the old

French stock pot. Inexpensive to mid-priced. Mon–Fri 7.30am–11pm; Sat 7.30am–3pm.

Rhebokskloof Restaurant Rhebokskloof winery, Rhebokskloof Minor Rd ☎021 869 8386. Intimate outdoor established recommended for the outstanding setting as well as the food. Overlooking a lake, it has a shaded terrace for summer lunches, offering expensive gourmet meals with thrilling combinations of flavours, both Cape and international. It's also a good place for morning or afternoon teas. Daily 9am–11.30am, noon–5pm & 6pm till late.

Terra Mare 90a Main St ☎021 863 4805. Straightforward, mid-priced food, such as Karoo lamb chops with spring rolls or pasta and pesto, using local ingredients and infused with considerable flair, served in a glass and steel restaurant with great sweeping views of the Paarl Valley. Tues–Sat 10am–2pm & 6–10pm.

Franschhoek

Between 1688 and 1700 about two hundred French Huguenots, desperate to escape religious persecution in France, accepted a Dutch East India Company offer of passage to the Cape and the grant of lands. They made contact with the area's earliest settlers, groups of Khoikhoi herders. Conflict between the French newcomers and the Khoikhoi followed familiar lines, with the white settlers gradually dispossessing the herdsmen, forcing them either further into the hinterland or into servitude on their farms. The establishment of white hegemony was swift and by 1713 the area was known as *de france hoek*. Though French-speaking died out within a generation because of explicit Company policy, many of the estates hereabouts are still known by their original French names. **FRANSCHHOEK** itself, 33km from Stellenbosch and 29km from

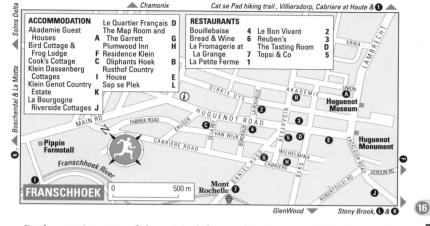

Chamonix　　　Cat se Pad hiking trail , Villiersdorp, Cabriere at Haute & ❶

ACCOMMODATION
Akademie Guest
　Houses　　　　　　　　**A**
Bird Cottage &
　Frog Lodge
Cook's Cottage　　　　　**C**
Klein Dassenberg
　Cottages
Klein Genot Country
　Estate　　　　　　　　**K**
La Bourgogne
　Riverside Cottages　**J**
Le Quartier Français　**D**
The Map Room and
　The Garrett　　　　　**G**
　Plumwood Inn　　　　**H**
Residence Klein　　　　**F**
　Oliphants Hoek　　　**B**
Rusthof Country
　House　　　　　　　　**E**
Sep se Plek　　　　　　**L**

RESTAURANTS
Bouillebaise　　　　　**4**
Bread & Wine　　　　　**6**
La Fromagerie at
　La Grange　　　　　　**7**
La Petite Ferme　　　　**1**
Le Bon Vivant　　　　**2**
Reuben's　　　　　　　**3**
The Tasting Room　　**D**
Topsi & Co　　　　　　**5**

FRANSCHHOEK　　　0　　　　500 m

Huguenot
Museum

Huguenot
Monument

Mont
Rochelle ❼

Pippin
Farmstall

Franschhoek River

GlenWood ▼　　Stony Brook, ❶ & ❷

Paarl, occupies parts of the original farms of La Cotte and Cabrière and is relatively young, having been established around a church built in 1833.

If sybaritic indulgence is what the Winelands is really about, then Franschhoek is the place that does it best. Despite being a fairly small *dorp*, it has managed to establish itself as the culinary capital of the Western Cape, if not the whole country. Its late Victorian and more recent Frenchified rustic architecture, the terrific setting (it's hemmed in on three sides by mountains), the vineyards down every other backstreet, and some vigorous myth-making have created a place you can really lose yourself in, a set piece that unashamedly draws its inspiration from Provence.

The town and around

Away from wining and dining, Franschhoek's attractions include hiking, horse-riding or cycling in the valley, or visiting the institutionalized **Huguenot Monument** and adjacent museum, which together occupy a prime position at the head of Huguenot Road, the main road through town, where it forms a T-junction with Lambrecht Street. The monument consists of three skinny, interlocking arches symbolizing the Holy Trinity, while the **Huguenot Memorial Museum** (Mon–Sat 9am–5pm & Sun 2–5pm; R5) gives comprehensive coverage of Huguenot history, culture and of their contribution to modern South Africa.

The best **hike** in the vicinity is the Cat se Pad' (Cat's Path), which starts on your left just under a kilometre from the museum as you head out of town up the Franschhoek Pass. The walk leads into *fynbos* with proteas, and gives instant access to the mountains surrounding the valley, with good views. The first two-kilometre section gets you to the top of the pass, and you can keep going for another 10km in the direction of Villiersdorp (though you don't actually reach it).

A great way to take in the beauty of Franschhoek (and some wine) is in the saddle – a couple of operators offer guided **equestrian tours**, for about R100 an hour, both taking in Rickety Bridge and Mont Rochelle wineries, with more straightforward outrides or longer or purely scenic rides also available. Contact Mont Rochelle Equestrian Centre, Mont Rochelle Estate (☎083 300 4368), or Paradise Stables, Roberstsvlei Road (☎021 876 2160 ⓦwww.paradisestables.co.za).

Museum van de Caab

Twelve kilometres north of Franschhoek along the R45, at the Solms Delta Wine Estate (see below), the highly recommended **Museum van de Caab** (daily 9am–5pm; free) gives a condensed and riveting slice through South African vernacular history as manifested on the farm and its surrounds. Housed alongside the atmospherically understated tasting room in the original 1740s gabled Cape Dutch cellar, the display begins with Stone Age artefacts found on the site and goes on to trace the arrival of the aboriginal Khoisan people, their colonization by Europeans, the introduction of slavery and how this eventually evolved into the apartheid system and its eventual demise.

The wineries

Franschhoek's **wineries** are small enough and sufficiently close together to make it a breeze to visit two or three in a morning. Heading north through town from the Huguenot Monument, you'll find most of the wineries signposted off Huguenot Road and its extension, Main Road; the rest are off Excelsior Road and the Franschhoek Pass Road.

Boschendal Pniel Rd, just after the junction of the R45 and R310 to Stellenbosch ⓦ www.boschendal .com. One of the world's longest-established New World wine estates, *Boschendal* draws busloads of tourists with its impressive Cape Dutch buildings, tree-lined avenues, restaurants and cafés, and of course its wines. Tasting takes place at the *Taphuis*, where you can sit indoors or sip under shady trees. Daily 8.30am–6.30pm; R15.

Cabrière at Haute Cabrière About 2km from town along the Franschhoek Pass Rd ⓦ www .cabriere.co.za. Atmospheric winery notable for its Pinot Noirs and colourful wine-maker Achim von Arnim, whose presence guarantees an eventful visit; try to catch him or one of his sons when they demonstrate sabrage – slicing off the upper neck of a bubbly bottle with a sabre, sending flying the neatly detached cork encased in the severed top ring of glass. Mon–Fri 9am–4.30pm, Sat 10am–4pm; R30.

GlenWood Robertsvlei Rd, signposted off the R45 ⓦ www.glenwoodvineyards.co.za. Small winery in a beautiful setting about ten-or-so minutes' drive from the village throng, which feels surprisingly remote; vineyard and cellar tours are frequently conducted by the owner. Mon–Fri 11am–4.30pm plus Sept–April Sat & Sun 11am–3pm; tasting R20, tasting and cellar tour R30.

Mont Rochelle Dassenberg Rd ⓦ www .montrochelle.co.za. Set against the Klein Dassenberg, Mont Rochelle has one of the most stunning settings in Franschhoek and an unusual cellar in a converted nineteenth-century fruit-packing shed, edged by eaves decorated with fretwork, stained-glass windows and chandeliers. A wholly black-owned winery – unusual for South Africa – its best wines are its whites. Daily 10am–6pm; R15.

Solms Delta Wine Estate & Museum 13km north of Franschoek along the R45 ⓦ www.solms-delta.co.za. Pleasingly bucolic Solms produces unusual and consistently outstanding wines which, on a summer's day, you can taste under ancient oaks at the edge of the vineyards. You can also order a picnic basket to enjoy on the banks of the stream that traces the estate's boundary. There's a fascinating museum here too (see above). Half the profits from the wines produced go into a trust that benefits residents of the farm and the Franschhoek Valley. Daily 9am–5pm; free.

▼ Haute Cabrière

Stony Brook Vineyards About 4km from Franschhoek, off Excelsior Rd ⓦ www .stonybrook.co.za. Family-run boutique winery, with just 140,000 square metres under vine, that produces first-rate wines, including its acclaimed flagship Ghost Gum Cabernet Sauvignon, which takes its name from a magnificent old tree outside the house and informal tasting room. Tastings are convivial affairs conducted by the owners. Mon–Fri 10am–3pm & Sat 10am–1pm; R20.

Practicalities

There's no public transport to Franschhoek or in the town itself. The buzzing **tourist office** is at 68 Huguenot Rd (summer Mon–Fri 9am–5pm, Sat & Sun 10am–6pm; winter Mon–Fri 9am–5pm, Sat & Sun 10am–4pm; ☎021 876 3603, ⓦwww.franschhoek.org.za), just north of the junction with Kruger Street; it can provide activities in the area and some excellent maps of the village and its winelands.

Accommodation

On the whole, guesthouse **accommodation** here is on the pricey side, but the rooms are of high quality and frequently in unparalleled settings; budget accommodation is hard to find, but there are a couple of reasonably priced self-catering cottages (listed here).

Akademie Guest Houses 5 Akademie St ☎021 876 3027, ⓦ www.aka.co.za. A beautiful room with a balcony and three characterful cottages (one of which is actually a double-storey house with a wraparound balcony and an outdoor bath) decorated with original artworks and each with its own garden and pond. Privacy is high on the agenda. There's also a huge room with a balcony. From R800 per cottage.

Bird Cottage and Frog Lodge Verdun Rd, 4.5km from town ☎021 876 2136, ⓔcindy@kingsley .co.za. Two very artistically furnished cottages surrounded by beautiful indigenous gardens close to the mountains in the midst of farmland. About as remote as you'll find this close to Franschhoek and very good value. R380 per cottage.

Cook's Cottage On the corner of De La Rey and Van Wyk sts ☎021 876 4229, ⓦwww .cookscottage.co.za. Spacious, beautifully decorated double-storey Victorian house in the centre of town with two bedrooms and a huge open-plan kitchen, dining room and lounge with a fireplace. Sleeps up to four people. R1300.

Klein Dassenberg Cottages Off Huguenot Rd ☎021 876 2107, ⓦ www.kleindassenberg.co.za. Self-catering cottages in a peaceful and beautiful setting. Two of the cottages are ideal for a couple, while the other pair sleeps four and can accommodate families.

Minimum two nights' stay over weekends. From R500 per cottage.

Klein Genot Country Estate Green Valley Rd ☎021 876 2738, ⓦ www.kleingenot.com. Indulgent boutique lodgings in huge grounds away from the main drag, done out in *Boere* Baroque style – pastiche Cape Dutch architecture, thatched roofs, heavy drapes and walls dripping with original South African artwork. Rooms are arranged along the length of a koi pond, whose fishy inhabitants poke their heads out to greet guests. There's a spa on site with three therapy rooms. Doubles R2700.

La Bourgogne Riverside Cottages Excelsior Rd ☎021 876 3245, ⓦ www.labourgogne.co.za. Six converted labourers' cottages set in indigenous gardens along a river on a working fruit farm. From R750 per cottage.

Le Quartier Français 16 Huguenot Rd ☎021 876 2151, ⓦ www.lequartier.co.za. A luxurious place with six suites (two with their own private walled garden and pool) and fifteen huge rooms decorated with sunny fabrics, all arranged around herb and flower gardens and a swimming pool. Child-friendly. Rated one of the world's top hundred hotels in 2007 by *Travel & Leisure* magazine. Also has one of the consistently best restaurants in the country (see p.185). Doubles from R3350.

The Map Room and The Garrett 21 Cabriere St ☎021 876 4229, ⓦ www.the maproom.co.za. Two adjoining and imaginatively decorated self-catering units in the centre of the villlage. *The Garrett* makes a cosy spot for a couple with great views and its own private garden with a pool, while the double-storey *Map Room* is an unusual, romantic bolt-hole for two. The bedroom spreads over the ground floor, with a spiral staircase leading to the expansive living area upstairs, with dramatic views over the vineyards and mountains.R1300 per unit.

Plumwood Inn 11 Cabriére St ☎021 876 3883, ⓦwww.plumwoodinn.com. Unfailingly excellent boutique guesthouse which makes a break from Franschhoek's Francophilia with its ethnic African-inspired decor. Detail is everything – from the custom-made cotton tablecloths to the luxurious beds covered with a sea of cushions, and impeccable service from Dutch owners Roel and Lucienne Rutten. Doubles from R990.

Residence Klein Oliphants Hoek 14 Akademie St ☎021 876 2566, ⓦwww.kleinoliphantshoek .co.za. Atmospheric eight-roomed guesthouse in a former double-storey Victorian mission station, where the massive reception room has soaring ceilings and the classrooms and mission-ary's quarters have been turned into bedrooms of varying size and luxury. The morning meal is taken in the breakfast room and adjoining terrace which overlooks a formal herb and rose garden. Doubles from R990.

Rusthof Country House 12 Huguenot St ☎021 876 3762, ⓦwww.rusthof.com. Modern eight-roomed guesthouse along the main drag (although it doesn't feel like it) in spitting distance of some of Franchhoek's top eateries. Rooms open onto a rose garden. Service is superb. Doubles from R1400.

Sep se Plek Excelsior Rd ☎083 459 9534 or 083 444 2477, ⓔladboer@mweb.co.za. Possibly the only bargain you'll find in Franschhoek in the form of three fully equipped, two-bedroom cottages on the edge of a small tranquil tree-lined lake on a working fruit farm. R400 per cottage.

Eating and drinking

Eating and drinking is what Franschhoek is all about, so plan on sampling at least one or two of its excellent **restaurants**, some of which rate among the Cape's best. Franschhoek's cuisine tends to be French–inspired, but includes salmon trout as a local speciality. Restaurants in town are concentrated along Huguenot Road, but there are a number of excellent alternatives in the more rustic environment of the surrounding wine estates. **Booking** is essential.

Bouillebaisse 38 Huguenot St ☎021 876 4430. Performance cooking at its best turns great food into a wonderful evening's entertainment at this intimate bistro, where the galley kitchen, in full view, runs the length of the eatery. Although there are main courses, the strongly Asian-influenced menu is best enjoyed tapas-style – a range of flavours, served as small helpings. Ask for ringside seats – and on no account miss out on the home-made sorbets: lime-basil, orange-sweet chilli and ginger-lemongrass. Expensive. Mon–Sat 10am–10pm.

Bread & Wine Môreson Farm, Happy Valley Rd, La Motte ☎021 876 3692. Signposted off the R45 is this moderately priced, genial and child-friendly venue surrounded by lemon orchards and vineyards. It serves imagina-tive modern Mediterranean-style country cuisine lunches (try the braised tomatoes with aubergine ravioli) accompanied by a variety of breads and the estate's own wines. Daily noon–3pm.

La Fromagerie at La Grange 13 Daniel Hugo St ☎021 876 2155. Sample platters of South African cheeses accompanied by local wines in the gardens here, overlooking vineyards, or sit down for tea or lunches that include savoury tarts, terrines and soufflés. Daily for lunch and tea as well as cheese tasting noon–4pm. On summer weekends this family-friendly spot becomes a buzzing jazz venue.

La Petite Ferme Franschhoek Pass Rd ☎021 876 3016. A multiple award-winner rated by *Condé Nast Traveler* as one of the world's top fifteen "best value" establishments, boasting delicately flavoured, rustic contem-porary cuisine and unparallelled views across a vineyard-clad valley, *La Petite Ferme* is, not surprisingly, popular. Among its specialities are home-smoked trout, roasted Karoo lamb and spiced roulade of ostrich. Meals are served with wines made in the restaurant's cellar. Expensive. Daily noon–4pm.

Le Bon Vivant 22 Dirkie Uys St ☎021 876 2717. Well-priced and consistently excellent establishment serving two-to-five-course nouvelle cuisine set meals as well as an à la carte menu with a splash of Dutch influence. Daily except Wed noon–3 & 6.30pm till late.

Reuben's 19 Huguenot Rd ☎021 876 3772. Minimalist chic decor and a relaxed ambience set the tone at one of Franschhoek's top eateries, with an inspired, eclectic menu that varies from day to day. Venison features big and there's always poultry, lamb, pork, seafood and a vegetarian option, all spiced up with a touch of Indian, Japanese and other Asian accents. The starters, which have included spiced beef tartar and chilli-salted squid, are

quite superb. Expensive. Daily 8am till last customers leave (kitchen closes 8.30pm).

The Tasting Room at Le Quartier Français 16 Huguenot Rd ☎021 876 2151. The place that made Franschhoek synonymous with food remains consistently one of South Africa's best restaurants (rated among the world's Top 50 by the UK's *Restaurant* magazine), offering excellent formal evening meals with a contemporary, global flavour. There are always vegetarian options and delicious desserts. Moderate. Daily 7–10pm.

Topsi & Co 7 Reservoir St West ☎021 876 2952. Run by one of South Africa's most eccentric and best-known chefs, Topsi Venter, this is a bag of surprises. There's no set menu, but you'll always find unlikely flavours being combined to great effect. A talking parrot called Dr Arnoldus Pannevis wanders around checking that everything is all right. Expensive. Mon & Wed–Sun noon–2.30pm & 7–9pm.

17

The Whale Coast and Overberg Interior

From about July, southern right whales start appearing in the warmer sheltered bays of the Western Cape, and the southern Cape coast – shown on the Garden Route (West) map at the back of this book – is prime territory for land-based whale-watching. The **Whale Coast**, as the section from roughly Kleinmond to De Hoop has come to be known, is close enough for an easy outing from Cape Town, yet is surprisingly undeveloped, with the exception of popular **Hermanus**, 112km east of Cape Town. The town trumpets itself as the **whale capital** of South Africa, and to prove it, an official whale crier (purportedly the world's only one) struts around armed with a mobile phone and a dried kelp horn through which he yells the latest sightings. The hype aside, the bay on which Hermanus sits does provide some of the finest shore-based whale-watching in the world and, even if there are better spots nearby, the town is the best geared-up place in the country to exploit it.

North of Hermanus are some **wineries** you can visit, while due east of Walker Bay, the inland hamlet of **Stanford** on the banks of the Klein River has managed to retain its historic village feel; it's a quieter base than Hermanus, while being near enough to the whale capital for a meal and sightseeing. Southeast down the bay from Hermanus, the unprepossessing town of **De Kelders** outshines its smarter neighbour as a whale-watching spot, but at nothing much else; and just inland of it, the very upmarket **Grootbos Nature Reserve** is a honeymoon destination. Heading further down the bay, you hit the fishing town of **Gansbaai** (Afrikaans for "goose bay"), which these days is far better known for its shark-cage diving than its waterfowl. Curving back to Hermanus, Danger Point is the promontory that indicates Walker Bay's southern extent, and marks the spot where HMS *Birkenhead* literally went down in history (see p.196).

An easy excursion from Hermanus takes you through attractive farming country to **Bredasdorp**, a junction town on the R316 that gives you the choice of branching out to Africa's southern tip at **Cape Agulhas**; the well-preserved Moravian mission town of **Elim**; or the fishing village of **Arniston**, which is the least-developed town along the Whale Coast. The real jewel of the coastline, though, is further to the east at the **De Hoop Nature Reserve**, an exciting wilderness of bleached dunes, craggy coast and more whales.

The **Overberg interior** – the stretch as far as Swellendam, along the N2 towards the Garden Route – is dominated by the towns of **Caledon**, only worth a stop for its rejuvenating hot springs, **Greyton**, a peaceful, oak-lined country town 35km off the main road, and **Swellendam** itself, brimming with historical guesthouses and with a good museum, decent restaurants and recommended horse-riding, as well as antelope viewing at the **Bontebok National Park**.

Public **transport**, such as there is, serves Hermanus. **Splash Bus** (☎082 658 5375, ✉splash@hermanus.co.za) runs at least once daily between Cape Town train station and Hermanus, and can collect visitors from their accommodation in central Cape Town. The **Baz Bus** drops people off at **Bot River**, 28km to the north on the N2, from where you can arrange to be collected by a shuttle operated by *Moby's Travel Lodge* in Hermanus, whether you're staying there or not; booking is recommended, but the Baz carries a mobile phone and can call ahead while you're en route.

Whale-watching

The Southern Cape, including Cape Town, provides some of the easiest and best places in the world for **whale-watching**. You don't need to rent a boat or take a pricey tour to get out to sea; if you come at the right time of year, whales are often visible from the shore, although a good pair of binoculars will come in useful for when they are far out.

All nine of the great whale species of the southern hemisphere pass by South Africa's shores, but the most commonly seen off Cape Town are **southern right whales** (their name derives from being the "right" one to kill because of their high oil and bone yields and the fact that, conveniently, they float when dead). Southern right whales are black and easily recognized from their pale, brownish **callosities**. These unappealing patches of raised, roughened skin on their snouts and heads have a distinct pattern on each animal, which helps scientists keep track of them.

Female whales come inshore to calve in sheltered bays, and stay to nurse their young for up to three months. **July to October** is the best time to see them, although they start appearing in June and some stay around until December. When the calves are big enough, the whales head off south again, to colder, stormy waters, where they feed on enormous quantities of plankton, making up for the nursing months when the females don't eat at all. Though you're most likely to see females and young, you may see **males** early in the season boisterously flopping about the females, though they neither help rear the calves nor form lasting bonds with females.

What gives away the presence of a whale is the blow or spout, a tall smoky plume which disperses after a few seconds and is actually the whale breathing out before it surfaces. If luck is on your side, you may see whales **breaching** – the movement when they thrust high out of the water and fall back with a great splash.

Probably the best **whale watching tour** in Hermanus is with Marine Dynamics, which operates the Dyer Island cruises (☎028 384 0406, ✉bookings@whalewatchsa.com).

The Whale Coast's hottest whale spots

In **Hermanus**, the best vantage points are the concrete cliff paths which ring the rocky shore from New Harbour to Grotto Beach. There are interpretation boards at three of the popular vantage points (Gearing's Point, Die Gang and Bientang's Cave). This is, however, the most congested venue during the whale season – at their worst, the paths can be lined two or three deep with people – though there are equally good spots elsewhere along the Walker Bay coast. Aficionados claim that **De Kelders** (see p.194), some 39km east of Hermanus, is even better, while **De Hoop Nature Reserve** (see p.200), east of Arniston, is reckoned by some to be the ultimate place along the entire southern African coast for whale-watching, with far greater numbers of southern rights breaching here than anywhere else.

▲ A whale shows itself at Hermanus

Hermanus and the Walker Bay wineries

On the edge of rocky cliffs and backed by mountains, **HERMANUS** sits at the northernmost end of **Walker Bay**, an inlet whose protective curve attracts calving whales as it slides south to the promontory of Danger Point. There is still the barest trace of a once-quiet cliff-edge fishing village around the historic harbour and in some understated seaside cottages, but for the most part the town has gorged itself on its whale-generated income that has produced modern shopping malls, supermarkets and craft shops. Hermanus also has good swimming and walking **beaches** and opportunities for **activities**.

Some of South Africa's top **wines** come from the **Hemel-en-Aarde Valley** along a few gravel kilometres of the **R320** to Caledon, which branches off the main road to Cape Town 2km west of Hermanus. The wineries here are worth popping into for their intimate tasting rooms and first-class wines, with views of the stark scrubby mountains just inland.

Arrival and information

There are two routes to Hermanus from Cape Town. It's more direct to take the N2 and head south onto the R43 at Bot River (a 1hr 30min drive), but the winding road that hugs the coast from Strand, leaving the N2 just before Sir Lowrie's Pass, is the more scenic (2hr). There's a helpful **tourist office** (Mon–Sat 9am–5pm, plus in summer Sun 10am–3pm; ☎028 312 2629, ⓦ www.hermanus .co.za) at the old station building in Mitchell Street, with maps, useful brochures about the area and an **Internet café**. It operates a free accommodation-finding service and can take bookings for boat-based and aerial whale-watching, as well as shark-cage diving trips.

Over the last weekend in September the town puts on a fun show of anything that's got a whale connection, even tenuously. To find out what's on – events range from ecology talks to classical recitals – check ⓦ www.whalefestival.co.za.

Accommodation

Unsurprisingly, accommodation on the shore is in high demand and tends to be more expensive than places set back. If there are more than two of you, the best option may be to rent a whole house or apartment through Hermanus Accommodation Centre, on the corner of Church and Myrtle lanes (☎028 313 0004, ⓦwww.hermanusaccom.co.za). If you want something more countrified, head off to Stanford, twenty minutes' drive away.

Auberge Burgundy 16 Harbour Rd ☎028 313 1201, ⓦwww.auberge.co.za. An imitation Provençal country house in the town centre, projecting a stylish Mediterranean feel, with imported French fabrics and a lavender garden. Breakfast is served across the road at the Burgundy restaurant. Doubles R1080.

Eastbury Cottages 36 Luyt St ☎082 658 4945, 028 312 1258, ⓦwww.eastburycottage.co.za. Three very reasonably priced, fully equipped self-catering cottages close to the *Marine Hotel*. No credit cards. Prices are in the R350–600 range per cottage, depending on how many people there are.

Forty Five Marine Drive 45 Marine Drive ☎028 312 3610, ⓕ028 313 1125. Cliffside self-catering luxury apartments next to the *Windsor Hotel*, with two bedrooms, two bathrooms, a kitchen and terrific views across the bay. Overflow guests may be shunted off to its far less comely relative, the *Esplanade*. Apartments R900/R570 at the *Esplanade*.

Moby's Travellers Lodge 9 Mitchell St ☎028 313 2361, ⓦwww.mobys.co.za. Centrally located hostel with doubles, dorms and a family suite as well as a cosy pub and inviting relaxation areas, including a rock pool. They provide breakfast and dinner at reasonable rates, or you can self-cater. They'll organize all tours and outings, and arrange transport to and from the Baz Bus drop off in Bot River. Dorms R100, doubles R200 per person.

Robin's Nest Meadow Ave ☎ 028 316 1597, ⓦwww.hermanus.co.za/accomm/10robinsnest. Three fully equipped, self-catering studio flats in the gardens of what was once Rheezicht Farm, 4km west of the centre. Reached through the Hemel-en-Aarde shopping village, these purpose-built, two-storey flats sleep two and open onto a communal courtyard. A semi-rural alternative to staying in town. R260 per person.

Windsor Hotel 49 Marine Drive ☎028 312 3727, ⓦwww.windsorhotel.co.za. A seafront hotel, offering a full range of accommodation on the very edge of Walker Bay. The *Windsor* is ideally situated in the centre of Hermanus and guests have sea views from the dining room, lounges and nearly half of the bedrooms. Buffet breakfast is included. Sea-facing doubles R1040.

The Town

Main Road, the continuation of the R43, meanders through Hermanus, briefly becoming Seventh Street. **Market Square**, just above the old harbour and to the south of Main Street, is the closest thing to a centre, and it's here you'll find the heaviest concentration of restaurants, craft shops and flea markets – the principal forms of entertainment in town when the whales are taking time out.

Just below Market Square is the **Old Harbour Museum** (Mon–Sat 9am–4.30pm, Sun noon–4pm; R5) where, among the uncompelling displays, you'll find lots of fishing tackle and some sharks' jaws. Outside, a few colourful boats, used by local fishermen from the mid-eighteenth to mid-nineteenth centuries, create a photogenic vignette in the tiny harbour.

An almost continuous five-kilometre cliff path through coastal *fynbos* hugs the rocky coastline from the old harbour to Grotto Beach in the eastern suburbs. For one short stretch the path heads away from the coast and follows Main Street before returning to the shore. East of the Old Harbour, just below the *Marine Hotel*, a beautiful tidal pool offers the only **sea swimming** around the town centre's craggy coast; it's big enough to do laps. For **beaches**, you have to

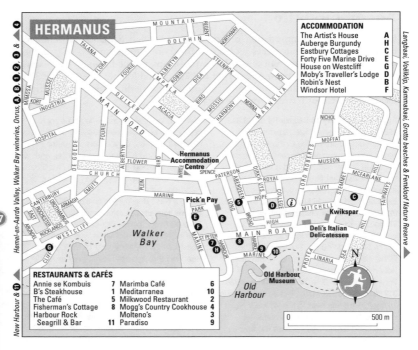

ACCOMMODATION

The Artist's House	A
Auberge Burgundy	H
Eastbury Cottages	C
Forty Five Marine Drive	E
House on Westcliff	G
Moby's Traveller's Lodge	D
Robin's Nest	B
Windsor Hotel	F

Langbaai, Voëlklip, Kammabaai, Grotto beaches & Fernkloof Nature Reserve

Hemel-en-Aarde Valley, Walker Bay wineries, Onrus, ⓐ ❶ ❷ ❸ 8

New Harbour & ⓫

THE WHALE COAST AND OVERBERG INTERIOR | Hermanus

RESTAURANTS & CAFÉS

Annie se Kombuis		Marimba Café	6
B's Steakhouse	7	Meditarranea	10
The Café	1	Milkwood Restaurant	2
Fisherman's Cottage	5	Mogg's Country Cookhouse	4
Harbour Rock	8	Molteno's	3
Seagrill & Bar	11	Paradiso	9

head out east across the Mossel River to the suburbs, where you'll find a decent choice, starting with secluded **Langbaai**, closest to town, a cove beneath cliffs at the bottom of Sixth Avenue that has a narrow strip of beach and is excellent for swimming. **Voëlklip**, at the bottom of Eighth Avenue, has grassed terraces, toilets, a nearby café for tea and is great for picnics if you prefer your sandwiches unseasoned with sand. Adjacent is **Kammabaai**, with the best surfing break around Hermanus, and 1km further east, **Grotto Beach** (which despite its name is not a rocky cove), marking the start of a twelve-kilometre curve of dazzlingly white sand that stretches all the way to De Kelders.

Also on the east side of town, the **Fernkloof Nature Reserve** (dawn–dusk; free) encompasses fifteen square kilometres of mountainous terrain and offers sweeping views of Walker Bay. This highly recommended wilderness area is more than just another nature reserve on the edge of town – it has some 40km of **waymarked footpaths**, including a 4.5-kilometre circular nature trail. Visiting is an excellent way to get close to the astonishing variety of delicate montane coastal *fynbos* (over a thousand species have been identified in the reserve), much of it flowering species that attract scores of birds, including brightly coloured sunbirds and sugarbirds endemic to the area.

A couple of kilometres west of town along Westcliff, the **New Harbour** is a working fishing harbour, dramatically surrounded by steep cliffs, projecting a gutsy counterpoint to the more manicured central area. Whales sometimes enter the harbour – and there's nowhere better to watch them than from the *Harbour Rock* (see p.192).

On the eastern edge of Hermanus, **Rotary Way** is a fantastic ten-kilometre drive that follows the mountain spine through beautiful montane *fynbos* offering sweeping views of the town, the Hemel-en-Aarde Valley and Walker Bay from Kleinmond to Danger Point. To get there from town, turn right just after the sports ground, and take a track straddled by a pair of white gateposts labelled "Rotary Way". The road is tarred for part of the way, then becomes a dirt track, eventually petering out altogether, which means you have to return the same way.

Hemel-en-Aarde Valley: the Walker Bay wineries

About fifteen minutes by car west of Hermanus, the vineyards of the Hemel-en-Aarde Valley date back to the early nineteenth century, when the Klein Hemel-en-Aarde Vineyard was part of a Moravian mission station, though winemaking is a relatively recent phenomenon, established here for not much more than a decade. Closest to town of the wineries is **Whalehaven** (Mon–Fri 9.30am–5pm, Sat 10.30am–1pm; free; ⓦ www.whalehavenwines.co.za) which has seen its reputation grow since its first vintage was released a decade ago; it's a couple of hundred metres after the Caledon turn-off. The longest established of the Walker Bay wineries is **Hamilton Russell** (Mon–Fri 9am–5pm, Sat 9am–1pm; free), which produces some of South Africa's priciest wines. Adjacent to Hamilton Russell, towards Caledon, **Bouchard Finlayson** (Mon–Fri 9am–5pm, Sat 10.30am–12.30pm; ⓦ www.bouchardfinlayson.co.za) is another establishment with a formidable reputation, and a wider range of wines than its neighbour. Furthest from town and newest of the wineries is **Cape Bay** (Mon–Fri 9am–4pm & summer only Sun 9am–noon), just under 7km from the Hemel-en-Aarde turn-off and about half a kilometre after the tar ends.

Across the road from Whalehaven Winery, in Hemel-en-Aarde Village, is possibly the best wine shop in South Africa, the **Wine Village** (Mon–Sat 9am–6pm & Sun 10am–3pm), with a staggering selection of labels from all the country's various wine-producing districts, covering a vast price range.

Hermanus activities

There's more to Hermanus than whales. The surrounding Raednagael Mountains serve as a great launching pad for **paragliding**; Para-Pax offer tandem flights (☎82 881 4724; R850). The coastline, a marine reserve stretching 500m out to sea, boasts some of the best **coral reefs** in Southern Africa, viewed by flashlight because of the lack of light permeating the plankton-rich water. **Scuba Africa**, The New Harbour, Westcliff Drive (☎028 316 2362, ✉aron@scubaafrica.co.za), runs **diving tours** (R330 for a dive and full gear rental) for anyone who arrives with proof of certification and a log book. The water is too cold for tropical fish, but if you're lucky a whale might come over to see what you're up to. You can also see the whales from horseback; **Horse Trail Safaris** (☎082 729 7776), based in Hermanus, does a dune and beach ride for experienced riders (2hr R360), and an hour-long mountain ride for novices (R180), while **African Horse Co** (☎082 667 9232), based in Stanford, offers a 20-kilometre half-day beach and lagoon ride (R400) for more experienced riders.

After indulging in all the activities on offer, you may want to relax for a half day at the luxury *Arabella Sheraton Western Cape Hotel & Spa* (take the R43 in the direction of Cape Town and the N2, and turn left at the Kleinmond turn-off). The spa here is worth a visit: for R250 you get four hours of sheer pleasure in the Turkish bathhouse with its flotation pool, Jacuzzis, steam rooms and saunas. All the regular body treatments are available at hefty prices (R430 for a one-hour Swedish massage, for instance); booking is essential (☎028 284 0000, ⓦwww.arabellasheraton.co.za).

Eating and drinking

Although **seafood** is the obvious thing to eat in Hermanus – and you'll find plenty of good restaurants serving it – there's a wide range of cuisine available here, with some gourmet **restaurants** to try.

There's no nicer way to eat on a beautiful day in Hermanus than to do a bit of self-catering or buy some fish and chips and eat out on the wall of the old harbour. *Hermanus Fish Shoppe* in Market Square does takeaway fish and chips – the best in town – as well as seafood salads and fresh seafood to cook yourself. Grub features large at the **market** held every Saturday morning on Market Square, where you'll find excellent home-made cheeses from Bot River as well as home-made pasta, pesto, marinated cheeses, muffins, houmus and baked goods. As for **delis**, try *Deli's Italian Delicatessen*, 181 Main Rd, a pukka Italian place selling pastas, sauces, cheeses, meats, and good Italian coffee. Central **supermarkets** include Kwikspar at 247 Main Rd (daily 7am–7pm) and Pick 'n Pay at 81 Main St (Mon–Sat 8am–6pm, Sun 9am–4pm).

Restaurants and cafés

Annie se Kombuis Warrington Place, Harbour Rd ℡ **028 313 1350.** Small, simple place serving inexpensive, traditional South African fare, such as *bobotie* and *koeksisters* (plaited syrupy doughnuts), Tues–Sat lunch & dinner, Sun lunch only.

B's Steakhouse Hemel-en-Aarde Village ℡ **028 316 3625.** A friendly, buzzing steakhouse – not part of a chain – serving brilliantly prepared, reasonably priced slabs of beef (staff hasten to tell punters they don't do burgers). Its formidable wine list and child-friendliness makes it an obvious choice for families. Tues–Sun dinner, Fri & Sun also lunch.

The Café 14 Aberdeen St. Fresh salads, quiches and breads in summer, soups and stews in winter, charged by the weight of your plate. Order your coffees and drinks from the counter, and help yourself to delicious cakes and desserts. Moderate. Mon–Sat 8.30am–5pm, Sun 10am–5pm.

Fisherman's Cottage Lemms Corner. An excellent spot for drinks, though the food – salads, fish and chips, and burgers – is pretty average. It's housed in an old rustic cottage off Market Square, with veranda seating. Moderate. Tues–Sat 11am–11pm, Sun lunch only.

Harbour Rock Seagrill & Bar New Harbour ℡ **028 312 2920.** Fish and chips and other mid-priced seafood dishes with stunning views from the cliffs, best at sundown. Daily breakfast, lunch & dinner.

Marimba Café 9 Royal Centre, Main Rd ℡ **028 312 2148.** Lively place with a constantly changing, mid-priced menu from across

Africa – the likes of Ethiopian roast lamb seasoned with cardamom and ginger, and *yassa* – Senegalese-style chicken. Booking essential. Daily evenings only.

Meditarranea Marine Drive ℡ **028 313 1685.** One of the best restaurants in town, with good views of Walker Bay. The Mediterranean-style food is pricey, but worth the treat. Tues–Sun evenings.

Milkwood Restaurant Atlantic Drive, Onrus ℡ **028 316 1516.** A 15-min drive west of Hermanus, *Milkwood* is especially recommended for its deck in an unsurpassed setting on a seaside lagoon, and does medium-priced steaks and excellent freshly caught fish. A good family venue. Daily noon–10.30pm.

Mogg's Country Cookhouse Hemel-en-Aarde Valley ℡ **028 312 4321.** A most unlikely location for one of Hermanus's most successful restaurants – on a working farm in the back country – with superb views across the valley. *Mogg's* is an intimate place that's always full and unfailingly excellent, serving whatever country-cooking surprises take the fancy of chefs Jenny Mogg and her daughter Julia, but there's always a choice of three starters, main courses and desserts, all moderately priced. Booking essential. Wed–Sun lunch, plus Fri & Sat evenings.

Molteno's Molteno St, Onrus River ℡ **028 316 2658.** A 15-min drive out of Hermanus, *Molteno's* is highly recommended for its ambience, its family-friendly meals, including pizzas and burgers, and its heaving Sunday-lunch carvery. Special theatre nights are

THE WHALE COAST AND OVERBERG INTERIOR | The Walker Bay wineries held once or twice a month with well-known artists invited to perform. Booking essential. Moderate prices. Mon & Wed–Sat bar open from 3pm, food served from 6pm till late, Sun lunch only, closed Tues.

Paradiso **83 Marine Drive** ☎ **028 313 1153.** Situated behind the village square this Italian restaurant offers two-for-the-price-of-one meals from Tues – Thursy. Tues–Sun lunch & dinner.

Listings

Emergencies Fire ☎ 028 361 0000; police (enquiries) ☎ 028 312 2626. See also p.163.
Hospital Hermanus Private Hospital, Hospital St, off Main Rd (☎ 028 313 0168), has a 24-hr casualty service.
Internet access There's an Internet café at the tourist office and at 69 Main Rd (Mon–Fri 7.30am–6pm, Sat 9am–4pm, Sun 10am–2pm).

Pharmacy Hermanus, 145 Main Rd (☎ 028 312 4039 or 312 233) is open Mon–Fri 8am–6.30pm, Sat 8am–1pm and Sun 10am–noon & 6.30–7.30pm.
Taxis Bernardus shuttle service (☎ 028 316 1093 or 083 658 7848) runs buses to and from Cape Town (R140 per person sharing one way), and can get you around town.

Stanford

East of Hermanus, and 150km from Cape Town, the R43 takes a detour inland around the Klein River Lagoon, past the pretty riverside hamlet of **STANFORD**, fifteen minutes away, in a wide, flat valley. Despite its proximity to hyped-up Hermanus, this historic village, established in 1857, has become something of a refuge for arty types seeking a tranquil escape from the urban rat race. To keep visitors racing around Stanford, the hamlet's residents have created an **arts and crafts route** that takes in over a dozen artists' studios. There are some decent **restaurants**, including a legendary one in a country cottage which requires booking several months in advance. But Stanford's principal attraction is its travel-brochure streetscape of simple **Victorian architecture** that includes lime-washed houses and sandstone cottages – as well as an Anglican church – with thatched roofs that glow under the late afternoon sun.

The town's northern boundary is the attractive Klein river, with a couple of great places to stay along the river, further out of town, as well as a **boat trip** on the river (Platanna River Cruises ☎ 028 341 0701; times by arrangement). There's rich birdlife in and among the rustling reed beds lining the river banks and you stand a good chance of spotting the flashy malachite kingfisher.

Although the **Birkenhead Brewery** (tasting Mon–Sat 11am–4pm, free tours Mon–Fri) just across the R43 from the village (along the R326) bills itself as a "craft brewery estate", the gleaming stainless steel pipes and equipment inside soon dispel any images of bloodshot hillbillies knocking up a bit of moonshine on the quiet. This is a very slick operation and a good place to go for a pub lunch (daily 11am–3pm) or to sample and buy beers which put those of SAB, South Africa's big brewing near-monopoly, in their place.

Two kilometres beyond the brewery is the award-winning **Klein River Cheese Farm** (Mon–Fri 9am–5pm, Sat 9am–1pm), which offers tastings of its famous Gruyere, Leiden, Colby and Dando cheeses. Buy one of its **picnic** baskets to have under the trees next to the river (Sept 15–May 15 daily 11am–3pm). Stanford's best wine, under the Raka label, is sold from the **Erica Vineyards** (Mon–Fri 9am–6pm), 4km further along the R326.

Practicalities

There is no public transport to Stanford, but once there you'd have no problem getting around this tiny hamlet on foot. The enthusiastic **tourist office** (Mon–Fri 8am–4pm & Sat 10am–5pm; ☎028 341 0340, ⓦ www.stanfordinfo.co.za), next to the library and opposite the Spar **mini-supermarket** in the middle of the village, has brochures about Stanford and can help with finding **accommodation**, of which Stanford has a fair selection – well-run B&Bs and self-catering cottages at reasonable prices. There is also a brochure for a walkabout you can do, taking in the various historical houses in the village.

Accommodation

B's Cottage 17 Morton St ☎028 341 0430, ⓔ milkwood@hermanus.co.za. A small open-plan self-catering thatched house, sleeping two, right in the centre, in an English-style country garden. Book well ahead as it's deservedly popular. R350 for the cottage.

Klein River Cheese Farm Cottage 7km on the R326 ☎028 341 0693 Charming three-bedroomed/two-bathroomed Victorian cottage on the river at the Cheese farm with a fireplace for the winter. Minimum stay is two nights. From R165 per person, and a minimum charge of R375 per night.

Mosaic Farm 10km from the centre, exit from Queen Victoria St ☎028 3410181, ⓦ www .mosaicfarm.com. Luxury stone, canvas and thatch chalets on the river, with 4km of lagoon frontage where you can canoe or kayak, on a large farm, with plenty of walks and groves of old milkwood trees. Meals are served safari-style in the outside lapa. R990 per person for accommodation and all meals, as well as some guided walks and kayaking, while self-catering in one of two cottages, costs R350 per person.

Stanford River Lodge 4km from the centre, exit from Queen Victoria Street ☎028 341 0444 or 082 378 1935, ⓦ www .stanfordriverlodge.co.za. Newly built, upmarket self-catering cottages or B&B on the river, perfect for swimming and canoeing in summer, with uninterrupted views and a swimming pool too. All the units are sunny, bright, airy and modern, and owners Mike and Valda Finch will make sure you have a good time. Doubles from R700.

Restaurants

Mariana's Bistro and Home Deli Du Toit St ☎028 341 0272. Innovative and reasonably priced country food in the owners' Victorian cottage, with meals taken under the vines on the veranda. Food and wines are local, and many of the vegetables are picked from Mariana and Peter's garden. Good enough to draw Cape Town gourmands out for the day, and you'll need to book a couple of months beforehand. Thurs–Sun noon–4pm, with last lunch order at 2pm.

Paprika Shortmarket St ☎028 341 0662. Delicious Mediterranean-style dinners made using local ingredients, including salmon. There are two vegetarian dishes, and home-baked bread. Nightly except Tues.

Peregrine Farm Stall Queen Victoria St ☎028 341 0386. Besides selling vegetables and breads, and local wines, this has a café serving breakfast and light lunches, including a traditional Sun roast. Daily 8.30am–4pm.

Stanford Gallery Art Café Queen Victoria St. Daytime venue where you can enjoy coffee and cake surrounded by locally produced artworks.

De Kelders

Continuing around Walker Bay, **DE KELDERS**, a haphazard and treeless settlement, stares from bleak cliffs across the bay to fashionable Hermanus. It surpasses the latter as whale-watching venue and has a marvellous, long, sandy beach, but is too recently established to draw the crowds.

At the end of Cliff Road is a car park from which you can clamber down to the **Klipgat Strandloper Caves**, excavated in the early 1990s, when evidence was unearthed of modern human habitation from 80,000 years ago. The caves became unoccupied for a few thousand years, after which they were used again by Khoisan people, 20,000 years ago. Shells, middens, tools and bones were uncovered, some of these now displayed in the South African Museum in Cape Town. From the caves, the waymarked **Duiwelsgats hiking trail** runs east for 7km as far as Gansbaai and is a good way to explore this beautiful coastline.

A few kilometres to the east is one of the most beautiful and expensive stays along this coastline. **Grootbos Private Nature Reserve** (☎028 384 8000, ⓦ www.grootbos.co.za; full board including all activities R2750 per person; minimum stay two nights) promotes itself as a "*fynbos* lodge", where experts guide you through the Western Cape's unique and richly varied plant kingdom. Garden Lodge, set in *fynbos*, has self-contained stone cottages with ethnic-chic furnishings, polished granite kitchen surfaces, temperature-controlled showers, multiple sun decks and views of the mountain from one side and the sea from the other. The rate includes a three-course dinner served in the main lodge, breakfast in your own cottage and a choice of activities, including guided horse-rides, walks or drives through the *fynbos* and conducted beach hikes. The other place to stay on the property is Forest

---

Dyer Island, Shark Alley and diving for denizens

How a black American came to be living on an island off South Africa in the early nineteenth century is something of a mystery. But according to records, Samson **Dyer** arrived here in 1806 and made a living collecting guano on the island that subsequently took his name.

Dyer Island is home to substantial **African penguin** and **seal breeding colonies**, both of which are prized morsels among great white sharks. So shark-infested is the channel between the island and the mainland at some times of year that it is known as **Shark Alley**, and these waters are used extensively by operators of great white viewing trips. In 1996 a group of West African castaways washed up here, having been put out to sea by the unscrupulous skipper of a Taiwanese merchant vessel whom they had paid to take them to the Far East, where they hoped to find work. One of them drowned in the process, but the rest (amazingly) survived five days at sea, including a stint down Shark Alley, clinging to pieces of timber and barrels.

Whale-watching and shark-cage diving operators

African Wings ☎028 312 2701, ⓦ www.africanwings.co.za. Popular whale-watching flights as well as one-day trips to see the Big Five, charter flights and safaris throughout Southern Africa.

Great White Adventure Centre ☎028 384 3846, ⓦ www.adventure-centre.co.za. Trips around a series of underground caves beneath the Hermanus/Gansbaai cliffs, which, in a bid to conserve their natural beauty, are not open to the general public. An unforgettable experience.

Marine Dynamics in the Great White House, Geelbek St, Kleinbaai, between De Kelders and Gansbaai ☎028 384 0406, ⓦ www.whalewatchsouthafrica.com. Take an unforgettable journey into the domain of the southern right whale. Sightings guaranteed July–Dec.

Shark Diving Unlimited Swart St, Kleinbaai ☎028 384 2787, ⓦ www.sharkdivingunlimited .com. Four-hour trips hours depending on how long the sharks take to show up.

Lodge, alongside a grove of milkwood trees. If you don't want to stay, you can experience the place on one of their **day excursions** from Grootbos (R950), led by a professional guide; morning and afternoon tea and a gourmet lunch are included in the price.

Practicalities

De Kelders has few facilities, but it is gradually beginning to shake off its reputation as the backwater of the Whale Coast, with a number of decent **places to stay**. For **refreshments** the only place is *Coffee on the Rocks* (☎028 384 2017; winter Wed–Sun 9am–5pm; summer 9am–late) on Cliff Street, a small, quirky eatery that does great coffee, cakes and light meals, with a deck in an unsurpassed position for whale watching. Booking is absolutely essential as it is very popular.

Accommodation

Ama-Krokka 28 Vyfer St ☎ 028 384 2776, ⓦ www.ama-krokka.co.za. B&B accommodation in two private suites in a house situated in a nature reserve with views of bird life and *fynbos*. Doubles R600.

Cliff Lodge 6 Cliff St ☎ 028 384 0983, ⓦ www.clifflodge.co.za. A stylish seafront guesthouse, perched on the cliffs of De Kelders, with breathtaking views from all four luxurious bedrooms and spacious penthouse suite. You can walk to the

secluded beach and swim in the ocean, frolic in the splash pool, or enjoy cappuccinos while whale-watching from the deck. Doubles from R1100.

De Kelders B&B Steyn St ☎ 028 384 0045, ⓦ www.dekelders.co.za. Simply furnished rooms in a house perched on the water's edge with superb views of Walker Bay from your very own viewing deck. Doubles from R800.

Gansbaai and Danger Point

GANSBAAI is a workaday place, economically dependent on its fishing industry and the seafood canning factory at the harbour. This gives the place a more gutsy feel than the surrounding holiday lands, but there's little reason to spend time here unless you want to engage in **great white shark safaris**, Gansbaai's other major industry, an appropriately competitive and cut-throat business with operators engaged in a blind feeding frenzy to attract punters. Boats set out from Gansbaai to **Dyer Island** (see box, p.195), east of Danger Point, where great white sharks come to feed on the resident colony of seals. Sharks are baited, but while you do stand a chance of seeing one, sightings are certainly not guaranteed, but boat trips usually emphasize other marine life sightings. For more information, contact the Gansbaai **tourist office** (Mon–Fri 9am–1pm & 2–5pm, Sat 10am–2pm; ☎028 384 1439, ⓦ www.gansbaaiinfo.com).

Danger Point, the southernmost point of Walker Bay, is where British naval history was allegedly made. True to its name, the Point lured the ill-fated HMS *Birkenhead* onto its hidden rocks on February 26, 1852. As was the custom, the captain of the troopship gave the order "Every man for himself." Displaying true British pluck, the soldiers are said to have lined up in their ranks on deck where they stood stock-still, knowing that if one man broke ranks it would lead to a rush that might overwhelm the lifeboats carrying women and children to safety. The precedent of "women and children first", which became known as the **Birkenhead Drill**, was thus established, even though 445 lives were lost in the disaster.

The Whale Coast interior: Elim and Bredasdorp

A good reason to venture along the network of dirt roads that crisscrosses the Whale Coast interior is to visit **ELIM**, a Moravian mission station 40km northwest of Agulhas, founded in 1824. The whole village is a National Monument of streets lined with thatched, whitewashed houses and fig trees. There's nothing twee about this very undeveloped and untouristy place – there isn't even a bottle store, and facilities amount to a couple of tiny shops.

The **tourist office** in Church Street (Mon–Sat 9am–12.30pm & 1.30–5pm; ☎028 482 1806) provides brochures about the area. **Tours** (R35, by arrangement) of the village start at the tourist office and take in the oldest house in the settlement, the church, the restored water mill where wheat is still ground, and the pottery studio. There's also a memorial commemorating the **emancipation of slaves** in 1834, the only such monument in South Africa; its presence reflects the fact that numerous freed slaves found refuge in mission stations like Elim.

The only **accommodation** is the community-run *Elim Guesthouse* (☎028 482 1715; doubles R320; dinner available on request), a newly renovated 1901 thatched home. For a cup of tea or a **snack**, try the *Old Mill Tea Room* (also run by the community, and open by arrangement; contact the tourist office).

Bredasdorp

BREDASDORP lies on the main routes to Cape Agulhas, Arniston and De Hoop Nature Reserve. The **tourism bureau** (☎028 435 7185, ⓦwww .tourismcapeagulhas.co.za), in Long Street, serves the entire region and produces an excellent booklet with all the information and maps you could desire to explore it. Although it doesn't merit an overnight stay Bredasdorp does offer two good reasons to stop off. One is **Kapula Candles**, at the corner of Petterson Road and First Avenue, (Mon–Fri 9am–5.30pm, Sat 9am–1pm; ☎028 424 2829, ⓦwww.kapulacandles.com), which started as a cottage industry and now supplies its beautifully crafted candles to shops throughout South Africa, with outlets in Germany. The factory shop has a café where you can get a decent cup of coffee surrounded by colourful candles, or outside in the herbarium. Close to Kapula is **Bel Don**, with quality goose-down products – from duvets to African-print tea-cosies. The **Shipwreck Museum** at 6 Independent St (Mon–Fri 9am–4.45pm, Sat & Sun 11am–4pm; R10) displays an interesting array of items retrieved from the many dashed vessels that have gone down off the treacherous coastline.

At 22 All Saints St (R319 to De Hoop), the earthy orange and purple *Julian's* (☎028 425 1201; Mon–Sat 9am–5pm & 6.30–8pm) serves light **lunches** such as grilled sardine fishcakes, and chicken and sweetcorn soup, and frothy lemon meringue tarts with coffee, in a large sunny building which doubles as a gallery, with paintings by local artists for sale. It also houses a ceramics workshop with pieces for sale. Should you want to stay over, you'll find the most stylish **rooms** in town here (doubles from R560).

Cape Agulhas and around

Along the east flank of the Danger Point promontory, the rocky and shallow coastline with heavy swells and strong currents makes this one of South Africa's most treacherous stretches of coast – one that has claimed over 250 wrecks and around 2500 lives. Its rocky terrain also accounts for the lack of a coastal road from Gansbaai and Danger Point to **Cape Agulhas**, the southernmost tip of Africa.

The plain around the southern tip has been declared the **Agulhas National Park** to conserve its estimated two thousand species of indigenous plant and marine and intertidal life as well as a cultural heritage which includes shipwrecks and archeological sites – stone hearths, pottery and shell middens have been discovered. There are no facilities apart from a **tea shop and restaurant** inside the terrific **Agulhas Lighthouse** (daily 8am–5pm; R15), commissioned in 1849. At the top, reached by a series of steep ladders, there are vertiginous views and some interesting exhibits about lighthouses around South Africa and elsewhere in the world. Dinners here at the *Lighthouse Restaurant* (T 028 435 7580; daily 8am–10pm) are charming, punctuated by flashes from the lighthouse beam.

The actual tip of the continent is marked by a rock and plaque about 1km from the lighthouse, towards Suiderstrand. Following the dirt road to **Suiderstrand** itself takes you to some beautiful, undeveloped beaches with rock pools to explore, and is definitely the best part of Agulhas.

Struisbaai, a small collection of holiday homes, about 6km east of Agulhas, has a nice harbour and long sandy beaches, but is unappealing when it's crowded in the summer. You're better off staying in Agulhas itself, unless you're **backpacking** – *Cape Agulhas Backpackers* (T 082 372 3354, W www.capeagulhasbackpackers.com; dorms R80, doubles R200, en-suite doubles R250, cottages sleeping two R350) is the only budget place around Agulhas, with camping, dorms, doubles and self-catering cottages with a pool, garden and good bedding throughout. It's run by a couple who are big on helping you enjoy the outdoors and will organize boating, kiteboarding, riding and other activities around Struisbaai, and also arrange pick-ups from Botrivier or Swellendam for those without their own transport.

Practicalities

L'AGULHAS, the rather windblown settlement associated with the southern tip, consists of a small collection of holiday houses and a few shops. It's reached by heading inland on the R316 to Bredasdorp, where the road splits, the more westerly branch (the R319) continuing 43km on to Agulhas, while the other fork leads to Arniston.

The smartest **accommodation** in town is the *Agulhas Country Lodge* on Main Road (T 028 435 7650, W www.agulhascountrylodge.com; doubles from R800), in a relatively grand stone building perched halfway up a hillside. All rooms have sea views from private balconies; excellent seafood **dinners** provide another inducement to stay. Uniquely positioned on the edge of the Agulhas National Park, with miles of undeveloped beach to explore to the west, is the sea-facing 🌿 *Pebble Beach* (T 028 435 7270 or 082 774 5008, W www .pebble-beach.co.za; doubles R600), in Suiderstrand (follow signs to the Southern Tip of Africa and then 4km beyond for Pebble Beach), with two en-suite rooms, in a modern thatched house with white beds and wooden floors, where you can smell the *fynbos* wafting in from the dunes in front of your room. They also rent a self-catering thatched cottage right on the strand, which sleeps six people. *Southermost* B&B, on the corner of Van Breda and Lighthouse streets (℡028 435 6565, ⓦwww.southermost.co.za; closed winter months; doubles R490), is a well-loved and rather dilapidated historic beach cottage opposite the tidal pool with an indigenous garden sloping down to the water's edge, but doesn't welcome smokers, kids or pets. Breakfasts are vegetarian.

Arniston

After the cool deep blues of the Atlantic to the west, the azure of the Indian Ocean at **ARNISTON** is startling, made all the more dazzling by the white dunes interspersed with rocky ledges. Reached on the R316, 24km southeast of Bredasdorp, and 220km from Cape Town, Arniston is one of the best places to stay along the Whale Coast– if you want nothing more than beach life. The colours may be tropical, but the wind can howl unpredictably here, as anywhere else along the Cape coast, and when it does, there's nothing much to do. The village is known to locals by its Afrikaans name, Waenhuiskrans ("wagon-house cliff"), after a cliff containing a huge cave 1500m south of town, which *trekboers* reckoned was spacious enough for a wagon and span of oxen (the largest thing they could think of). The English name derives from a British ship, the *Arniston*, which hit the rocks here in 1815.

The shallow seas, so treacherous for vessels, provide Arniston with the safest swimming waters along the Whale Coast. Apart from sea bathing, the principal attraction is **Kassiesbaai**, a district of starkly beautiful limewashed cottages, now declared a National Monument and home to coloured fishing families that have for generations made their living here. Its beautifully simple dwellings invariably show up in coffee-table books whenever picturesque images of fishing villages are called for. But Kassiesbaai sits a little uneasily as a living community, as it's also a bit of a theme park for visitors stalking the streets with their cameras. More positively, all the holiday accommodation is in the adjacent new section of town where you'll find a number of exclusive holiday homes all built in the whitewashed, thatched-roof cottage style of the area. The only regular entertainment here is wandering down to the harbour at high tide to watch fishing boats being shoved down the slipway by a tractor that ends up half submerged. You can swim next to the slipway or at **Roman Beach**, the main swimming beach, just along the coast as you head south from the harbour. In season, keep your eyes open for **southern right whales**.

Heading north through Kassiesbaai at low tide, you can walk 5km along an unspoilt beach unmarred by buildings until you reach an unassuming fence – resist the temptation to climb over this, as it marks the boundary of the local testing range for military material and missiles. Heading south of the harbour for 1500m along spectacular cliffs, you'll reach the vast **cave** after which the town is named. The walk is worth doing simply for the *fynbos*-covered dunes you'll cross on the way. From the car park right by the cave, it's a short signposted walk down to the dunes and the cave, which can only be reached at low tide. The rocks can be slippery and have sharp sections, so be sure to wear shoes with tough soles and a good grip.

Practicalities

There's no public transport to Arniston. The choice for **eating** is limited. *Die Waenhuis* (Mon–Sat 8am–6.30pm), on Du Preez Street (a continuation of the national road), is decorated to resemble a fishermen's tavern and serves good fish and chips. The Arniston fishermen's wives run a small eating place in the Kassiesbaai Craft Shop (booking required on ☎028 445 9760; ask for Lilian Newman), where they'll cook up a three-course traditional fisherman's meal with the catch of the day brought in by their menfolk. The *Arniston Hotel* has outdoor seating to take in the sea views, and does fabulous, blow-out breakfasts, and pleasing fresh fish dinners; it also holds the town's only **bar**.

You can buy fresh fish from the fishermen at the slipway near the hotel. There's a small **supply store** attached to *Die Waenhuis* selling basics, but if you're self-catering it's best to stock up at the Super Spar on Church Street in Bredasdorp.

Accommodation

Accommodation is limited to one hotel – the best place to stay if your budget allows it – some self-catering cottages and a handful of B&Bs, which get snapped up quickly during school holidays and over weekends. The village is small and not all properties are numbered, so be sure to get directions from the main road if you're renting a house. Etna (☎028 445 9657, ⓦwww.arniston-etnas.co.za) rents out a number of cottages in the area.

Arniston Hotel ☎028 445 9000, ⓦwww .arnistonhotel.com. A luxurious and well-run hotel, dominating the seafront, with every comfort for a dreamy seaside night, including a spa with massage and beauty treatments. The best rooms have a fireplace, or a sea-facing balcony. If it's way out of your budget, go during the week or in winter months when prices drop. *Doubles R1100 pool-facing, R1400 sea-facing.*

Arniston Seaside Cottages Well signposted from the national road, along the street behind the hotel ☎028 445 9772, ⓦwww.arniston-online.co.za. Limewashed self-catering cottages, fully equipped and serviced. Out of season rates are per person, but in season (Jan, Easter school holidays & Dec) you pay for the number of beds in the unit. R220 per person.

Kassiesbaai Cottage Kassiesbaai ☎028 445 9760. Lilian Newman rents out her

modestly furnished traditional fisherman's cottage, which contains three double rooms for self-catering. R450 for six people, extra for bedding.

Southwinds Huxham St, just behind the *Arniston Hotel* ☎028 445 9303, ⓦwww .arniston-info.co.za. Well-appointed double suites, looking onto a courtyard garden. The owners are friendly and prices drop in winter. B&B doubles R660.

Waenhuis Caravan Park Along the mainroad into Arniston, 300m from the centre ☎028 445 9620. Pitch your own tent or stay in one of the four- or six-bed en-suite bungalows. The cheaper, older ones don't provide linen, and you'll pay a bit more to have all the mod cons including TV. The place can get crowded and very noisy over weekends and peak season. R324 per four-person bungalow.

De Hoop Nature Reserve

De Hoop (daily 7am–6pm; R24) is the **wilderness highlight** of the Western Cape. Although the reserve could technically be done as a day-trip from Hermanus, you'll find it far more rewarding to come here for a night or more. The five-day, portered **Whale Trail** hike is one of South Africa's best walks and among the finest wildlife experiences in the world, though, inevitably, it is heavily booked out.

The breathtaking coastline is edged by bleached sand dunes standing 90m high in places, and rocky formations that at one point open to the sea in a

▲ De Hoop Nature Reserve

massive craggy arch. The flora and fauna are impressive, too, encompassing 86 species of mammal, 260 different birds and 1500 varieties of plants, and it's reckoned to be the ultimate place in South Africa (surpassing even Hermanus and De Kelders) to see **southern right whales**. If you're here for a couple of days in season, you will not fail to see whales, and sometimes dozens of whales are in evidence at one time, as well as dolphins. July to October is the best time, but you stand a very good chance of a sighting from June through to November. Inland, rare **Cape mountain zebra**, **bontebok** and other **antelope** congregate on a plain near the reserve accommodation. Apart from bathing, and scrambling over rocks and sand dunes, there are mountain-biking trails (bring your own bike as there's nowhere to rent one). The huge rock pools at Koppie Allen provide hours of pleasure.

The five-day, four-night **Whale Trail** (☎028 425 5020, ⓦwww.capenature .org.za) follows a spectacularly beautiful route from the Potberg Mountains 55km along the coast to Koppie Alleen. Only moderately difficult, it's also marvellously quiet: besides your own group (and the whales) you won't see another soul and the only prints you'll come across are those of eland, baboons and ostriches. Even the porters invisibly pick up your goods and desposit them ahead of you, at huts of two or three rooms with bunk beds, idyllically located along the deserted coast. To go in whale season, though, you'll need to book a year in advance and take any date offered. Bookings are for a minimum of six and maximum of twelve people (with no children under 8), and you pay for six even if there are just two of you. You have to undertake the whole trail, not join it for a day or two. Prices are between R700 and R850 per person with R300 extra for portage.

Practicalities

De Hoop is along a signposted dirt road that spurs off the R319 as it heads out of Bredasdorp, 50km to its west. **Accommodation** (Mon–Fri 7.30am–4pm;

☎021 659 3500, ⓦwww.capenature.co.za), usually booked up at weekends, includes a **campsite** with each site shaded by a milkwood tree, and two-bedroomed **self-catering cottages** (R480) with a cooker, fridge and kitchen utensils and bedding. More expensive, but far more spacious, sleeping six, are the three thatched cottages on the lip of the estuary, also with two bedrooms, but with more privacy and a large comfortable living room (R950); it's a twenty-minute drive from here to the coast. Best of all, if there's a group of you, at the beach itself, is the newly renovated, splendidly isolated huddle of ⚡**thatched cottages** at Koppie Alleen. The site couldn't be more thrilling, overlooking a bay full of whales (R3750 per night for six people, and R500 per person for up to two additional people).

Overnight visitors are required to reach the reserve by 4pm. There are **no food supplies** at De Hoop, so be sure to stock up with everything before you come – the nearest shop is 15km away, in the hamlet of **Ouplaas**.

If accommodation is full within De Hoop, there are some options outside the reserve. Closest to the gates, and offering full catering, is *Buchu Bushcamp* (☎028 542 1602, ⓦwww. buchu-bushcamp.com; B&B doubles R930) in five open-plan timber and thatch chalets, three of them sleeping four, with good linen and fittings, connected by a wooden walkway to a central dining room, lounge and bar. The whole feel is of a gracious, thatched safari-camp, set in *fynbos*. There is also a guide who can help plan your day or take you out on a nature walk. The coast itself is some 15km off. Prices, as elsewhere, are higher in summer, but surprisingly low during whale season itself. East of Buchu, and 4km beyond the hamlet of Ou Plaas towards Potberg, is *Verfheuwel Farm* (☎028 542 1038, ⓔverfheuwel@xsinet.co.za; from R250) with very reasonable self-catering or B&B rates in a cottage attached to the main farmhouse. It's run by hospitable Afrikaner farming folk who can bring dinner to your cottage if you ask in advance. The country-style cottage sleeps a couple, with beds in the living area for children. The garden is beautiful and has a swimming pool. If *Verfheuwel* is full, owner Matti can direct you to other friends and relatives in the area with farm accommodation.

The Overberg interior

Along, and just off the N2, **Caledon** merits a quick visit for its refreshing hot springs, while a few towns are worth visiting for a night or two. Closer to Cape Town, **Greyton** makes a perfect weekend break, with enough good food, walks and lounging in garden cafés to occupy you for two nights. Nearby, South Africa's oldest mission station, **Genadendal**, a six-kilometre excursion west of Greyton, is also worth a look around. **Swellendam**, futher along the N2 is often treated as the first night stop along the Garden Route, but can be used as a base to visit **De Hoop Nature Reserve** for the day, or to see some antelope and ostriches in the **Bontebok National Park**.

Caledon

The first impression of **CALEDON**, some 111km east of Cape Town on the N2, is of huge, cathedral-like grain silos that dwarf its church spires. It's worth a stop to indulge in its hot spring, the Caledon **spa** (Tues–Sat 10am–7pm; R100; ☎028 214 5100), which offers a gamut of physical indulgences –

wonderfully relaxing and rejuvenating, though in an artificial setting. The swimming pools, and use of the saunas, steam room and gym are all included in the price; towels are provided and robes can be rented. When you arrive, the crowds you'll see are not going to the spa, but to the next-door casino. If you fancy a flutter, you can try your luck at one of the scores of slot machines lined up inside the large gambling hall, which also has a number of gaming tables.

Greyton

GREYTON, a tranquil village 46km north of Caledon, and 145km from Cape Town, is a favourite weekend destination for Capetonians, based around a core of Georgian and Victorian buildings, shaded by grand old oaks, and tucked away at the edge of the Riviersonderend (meaning "river with no end") Mountains. With good guesthouses, it is a great place to unwind, stroll and potter about in the handful of galleries, antique shops and cafés, and sample locally produced Von Geusau Belgian chocolates and chocolate cakes. It also boasts some good places to walk, most notably the superb **Boesmanskloof Traverse** hike, which crosses the mountains to a point 14km from McGregor.

The Boesmanskloof Traverse

The fourteen-kilometre **Boesmanskloof Traverse** takes you from the gentle, oak-lined streets of **Greyton** across the Riviersonderend mountain range to the glaring Karoo scrubland around the town of **McGregor** (p.251). The stark contrast over so short a distance is staggering, made all the more so by the fact that no direct roads connect the two towns; to drive from one to the other involves a circuitous two-hour journey.

The classic way to cover the Traverse is to walk from Greyton to **Die Galg** (14km from McGregor), where people commonly spend the night, returning the same way to Greyton the following day. The Traverse rises and falls a fair bit, so you'll have to contend with a lot of uphill walking, but the route can easily be completed in a day if you're reasonably fit, and you can still have a rewarding outing venturing only part of the way and returning to Greyton for the evening. A decent day's walk takes you to **Oak Falls**, 9km from Greyton. Composed of a series of cascades, it's the highlight of the route, its most impressive feature being a large pool where you can rest and swim in cola-coloured water.

The walk takes you through numerous species of wonderful montane *fynbos*, and between July and October you can find yourself walking through magnificent groves of flowering king proteas. Mammals include small antelope, caracals, baboons and dassies, though it's unlikely you'll see many of them.

Trail practicalities

You're free to walk the first 5km of the trail and back, but to complete the whole route from Greyton to Die Galg – numbers are limited to fifty people per day – you will need a **permit** (R25 per person per day). Over weekends, the trail gets extremely full and permits must be arranged in advance through the Greyton Tourism Bureau. You get a **map** when you buy the permit, although you don't really need one as the Traverse is very clearly marked out. The walk can be strenuous, so make sure you're fit and have good shoes. It's also worth noting that this is an area of winter rainfall; summers are hot and dry.

As for **accommodation**, there's *Whipstock Farm* (see p.252) 4km beyond Die Galg (the owner can collect you free of charge from Die Galg), or the overnight dorms at Die Galg (☎023 625 1735; ask for Mr Oosthuizen), equipped with a fridge, cooker and beds (but no bedding).

There's no public transport to Greyton. The best driving route is to take the signposted, sealed R406 from the N2, just west of Caledon. The **Greyton Tourism Bureau** at 29 Main St (Mon–Sat 10am–5pm, Sun 10am–3pm; ☎028 254 9414, ⓦ www.greyton.net), along the main road as you come into town, has lists of accommodation and rents out bicycles for R15 an hour.

Accommodation

It's worth staying somewhere with a fireplace if you're here in winter, as it can be cold in this mountainous terrain, and conversely look for a pool in summer. Most places charge more for a one-night stay, as it is primarily a weekend destination, not on the way to anywhere else, and there's little accommodation to be found in the lower price ranges.

Acorns On Oak 2 Oak St ☎028 254 9567, ⓦ www.acorns-on-oak.co.za. Five luxurious rooms each with underfloor heating, espresso machine, loft lounge and garden-facing patio on this riverfront property. Well-priced choice for a romantic weekend, with no children allowed. There's also a 12-metre heated pool and loungers in a lovely garden. Doubles R750.

Auberge Greyton On the corner of Oak St and Main Rd ☎028 254 9192. Simple, uncluttered farm-style rooms – if you're planning on hiking and just need a bed for the night (or two), this friendly and reasonable B&B is a good bet. Doubles R450 for one night only, R360 if you stay for two nights or longer.

Barnards Boutique Hotel 16 Main Rd ☎028 254 9394, ⓦ wwwbarnardshotel.co.za. Modern and comfortable rooms in a new and fashionable gay-owned establishment with a lovely pool and a great bar. Doubles R650–950.

Guinea Fowl Ds Botha St ☎028 254 9550. Guesthouse with en-suite rooms and serving a full English breakfast. Doubles R550.

High Hopes 89 Main Rd ☎028 254 9898, ⓦ www.highhopes.co.za. One of the best B&Bs in town, in a beautiful country-style home set in magnificent gardens with a huge ornamental pond and a swimming pool. Besides three rooms, there's a self-contained unit with a kitchen, which can be taken on a B&B or self-catering basis. A variety of therapies including massage, are on offer too, and it's ideal for women travelling alone. Doubles R640–950.

Eating and drinking

The town has a Saturday **market** at the corner of Main Road and Cross Market Street (10am–noon), to which locals bring their produce: organic vegetables, fabulous and well-priced cheeses, decadent cakes, breads, biscuits and preserves; also on sale are secondhand books and bric-a-brac. Otherwise, there is a limited range of food on sale at the small deli at the *Oak and Vigne Café*. The nicest place for a **drink** is at *Barnard's Boutique Hotel* on Main Road. Food at the restaurants tends to be quite sophisticated, creative, nouvelle cuisine.

254 8 Ds Botha St ☎028 254 9373. Book a candlelit veranda table for fine, innovative food, fun and a welcoming atmosphere. There is always something delicious for vegetarians too. Moderate prices. Wed, Fri & Sat dinner only, booking essential.

Abbey Rose Main Rd ☎028 254 9470. Garden setting to enjoy salads or tea and scones. Open daily 9am–4.30pm, plus dinner Fri & Sat.

Barnard's Boutique Hotel 16 Main Rd ☎028 254 9394. Nice setting for a sundowner, with wine and tapas on the *stoep*, or a fireplace inside. The big screen at the pub draws sports fans.

Jam Tin In the township 2km south of town ☎028 254 9075 or 076 875 8737. From her humble 200-year-old family home, Dora cooks a traditional, inexpensive, three-course Cape Malay meal in the evening. Booking necessary and directions given to her home.

Oak and Vigne Café Ds Botha St ☎028 254 9037. Highly popular, situated in an old cottage with an oak-shaded terrace where you can savour reasonably priced Mediterranean-influenced country breakfasts, teas & gourmet lunches daily.

Genadendal

GENADENDAL, whose name means "valley of grace", was founded in 1737 by Moravians, and some of the ochre and earthy-pink architecture hints at Central European influences. Just 6km from Greyton, it's definitely worth roaming around. The village's focus is around **Church Square**, dominated by a very Germanic church building dating back to 1891. The old bell outside dates back to the eighteenth century, when it became the centre of a flaming row between the local farmers and the mission station. The scrap broke out when missionary Georg Schmidt annoyed the local white farmers by forming a small Christian congregation with impoverished Khoi – who were on the threshold of extinction – and giving refuge to maltreated labourers from local farms. What really got the farmers' goat was the fact that while they, white Christians, were illiterate, Schmidt was teaching native people, whom they considered uncivilized, to read and write. The Dutch Reformed Church, under the control of the Dutch East India Company, waded in when Schmidt began baptizing converts, and prohibited the mission from ringing the bell which called the faithful to prayer.

In 1838 Genadendal established the first teacher training college in the country, which the government closed in 1926, on the grounds that coloured people didn't need tertiary education and should be employed as workers on local farms – a policy that effectively ground the community into poverty. In 1995, in recognition of the mission's role, Nelson Mandela renamed his official residence in Cape Town "Genadendal".

Today, the population of this principally coloured town numbers around four thousand people, adhering to a variety of Christian sects – no longer just Moravianism. The **Mission Museum** (Mon–Thurs 9am–1pm & 2–5pm, Fri 9am–3.30pm, Sat 9am–noon) adjacent to Church Square, is moderately interesting, as is a wander through the town, down to the rural graveyard, spiked with old tombstones.

Swellendam and around

On the N2, 97km east of Caledon and 220km from Cape Town, **SWELLENDAM** is an attractive historic town at the foot of the Langeberg. With one of the best country museums in South Africa, it's a congenial stop along the N2 between Cape Town and the Garden Route. And because of its ample supply of good accommodation and its position – poised between the coastal De Hoop Nature Reserve and the Langeberg – it's a suitable base for spending a day or two exploring this part of the Overberg, with the Bontebok National Park, stomping ground of an attractive type of antelope, close at hand to the south.

South Africa's third-oldest white settlement, Swellendam was established in 1745 by Baron Gustav van Imhoff, a visiting Dutch East India Company bigwig. He was deeply concerned about the "moral degeneration" of burghers who were trekking further and further from Cape Town and out of Company control. Of no less concern to the Baron was the loss of revenue from these "vagabonds", who were neglecting to pay the company for the right to hold land and were fiddling their annual tax returns. Following a brief hiccup in 1795, when burghers declared a "free republic" (quickly extinguished when Britain occupied the Cape), the town grew into a prosperous rural centre known for its wagon-making, and for being the last "civilized" port of call for trekboers heading out into the interior. The income generated from this helped build Swellendam's gracious homes, many of which went up in smoke in the fire of 1865, which razed much of the town centre.

Arrival, information and activities

Greyhound, Intercape and Translux **buses** between Cape Town and Port Elizabeth pull in diagonally opposite the *Swellengrebel Hotel*, 91 Voortrek St, in the centre of town, while the Baz Bus will drop you off at any of the central accommodation. Swellendam has a very switched-on **tourist office** at 36 Voortrek St (Mon–Fri 9am–5pm, Sat & Sun 9am–1pm; ☎028 514 2770, @infoswd@swellenmun.co.za), which provides frank and helpful advice about local attractions and can book accommodation. The town is built along a very long main road with no traffic lights; it's most attractive at either end, with a mundane shopping area in the middle. The eastern end is dominated by the museum complex, and is nearest to the mountain reserve for hiking or horse-riding. This is also the area where you'll find the backpacker lodge.

The best thing to do in Swellendam is to go **horse-riding** in the forests and mountains at the eastern edge of town, securely seated in a western-style saddle. Two Feathers Horse Trails (☎082 494 8279 or 082 485 4379, @www.twofeathers.co.za) offers riding by the hour, or you can do a full-day outing with picnic lunch included. The horses are well cared for, the guide, Barry, patient and responsive, and there are mounts suitable for beginners or experienced riders.

The Town

The only building in the centre to survive the town's 1865 fire is the Cape Dutch-style **Oefeningshuis**, 36 Voortrek St, which now houses the tourist office. Built in 1838, it was first used as a place for religious activity, then as a school for freed slaves, and has surreal-looking clocks with frozen hands carved into either gable end, below which there's a real clock above the entrance. Diagonally opposite and slightly east at no. 11, the **Dutch Reformed Church**, dating from 1910, incorporates Gothic windows, a Baroque spire, Renaissance portico elements and Cape Dutch gables into a wedding cake of a building that agreeably holds its own, against the odds, and certainly still draws a good crowd on Sundays.

On the east side of town, a short way from the centre, is the excellent **Drostdy Museum**, 18 Swellegrebel St (Mon–Fri 9am–4.45pm, Sat & Sun 10am–3.45pm; R15). It's a collection of historic buildings arranged around large grounds, with a lovely nineteenth-century Cape garden. The centrepiece is the *drostdy* itself, built in 1747 as the seat of the *landdrost*, a magistrate-cum-commissioner sent out by the Dutch East India Company to control the outer reaches of its territory. The building conforms to the beautiful limewashed, thatched and shuttered Cape Dutch style of the eighteenth century, but the furnishings are of nineteenth-century vintage. From the rear garden of the *drostdy* you can stroll along a path and across Drostdy Street to **Mayville**, a middle-class Victorian homestead from the mid-nineteenth century with an old rose garden. The **Old Gaol**, with thatched roof, and thick, whitewashed walls has been converted into the best daytime eatery in town, while the **Utamaduni Gallery** next door with good crafts for sale.

On a far flightier note, the **Sulina Faerie Sanctuary**, 33 Buitenkant St (Thurs–Sun 9am–4.30pm; R10), is the result of one Swellendam resident's obsession, housing hundreds of fairy statuettes and images. Its mystical garden has gnomes, pixies and miniature castles hidden in the overgrowth.

Accommodation

Anyone who enjoys the atmosphere of historic houses will be spoilt for choice in Swellendam, where places to stay in Cape Dutch and Georgian houses are ten a penny, and rates tend to be pretty reasonable.

Augusta de Mist 3 Human St ☏ 028 514 2425, ⓦ www.augustademist.co.za. A 200-year-old homestead with three beautifully renovated cottages, two garden suites and a family unit, mostly with fireplaces and all with percale linen. A rambling terraced garden and a pool complete the picture. R700–1200 per person.

Cypress Cottage 3 Voortrek St ☏ 028 514 3296, ⓦ www.cypresscottage.co.za. Five charming rooms, decorated with antiques, in the back garden of a grand house, one of the oldest in town, as well as two rooms inside the main house. Good value. Doubles R600.

Eenuurkop Huisie 8km from town on the Ashton road ☏ 028 514 1447. Two self-catering cottages, one with three bedrooms, the other with one, in a stunning setting with great views and access to mountain walks. R600 per small cottage.

Herberg Roosje Van De Kaap 5 Drostdy St ☏ 028 514 3001, ⓦ www.roosjevandekaap.com. A popular B&B in a beautiful house right near the museum, with a pool, excellent and friendly service and a good reputation for candlelit dinners, though some of the rooms are rather small. Discounts for cash payments. Doubles R600.

Klippe Rivier Homestead Signposted off the western end of town ☏ 028 514 3341, ⓦ www.klipperivier.com. Swellendam's most formal and luxurious accommodation, in a beautiful 1825 Cape Dutch homestead with six utterly comfortable country-style bedrooms, each with a patio or veranda, a secluded cottage and saltwater swimming pool, gorgeous gardens and fabulous breakfasts. No under-10s. Doubles R2000.

Lulu's B&B 10 Voortrek St ☏ 028 514 2202 or 082 847 9523. A well-run B&B, centrally located, with two en-suite rooms and a self-catering loft apartment (sleeping up to eight) above. Doubles R350, apartment R150 per person for four people.

Swellendam Backpackers 5 Lichtenstein St ☏ 028 514 2648, ⓦ www.swellendambackpackers.co.za. Swellendam's only hostel is a friendly place, well situated near the Marloth Nature Reserve and museum, with a large campsite, dorms and decent doubles; staff can also arrange activities including horse-riding, mountain biking and canoeing. Children are also welcome, as there's lots of space, and while this isn't a big party place, there is a bar conveniently on the premises. En-suite doubles R250, dorms R80.

Swellendam Country Lodge 237 Voortrek St ☏ 028 514 3629, ⓦ www.swellendamlodge.com. Six rooms with separate entrances, reed ceilings, and elegant, uncluttered decor in muted hues. B&B doubles R500–660.

Eating

There's no shortage of decent places to eat in Swellendam – ranging from snack bars to formal restaurants where you can enjoy a romantic candlelit dinner – many of them in delightful old buildings. Most are on either end of the long main road.

The Old Gaol Coffee Shop Drostdy Museum, 26 Swellengrebel St ☏ 028 514 3847. Not the usual run-of-the-mill museum snack bar, this is a great place with indoor and outdoor seating where you can get fantastic coffee and cake, milk tart in a copper pan, and *roosterkoek* – traditional bread made on an open fire, with nice fillings. Open 8.30am–6pm.

The Old Mill 241–243 Voortrek St, west end ☏ 028 514 2790. Pleasant spot with daytime garden seating; satisfying, well-presented dinners, including starters such as deep-fried camembert with sesame seed coating, and main dishes of fish, pasta and game, with the advantage of a fireplace in winter. Moderately priced.

Roosje Van De Kaap 5 Drostdy St ☏ 028 514 3001. A highly rated, expensive restaurant offering traditional Cape food, with a great wine list – a good choice for a romantic candlelit dinner. Booking essential. Tues–Sun 7–11pm.

fare. Good for vegetarians. Moderate. Daily 9.30am–9pm, closed Sun eves.

Bontebok National Park

Just 6km south of Swellendam along the Breede River, the **Bontebok National Park** (May–Sept 7am–6pm; Oct–April 7am–7pm; ☎028 514 2735; day visitors R20, overnight visitors free) is a compact 28-square kilometre reserve at the foot of the Langeberg range that makes a relaxing overnight stop between Cape Town and the Garden Route. The park was established in 1931 to save the Cape's dwindling population of bontebok, an attractive antelope with distinctive cappuccino, chocolate-brown and white markings on its forehead and hindquarters. By 1930, hunting had reduced the number of animals to a mere thirty. Their survival has happily been secured and there are now three hundred of them in the park, as well as populations in other game and nature reserves in the province. There are no big cats in the park, but **mammals** you might encounter include rare Cape mountain zebra, red harte-beest and grey rhebok, and there are more than 120 **bird species**. It's also a rich environment for **fynbos**, with nearly five hundred species here, including erica, gladioli and proteas. Apart from game viewing, there are opportunities to swim in the Breede River, hike a couple of short nature trails and fish.

Self-catering 🏃 **accommodation** is available in ten, newly built, fully equipped chalets (R580 for two) or you can camp next to the river in your own tent. A **shop** at the park entrance sells drinks and sweets, but you'll need to bring your own food with you.

The Garden Route

The **Garden Route**, a slender stretch of coastal plain on the **N2** between **Mossel Bay** and **Storms River Mouth**, has a legendary status as South Africa's paradise – reflected in local names such as Garden of Eden and Wilderness. This soft, green, forested swath of nearly 200km, mapped in the colour section at the back of this book, is cut by rivers from the mountains to the north, tumbling down to its southern rocky shores and sandy beaches.

The **Khoikhoi** herders who lived off its natural bounty considered the area a paradise, calling it Outeniqua ("the man laden with honey"). Their Eden was quickly destroyed in the eighteenth century with the arrival of Dutch **woodcutters**, who had exhausted the forests around Cape Town and set about doing the same in Outeniqua, killing or dispersing the Khoikhoi and San in the process. Birds and animals suffered too from the encroachment of Europeans. In the 1850s, the Swedish naturalist Johan Victorin shot and feasted on the species he had come to study, some of which, including the endangered narina trogon, he noted were both "beautiful and good to eat".

Despite the dense appearance of the area, what you see today are only the remnants of one of Africa's great **forests**; much of the indigenous hardwoods have been replaced by exotic pine plantations, and the only milk and honey you'll find now is in the many shops servicing the Garden Route coastal resorts. **Conservation** has halted the wholesale destruction of the indigenous woodlands, but a huge growth in tourism and the influx of urbanites seeking a quiet life in the relatively crime-free Garden Route towns threatens to rob the area of its remaining tranquillity.

The Garden Route coast is dominated by three inlets – Mossel Bay, the Knysna lagoon and Plettenberg Bay – each with its own town. Oldest of these and closest to Cape Town is **Mossel Bay**, an industrial centre of modest charm, which marks the official start of the Garden Route. **Knysna**, though younger, exudes a well-rooted urban character and is the nicest of the coastal towns, with one major drawback – unlike **Plettenberg Bay**, its eastern neighbour, it has no beach of its own. A major draw, though, is the **Knysna forest** covering some of the hilly country around Knysna.

Between the coastal towns are some ugly modern holiday developments, but also some wonderful empty beaches and tiny coves, such as **Victoria Bay**, **Buffels Bay** and **Nature's Valley**. Best of all is the **Tsitsikamma National Park**, which has it all – indigenous forest, dramatic coastline, the pumping **Storms River Mouth** and South Africa's most popular hike, the **Otter trail**. If you're intending to use national-park accommodation at any of the parks in this chapter, consider booking in advance through SANParks (see p.40).

Most visitors take the Garden Route as a journey between Cape Town and **Port Elizabeth** (covered in Chapter 20), dallying for little more than a day or two for shopping, sightseeing or a taste of one of the many adventure sports on offer. The rapid passage cut by the excellent N2 makes it all too easy to have a fast scenic drive – and end up disappointed because you don't see that much from the road. To make the journey worthwhile, you'll need to slow down, take some detours off the highway and explore a little. To avoid having to drive the N2 in both directions, consider flying one of the legs (see below) or tackling the interior **Route 62** (see Chapter 19).

Travel practicalities

The **Garden Route** is probably the best-served stretch of South Africa for **transport**. Most user-friendly among the public transport options is the daily **Baz Bus** service between Cape Town and Port Elizabeth (℡021 439 2323, Ⓦwww.bazbus.co.za), which picks up passengers daily from accommodation at either end (7.15–8.30am). It provides a door-to-door service within the central districts of all the towns along the way, and has the advantage over the large intercity lines that it will happily carry outdoor gear, such as surfboards or mountain bikes. Although the buses take standby passengers if there's space available, you should book ahead to secure a seat.

Intercape, Greyhound and Translux **intercity buses** from Cape Town and Port Elizabeth are better for more direct journeys, stopping only at Mossel Bay, George, Wilderness, Sedgefield, Knysna and Storms River (the village, but not the Mouth, which is some distance away). These buses often don't go into town, letting passengers off at filling stations on the highway instead.

More of a day out than serious transport, the **Outeniqua Choo-Tjoe** is a goods train with passenger carriages attached, running the 30km between George and Mossel Bay (Mon–Sat: summer 2 daily, less frequently at other times; 2hr 45min; R65 single, R75 return) in both directions. The route changed in 2006 after serious flooding affected the scenic route to Knysna, and the new route isn't a patch on the old. You need to book your tickets a day ahead on ℡044 382 1361 or 044 801 8202. And finally, if time is tight, you may want to go by **air** to George at the west end of the Garden Route, served by scheduled flights from Cape Town, Johannesburg, Durban and Port Elizabeth.

Mossel Bay and around

MOSSEL BAY, a midsized town 397km east of Cape Town, gets a bad press from most South Africans, mainly because of the huge industrial facade it presents to the N2. Don't panic – the historic centre is a thoroughly pleasant contrast, set on a hill overlooking the small working harbour and bay, with one of the best **swimming** beaches along the southern Cape coast and an interesting museum. The town takes on a strong Afrikaans flavour over Christmas, when Karoo farmers and their families descend in droves to occupy its caravan parks and chalets. While Mossel Bay's modest attractions are unlikely to hold you for more than a night, it has some decent accommodation and a first-class restaurant, which make it a good place to pause before launching out along the Garden Route.

From Mossel Bay the R328 heads inland to connect with Oudtshoorn, 85km away (see p.256). A short way along this route is the **Robinson Pass** where there is a great family holidaying spot at the *Eight Bells Inn*, and the possibility of seeing game at **Botlierskop Private Game Reserve**.

The Garden Route is fast losing its reputation as the place to go for sun-soaking idleness or to commune with nature. Adrenaline and adventure are elbowing out these passive pursuits and now thrill-junkies go expressly to throw themselves off bridges, to gape into the jaws of great white sharks and to freewheel down scary mountain passes. The choice is broad – and widely spread across the entire length of the Garden Route. To help you plan, here are some highlights.

Abseiling Drop down a cliff face at the private Featherbed Nature Reserve (box on p.230), the entrance to the Knysna lagoon, or along the Kaaimans River gorge in Wilderness (p.221).

Bungee jumping The world's highest commercial jump is at Bloukrans Bridge (see box, p.240); you can also try bungee swinging, a jump with a twist, at Gouritz River Bridge near Mossel Bay (see p.216).

Canopy tours and ziplining Monkey around swinging from tree to tree in an indigenous forest, 30m above the forest floor (see box, p.248), or zing over waterfalls and across a river gorge (p.248).

Hiking There's a terrific circular one-day hike along the edge of the Robberg Peninsula (p.240), with a chance of seeing whales, dolphins and seals. Otherwise, there are quite a few longer and more challenging trails to attempt; see the box on pp.214–215.

Horse-riding Sit cowboy-style in a deep saddle at *Southern Comfort Western Horse Ranch*, between Knysna and Plettenberg Bay (see p.228). Or head out with an English saddle through African countryside near Plettenberg Bay, for *fynbos* and forest trails.

Mountain biking Tear down the hair-raising Swartberg Pass, starting out from Knysna or Oudtshoorn (p.256), or pedal your way in a slightly calmer fashion round the Homtini Cycle Route in the Knysna forest (see box, p.333).

River boat Go for a leisurely ferry ride down the spectacular Keurbooms river estuary where bird life is in abundance (see box, p.241).

Scenic excursions The Outeniqua Choo-Tjoe steam train passes through beautiful back-country between George and Mossel Bay (see opposite). With your own transport, try taking the old road just east of The Crags, winding your way down the fantastically scenic route to Nature's Valley (see p.244).

Whale, dolphin and shark encounters Take to the water on a well-informed eco-tour that could encounter a variety of whales and dolphins at Plettenberg Bay (p.241), or enter a shark cage for a first-hand encounter with Jaws at Mossel Bay (see p.216).

Wildlife spotting There's family fun in the forest, looking for apes from around the world at Monkeyland (p.243) or avifauna at the adjacent Birds of Eden (see p.243); or coming face to face with the world's largest land mammal at the Knysna Elephant Sanctuary (see p.243) and the Knysna Elephant Park (see p.234).

Ziplining See canopy tours (above).

Mossel Bay bears poignant historical significance as the place where indigenous Khoi cattle herders encountered the Europeans in a bloody spat that symbolically set the tone for five hundred years of race relations on the subcontinent. A group of Portuguese mariners under captain **Bartholomeu Dias** set sail from Portugal in August 1487 in search of a sea route to the riches of India, and months later rounded the Cape of Good Hope. In February 1488, they became the first Europeans to make landfall along the South African coast, when they pulled in for water to the safety of an inlet

▲ Boats at Mossel Bay

they called Aguado de São Bras ("watering place of St Blaize"), now Mossel Bay. The Khoikhoi were organized into distinct groups, each under its own chief and each with territorial rights over pastures and water sources. The Portuguese, who were flouting local customs, saw it as "bad manners" when the Khoikhoi tried to drive them off the spring. In a mutual babble of incomprehension the Khoi began stoning the Portuguese, who retaliated with crossbow fire that left one of the herders dead.

Arrival, information and accommodation

The N2 bypasses Mossel Bay and, of all the buses, only the **Baz Bus** comes right into town, dropping you off anywhere on request. The large **intercity buses** all stop at Shell Voorbaai Service Station, 7km from the centre, at the junction of the national highway and the road into town. The town itself is small enough to negotiate on foot, but should you need transport, Jordaan runs a **taxi** service (℡082 673 7314). The busy **tourist office** (Mon–Fri 8am–6pm, Sat 9am–4pm; ℡044 691 2202, @www.visitmosselbay.co.za), bang in the centre on the corner of Church and Market streets, has shelves of brochures about Mossel Bay and the rest of the Garden Route, and a **map** of the town.

Accommodation

Mossel Bay has a broad range of **accommodation**, including a number of reasonable B&Bs that can be booked through the tourist office should our recommendations be full. There's **camping** at the municipal site, *De Bakke*, at George Road just back from the beach (℡044 691 2915, @www.mosselbaymun.co.za), which also has good self-catering chalets sleeping four (R500). *Point Caravan Park* in Point Road (℡044 690 3501; R155 for sea-facing caravans), along the rocky point, is not as nice as the bay's main beach for swimming, but it's close to the start of the St Blaize hiking trail.

Edward Charles 1 Sixth Ave ☎ 044 691 2152, Ⓦ www.edwardcharles.co.za. An upmarket guesthouse in a central location overlooking Santos Beach with a swimming pool. Doubles from R650.

Green Door 49 Marsh St ☎ 044 691 3820, Ⓦ www.greatbrakriver/greendoor. Central B&B in a charming 100-year-old sandstone building. The older family rooms, which sleep four, are less attractive than the newer doubles, but are good value if there are more than two of you. Doubles R450.

Highview Lodge 76 Rodger St ☎ 044 691 9038, Ⓦ www.highviewlodge.co.za. Very reasonably priced B&B rooms with exceptional views of the bay and the mountains. Doubles from R350.

Huisj Te Marquette 1 Marsh St ☎ 044 691 3182, Ⓔ marquette@pixie.co.za. Twelve guest rooms in a very well-run establishment near the Point, with an adjoining backpackers with dorms and doubles. Dorm beds R100, doubles R260, en-suite doubles R300, guest rooms from R350 per person sharing.

Mossel Bay Guest House 61 Bruns Rd ☎ 044 691 2000. Comfortable rooms in an Afrikaner suburban home, not far from Santos Beach. Doubles R700.

Protea Hotel Mossel Bay Bartholomeu Dias Museum Complex, Market St ☎ 044 691 3738, Ⓦ www.proteahotels.com/mosselbay. Opposite the tourist office, in an old Cape Dutch manor house, this quaint place has breakfast served at *Café Gannet*, Mossel Bay's nicest restaurant. Doubles from R875 without breakfast.

Santos Express Santos Beach ☎ 044 691 1995. A stationary train with a great location – on the beach, just metres from the surf. Accommodation is in four-person train compartments, but you'll have one to yourself if you're a couple or a family. Morning coffee and continental breakfast is included. The restaurant is good value. R115 per person sharing.

Valhalla Guest House 86 Montagu St ☎ 044 691 1075. An inexpensive B&B near the town centre, though a bit of a walk to the beach, with breakfast outdoors, and sea views owing to its elevation on the hillside. Doubles R350 self-catering, R400 B&B.

The Town

Mossel Bay's main urban attraction is the **Bartholomeu Dias Museum Complex**, housed in a collection of historic buildings well integrated into the small town centre, all near the tourist office and within a couple of minutes' walk of each other. The highlight is the **Maritime Museum** (Mon–Fri 8.15am–4.45pm, Sat & Sun 9am–4pm; R12), a spiral gallery with displays on the history of European, principally Portuguese, seafaring, arranged around a full-size replica of Dias' original caravel. The ship was built in Portugal and sailed from Lisbon to Mossel Bay in 1987 to celebrate the five hundredth anniversary of Dias' historic journey. You can't fail to be awed by the idea of the original mariners setting out on the high seas into terra incognita on such a small vessel – particularly as the crew were accommodated above deck with only a sailcloth for protection against the elements.

The one Mossel Bay attraction that most South Africans have heard of is the **Post Office Tree**, just outside the Maritime Museum. Sixteenth-century mariners used to leave messages for passing ships in an old boot under a milkwood tree somewhere around here, and the plaque claims that "this may well" be the same tree. You can post mail here in a large, boot-shaped letterbox and have it stamped with a special postmark.

Of the remaining exhibitions, the **Shell Museum and Aquarium** (Mon–Fri 9am–4.45pm, Sat & Sun 10am–4pm; donation) next to the Post Office Tree is the only one worth taking time to visit. This is your chance to see some of the beautiful shells found off the South African coast, as well as specimens from around the world. The fascinating displays of living shellfish include cowries with their inhabitants still at home.

If you're keen on walking and the outdoors, and want to schedule in at least one long walk somewhere in the country during your holiday, the Garden Route provides some fine possibilities. Indeed, walking is the only way to really experience the Garden Route's forests and coast and escape the clutter of holiday homes and the noisy N2.

The waymarked **hikes** listed below are two to five days long. You'll need to carry all your food, a sleeping bag for use in the communal hiking huts (mattresses are provided), lightweight cooking utensils and stove, and waterproofs. You should also wear proper worn-in hiking boots. For day-hikes and walks lasting only a couple of hours, consult Judith Hopley's On Foot in the Garden Route, available from Knysna's tourist office and several other outlets on the Garden Route. If you've no appetite for dried food and a heavy pack, note that the marvellous Dolphin trail is portered.

Dolphin trail

Start: Sandrif River Mouth, Tsitsikamma National Park
End: Storms River Mouth, Tsitsikamma National Park
Distance: 20km
Duration: two and a half days
Booking: ☏042 281 1607 extension 219
Cost: R3000 per person, including food, accommodation and permits
This is the Garden Route's luxury trail. Backpacks are transported to overnight stops where you're greeted with comfortable accommodation and cooked meals. The terrain through the Tsitsikamma National Park is breathtaking, covering the rugged coastal edge and the natural forest. The price includes a guide, a boat trip up the Storms River Gorge, and a 4WD drive through the Storms River Pass.

Harkerville Coast hiking trail

Start and end: Harkerville Forestry Station, 12km west of Plettenberg Bay, signposted off the N2
Distance: 26.5km
Duration: two days
Permit and booking: ☏044 302 5606
Cost: R100 per person
Closer to the roads, this circular trail doesn't feel as remote as the Otter trail (see below) but is a good second-best, taking in magnificent rocky coastline, indigenous forest and fynbos. Lots of rock scrambling and some traversing of exposed, narrow ledges above the sea is required, so don't attempt this if you're unfit or scared of heights. Monkeys, baboons and fish eagles are commonly seen, and you may also spot dolphins or whales.

A short walk north down the hill from the Maritime Museum gets you to **Santos Beach**, the main town strand, and purportedly the only north-facing beach in South Africa – which gives it exceptionally long sunny afternoons. Adjacent to the small town harbour, the beach provides some of the finest swimming along the Garden Route, with uncharacteristically gentle surf, small waves and a depth perfect for practising your crawl.

East of the harbour, the coast bulges south towards the **Point**, which has several restaurants and a popular bar/restaurant (see p.217) with a deck at the ocean's edge, from which you may see dolphins cruising past, as well as a surreal five-hundred-metre rocky channel known as the aquarium, which is used as a natural **tidal pool**. Adjacent to this, the Department of Marine and Coastal Management has installed an **Aquarium** (Mon–Fri 9am–4pm, Sat & Sun 9am–12.30pm; donation) under Tidals pub, which showcases local lobsters,

Otter trail

Start: Storms River Mouth, Tsitsikamma National Park
End: Nature's Valley, Tsitsikamma National Park
Distance: 42km
Duration: five days
Booking: Through South African National Parks, up to twelve months in advance (☏012 426 5111). The maximum number of people on the trail is twelve.
Cost: R525 per person.
South Africa's first established hiking trail, this is a coastal walk crossing rivers, tidal pools and indigenous forest. You may see dolphins, whales and seals, and the spoor of the Cape clawless otter – although virtually impossible to spot, the creatures are certainly around. The short stretches between log-hut nightstops mean you can take things slowly, and enjoy the vegetation and birds. The Bloukrans River has to be crossed by wading or swimming: go at low tide and waterproof your backpack. Some parts of the hike are steep, so you need to be fit.

Outeniqua trail

Start: Beervlei (the old forest station – eight overnight huts); directions are given when you book
End: Harkerville Forestry Station, 12km west of Plettenburg Bay
Distance: 108km
Duration: seven days (shorter versions possible)
Permit: ☏044 302 5606
Cost: R50 per person per day
The main draw here is the indigenous forest, including giant yellowwood trees, pine plantations and gold-mining remains at Millwood in the Goudveld State Forest.

Tsitsikamma trail

Start: Nature's Valley Caravan Park, Tsitsikamma National Park
End: Storms River Bridge, Tsitsikamma National Park
Distance: 64km
Duration: five days (shorter versions possible)
Permit: ☏012 426 5111
Cost: R60 per person per night
Features: Not to be confused with the Otter trail, this is an inland walk through indigenous forest, long stretches of open *fynbos* and the Tsitsikamma mountain range. Five overnight huts accommodate thirty people. It's not a difficult hike, and you won't cover more than 17km or so per day – although after heavy rains the rivers can be hard to cross.

crabs and fish found off this coast in a handful of small tanks, as well as a pair of Amazon piranhas.

A couple of hundred metres to the south at the top of some cliffs, the **St Blaize Lighthouse**, built in 1864, is still in use as a beacon to ships. Below it, the **Cape St Blaize Cave** is both a marvellous lookout point and a significant archeological site. A boardwalk leads through the cave past three information panels describing the history of the interpretation of the cave as well as the modern understanding of it. In 1801 Sir John Barrow insisted that shells found at the site had been brought by seagulls, while others argued that they were relics of human habitation. It turned out that Barrow's opponents were right, but it wasn't till 1888 that excavations uncovered stone tools and showed that people had been using the cave for something close on 100,000 years. The path leading up to the cave continues onto the Cape St Blaize trail (see p.216).

Activities

Given that the seals of **Seal Island**, about 10km northwest of Santos Beach, are a popular delicacy for great white sharks, you'd be forgiven for wondering why scuba diving remains so popular off Mossel Bay. In 1990, the unfortunate Monique Price became the first fully kitted scuba diver to die in a great white attack – just off the island – and divers are warned to avoid its immediate environs. There are, however, several rewarding **diving and snorkelling** spots around Mossel Bay, and full facilities, including open-water certification courses (around R1900) and one-off dives are available from Electro Dive (☎ & ⓕ044 698 1976 or ☎082 561 1259). Electro Dive rents out gear and provides shore-based and boat-based dives (R320 including kit). It also does parasailing and jetskiing. These aren't tropical seas, so don't expect clear warm waters (although temperatures tend to be warmer than at other Garden Route resorts), but with visibility usually between 4m and 10m you stand a good chance of seeing octopus, squid, sea stars, soft corals, pyjama sharks and butterfly fish.

For those who want to see **great white sharks** face to face there are a couple of outfits offering cage dives. The best months for sightings are March to November, and the worst January and February, but at no time are encounters guaranteed. One of the better operations in the country is Shark Africa, located on the corner of Church and Market streets (☎044 691 3796, ⓦwww.sharkafrica.co.za), with whom you can either observe from a boat or go underwater in a cage for R800, with the assurance that if the sharks don't show you get half your money back. If you're unlucky the first time and choose to try again on another day, you'll only be charged the amount you were refunded.

Cruises around Seal Island to see the African penguin and seal colonies can be taken on the *Romonza* (hourly 10am–4pm; R70; ☎044 690 3101) a medium-sized yacht that launches from the yacht marina in the harbour. On the mainland you can check out the coast on the **St Blaize hiking trail**, an easy fifteen-kilometre walk (roughly 4hr each way; a map is available from the tourist office) along the southern shore of Mossel Bay. The route starts from the Cape St Blaize Cave, just below the lighthouse at the Point, and heads west as far as Dana Bay, taking in magnificent coastal views of cliffs, rocks, bays and coves.

If jumping off bridges is your bag, **bungee jumping** at the old Gouritz River Bridge, about 40km west of Mossel Bay along the N2, offers a considerably cheaper alternative (R180) to the Bloukrans Bridge (see box, p.240) near Nature's Valley. If you're interested, just turn up and talk to Face Adrenalin at the bridge, though booking in advance will get you the time you want (☎044 697 7001). Gouritz also offers the option of a **bungee swing** (again run by Face Adrenalin; R180), in which the bungee is attached to the back of the same bridge causing you to swing down and under. Prices are the same whether you go alone or in tandem, with photos included.

Eating and drinking

With the notable exception of the *Café Gannet*, the **Lighthouse Restaurant** at the *Point Hotel* is the nicest place for food and drinks, mainly because of the large stretch of sea frontage it offers, though there has been an upsurge of development here. The small Point Village shopping development at the north end has a couple of inexpensive to mid-priced family restaurants, opening daily from the morning until 11pm-ish.

Café Gannet Market St ☎044 691 1885. Close to the Bartholomew Dias Museum Complex is Mossel Bay's top restaurant, with moderately priced seafood lunches and dinners, served in a stylish garden with glimpses across the harbour, and a good spot for sundowners. Daily 7am–11pm.

Delfino's Espresso Bar and Pizzeria Point Village ☎044 690 5247. Italian food at reasonable prices, plus a view.

King Fisher Point Village ☎044 690 6390. A relaxed joint above *Delfino's*, specializing in moderately priced seafood and offering good views.

Lighthouse Restaurant *Point Hotel*, **Point Rd** ☎044 691 3512. A wide ranging à la carte menu in a fabulous setting, with some veggie options. Daily 7am–10pm.

Santos Express Santos Beach. The restaurant attached to the train carriage on the beach, with an adjoining pub, is a lively venue with good calamari and burgers, at keen prices.

Tidals Waterfront Tavern & Pub South side of the Point. Mossel Bay's rowdiest drinking spot buzzes until the early hours on Fridays and Saturdays, in a stunning seaside location. overlooking cliffs and the open sea.

Around Mossel Bay: Robinson Pass to Oudtshoorn

Heading inland towards Oudtshoorn from Mossel Bay on the R328 takes you over the forested coastal mountains over the **Robinson Pass** into the desiccated Little Karoo. Close to the top, 35km from Mossel Bay, and a compelling stop for a meal or drink, is the *Eight Bells Mountain Inn* (☎044 631 0000, Ⓦwww.eightbells.co.za; doubles R790), a firm favourite with well-heeled families wanting a fully catered hotel-style holiday with all sorts of activities laid on for children, and rest time for adults. The atmosphere is friendly and it's superbly run with special meals and meal times for younger children, horse-riding, swimming, tennis and walking. Out of school holidays it remains a restful stop-off with lovely gardens and extensive grounds.

On a nearby property, the **Botlierskop Private Game Reserve** (☎044 696 6055, Ⓦwww.botlierskop.co.za) does game drives for day visitors at 10am and 3pm (R390, children R198) and elephant-back rides at 10am and 11am (R500, children R250) as well as horse-rides (R150 an hour). Staying over in a luxury tent with meals and game drives will set you back R2500. Though it's no substitute for a safari in Kruger, and there's nothing wild about it, you will mostly (but not always) see lions in their huge enclosure, and there's a good chance of spotting elephants, rhinos, giraffes and antelope too. All activities and accommodation must be booked in advance as numbers are limited.

George, Victoria Bay and Wilderness

There's little reason to visit **GEORGE**, 66km northeast of Mossel Bay, unless you need what a big centre offers – airport, hospital and shops – and it does lie conveniently halfway between Cape Town and Port Elizabeth. Sadly the Outeniqua Choo-Tjoe, which once lured people into George, is no longer doing its spectacular rail route to Knysna due to severe flooding, though it still runs to the less attractive destination of Mossel Bay. However, a cable car up to the top of George Peak is planned for 2010, which should be a reasonable attraction.

A large inland town, surrounded by mountains, George is a five-kilometre detour northwest off the N2, and 9km from the nearest stretch of ocean at

Victoria Bay. Sadly, all that's left of the forests and quaint character that moved Anthony Trollope, during a visit in 1877, to describe it as the "prettiest village on the face of the earth" are some historic buildings, of which the beautiful **Dutch Reformed Church**, in Davidson Street at the top end of Meade Street, is the most notable. Completed in the early 1840s, the church is definitely

President Botha: the King Canute of apartheid

Pieter Willem Botha is credited with setting up an autocratic "Imperial Presidency" in South Africa, but in retrospect he was actually the King Canute of apartheid, closing his eyes to the incoming tide of democracy and believing that by wagging his finger (his favoured gesture of intimidation) he could turn it back.

A National Party hack from the age of 20, Botha worked his way up through the ranks, getting elected an MP in 1948 when the first apartheid government took power. He became leader of the National Party in the Cape Province and was promoted through various cabinet posts until he became **Minister of Defence**, a position he used to launch a palace coup in 1978 against his colleague, Prime Minister John Vorster. Botha immediately set about modernizing apartheid, modifying his own role from that of a British-style prime minister, answerable to parliament, to one of an executive president taking vital decisions in the secrecy of a President's Council heavily weighted with army top brass.

Informed by the army that the battle to preserve the apartheid status quo was unwinnable purely by force, Botha embarked on his **Total Strategy**, which involved reforms to peripheral aspects of apartheid and the fostering of a black middle class as a buffer against the ANC, while pumping vast sums of money into building an enormous military machine that crossed South Africa's borders to bully or crush neighbouring countries harbouring groups opposed to apartheid. South African refugees in Botswana and Zimbabwe were bombed, Angola was invaded, and arms were run to anti-government rebels in Mozambique, reducing it to ruins – a policy that has returned to haunt South Africa with those same weapons now returning across the border and finding their way into the hands of criminals. Inside South Africa, security forces enjoyed a free hand to murder, maim and torture **opponents of apartheid** on a scale that only fully emerged between 1996 and 1998, under the investigations of the Truth and Reconciliation Commission.

Botha's intransigence led to his greatest blunder in 1985, when he responded to international calls for change by hinting that he would announce significant reforms at his party congress that would irreversibly jettison apartheid. In the event, the so-called **Rubicon speech** was a disaster, as Botha proved to have insufficient steel to resist pressure from white right-wing extremists. The speech shrank away from meaningful concessions to black South Africans, the immediate result of which was a flight of capital from the country and intensified sanctions. Perhaps worst of all for the apartheid regime, the **Chase Manhattan Bank** refused to roll over its massive loan to South Africa, leaving the country an uncreditworthy pariah.

Botha blustered and wagged his finger at the opposition through the late 1980s, while his bloated military sucked the state coffers dry as it prosecuted its dirty wars. Even National Party stalwarts realized that his policies were leading to ruin, and in 1989, when he suffered a stroke, the party was quick to replace him with **F.W. de Klerk**, who immediately proceeded to announce the reforms the world had expected four years earlier from Botha's Rubicon speech.

Botha lived out his unrepentant retirement near George, declining ever to apologize for any of the brutal actions taken under his presidency to bolster apartheid. Curiously, when he died in 2006, he was given an uncritical, high-profile state funeral, broadcast on national television and attended by members of the current government, including President Thabo Mbeki.

worth a stop if you happen to be passing through, with its elegantly simple classical façade, Greek-cross plan with an impressive centrally placed pulpit and wonderful domed ceiling, panelled with glowing yellowwood. **St Mark's Cathedral**, in Cathedral Street, consecrated in 1850, is also worth seeing, but unlike the Dutch Reformed Church which is open to the public it can only be visited by appointment. Other than that, George's claim to recent fame (or notoriety) is the fact that it was the parliamentary seat of former State President **P.W. Botha** (see box opposite), the last of South Africa's apartheid hardliners. The George Museum once housed the P.W. Botha collection, an exercise in blind adulation for one of the most ruthless proponents of apartheid. The collection was regarded as unsuitable for a museum in the "New South Africa" and was removed in the 1990s.

Practicalities

The small George **airport** is 10km west of town on the N2. A Zeelie's **taxi** (☎044 874 6707) into town will set you back R50 from the airport; most tourists flying in rent a car from one of the rental companies here and set off down the Garden Route. Outeniqua Choo-Tjoe **trains** (see p.210) arrive at the Outeniqua Railway Museum, 2 Mission Rd, just off Knysna Road (☎044 801 8202). Intercape, Translux and Greyhound **intercity buses** pull in at George station, adjacent to the railway museum. The **Baz Bus** drops off at *McDonald's* on Courtenay Street. George's **tourist office**, 124 York St (Mon–Fri 8am–5pm, Sat 9am–1; ☎044 801 9295, ⓦwww.georgetourism.co.za), can provide town **maps** and help with accommodation bookings.

Accommodation

10 Caledon Street 10 Calendon St ☎044 873 4983, ⓦwww.10caledon.co.za. The pick of the mid-priced B&Bs, in a spotless guest-house in a quiet street around the corner from the museum, featuring balconies with mountain views and a garden. Doubles R600.
Arbour Lodge On the corner of Davidson and Arbour rds ☎044 874 7592 or 082 412 4114, ⓦwww.ashmole.com. A modern suburban home with three large en-suite rooms with kitchenettes, close to the centre on the busy road to Oudtshoorn. It's hosted by an extremely friendly and obliging couple, who welcome children. Self-catering R380, B&B R500.

Die Waenhuis 11 Caledon St ☎044 874 0034, ⓔdiewaenhuis@lantic.net. Mid-nineteenth-century home that has retained its period character. English breakfasts are served in a sunlit dining room. Doubles R1180.
George Tourist Resort York St ☎044 874 5205. En-suite chalets (R620/R910 sleeping four/ eight) and rondavels (R500 sleeping four) in well-kept pleasant gardens, with a swimming pool, children's playground, shop and laundry facilities.
Oak Tree 30 Caledon St ☎082 563 9952 or 044 874 5931, ⓦwww.oaktreebnb.co.za. This Victorian home has two comfortable rooms, with white linen and well-appointed bathrooms. Both rooms have separate entrances. Doubles R1100.

Eating and drinking

Fong Ling Taiwanese Corner of York and Fichat sts ☎044 884 0088. Quick mid-priced lunches or evening marathons. Daily from 11.30am–3pm & 5.30–10.30pm.
La Capannina 122 York St ☎044 874 5313. Italian restaurant with excellent pizzas.

Open lunch & dinner daily, except Sat & Sun lunch.
The Old Town House Corner of York and Market sts ☎044 8874 3663. Lovely ambience in this original town house, where the moderately priced food is well cooked with attention to

detail in an intimate setting. Open lunch & dinner daily, closed Sun.

Travel Bugs 111 York St. Good coffee, breakfasts and light lunches in a shaded courtyard. Mon–Fri 8am–4.30pm, Sat 9am–noon.

Zanzibar Sports Pub Next to the museum, in two old railway carriages. Beer and a big screen, mainly enjoyed by a younger crowd. Mon–Sat 11am till after midnight.

Victoria Bay

Some 9km south of George and 3km off the N2 lies the minuscule hamlet of **VICTORIA BAY**, on the edge of a small sandy beach wedged into a cove between cliffs, with a grassy sunbathing area, safe swimming and a tidal pool. During the December holidays it packs out with day-trippers, and rates as one of the top **surfing** spots in South Africa. Because of the cliffs, there's only a single row of buildings along the beachfront, with some of the most dreamily positioned guesthouses along the coast (and therefore some of the priciest for what you get).

There's no public **transport** to Victoria Bay, although many people hitch the few kilometres from the N2. Arriving by **car**, you'll encounter a metal barrier as you drop down the hill to the bay, and you'll have to try and park in a car park that's frequently full (especially in summer). If you're staying at one of the B&Bs, leave your car at the barrier and collect the key from your lodgings to gain access to the private beach road. The only places to buy **food** are a small beachside kiosk selling light refreshments and a casual restaurant where you can stroll down in flip-flops and shorts. However, the resort's B&Bs are served by Mr Delivery, a company that will collect from about ten fast-food joints in George and will also fetch groceries and even videos.

Accommodation

Besides the places to stay reviewed here, there's magnificently located **camping** on the clifftop overlooking the beach, at the *Victoria Bay Caravan Park*, on the left as you approach the beach (☎044 889 0081).

Land's End Guest House The Point, Beach Rd ☎044 889 0123, ⓦwww.vicbay.com. Two self-catering studio apartments at the end of the road, sleeping two, plus two flats on a B&B basis. B&B doubles from R900.
Pier Plesier Beach Rd ☎044 889 0051, ⓔianwesson@mjvn.co.za. A well-run modern brick building with upstairs and downstairs en-suite flats overlooking the sea, just 6m from the high-water mark. The flats have either one or two rooms, and can sleep four. The cheapest unit has no sea view. Self-catering from R390, B&B from R500.

Sea Breeze Holiday Resort Along the main road into the settlement ☎044 889 0098, ⓦwww .seabreezecabanas.co.za. A variety of budget self-catering units, including modern two-storey holiday huts and wooden chalets, sleeping two, four or eight people. The huts have no sea views, but it's an easy stroll to the beach. From R620 per cabana.
The Waves 7 Beach Rd ☎044 889 0166, ⓦwww.gardenroute.co.za/vbay/waves. Two comfortable suites in a high-ceilinged Victorian house. Suites R1500.

Wilderness

East of Victoria Bay, across the Kaaimans River, the beach at **WILDERNESS** is so close to the N2 that you can pull over for a quick dip with barely an interruption to your journey, though African wilderness is the last thing you'll find here. Wilderness village earned its name, so the story goes, after a young man called Van den Berg bought the property in 1830 for £183 as a blind lot at a Cape Town auction. When he got engaged, his fiancée insisted that their first year of marriage should be spent out of town in the wilderness, so he romanti-cally (or perhaps opportunistically) named his property Wilderness and built a hut on it.

If the hut still exists, you'll struggle to find it among the sprawl of retirement homes, holiday houses and thousands of beds for rent in the vicinity. The beach, which is renowned for its long stretch of sand, is backed by tall dunes, rudely blighted by holiday houses. Once in the water, stay close to the shoreline: this part of the coast is notorious for its unpredictable currents.

The main attraction of the area, though, is the Wilderness National Park, whose river is lovely to paddle along, with good bird-spotting. Wilderness's tiny **village centre**, on the north side of the N2, has a filling station, a few shops, restaurants and a **tourist office** in *Milkwood Village Mall*, Beacon Road, off the N2 opposite the Caltex Garage (May–Sept Mon–Fri 8am–5pm, Sat 9am–1pm; Oct–April Mon–Fri 8am–6pm, Sat 8am–1pm, Sun 3–5pm; ☏044 877 0045, Ⓦwww.visitwilderness.co.za).

Eden Adventures (☏044 877 0179 or 083 628 8547) runs half-day **canoeing**, **cycling**, **abseiling** or **kloofing** trips along the nearby Kaaimans River and its gorge (R250). Explore the river yourself by renting a two-seater canoe from them (R120 for 3hr including park fees). Wilderness Adventures (☏044 850 1008) runs mountain **horse-riding** tours (R150 an hour). To see it all from the air, sign up with the recommended Cloudbase Paragliding Adventures (☏044 877 1414) for a tandem **paragliding** jump that clocks in at R450. You fly for a minimum of fifteen minutes, but you'll only be taken up when the weather offers absolutely safe conditions.

When it comes to **eating**, *The Girls* on George Road (☏044 877 1648; lunch & dinner daily except Sun) in the village centre is the place to come for fusion Mediterranean food. Combining middle-European and local flavours, at moderate prices, *Palms* is the best restaurant at the Swiss-owned *Palms Wilderness Guest House*, Owen Grant Road (☏044 877 1420; dinner daily), 3km from town. For an informal meal that might include smoked salmon omelette, pizza or steak, try the *Wilderness Grill* on George Road (open daily for breakfast, lunch & dinner), with seating outside under parasols or indoors by the fire. If you're at **Milkwood Village**, there are several places to eat, one of the best being *Pomodoro*, an Italian restaurant with a pleasant ambience.

Accommodation

The Albatross Sixth Ave, take South St exit off the N2 ☏044 877 1716. Guesthouse in easy walking distance from the beach, with large balconies and perfect dolphin-watching views. Doubles from R550.

Fairy Knowe Backpackers ☏044 877 1285, Ⓔfairybp@mweb.co.za. The oldest home (built 1897) in the area, with a wraparound balcony and set in the quiet woodlands near the Touws River, though nowhere near the sea; to reach the site, 6km from the village, follow signs from the N2 east of Wilderness. The Baz Bus will drop off here. Dorms R90, rooms R240.

Island Lake Holiday Resort Lakes Rd, 2km from the Hoekwil/Island Lake turn-off on the N2 ☏044 877 1194. Camping and self-catering

bungalows that sleep four (R485), on one of the quietest and prettiest spots on the lakes.

Mes-Amis Homestead Buxton Close, signposted off the N2 on the coastal side of the road, directly opposite the national park turn-off ☏044 877 1928, Ⓦwww.mesamis.co.za. Nine double rooms, each of which has its own terrace, offering some of the best views in Wilderness. B&B doubles R960.

The Tops Hunts Lane, on a hill about 500m from the tourist office ☏044 877 0187 or 083 631 2339. Four airy en-suite bedrooms, three of which have sea views and French doors opening onto a deck. B&B doubles R570.

Wilderness Bush Camp Heights Rd (follow Waterside Rd west for 1600m up the hill)

⊕ **044 877 1168**, ⊛ **www.boskamp.co.za**. Six
self-catering timber units with loft
bedrooms, thatched roofs and ocean

views. The camp is part of a conservation
estate that you're free to roam around.
From R300 per unit.

Wilderness National Park

Stretching east from Wilderness village is the **Wilderness National Park**
(reception open 24hr; ⊕044 877 1197; R60), the least aptly named national
park in South Africa, as it never feels very far from the rumbling N2. Although
the park takes in beach frontage, it's the **forests** you should come for, as well as
the 16km of inland waterways; the variety of habitats here include coastal and
montane *fynbos* and wetlands, attracting 250 species of **birds** – as well as many
holidaymakers.

There are two **restcamps**, both on the west side of the park and clearly
signposted off the N2. *Ebb and Flow North* (rondavels from R200), right on the
river, is cheap, old-fashioned and away from the hustle. It offers camping, fully
equipped two-person bungalows with their own showers, and slightly cheaper
huts with communal washing and toilet facilities. *Ebb and Flow South*, signposted
close by, has camping and modern accommodation in spacious log cabins on
stilts and brick bungalows which, although dearer than *North* camp, represent
good value if there are more than two of you (you pay R690 for a minimum
of four people) for its fully equipped, self-contained family brick bungalows or
log cabins on stilts. There are also cheaper en-suite forest huts (R375) with
communal kitchens for two people. Seasonal discounts of twenty percent are
offered on accommodation (apart from the forest huts and camping) from mid-
January to mid-March and from May to November. There is a **shop** selling
milk, bread and basic groceries at reception, a coin-operated **laundry**, and a
small children's playground.

Activities

To take advantage of all the water, you can rent **canoes** and **pedaloes** from
reception. There are also several waymarked walking trails, well worth doing to
get a feeling of the indigenous vegetation and escape the N2 and holiday homes
– the reception issues trail **maps**. The **Giant Kingfisher trail** is an easy seven-
kilometre walk that starts at *Ebb and Flow North* camp and passes through the
forest along the eastern bank of the Touws River to some rock pools teeming
with little sea creatures, returning along the same route, taking three hours for
the round trip. Another hike of about three hours is the six-kilometre **Cape
Dune Molerat trail**, a circuit along the dunes separating Rondevlei and
Swartvlei lakes, with good views onto both. It offers excellent birding opportunities and you'll see wild flowers during winter and spring. To get there, take
the N2 east towards Sedgefield for 16km, take the Swartvlei turn-off and
continue down a dirt road; after 2.8km turn right and continue for just over a
kilometre to the conservation station and trail starting point.

Sedgefield, Goukamma and Buffels Bay

The drive between Wilderness and Sedgefield gives glimpses on your left of
dark-coloured lakes which eventually surge out to sea, 21km later, through a
wide lagoon at **SEDGEFIELD**, a lacklustre holiday village a few kilometres off

the road, with a safe swimming **beach** that makes a refreshing pit stop. Until recently Sedgefield's unpromising appearance of shops, restaurants and B&Bs lining the highway hid a gloriously undeveloped beachfront. But the resort's authorities have woken up to the economic potential of development, and turned parts of the beachfront into a building site. At least accommodation prices are more reasonable here than at Knysna half an hour away (see p.224), making Sedgefield a potential base for exploring the area.

Sedgefield could be used as a base from which to explore **Goukamma Nature and Marine Reserve** and the western extent of **Groenvlei**, a freshwater lake that falls within the reserve's boundaries. An unassuming sanctuary of around 220 square kilometres, Goukamma ranges from near Sedgefield east as far as the small seaside resort of **Buffels Bay** to absorb 14km of beach frontage, some of the highest vegetated dunes in the country, and walking country covered with coastal *fynbos* and dense thickets of milkwood, yellowwood and candlewood trees.

The area has long been popular with anglers for Groenvlei's six **fish** species. Away from the water, you stand a small chance of spotting one of the area's **mammals**, including bushbuck, grysbok, mongoose, vervet monkeys, caracals and otters. Because of the diversity of coastal and wetland habitats, over 220 different kinds of **birds** have been recorded here, including fish eagles, Knysna louries, kingfishers and very rare African black oystercatchers. Offshore, southern right **whales** often make an appearance during their August to December breeding season, and bottlenose and common **dolphins** can show up at any time of year.

Apart from angling and bird-watching, the Goukamma offers a number of self-guided activities, including safe **swimming** in Groenvlei. There are several day-long hiking **trails** that enable you to explore different habitats – if you plan on hiking you should pick up the Cape Nature Conservation map from your guesthouse. A beach walk, which takes around four hours one way, traverses the 14km of crumbling cliffs and sands between the Platbank car park on the western side of the reserve and the Rowwehoek one on the eastern side. Alternatively, you can go from one end of the reserve to the other via a slightly longer inland trek across the dunes. There's also a shorter circular walk from the reserve office through a milkwood forest, as well as **horse-riding** trips run by Cherry Tree Christian Adventures (℡082 060 6751; R150 per hour).

Two roads off the N2 provide **access** to the reserve. At the westernmost side, a dirt road that runs down to Platbank Beach takes you past the tiny settlement of **Lake Pleasant** on the south bank of Groenvlei, which consists of little more than a hotel and holiday resort. On the eastern side, access is via the Buffels Bay road, halfway along which is the reserve office. There are no public roads within the reserve.

Accommodation

Among the forest of holiday homes in **Sedgefield**, you'll find some decent accommodation away from the N2. Another inexpensive alternative to Knysna is **Buffels Bay**, a haphazard little development at the east of the reserve; it's 10km down a turn-off along the N2, 13km east of Sedgefield.

At **Goukamma Nature and Marine Reserve** (bookings ℡021 659 3500) you can choose to stay at a basic bushcamp that sleeps up to eight people (R700 for first four, then R75 per additional person) or one of the thatched rondavels that sleep up to five (R300 for first two, then R150 per additional person). All have fully equipped kitchens, but you must bring your own bedding.

Coral Reef Guesthouse 28 Coral Reef Crescent, Cola Beach, Sedgefield ☎ 044 343 3133, ⓦ wwwcoralreef.co.za. Two double rooms, a triple and a family unit, all brightly decorated. There's a saltwater pool and a comfortable relaxing area. Discounts for stays of two or more nights. B&B doubles R700.
Lake Pleasant Chalets & Lodges Lake Pleasant, east of Sedgefield, south of the N2 ☎ 044 343 1985, ⓦ www.lake-pleasant.co.za. Self-catering timber chalets and slightly smaller four-person garden lodges at a family resort with a kids' play area and a trampoline. There's also a restaurant, a pub and a store selling basics, and they rent out mountain bikes, rowing boats and canoes. Doubles R530.
Warthog Wallow 11 Begonia St, Sedgefield ☎ 044 343 1965, ⓦ www.warthogwallow.co.za. Peaceful timber guesthouse with views of the nearby mountains. Doubles R390 self-catering, R450 B&B.

Knysna and the Knysna forests

South Africa's 1990s tourist boom rudely shook **KNYSNA** (pronounced "Nize-nuh") from its gentle backwoods drowse, which for decades made this the hippy and craftwork capital and quiet retirement village of the country. The town, 102km east of Mossel Bay, now stands at the hub of the Garden Route, its lack of ocean beaches compensated for by its hilly setting around the **Knysna lagoon**, its handsome **forests**, good opportunities for **adventure sports**, a pleasant **waterfront development** – and some hot marketing.

Knysna's distinctive atmosphere derives from its small historic core of Georgian and Victorian buildings, which gives it a character absent from most of the Garden Route holiday towns. Coffee shops, craft galleries, street traders and a modest nightlife add to the attractions, and you may find yourself tempted to stay longer than just one night. That the town has outgrown itself is evident from the cars and tour buses which, especially in December and January, clog Main Street, the constricted artery that merges with the N2 as it enters the town.

Some history

At the beginning of the nineteenth century, the only white settlements outside Cape Town were a handful of villages that would have considered themselves lucky to have even one horse. Knysna, an undeveloped backwater hidden in the forest, was no exception. The name comes from a Khoi word meaning "hard to reach", and this remained its defining character well into the twentieth century. One important figure was not deterred by the distance – **George Rex**, a colourful colonial administrator who placed himself beyond the pale of decent colonial society by taking a coloured mistress. Shunned by his peers in Britain, he headed for Knysna at the turn of the nineteenth century in the hope of making a killing shipping out hardwood from the lagoon.

By the time of Rex's death in 1839, Knysna had become a major **timber centre**, attracting white labourers who felled trees with primitive tools for miserly payments, and looked set eventually to destroy the forest. In 1872, **Prince Alfred**, on his visit to the Cape, made his small royal contribution to this wanton destruction when he made a special detour here to come elephant hunting. The forest only narrowly escaped devastation by far-sighted and effective conservation policies introduced in the 1880s.

By the turn of the twentieth century, Knysna was still remote, and its forests were inhabited by isolated and inbred communities made up of the impoverished

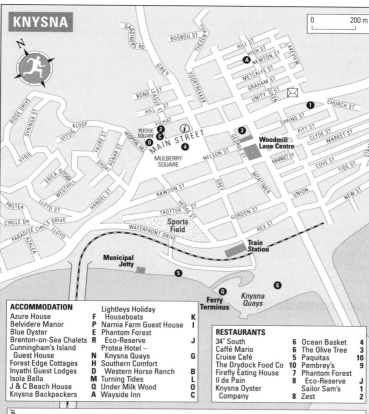

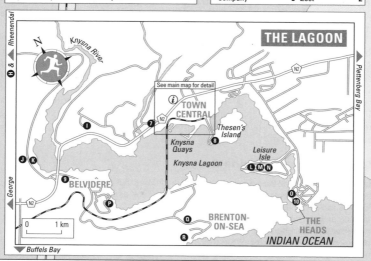

descendants of the woodcutters. As late as 1914, if you travelled from Knysna to George you would have to open and close 58 gates along the 75-kilometre track. Fifteen years on, the passes in the region proved too much for **George Bernard Shaw**, who did some impromptu off-road driving and crashed into a bush, forcing Mrs Shaw to spend a couple of weeks in bed at Knysna's *Royal Hotel* with a broken leg.

Arrival and information

Knysna wraps around the lagoon, with its oldest part – the town centre – on the northern side. The lagoon's narrow mouth is guarded by a pair of steep rocky promontories called **The Heads**, the western side being a private nature reserve and the eastern one an exclusive residential area (confusingly, it's also called The Heads), along dramatic cliffs above the Indian Ocean.

Greyhound, Intercape and Translux **buses** drop passengers off at the **train station** in Remembrance Avenue opposite Knysna Quays; the **Baz Bus** will drop passengers off at any of the town's accommodation. For local transport, there are a couple of **taxi** services (see "Listings" on p.231).

The **tourist office**, Knysna Tourism, at 40 Main St (Mon–Fri 8am–5pm, Sat 8.30am–1pm; slightly longer hours during the season; ☎044 382 5510, ⊛www .tourismknysna.co.za), provides maps and runs a desk for booking **activities** around Knysna – including cruises to and abseiling down The Heads and bungee jumping from the Bloukrans River Bridge.

Accommodation

Knysna has hundreds of accommodation establishments to choose from, though rates have become expensive over the years. The best places to stay in town are away from the main road, with views of the lagoon and The Heads. Out of town there are some excellent guesthouses and B&Bs as well as reasonably priced self-catering cottages right in the **forest**, where you can get well away from the town buzz. For somewhere quieter on the lagoon, make for the western edge at **Brenton-on-Sea**. It is possible to stay here or a few kilometres inland in the quaint and very upmarket settlement of **Belvidere**, through which visitors are prohibited from driving.

For something different, you can rent a **houseboat** from Lightleys, moored at the Belvidere turn-off from the N2 (☎044 386 0007, ⊛www.houseboats.co.za; R1045 for two people or R1245 for four in a four-berth Leisure Liner, R1735 for a six-berth Aqualiner). Its houseboats let you explore the lagoon's 20km of navigable water and are fully equipped, with interiors resembling those of caravans. Another option is a **township homestay**, arranged through Knysna Tourism; it runs a busy accommodation office (☎044 382 6960, ⊛booking @mweb.co.za) and can help you book homestays and any other type of accommodation in the vicinity.

Town centre and Knysna Quays

Knysna Backpackers 42 Queen St ☎044 382 2554, ⊛www.knysnabackpackers.co.za. Spotless, well-organized hostel in a large, rambling and centrally located Victorian house that has been declared a national monument. Totally renovated in 2007, this tranquil establishment has five rooms rented as doubles (but able to sleep up to four people) and a dorm that sleeps eight. Doubles R230, dorms R80 per person.
Protea Hotel – Knysna Quays Waterfront Drive ☎044 382 5005, ⊛www.proteahotels.com /protea-hotel-knysna-quays.html. A 122-room, nautically themed luxury hotel in a fabulous

spot on the waterfront, within walking distance of the centre. Rooms either have views of the lagoon and the yacht basin or of the train station. Doubles from R880 per room without breakfast.

Wayside Inn Pledge Square, 48 Main Rd ☎044 382 6011, ⓦ www.waysideinn.co.za. A smart

overnight stop right in the centre done out in sisal matting, wicker furniture and white linen on black wrought-iron bedsteads. A continental breakfast is served in your room or on the deck outside. Doubles R600.

Eastern suburbs, Leisure Isle and The Heads

Cunningham's Island Guest House
3 Kingsway, Leisure Isle ☎044 384 1319, ⓦ www.islandhouse.co.za. Purpose-built two-storey, timber-and-glass guesthouse with eight suites, decked out in dazzling white relieved by a touch of blue and some ethnic colour (stripey cushions and African baskets). Each room has its own entrance leading to the garden, which has a swimming pool shaded by giant strelitzias. Stylish and comfortable, its only drawback is the lack of views. Doubles from R695.

Isola Bella 21 Hart Lane, Leisure Isle ☎044 384 0049, ⓦ www.isolabella.co.za. You can't help but gasp at The Heads views through the huge windows of this imposing guesthouse at the lagoon's edge. You'll either love or loathe the mildly operatic decor – repro furniture, lots of oil paintings and some floral fabrics. Either way, the rooms are undeniably luxurious. Breakfast is served on the spectacularly positioned balcony

overlooking the water. From R1400 per person sharing.

Turning Tides 19 Woodbourne Drive, Leisure Isle ☎044 384 0302, ⓦ www.capetown.at/turningtides. Comfortable, simply furnished double-storey B&B run by a friendly couple – he a retired doctor, she a nutritional scientist (special dietary needs catered for). Each of the three rooms in this child-friendly home has its own balcony with lagoon views. Doubles R640.

Under Milk Wood George Rex Drive, The Heads ☎044 384 0745, ⓦ www.milkwood.co.za. Luxury self-catering accommodation on the lagoon at the foot of The Heads with its own private beach – safe for swimming – and terrific views of the mountains and water. The two-bedroom self-catering units, with their own sun decks, are surrounded by milkwood trees; rates vary depending on whether the unit is on the lagoon, the hillside or between. There are also two B&B rooms. Chalets from R945.

West of town

Azure House 65 Circular Drive ☎044 382 1221, ⓦ www.azurehouse.com. Lime-washed whites, blues and pale yellows are the signature colours in these upmarket self-catering rooms, each en suite, with a small lounge. Breakfast (optional) is served on a wicker tray on your private balcony overlooking the lagoon. B&B R780 per room.

Blue Oyster Corner of Rio and Stent sts ☎044 382 2265, ⓦ www.blueoyster.co.za. Hospitable three-storey, vaguely Greek-themed B&B set high on one of the hills that rise up behind Knysna, offering fabulous panoramas across the lagoon to The Heads. The four comfortable double rooms, of which the ones on the top floor have the best views, are done out in white and blue. Doubles from R640.

Narnia Farm Guest House Signed off Welbedacht Lane, 3km west of Knysna

☎044 382 1334, ⓦ www.narnia.co.za. On a hillside with views of the lagoon, this is an immensely fun stone and rough-hewn timber farmhouse in a glorious garden, set among protea plantations. Two en-suite B&B rooms upstairs have their own balconies and swinging chairs and are decorated in a rustic-chic style, as is a comfortable semi-detached two-bedroom cottage downstairs which has a lounge, fireplace and kitchenette. The *Pool House* (so called because it opens onto a gorgeous, deck-surrounded swimming pool and its spacious lounge has its own pool table) is a one-bed-room cottage not far from the house, while the *Shed* (R1000 for the whole unit) is a short walk from the main house and has two bedrooms. Walks on the property include one down to a small lake. Self-catering from R850, B&B from R1000 per room.

Phantom Forest Eco-Reserve Phantom Pass Rd, west of town off the N2 ☎044 386 0046, ⓦwww.phantomforest.com. Breathtaking, tranquil forest lodge making extensive use of timber and glass, set on a hill in indigenous forest, with fabulous lagoon views. African fabrics and pure cotton linen help reinforce the sense of unbridled luxury.

Timber boardwalks wind through the forest to connect the suites to the main buildings, which feature a safari-style dining room, an open-air hot tub, a massage suite and a Jacuzzi. The swimming pool teeters on the edge of the hill, cocooned by vegetation, with vervet monkeys frolicking in the forest canopy. Doubles from R2400 half board.

The forest

Forest Edge Cottages Rheenendal turn-off, 16km west of Knysna on the N2 ☎082 456 1338, ⓦwww.forestedge.co.za. Ideal if you want to be close to the forest itself, these traditional tin-roofed, two-bedroomed cottages have verandas built in the vernacular tin-roofed style. Self-contained, fully equipped and serviced, the cottages sleep four. Forest walks and cycling trails start from the cottages, and you can also rent mountain bikes. Cottages from R650.

Southern Comfort Western Horse Ranch 3km along the Fisanthoek road, 17km east of Knysna en route to Plettenberg Bay ☎044 532 7885, ⓦwww.schranch.co.za. Very basic double rooms, dorms and a tree house, on a farm adjacent to the eastern section of the Knysna forest; staff can pick you up from the N2. Horse-riding (R150/hr, R590 for overnight forest trails) – and massages for the saddle-weary – are on offer. You can self-cater or take the meals provided. Doubles from R220.

Belvidere and Brenton-on-Sea

Belvidere Manor Duthie Drive, Belvidere Estate ☎044 387 1055, ⓦwww.belvidere.co.za. A collection of tin-roofed repro Victorian cottages, nicely positioned on the water's edge. Although they're spacious and were once quite smart, the feel now is of Laura Ashley let loose in a Holiday Inn. However, this is the only accommodation in this unique area. Doubles from R1860.
Brenton-on-Sea Chalets C.R. Swart Drive, Brenton beachfront ☎044 381 0081, ⓦwww.abalonelodges.co.za. A 15min drive from

Knysna and overlooking the long curve of Brenton Beach, which swings round to Buffels Bay. The three-bedroom, self-catering chalets sleep six people, and are well equipped and comfortably furnished. R950.
J&C Beach House 116 Watsonia Ave, Brenton ☎044 381 0107, ⓦwww.jcbeachhouse.co.za. Simple and elegant rooms, each with views of the ocean from the balcony. You can sun yourself at the pool or on nearby Brenton beach. From R910 per room.

The town and beaches

Main Street, which used to be hub of the Knysna, lost some of its status as the heart of the town with the development of the waterfront area. But it has begun fighting back, with extensive redevelopment that has brought with it trendy coffee shops, restaurants and shops.

About 500m south of Knysna Tourism, at the end of Grey Street lies the **Knysna Quays**, the town's waterfront complex and yacht basin. Built at the end of the 1990s, this elegant two-storey steel structure with timber boardwalks resembles a tiny version of Cape Town's V&A Waterfront – but probably owes its inspiration as much to New England or Seattle, and blows away Knysna's hippy cobwebs with a breath of upmarket supercool. Here you'll find the luxury *Protea Hotel*, some clothes and knick-knack shops and a couple of good eating places, including a stunning deli-style bistro, *34° South*, with outdoor decks, from which you can watch yachts drift past. Riding on the success of the Quays, **Thesen's Island**, reached by a causeway at the south end

of Long Street, has some stylish shops and eateries, among them the Knysna Oyster Company, one of the best spots for feasting on shellfish – on the edge of the lapping lagoon.

The beaches

Don't come to Knysna for a beach holiday: the closest beach is 20km from town at **Brenton-on-Sea**. A tiny settlement on the shores of Buffels Bay, it does admittedly have a quite exceptional beach. Although **Buffels Bay** (see p.120), the next beach to the west, is along the same continuous stretch of sand as Brenton-on-Sea, there's no direct route there; you have to return to the N2 and proceed from there. In the opposite direction from Knysna, the closest patch of sand is at **Noetzie**, a town known more for its eccentric holiday homes built to look like castles than for its seaside.

Eating, drinking and nightlife

As far as food goes, oysters are an obvious choice, with the Knysna Oyster Company here being one of the world's largest oyster farms, but you'll also find a lot of good **restaurants** catering to other palates and one or two excellent **coffee shops**. With so many forests, waterways and beaches, you may be tempted to have a **picnic**, and there's no shortage of tempting deli food in town.

Knysna has a livelier atmosphere than you might expect from a Garden Route town. At night *Stones*, on the corner of St George's and Main roads, is where to head for local and visiting **bands** from across the country.

34° South Knysna Quays. An outstanding, moderately priced deli and eating place, with imported groceries, home-made fare and seafood; from here you can watch the drawbridge open to let yachts sail through. Daily 9am–1pm.

Caffé Mario Knysna Quays ☎044 382 7250. An intimate Italian waterside restaurant with outdoor seating, and *paninoteca* and *tramezzini* on its snack menu as well as great pizza and pasta. Excellent value. Daily from 9am for breakfast, lunch and dinner.

Cruise Café Featherbed Ferry Terminal, off Waterfront Drive. Relaxed eatery that fuses African and Asian flavours to bring forth starters such as *bobotie* spring rolls. Moderately priced main courses include Karoo lamb with mint and cranberry reduction and

Knysna cruises and activities

One of the obligatory excursions around Knysna is a **cruise** across the lagoon to The Heads. Knysna Featherbed Company (℡044 382 1693) runs several 75-minute trips a day from Knysna Quays to The Heads (R80), a ninety-minute trip on the double-decker M/V *John Benn* (R90) as well as a dinner cruise (R295) on purportedly the only paddle-driven vessel in the country. For travel beyond The Heads, you can take a sailing trip (1hr 30min; R200) and a sunset cruise (2hr 30min; R440) with delicious food and wine. The only way to reach the private **Featherbed Nature Reserve** on the western side of the lagoon is on a four-hour Featherbed Nature Tour (R300), which includes the boat there and use of a 4WD shuttle to the top of the western Head, with the option of walking 2km back downhill to enjoy spectacular views and see flora and fauna, including Knysna louries; a buffet meal is included as well. There's a slightly shorter version (3hr 30min) which excludes the meal (R190). **Bookings** are essential, and can be made at the kiosk on the north side of Knysna Quays; **departures** are from the Waterfront Jetty and municipal jetty on Remembrance Avenue, 400m west of the quays and station.

Activities and adventure sports

Seal Adventures (℡044 382 5599, ⓦwww.sealadventures.co.za) runs **abseiling** and **rap jumping** trips (the latter involving running down a mountainside while harnessed; R300) in the Featherbed Nature Reserve, **canoeing** trips on the lagoon (R180, and **quad biking** (R350) in the forests. Knysna Forest Tours and Mountain Biking Africa (see pp.231–232) offers a range of guided forest and coastal hikes and mountain-biking trips in Knysna's forests and along the beaches as well as bird-watching and fly fishing.

Customized tours can be arranged by Deep South (℡044 382 2010 or 083 250 9441, ⓦwww.deepsoutheco.com), allowing you to combine, for example, mountain biking and a lagoon cruise (R630 per person for 2–6 people; cost includes lunch). It will also do standalone mountain biking trips or cruises.

venison loin in pastry with rosemary and cranberry reduction. Afro-Asian prawn curry and grilled calamari steak with smoked oyster and sun-dried tomatoes are among the seafood offerings. The waterside deck here is one of the best places in town to sink a drink while watching the setting sun. Mon–Sat 11.30am–11pm & Sun 11.30am–4pm.
The Drydock Food Co Knysna Quays ℡044 382 7310. Reckoned by many to be the best place to eat in town, with a great mid-priced seafood menu that has coastal oysters and local salmon trout as starters and main courses of prawns, East Coast sole and meat dishes. Daily lunch and dinner.
Firefly Eating House 152a Old Cape Rd ℡044 382 1490. Relaxed little eatery whose fiery red decor and sparkling fairy lights match the mid-priced spicy menu. Dishes draw their inspiration from Malaysia, Thailand and East and South Africa. Recommended if you like it hot. Tues–Sat 6.30–10pm.
Il de Pain Thesen Island. Trendy restaurant in a bakery, with an inexpensive menu of

salads, baguettes, oysters and pastas, written up on a blackboard. Try the thick crusty bread baked in a woodfired oven with butter and preserve for breakfast or settle for one of the delicious pastries with coffee. Tues–Sat 8am–3pm & Sun 9am–1.30pm.
Knysna Oyster Company Thesen Island. Run by the firm of the same name which has been in operation since 1949, this restaurant serves oysters harvested by the parent company from beds in the Knysna River Estuary. Don't worry it you're not an oyster eater – they also serve medium-priced steaks, chicken and freshly caught fish. Daily 10am–9pm.
Ocean Basket Knysna Mall, corner of Main Rd and Grey St. A reliably predictable family-friendly seafood restaurant chain with everything from freshly caught fish to hake and chips, at reasonable prices. Mon–Thurs noon–10pm, Fri–Sun noon–11pm.
The Olive Tree 12 Main Rd. This local favourite offers a great buffet lunch, cooked on the

day. Choice depends on the whim of the chef and the availability of ingredients. The well-priced spread can consist of spicy chickpeas, chicken wings – you name it – and a range of fresh salads. Toasted sandwiches and coffee are also on offer. Daily 8am–5pm.

Paquitas Knysna Heads ☏ 044 384 0408. Burgers, ribs and pizzas in a restaurant fabulously located on the rocks beneath The Heads, where kids can run onto the beach. Daily lunch and dinner.

Pembrey's Brenton Rd, Belvidere ☏ 044 386 0005. Small, unpretentious and highly rated restaurant that fuses country cooking with haute cuisine. You'll find venison, duck confit and prawns on the moderately priced menu alongside offal. Booking essential. Wed–Sun 6.30pm till the last person leaves.

Phantom Forest Eco-Reserve Phantom Pass Rd ☏ 044 386 0046. Eating is secondary to being in one of the most beautiful places in South Africa, in a forest with views of the whole estuary. The expensive Pan-African set menu ranges from ostrich medallions marinated in orange and ginger to forest mushrooms with garlic rocket and Knysna cheese, and tempting desserts such as brandy snap baskets. Dinner daily.

Sailor Sam's Main Rd, opposite the post office. A warm-hearted, old-fashioned chippy that offers incredible value, brilliant fish and chips and the cheapest oysters in town (but don't tell a soul: the delicious shellfish aren't local, they're shipped in from the West Coast). Mon–Sat 11am–8.30pm & Sun 11am–3pm.

Zest Pledge Square, Main Rd. Relaxed, stylish dining at a mid-priced eatery influenced by Australian fusion food. Local seasonal produce goes into an eclectic range of dishes from Moroccan chicken to Thai-style seafood. There's always venison and ostrich and lots of daily specials. Nov–March daily 5–10pm; April–Oct Mon–Sat 5–10pm.

Listings

Car rental Avis, on the corner of Long St and Main Rd ☏ 044 382 2222; Tempest, 14 Gray St ☏ 044 382 0354.
Emergencies Tourist victim support ☏ 044 878 2139 or 082 492 3968. See also p.163.
Hospital Knysna Private Hospital, Hunters Drive (☏ 044 384 1083), is well run and has a casualty department open to visitors.

Pharmacy Marine Pharmacy, on the corner of Main and Grey sts ☏ 044 382 5614 (Mon–Fri 8am–8pm, Sat 8am–1pm & 5–8pm, Sun 9.30am–1pm & 5–8pm).
Taxis Benwill Shuttle (☏ 083 728 5181; after hours ☏ 044 384 0103) is handy for transport around town, but take care to agree the fare before getting inside.

The Knysna forests

The best reason to come to Knysna is for its **forests**, shreds of a once magnificent woodland that was home to **Khoi** clans and harboured a thrilling variety of wildlife, including elephant herds. The forests attracted European explorers and naturalists, and in their wake woodcutters, businessmen like George Rex and gold-diggers, all bent on making their fortunes here.

The French explorer Francois Le Vaillant was one of the first **Europeans** to sample the delights of these forests. He travelled through in the eighteenth century with Khoi trackers, who shot and cooked an elephant; the explorer found the animal's feet so "delicious" that he wagered that "never can our modern epicures have such a dainty at their tables". Two hundred years later, all that's left of the Khoi people are some names of local places. The legendary Knysna elephants have hardly fared better and are teetering on certain extinction.

Eleventh-hour **conservation** has ensured that some of the hardwoods have survived to maturity in reserves of woodland that can still take your breath away. A number of walks have been laid out in several of the forests – yet the effects of the nineteenth-century timber industry means that all these reserves are some distance from Knysna itself and require transport to get to. **Knysna Forest**

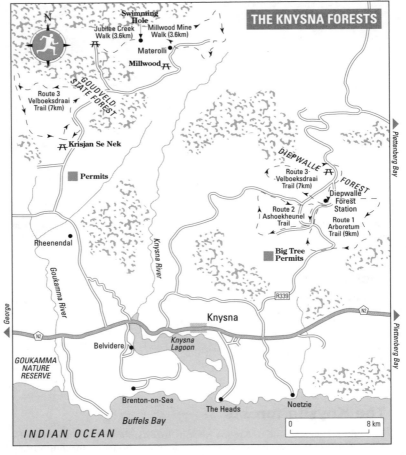

THE KNYSNA FORESTS

Swimming Hole
Jubilee Creek Walk (3.6km)
Millwood Mine Walk (3.6km)
Materolli
Millwood

GOUDVELD STATE FOREST

Route 3 Velboeksdraai Trail (7km)

Krisjan Se Nek

Permits

DIEPWALLE FOREST

Route 3 Velboeksdraai Trail (7km)

Diepwalle Forest Station

Route 2 Ashoekheunel Trail

Route 1 Arboretum Trail (9km)

Big Tree Permits

Rheenendal

Knysna River

Goukamma River

R339

N2

Knysna

Belvidere

Knysna Lagoon

GOUKAMMA NATURE RESERVE

Brenton-on-Sea

The Heads

Noetzie

Buffels Bay

INDIAN OCEAN

George

Plettenberg Bay

0   8 km

Tours and Mountain Biking Africa (Tony ☎082 783 8392 or Rolf ☎073 191 5420; Ⓦwww.mountainbikingafrica.co.za or www.knysnaforesttours .co.za) is an adventure company offering guided forest and coastal **hikes and mountain biking trips** in the area as well as bird-watching and fly fishing. Half-day hikes and biking trips start at R350 per person including refreshments. For self-guided trips, buy the second edition of the excellent book by Judith Hopley, *On Foot in the Garden Route*, available from Knysna's tourist office.

Goudveld State Forest

The beautiful **Goudveld State Forest** (daily sunrise–sunset; R4 if attendant is present, otherwise by self-issued free permit), just over 30km northwest of Knysna, is a mixture of plantation and indigenous woodland. It takes its name from the gold boom (*goudveld* is Afrikaans for goldfields) that brought hundreds of prospectors to the mining town of **Millwood** in the 1880s. The six hundred small-time diggers who were here by 1886, scouring out the hillsides and panning Jubilee Creek for alluvial gold, were rapidly followed by larger syndicates, and a flourishing little town quickly sprang up, with six hotels, three newspapers and a music hall.

However, the singing and dancing was shortlived and bust followed boom in 1890 after most of the mining companies went to the wall. The ever-hopeful diggers took off for the newly discovered Johannesburg goldfields, and Millwood was left a deserted **ghost town**. Over the years, its buildings were demolished or relocated, leaving an old store known as Materolli as the only original building standing. Today, the old town is completely overgrown, apart from signs indicating where the old streets stood. In **Jubilee Creek**, which provides a lovely shady walk along a burbling stream, the holes scraped or blasted out of the hillside are still clearly visible. Some of the old mine works have been restored, as have the original **reduction works** around the cocopan track, used to carry the ore from the mine to the works, which is still there after a century.

The forest itself is still lovely, featuring tall, indigenous trees, a delightful valley with a stream, and plenty of swimming holes and picnic sites. To get there from Knysna, follow the N2 west toward George, turning right onto the Rheenendal road just after the Knysna River, and continue for about 25km, following the Bibby's Koep signposts until the Goudveld sign.

Diepwalle Forest

The **Diepwalle Forest** (daily 6am–6pm; small entry fee), just over 20km northeast of Knysna, is the last haunt of Knysna's almost extinct elephant population. The only elephants you can expect to see here are on the painted markers indicating the three main hikes through these woodlands. However, if you're quiet and alert, you do stand a chance of seeing vervet monkeys, bushbuck and blue duiker. To get there from Knysna, follow the N2 east towards Plettenberg Bay, after 7km turning left onto the R339, which you should take for about 16km in the direction of Avontuur and Uniondale. The **forest station** is 10.5km after the tar gives way to gravel. All trails begin at the forest station, which provides a map of them.

THE GARDEN ROUTE | Knysna and the Knysna forests

Goudveld hikes

A number of clearly **waymarked hikes** traverse the Goudveld. The most rewarding (and easy going) is along **Jubilee Creek**, which traces the progress of a burbling brook for 3.5km through giant woodland to a gorgeous, deep rock-pool – ideal for cooling off after your effort. It's also an excellent place to encounter **Knysna louries**; keep an eye focused on the branches above for the crimson flash of their flight feathers as they forage for berries, and listen out for their harsh call above the gentler chorus provided by the wide variety of other birdlife here. You can pick up a **map** directing you to the creek from the entrance gate to the reserve; note that the waymarked trail is linear, so you return via the same route. There's a pleasant **picnic site** along the banks of the stream at the start of the walk.

A more strenuous option is the circular **Woodcutter Walk**, though you can choose either the three- or the nine-kilometre version. Starting at **Krisjan se Nek**, another picnic site not far past the Goudveld entrance gate, it meanders downhill through dense forest, passing through stands of tree ferns and returns uphill to the starting point. The picnic site is also where the nineteen-kilometre **Homtini Cycle Route** starts, taking you through forest and *fynbos* and offering wonderful mountain views. Be warned though; you really have to work hard at this, with one particular section climbing over 300m in just 3km. The tourist office has maps of the area.

Traffic signs warning motorists about elephants along the N2 between Knysna and Plettenberg Bay are rather optimistic: there are few indigenous pachyderms left and, with such an immense forest, sightings are rare. But such is the mystique attached to the **Knysna elephants** that locals tend to be a little cagey about just how few they number. By 1860, the thousands that had formerly wandered the once vast forests were down to five hundred, and by 1920 (twelve years after they were protected by law), there were only twenty animals left; the current estimate is three. Loss of habitat and consequent malnutrition, rather than full-scale hunting, seems to have been the principal cause of their decline.

An attempt was made in 1995 to create a breeding herd by introducing three young cows from the Kruger National Park, who it was hoped would breed with the forest's lone bull. The "bull" turned out also to be a cow and fled in terror when confronted with the three teenagers. In the chase that followed, one young elephant died from pneumonia, brought on by stress. By 1997, the two surviving aliens had moved east and were causing destruction to farmland near Plettenberg Bay. South African National Parks, working with local wildlife organizations, decided to relocate them to Shamwari Game Reserve (see p.278), some 300km to the east near Port Elizabeth, where they are doing well. The only elephants you're guaranteed to see near Knysna are at the **Knysna Elephant Park** (see below) or the **Knysna Elephant Sanctuary** (see p.243), both near Plettenberg Bay.

Diepwalle ("deep walls") is one of the highlights of the Knysna area and is renowned for its impressive density of huge trees, especially **yellowwoods**. Once the budget timber of South Africa, yellowwood was considered an inferior local substitute in place of imported pine, and found its way into the structure, floorboards, window frames and doors of thousands of often quite modest nineteenth-century houses in the Western and Eastern Cape. Today, its deep golden grain is so sought after that it commands premium prices at the annual auctions.

The three main hiking routes cover between 7km and 9km of terrain, and pass through flat to gently undulating country covered by indigenous forest and montane *fynbos*. If you're moderately fit, the hikes should take two to two-and-a-half hours. The nine-kilometre **Arboretum trail**, marked by black elephants, starts a short way back along the road you drove in on, and descends to a stream edged with tree ferns. Across the stream you'll come to the much-photographed **Big Tree**, a six-hundred-year-old Goliath yellowwood. The easy nine-kilometre **Ashoekheuwel trail**, marked by white elephants, crosses the Gouna River, where there's a large pool allegedly used by real pachyderms. Most difficult of the three hikes is the rewarding seven-kilometre **Velboeksdraai trail**, marked by red elephants, which passes along the foothills of the Outeniquas. Take care here to stick to the elephant markers, as they overlap with a series of painted footprints marking the Outeniqua trail, for which you need to have arranged a permit to use. Just before the Veldboeksdraai picnic site stands another mighty yellowwood regarded by some as the most beautiful in the forest.

Knysna Elephant Park

Heading east from Knysna along the N2, you come to the **Knysna Elephant Park** (daily 8.30am–5pm; ☎044 532 7732, ⍟www.knysnaelephantpark.co.za), 9km before Plettenberg Bay. The park was established in 1994 to provide a home for abandoned, orphaned and abused young elephants, and opened to the public in 2003. The youngest of its charges are reared by park staff, who hand-feed them forty litres of baby formula a day, and sleep next to them at night. The park offers **accommodation** in upmarket self-catering units (being upgraded; rates to be announced), which, as the management points out, are "situated on the second level of the elephant *boma* and as a result the sounds of the elephants and the cleaning of their stalls in the morning will be audible".

Of the **activities** on offer, the most popular are the roughly hour-long tours which leave every half hour (daily 8.30am–4.30pm; R130, children R65, bucket of feed R25), where you'll get the chance to touch and feed one of the pachyderms. You can also take a two-hour ride on an elephant or a guided nature walk of the same duration alongside one (R495, children R275; booking essential).

Plettenberg Bay and around

Over the Christmas holidays, forty thousand residents from Johannesburg's wealthy northern suburbs decamp to **PLETTENBERG BAY** (usually called Plett), 33km east of Knysna, and the flashiest of the Garden Route's seaside towns. It's wise to give it a miss at this time, with prices doubling and accommodation impossible to find. Yet, during low season, sipping champagne and sucking oysters while watching the sunset from a bar can be wonderful – the banal urban development on the surrounding hills somehow doesn't seem so bad because the bay views really are stupendous. Nevertheless it remains an expensive place to stay, with no cheap chalets or camping. For these you'll have to go to nearby **Keurbooms**. Further afield, the deep-blue **Tsitsikamma Mountains** drop sharply to the inlet and its large estuary, providing a constant vista to the town and its suburbs. The bay generously curves over several kilometres of white sands separated from the mountains by forest, which makes this a green and temperate location with rainfall throughout the year.

Southern right whales appear every winter, and are a seriously underrated attraction, while **dolphins** can be seen throughout the year, hunting or riding the surf, often in substantial numbers. **Swimming** is safe, and though the waters are never tropically warm they reach a comfortable temperature between November and April. River and rock **fishing** are rewarding all year long. One of the Garden Route's best short **hikes** covers a circuit round the Robberg Peninsula – a great tongue of headland that contains the western edge of the bay.

On the east of the bay lies the seaside resort of **Keurboomsstrand** and beyond that **The Crags** (both of them more or less suburbs of Plett) with its trio of wildlife parks: **Monkeyland**, **Birds of Eden** and the **Elephant Sanctuary**, all worth a visit, especially if you're travelling with kids.

Arrival, information and accommodation

Plettenberg Bay has an airport, but at the time of writing regular flights into it had been suspended. George airport, 95km away, is the closest place receiving scheduled **flights** (see p.219). Intercape, Greyhound and Translux **intercity buses** stop at the Shell Ultra City service station, just off the N2 in Marine Way, 2km from the town centre. As there's no transport around town, you'll need to arrange for your guesthouse to collect you. The **Baz Bus** drops passengers off at accommodation in town. Plett's lacklustre **tourist office**, Shop 35, Mellville

Whaling and gnashing of teeth

For conservationists, the monumental 1970s eyesore of the *Beacon Island Hotel* may not be such a bad thing, especially when you consider that previously the island was the site of a whale-processing factory established in 1806 – one of some half-dozen such plants erected along the Western Cape coast that year. Whaling continued at Plettenberg Bay until 1916. Southern right whales were the favoured species, yielding more oil and **whalebone** – an essential component of Victorian corsets – than any other. In the nineteenth century, a southern right would net around three times as much as a humpback caught along the Western Cape coast, leading to a rapid decline in the southern right population by the middle of the nineteenth century.

The years between the establishment and the closing of the Plettenberg Bay factory saw worldwide whaling transformed by the inventions of the industrial revolution. In 1852, the explosive harpoon was introduced, followed by the use of steam-powered ships five years later, making them swifter and safer for the crew. In 1863, Norwegian captain Sven Foyn built the first modern whale-catching vessel, which the inventive Foyn followed up in 1868 with the **cannon-mounted harpoon**. In 1913 Plettenberg Bay was the site of one of seventeen shore-based and some dozen floating factories between West Africa and Mozambique, which that year between them took about 10,000 whales.

Inevitably, a rapid decline in humpback populations began; by 1918, all but four of the shore-based factories had closed due to lack of prey. The remaining whalers now turned their attention to fin and blue whales. When the South African fin whale population became depleted by the mid-1960s to twenty percent of its former size, they turned to sei and sperm whales. When these populations declined, the frustrated whalers started hunting minke whales, which at 9m in length are too small to be a viable catch. By the 1970s, the South African whaling industry was in its death throes and was finally put out of its misery in 1979, when the government harpooned it by banning all activity surrounding whaling.

Corner, Main Street (Mon–Fri 8.30am–5pm, Sat 9am–1pm; ℡044 533 4065, ⓦwww.plettenbergbay.co.za), has photocopied maps of the town and may be able to help with finding accommodation.

Accommodation in town

An Ocean Watch 21 Plettenberg St ℡044 533 1700, ⓦwww.anoceanwatchguesthouse.co.za. A beautifully decorated beach-style home in which just about everything is shimmering white or cream. Four of the six rooms have sea views as does the heated swimming pool. Doubles from R840.

Anlin Beach House 33 Roche Bonne Ave ℡044 533 3694, ⓦwww.anlinbeachhouse.co.za. Two stylish and comfortably kitted out garden studios with kitchenettes, and a larger family unit with three bedrooms and a kitchen, in a garden setting close to Robberg Beach. Units are serviced daily. Doubles from R870.

Bayside Lodge 5 Sanganer Ave ℡044 533 0601, ⓦwww.baysidelodge.co.za. Modern two-storey brick house in a quiet suburban area about 500m from the beach with four en-suite rooms and a self-contained cottage. R950 per room or cottage.

Bright Water 15 Jackson St ℡044 533 0467, ⓦwww.brightwater.co.za. Three en-suite doubles in a centrally located, homely suburban house where you can rent the whole place or just a room, with use of the kitchen. Doubles from R590.

Cornerway House B&B 61 Longships Drive ℡044 533 3190, ⓦwww.cornerwayhouse.co.za. Five en-suite rooms in a comfortable bungalow decorated in English cottage-style and set in a pretty garden with a swimming pool. Doubles R780.

Lyell's 59 Beacon Way ℡044 533 5692. Three sparkling white en-suite B&B rooms (R700) in a suburban house, plus a budget

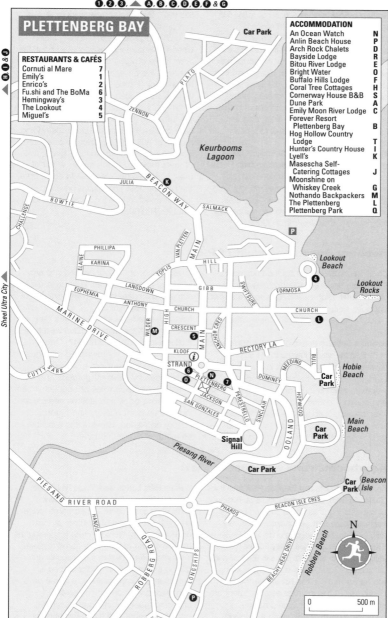

PLETTENBERG BAY

Car Park

RESTAURANTS & CAFÉS

Cornuti al Mare	7
Emily's	1
Enrico's	2
Fu.shi and The BoMa	6
Hemingway's	3
The Lookout	4
Miguel's	5

ACCOMMODATION

An Ocean Watch	N
Anlin Beach House	P
Arch Rock Chalets	D
Bayside Lodge	R
Bitou River Lodge	E
Bright Water	O
Buffalo Hills Lodge	F
Coral Tree Cottages	H
Cornerway House B&B	S
Dune Park	A
Emily Moon River Lodge	C
Forever Resort Plettenberg Bay	B
Hog Hollow Country Lodge	T
Hunter's Country House	I
Lyell's	K
Masescha Self-Catering Cottages	J
Moonshine on Whiskey Creek	G
Nothando Backpackers	M
The Plettenberg	L
Plettenberg Park	Q

Keurbooms Lagoon

Lookout Beach

Lookout Rocks

Shell Ultra City

Hobie Beach

Main Beach

Signal Hill

Piesang River

Car Park

Beacon Isle

N

Robberg Beach

0   500 m

18 THE GARDEN ROUTE

self-catering unit (R500). The upstairs living area has sea views.

Nothando Backpackers 5 Wilder St ☎ 044 533 0220, ✆ www.nothando.com. Top-notch child-friendly hostel run by a former schoolteacher. A 5min walk from Plett's main drag, the single-storey suburban house has seven double rooms (five en suite) and three dorms (two with four beds, the other with eight). Breakfast (of cereal, cheese, bread, muffins, yoghurt as well as bacon and eggs) is available for R35. Dorms R85, doubles R250, en-suite doubles R300, four-bed dorms R480.

The Plettenberg 40 Church St, Lookout Rocks ☎ 044 533 2030, ✆ www.plettenberg.com. Plett's prestige hotel is a large, luxurious establishment offering unbeatable views straight onto the ocean. But despite the sky-high rates you could still end up in a room overlooking the car park. Doubles from R3900.

Plettenberg Park Near the end of Robberg Rd, close to the airport ☎ 044 533 9067, ✆ www.plettenbergpark.co.za. Set in a private nature reserve and perched on a cliff edge above the swirling Indian Ocean, this stupendously located boutique hotel is the obvious choice for a romantic getaway. Seven suites have sea views and the remaining three look onto a beautiful little lake surrounded by *fynbos* inhabited by small game. The supremely luxurious rooms are furnished in supercool off-whites and oaty colours, with animal-skin rugs adding a dash of Africa. The shower in one room is surrounded on four sides by glass, two of them exposed to the ocean. A set of meandering timber steps leads down from the pool deck to an isolated private beach far below with a lovely natural rock pool. Doubles R4700.

Robberg Beach and west of Plett

Coral Tree Cottages Off the N2, 11km west of Plettenberg Bay ☎ 044 532 7822, ✆ www.coraltree.net. High-quality, spacious thatched cottages sleeping up to four, though unfortunately the roar of the N2 is never absent. From R700.

Hunter's Country House Off the N2, 10km west of Plett on the way to Knysna ☎ 044 532 7888, ✆ www.hunterhotels.com. Set in a woodland area, this is one of the best upmarket places to stay on the Garden Route, with an emphasis on country comfort rather than seaside glitz. Garden suite accommodation is in thatched cottages set in well-established gardens, each with an open fireplace,

private patio, underfloor heating and a/c, while the forest suites are larger and more sumptuous, each with its own private pool. From R2340 per suite.

Masescha Self-Catering Cottages 1km north off the N2, signposted 12km west from Plettenberg Bay ☎ 044 532 7647. Three plainly furnished, whitewashed cottages on a farm, with outdoor sitting areas surrounded by pleasant gardens and a forest. Good for families or couples, it has a swimming pool, and also on site are an indigenous plant nursery and natural-history bookshop. Breakfast is available as an extra. R350 per cottage.

Keurboomstrand and east of Plett

Arch Rock Chalets and Caravan Park Arch Rock ☎ 044 535 9409, ✆ www.archrock.co.za. A range of self-catering units and a caravan park-cum-campsite that get packed in summer with families. Self-catering units from R430.

Bitou River Lodge Bitou Valley Rd (the R340), about 4km from the N2 ☎ 044 535 9577, ✆ www.bitou.co.za. Great value in a lovely spot on the banks of the Bitou River. The five bedrooms at this intimate establishment are comfortable but unfussy and rooms overlook a pretty garden with a lily pond. B&B doubles R990.

Buffalo Hills Lodge and Safari Rietvlei Rd, Wittedrif Village ☎ 044 535 9739, ✆ www.buffalohills.co.za. Farm turned game lodge on the banks of the Bitou River, a 15min drive from Plett. No substitute for seeing the big five at one of the major game reserves, it nonetheless provides a thoroughly entertaining experience. The (dinner, bed & breakfast) package includes a game drive and guided walk on which you stand a chance of seeing rhino, buffalo, giraffe, bontebok, zebra and a number of other antelope. Accommodation in the main lodge, which resembles an old-style African farmhouse with animal skins thrown on a cement floor, is in four double rooms. A stone cottage a little away from the lodge sleeps four, while nine huge, luxury walk-in tents, pitched on their own decks, have spa baths. Breakfast is served on the lawn in front of the lodge, where you can watch animals graze while you do the same. DB&B R1100 per person.

Dune Park Keurboomstrand Rd, leading off the N2 and running along the shore to Keurbooms ☏044 535 9606, Ⓦwww.dunepark.co.za. Luxury hotel and self-catering cottages within spitting distance of the sea. Doubles from R1800.

Emily Moon River Lodge Rietvlei Rd, off the N2 (turn off at Penny Pinchers) ☏044 533 2982, Ⓦwww.emilymoon.co.za. That the owner of this highly imaginative and luxurious lodge, perched on a ridge looking across the Bitou Wetlands, is a dealer in ethnic art is plain to see. The place is not only littered with Batonga sculptures and Swazi crafts, it has in places been constructed out of artworks, such as the intricate Rajastani arched screen that is the entrance to the magnificently sited restaurant. Each of its chalets jetties out of the hillside to offer views from a private deck (and bathroom) of the oxbowing Bitou, along which small game can occasionally be seen. All chalets have fireplaces and TVs. There is a family suite that sleeps four in which kids are accommodated at a very discounted rate. Chalets R1860.

Forever Resort Plettenberg Bay 6km east of Plett and signposted off the N2 near Keurboomstrand ☏044 535 9309, Ⓦwww.foreversa.co.za /plettenberg. A sizeable family resort, with camping on the shady banks of the Keurbooms river, away from the sea, and a range of self-catering log cabins some with river views. Canoes and motorboats are available to rent, and there's a swimming pool. R830 for a one-bedroom cabin.

Hog Hollow Country Lodge Askop Rd, 18km east of Plettenberg Bay (turn south off the N2 at the signpost) ☏044 534 8879, Ⓦwww .hog-hollow.com. A touch of luxury in a private reserve where each of the chalets, done out in earthy colours and spiced up with African artefacts, has a bath or shower and its own wooden deck with vistas across the forest and Tsitsikamma Mountains; superb food is served as well. From here you could hike for a couple of hours through forest to Keurbooms Beach, or drive there in 15min. R2320 per chalet.

Moonshine on Whiskey Creek 14km east of Plettenberg Bay along the N2, signposted north of the N2 ☏044 534 8515 or 072 200 6656, Ⓦwww.whiskeycreek.co.za. Fully equipped bungalows, three wooden cabins and one creatively renovated labourers' cottage, nestled in indigenous forest, with a children's play area. One of the best reasons to come here is the access to a secluded natural mountain pool and waterfall at the bottom of nearby the gorge. From R550 per cabin.

The town and around

Plett's town **centre**, at the top of the hill, consists of a conglomeration of super-markets, swimwear shops, estate agents and restaurants aimed largely at the holiday trade. Visitors principally come for Plett's **beaches** – and there's a fair choice. Southeast of the town centre on a rocky promontory is **Beacon Island**, dominated by a 1970s hotel, an eyesore blighting a fabulous location. Beacon Island Beach, or **Main Beach**, right at the central shore of the bay, is where the fishing boats and seacats anchor a little out to sea. The small waves here make for calm swimming, and this is an ideal family spot. To the east is **Lookout Rocks**, attracting surfers to the break off a needle of rocks known as the Point and the predictable surf of **Lookout Beach**, to its east, which is also one of the nicest stretches of sand for bathers, body-surfers or sun lizards. Lookout Beach has the added attraction of a marvellously located restaurant (see p.242), from which you can often catch sight of **dolphins** cruising into the bay. From here you can walk several kilometres down the beach towards Keurbooms (see p.242) and the **Keurbooms Lagoon**.

Robberg Marine and Nature Reserve

One of the Garden Route's nicest walks is the four-hour, nine-kilometre circular route around the spectacular rocky peninsula of **Robberg**, 8km southeast of Plett's town centre. Here you can completely escape Plett's development and experience the coast in its wildest state, with its enormous horizons and lovely vegetation. Much of the walk takes you along high cliffs, from where you can often look down on seals surfacing near the rocks, dolphins arching through the water and, in winter, whales further out in the bay.

If you don't have time for the full circular walk, there is a shorter two-hour hike and a thirty-minute ramble. A **map** indicating these is available at the reserve gate when you pay to enter (daily: May–July 8am–6pm; rest of year 6.30am–8pm; R25). You'll need sturdy walking shoes, as the terrain is rocky and steep in parts, and the walk involves some serious rock-hopping on the west side. Bring a hat and a bottle of water, as there's no drinking water for much of the way and no tea rooms.

There's no public transport to the reserve; if you're staying at a backpacker lodge, ask about their transfers, which are generally reasonably priced. To **drive** there, take Strand Street towards Beacon Isle, turn right into Piesangs Valley Road, and 200m further on turn left into Robberg Road. Follow the airport signs, continuing for 3.5km, and look out for the Robberg turn-off to your left.

Whale-watching and other activities

A number of outfits run trips to see whales from the water, offering the chance of close encounters with a variety of whales and several dolphin species. Only **permitted whale watchers** are allowed to go within 50m of a whale; everyone must maintain a distance of 300m, and there are plans in the pipeline to increase this to 500m. In Plett, only Ocean Safaris and Ocean Blue (listed below) hold permits. Air-based trips have the additional attraction of spectacular aerial views of bays and river inlets.

Dolphin Adventures Central Beach ℡083 590 3405, ⊚www.dolphinadventures .co.za. Sea kayaking is one of the best ways to watch whales, and this outfit offers unforgettable trips with experienced and knowledgeable guides in two-person kayaks (2hr 30min; R250 including all equipment). Out of whale season it's still worth going out to see dolphins and seals.

Ocean Blue Central Beach ℡044 533 5083 or 083 701 3583, ⊚www.oceanblue .co.za. Sea-kayaking (R250) and boat-based whale-watching (R500) are among the offerings of this licensed outfit, which also runs township tours (see below).

Ocean Safaris Shop 3, Hopwood St ℡044 533 4963, ⊚www.oceansafaris.co.za. Tailor-made cruises from a licensed whale-watching company. Apart from southern rights, the trips run into common, bottlenose and humpback dolphins, as well as Bryde's and humpback whales – and the occasional minke and killer whale. The Close Encounter with Whales outing costs R500 per person and virtually guarantees sightings between July and November; the Discovery Cruise, which costs R300, is principally a dolphin-viewing excursion.

Other activities

Bungee jumping If you fancy swinging through the air, then pull in at Tsitsikamma Forest Village, 20km east of The Crags and Monkeyland turn-off along the N2, where you'll find the registration office for the world's highest commercial bungee jump. The jump takes place off the 216-metre Bloukrans River Bridge, 2km beyond the village down a signposted road that also brings you to a viewpoint. There's no need to book ahead for the jump, which costs R590 (including video) for the seven-second descent. For the not so brave there's a mesh catwalk over the jump site (R70), and a

Whale- and dolphin-watching

Elevated ocean panoramas give Plettenberg Bay outstanding vantages for watching **southern right whales** during their breeding season between June and October. An especially good vantage point is the area between the wreck of the Athene at the southern end of Lookout Beach and the Keurbooms River. The Robberg Peninsula is also excellent, looming protectively over this whale nursery and giving a grandstand view of the bay. Other good town viewpoints are from Beachy Head Road at Robberg Beach; Signal Hill in San Gonzales Street past the post office and police station; the *Beacon Island Hotel* on Beacon Island; and the deck of the *Lookout* restaurant on Lookout Beach. Outside Plett, the Kranshoek viewpoint and hiking trail offers wonderful whale-watching points along the route. To get there, head for Knysna, taking the Harkerville turn-off, and continue for 7km. It's also possible to view the occasional pair (mother and calf) at Nature's Valley, 29km east of Plett on the R102, and from Storms River Mouth. For more information about whales, see the box on p.236.

Eating, drinking and nightlife

Restaurants come and go in Plett at a similar lick to the tides, but one or two long-standing establishments have managed to remain afloat. Locally caught

160-metre flying fox – a zipline along which you slide while harnessed (R150, or R100 each for two people in tandem). For further information, contact Bloukrans Bungy (aka Face Adrenalin) at the bridge (℡042 281 1458, ⊛www.faceadrenalin.com).

Canoeing If you can tear yourself away from the beach, canoeing up the Keurbooms River gives an alternative perspective on the area. Cape Nature Conservation on the east side of the Keurbooms River Bridge along the N2 (℡044 533 2125) rents out fairly basic craft (R75 per day for a two-person canoe).

Elephant encounters The Knysna Elephant Park (see p.234) and Elephant Sanctuary (see p.243) offer the opportunity of close encounters with the large mammals.

Ferry trips and motorboating Keurbooms River Ferries, signposted on the east side of the Keurbooms River Bridge (℡083 254 3551, ⊛www.ferry.co.za), runs guided upriver boat trips (R90) with knowledgeable guides skilled at spotting rare birds, and also rents out motorboats (R80/hr; minimum 2hr). Be sure to bring a picnic for any of the boat trips; the river is dotted with little beaches that are a good place to stop for a swim and walk. The indigenous forest comes right down to the river edge, and the journey gets better the higher up you go, the gorge narrowing and the pleasure boats and water-skiers now left behind. Don't be put off by the river's cola colour (which comes from harmless oxides in the water): the water is quite fresh, and wonderful to swim in during the summer. While you're here, keep an eye out for the pink-flowering keurboom trees that lend their name to the river and resort.

Skydiving If you fancy a bit of an adrenaline rush, you can go tandem skydiving (no experience required) with Skydive Plettenberg Bay (℡082 905 7440, ⊛www .skydiveplett.com). It charges R1300 for a jump, with the option of paying extra for a DVD or video of the event.

Township tours Ocean Blue, Central Beach (℡044 533 5083 or 083 701 3583, ⊛www.oceanadventures.co.za), arranges relaxed tours into Plett's township with a guide who is a member of the community. Outings cost R100 per person and all the takings go into a development trust, which among other things, pays teachers' salaries and funds a creche.

fresh fish is the thing to look out for. And because the town is built on hills, you should generally expect terrific views.

Cornuti al Mare Seaview Properties,
1 Perestrella St ☎ 044 533 1277. Terrific pizzas – the best along the Garden Route – and also great pasta dishes that won't break the bank and endless views of sea and sky. Daily noon–11pm.

Emily's Rietvlei Rd, off the N2 (turn off at Penny Pinchers) ☎ 044 533 2982. Boutique restaurant attached to *Emily Moon's Lodge* that's widely regarded as the best eatery in the area, offering stunning views of the Bitou Wetland and classical French cuisine with an edge. There's no set menu as everything is based on what seasonal ingredients are locally available on the day, but there's always a choice of five or six starters and mains with a small range of desserts. Booking is essential. Expensive. Tues–Sun noon–3pm & daily 6–11pm.

Enrico's Main Beach, Keurboomstrand. Great, mid-priced Italian standards – thin-based pizzas, pasta and veal – to enjoy alfresco on the beach or in the stylish indoor restaurant. Daily 11.30am–10pm.

Fu.shi and **The BoMa** The Upper Deck, 3 Strand St. Two mid-priced eateries rolled into one right in the centre, surrounded by picture windows to make the most of the elevated views. As its name suggests *Fu.shi's* menu is Asian fusion, featuring sushi and various coquettishly named dishes – Nuggets of Pleasure (wasabi prawns with cashew salad), Flights of Fantasy (sliced duck breast with pak choi) and Cocubine's Whisper (chilli chocolate fondant with pistachio brittle). The *BoMa* is a cocktail bar cum breakfast and snack joint. Mon–Sat noon–5pm & 6pm–late, Sun 10am–5pm.

Hemingway's On the Bitou River, just off the N2 between Plettenberg Bay and Keurbooms ☎ 044 535 9445. Reasonably priced meals are served at this pleasant pub with outdoor seating on the edge of the calm lagoon. The fish and chips are especially recommended. Daily 11am–10pm.

The Lookout Lookout Beach. Marvellous bay views – if you're lucky, you'll see whales and dolphins rollicking in the surf – at this mid-priced, casual bar-restaurant focusing on seafood, including crayfish. Daily 9.30am–late.

Miguel's Melville's Corner, corner of Main and Marine sts ☎ 044 533 5056. Upmarket Portuguese cuisine, in a stunning location bang in the town centre with views of the ocean and passing trade. Its speciality is *espetadas* – beef, chicken or seafood cooked with jalapeno peppers and served on a large skewer. Open daily from 8am for breakfast, lunch and dinner.

Keurboomstrand and The Crags

Some 14km east of Plettenberg Bay by road, across the Keurbooms River, is the uncluttered resort of **KEURBOOMSTRAND** (Keurbooms for short), little more than a suburb of Plett, sharing the same bay and with equally wonderful beaches, but less safe for swimming. The safest place to take the waves is at **Arch Rock**, in front of the caravan park, though **Picnic Rock Beach** is also pretty good. A calm and attractive place, Keurbooms has few facilities, and if you're intending to stay here (see "Accommodation", pp.238–239) you should stock up in Plettenberg Bay beforehand. One of Keurbooms' highlights is **canoeing** or, if you feel less energetic, taking a ferry ride or motorboat up the Keurbooms River (see box, p.241).

The Crags, 2km east of Keurbooms, comprises a collection of smallholdings along the N2, a bottle store and a few other shops on the forest edge, but the reason most visitors pull in here is for the **Elephant Sanctuary**, **Monkeyland** and **Birds of Eden**. To reach them, look out for the BP filling station, then take the Monkeyland/Kurland turn-off and follow the Elephant Sanctuary/Monkeyland signs for 2km.

Elephant Sanctuary

The Elephant Sanctuary (daily 8am–5pm; ☎ 044 534 8145, ⓦ www.elephantsanctuary .co.za) offers a chance of close encounters with its half-dozen pachyderms, all of whom were saved from culling in Botswana and the Kruger National Park. On the popular one-hour Trunk-in-Hand programme (daily on the hour: 8am–noon & 1.30–3.30pm; R250, children R125) you get to walk with an elephant holding the tip of its trunk in your hand and also to stroke, feed and interact with it. The programme includes an informative talk about elephant behaviour. 15minute elephant-back rides (R595) are among the other packages on offer.

Monkeyland

Monkeyland (daily 8.30am–5pm; free entry to viewing deck; safaris into the forest: R115; combined ticket with Birds of Eden R184; ☎044 534 8906, ⓦwww.monkeyland.co.za), 400m beyond the Elephant Sanctuary, brings together primates from several continents, all of them orphaned or saved from a dismal life as pets. The place is a sanctuary, so none of the animals has been taken from the wild – and most wouldn't have the skills to survive there. Life is made as comfortable as possible for them and they are free to move around the reserve, looking for food and interacting with each other and their environment in as natural a way as possible. For your own safety and that of the monkeys, you are not allowed to wander around alone. Guides take visitors on walking "safaris", during which you come across water holes, experience a living indigenous forest and enjoy chance encounters with creatures such as ringtail lemurs from Madagascar and squirrel monkeys from South America. The safaris are entertaining and also feature an informed commentary covering issues such as the differences between monkeys and apes, primate communication and social systems. One of the sanctuary's highlights is crossing the Indiana Jones-esque rope bridge (at 128m, it's purportedly the longest such bridge in the southern hemisphere) spanning a canyon to pass through the upper reaches of the forest canopy, where a number of species spend their entire lives. For refreshments or meals, there's a restaurant with a forest deck at the day lodge.

Birds of Eden

Under the same management as Monkeyland and right next door, **Birds of Eden** (daily 8.30am–5pm; R115, combined ticket with Monkeyland R184) is a huge bird sanctuary which took four years to create. Great effort was taken to place netting over a substantial tract of virgin forest with as little impact as possible. The result is claimed to be the largest free-flight aviary in the world. As with Monkeyland, most of Birds of Eden's charges were already living in cages and are now free to move and fly around within the confines of the large enclosure (so large in fact that you can easily spend an hour slowly meandering along its winding, wheelchair-friendly, wooden walkway). Although it has come in for some criticism for cutting off local birds from their traditional turf and disrupting some migration routes, the result is quite remarkable, with little lakes, waterfalls and a wonderful suspension bridge along the way. Most of the birds are exotics, some impossibly brightly coloured (such as the incandescent scarlet ibis from South America and golden pheasant from China), but you'll also see a number of locals, such as the Knysna lourie and South Africa's national bird, the blue crane. Watch out for the cheeky cockatoos that may alight on your shoulder and steal buttons from your shirt or beads from round your neck. A **restaurant** by one of the lakes sells light meals and liquid refreshments.

Tsitsikamma National Park, Nature's Valley and Storms River

The **Tsitsikamma National Park,** roughly midway between Plettenberg Bay and Port Elizabeth, is the highlight of any Garden Route trip. Starting from just beyond Keurboomstrand in the west, the national park extends for 68km into the Eastern Cape along a narrow belt of coast, with dramatic foamy surges of rocky coast, deep river gorges and ancient hardwood forests clinging to the edge of tangled, green cliffs. You'd be crazy to pass up its main attraction, the **Storm's River Mouth**, the most dramatic estuary on this exhilarating stretch of coast. Established in 1964, Tsitsikamma is also South Africa's oldest marine reserve, stretching 5.5km out to sea, with an **underwater trail** open to snorkellers and licensed scuba divers.

Tsitsikamma has two sections: **De Vasselot** in the west and **Storms River Mouth** in the east. Each section can only be reached down a winding tarred road from the N2 (there's no way of getting from one to the other through the park itself). De Vasselot incorporates **Nature's Valley**, the only resort in the park, and the most low-key settlement on the Garden Route, with a fabulous sandy beach stretching for 3km. South Africa's ultimate hike, the five-day **Otter trail** (see box, p.215), connects the two sections of the park (see box, p.248).

The nearest settlement to Storms River Mouth, some 14km to its north at the top of steep winding road, is the confusingly named **Storms River Village**, which is outside the national park and some distance from any part of the river. While Storms River Village makes a convenient base for adventure activities in the vicinity and day-trips down to Storms River Mouth, the experience is very different from staying overnight at the coast.

Nature's Valley and De Vasselot

The **De Vasselot** section, at the western end of Tsitsikamma, extends inland into a rugged and hilly interior incised with narrow valleys and traversed by a series of footpaths. In fact De Vasselot is not a name that trips readily off South African tongues – most people know the section for **Nature's Valley**, a pleasingly old-fashioned settlement on the Groot River Lagoon with 20km of beach. Bypassed by the N2, and by intercity buses and tour parties, Nature's Valley, 29km east of Plettenberg Bay, down the lovely winding Groot River pass (along which you'll often encounter baboon troops), is the place to go if you're after a quiet time along the Garden Route.

There are plenty of good **walks** at Nature's Valley, many starting from the De Vasselot campsite, 1km north of the village, where you can pick up maps and information about birds and trees. One of the loveliest places to head for is **Salt River Mouth**, 3km west of Nature's Valley, where you can swim and picnic – though you'll need to ford the tannin–dark river at low tide. This walk starts and ends at the café at Nature's Valley. Also recommended is the circular six-kilometre **Kalanderkloof trail**, which starts at the De Vasselot campsite, ascends to a lookout point, and descends via a narrow river gorge graced with a profusion of huge Outeniqua yellowwood trees and Cape wild bananas.

Public transport to Nature's Valley is limited to the **Baz Bus**, which deposits passengers at their accommodation. The village centre is little more than an all-in-one restaurant, pub and small trading store that acts as an informal, but excellent, **information** bureau (☎ 044 531 6835, ⦿ www.natures-valley.co.za), and can help you find the limited **accommodation** available.

If you're **self-catering**, stock up on supplies before you get to Nature's Valley. The only place to buy a meal is at the **restaurant**, on the corner of Forest and St Michael streets, which serves seafood, steaks, burgers and toasted sandwiches, and provides the only nightlife apart from gazing at the stars.

Accommodation

Accommodation in Nature's Valley itself is pretty limited, which contributes to its low-key charm, but you'll find some choice options on the road leading off the N2 into the village, just before the switchbacks begin. Apart from the places listed below, self-catering accommodation can be rented through Karen van Rooyen (☎ 082 772 2972), who handles around eight cottages (R400–800 per cottage) in and around Nature's Valley – most of which sleep between six and eight people.

De Vasselot restcamp 1km to the north of the village. Bookings through South African National Parks (see p.40), or if you're already in Nature's Valley, the camp supervisor ☎ 044 531 6700. Campsites tucked into indigenous forest, and basic two-person forest huts with communal ablution facilities. R275 per hut.

Four Fields Farm Nature's Valley Rd; 3km from the N2 along the R102 and 6km from Nature's Valley. ☎ 044 534 8708, ⦿ http://cyberperk.co.za /fourfields. A welcoming, charmingly unpretentious former dairy farm, less than 10min drive from the sea at Nature's Valley. Five en-suite bedrooms (R600), simply furnished with beautiful old pieces, have French doors leading to their own private decks, which in turn open onto a lovely garden surrounded by fields. There's also a self-catering cottage sleeping four (R600).

Froggy Pond Second house on the right as you enter Nature's Valley ☎ 044 531 6835, ⦿ www .natures-valley.co.za. Self-catering accommodation in a two-storey timber and brick cottage. Downstairs is a self-contained flatlet with a double bedroom and living area that can sleep two adults and two children; upstairs are two double rooms with en-suite showers. Doubles R300.

Lily Pond Lodge 102 Nature's Valley Rd; 3km from the N2 along the R102 and 6km from Nature's Valley ☎ 044 534 8767, ⦿ www.lilypond .co.za. Probably the most memorable place to stay in the vicinity of Nature's Valley, the lodge distinguishes itself through its sharp sense of style and its commitment to luxury. Modernist in inspiration, its flowing spaces and enormous windows create a sense of supreme calm, which is echoed outdoors in the huge lily pond the lodge is named after. The four en-suite rooms have French doors opening onto private terraces, sound systems, TV and Wi-Fi access, while the two spacious luxury suites also have their own lounge, underfloor heating and king-sized beds. There are three even more luxurious garden suites and a honeymoon suite that has its own private garden. Doubles from R1050.

Nature's Valley Guest House 411 St Patrick's Ave ☎ 044 531 6805, ⦿ www .naturesvalleyguesthouse.co.za. A well-located and exceptionally well-priced B&B with six doubles, three of them en suite. A snooker table, TV lounge, canoe, surfboard and windsurfer are available for guests, and you can set out from the guesthouse on two- to six-hour hikes along the beaches or through the forest. Doubles from R400.

Tranquility Lodge 130 Saint Michael's St (next to the shop) ☎ 044 531 6663, ⦿ www .tranquilitylodge.co.za. If Nature's Valley has a centre then this comfortable lodge, next to the village's only shop, is bang in the middle of it. A two-storey brick and timber building set in a garden that feels as if it's part of the encroaching forest, it is just 50meters from the beach. Breakfast is served on an upstairs deck among the treetops. All rooms are en suite, the standard ones with a shower, the superior ones with a bath as well and satellite TV. There's also a larger honeymoon suite with a spa bath, double shower, fireplace and private deck. Doubles from R880.

Storms River Mouth

In contrast to the languid lagoon and long soft sands of Nature's Valley, **Storms River Mouth** (daily 7am–7pm; R80 per person; ☎042 281 1607), 55km from Plettenberg Bay, presents the elemental face of the Garden Route, with the dark Storms River surging through a gorge to battle with the surf. **Storms River Mouth Restcamp**, sited on tended lawns, is poised between a craggy shoreline of black rocks pounded by foamy white surf and steeply raking forested cliffs, and is without a doubt the ultimate location along the southern Cape coast. Don't confuse this with **Storms River Village** just off the N2, which is nowhere near the sea.

Walking is the main activity at the Mouth, and at the visitors' office at the restcamp you can get **maps** of short, waymarked coastal trails that leave from here. These include steep walks up the forested cliffs, where you can see 800-year-old yellowwood trees with views onto a wide stretch of ocean. Most rewarding is the **three-kilometre hike** west from the restcamp along the start of the Otter trail to a fantastic **waterfall** pool at the base of fifty-metre-high falls where you can swim right on the edge of the shore. Less demanding is the kilometre-long **boardwalk stroll** from the restaurant to the suspension bridge to see the river mouth. On your way to the bridge, don't miss the dank *strandloper* (beachcomber) **cave**. Hunter-gatherers frequented this area between 5000 and 2000 years ago, living off seafood in wave-cut caves near the river mouth. A modest display shows an excavated midden, with clear layers of little bones and shells.

If you're desperate to walk the **Otter trail** (see box, p.215), which begins at Storms River, and have been told that it is full, don't despair. A single person or a couple can stand a chance of getting in on the back of a last-minute cancellation, so it may be worth hanging out at the Mouth for a night or two.

Swimming at the Mouth is restricted to a safe and pristine little sandy bay below the restaurant, though conditions can be icy in summer if there are easterly winds and cold upwellings of deep water from the continental shelf. Hikes and other outdoor pursuits can be arranged through one of the local operators (see box, p.248).

Practicalities

Storms River Mouth is 18km south of **Storms River Bridge**. Most people stop at the bridge, on the N2, to gaze into the deep river gorge and fill up at the most beautifully located filling and service station in the country. Even if your time is limited and you can't spend the night at Storms River Mouth, it's still worth nipping down for a meal, a restorative walk or a swim in the summer. You'll need your own wheels, though, as there's no public transport to the Mouth. The only **eating** place is the restcamp restaurant, serving breakfasts and à la carte meals which, alas, are less memorable than the startling views.

A variety of **accommodation**, all with sea views, is available at **Storms River Mouth Restcamp** (☎042 281 1607), including superb campsites just metres from where the surf breaks on the rocks; incredibly good-value two-person cabins (R275 per cabin), which provide bedding and towels, share ablutions and have communal catering facilities; comfortable one-bedroom self-catering log cottages (from R530 per cottage), including breakfast; oceanette mini-apartments (R500) close to the sea, also including breakfast; and family oceanettes (R880) and a luxury cottage (R1740) for a minimum of four people. All are heavily subscribed in season, so advance booking through South African National Parks is essential (see p.40).

▲ Bridge over Storms River Mouth

Storms River Village

About a kilometre south of the national road, **STORMS RIVER VILLAGE** is a tranquil place crisscrossed by a handful of dirt roads and with about forty houses, enjoying mountain vistas. It offers a number of places to stay, several of which are backpacker lodges, a couple of general dealers selling basics, a liquor store and an adventure centre which runs zip-line tours though the forest canopy (see box below). While Storms River Village is an excellent base for adventure activities, it is well outside the national park and if you want to be at the seaside, is no substitute for staying at the River Mouth or Nature's Valley.

Storms River activities

Storms River Village makes a good base for numerous local adventure activities as well as those further afield. If you don't have your own transport, you can take advantage of the reasonably priced shuttle services operated for its guests by **Dijembe Backpackers** at Formosa and Assegai streets, Storms River Village (☎042 281 1842, ⓦwww.thedidge.co.za), which also acts as a central booking agency for a wide range of activities in the vicinity.

Boat trips SANParks (☎042 281 1607) runs trips (every 45min 9.30am–2.45pm; R40) about 1km up Storms River leaving from near the dive shop, just beneath the main building.

Canopy tour See zip line (below).

Mountain biking Dijembe Backpackers rents out mountain bikes for the day (R80 for guests, R100 for others).

Quad biking Bikes can be rented for R300 an hour from Tsitsikamma Adventure Park (☎082 578 1090, ⓦwww.tsitsikammaadventure.co.za).

Dolphin trail A wonderful 20-kilometre trail covered in two-and-a-half days and three nights, with luxury accommodation and no carrying of backpacks. The trail starts at Storms River Mouth, and winds its way eastwards through natural *fynbos* and virgin forest, over rugged rocks at the water's edge, to end on the banks of the Sandrif River at The Fernery. The package includes all meals, two well-trained local guides, a boat trip into the Storms River Gorge and a 4WD drive through the old Storms River Pass. Book through The Fernery (☎042 280 3588, ⓦwww.dolphintrail.co.za; R3300 per person).

Horse riding Dijembe Backpackers takes couples on guided two-and-a-half-hour hacks into the forest for R250, including lunch.

Snorkelling You can rent a wetsuit, snorkel, mask and flippers for R80 from the dive shop, just below the main building at Tsitsikamma National Park (☎042 281 1607).

Woodcutters' Journey A relaxed jaunt organized by Storms River Adventures (☎042 281 1836, ⓦwww.stormsriver.com; teatime trip R90, lunch trip R175), which has its headquarters next to the Storms River village post office. The trip takes you down through the forest to the river along the old Storms River Pass in a specially designed trailer, drawn by a tractor.

Zip line Run by Storms River Adventures (see Woodcutters' Journey, above), the Canopy Tour (R420), through the treetops, gives a bird's eye view of the forest as you travel 30m above ground along a series of interconnected cables attached to the tallest trees. The system has been constructed in such a way that not a single nail has been hammered into any tree. A faster, higher alternative, geared more to adrenaline junkies, is the zipline tour across the Kruis River at the Tsitsikamma Adventure Park (☎082 578 1090, ⓦwww.tsitsikammaadventure.co.za; R300), which at times is 50m above the ground and crisscrosses an awesome ravine, zipping over three waterfalls, with the longest slide measuring 211m.

As far as **eating out** goes the choice is between the restaurant at the *Village Inn* or *Rafters* at *The Armagh* (see below).

Accommodation

The Armagh Fynbos Ave ☎042 281 1512, ⓦwww.thearmagh.com. A hospitable guest-house in a beautiful garden that drifts off into the *fynbos*. The rooms include a rather tired looking honeymoon suite and four standard rooms, all of which open onto the garden. There's also a decent restaurant. Doubles from R650.

At the Woods Guest House 49 Formosa St, along the main drag into town ☎042 281 1446, ⓦwww.atthewoods.co.za. Friendly, modern guesthouse that's the nicest place in town, with traditional reed ceilings and large, comfortable rooms with king-sized beds and French doors that open onto garden verandas, or upstairs, onto private decks with mountain views. Three-course home-cooked dinners can be arranged. Doubles from R790.

Dijembe Backpackers Corner of Formosa and Assegai sts ☎042 281 1842, ⓦwww .thedidge.co.za. Chilled hostel with lots on offer, including bike rental, horse-riding and shuttles to all the local attractions as well as great-value accommodation. Dorms R80, doubles R220, en-suite double R260.

Tsitsikamma Lodge A couple of kilometres east of town along the N2, 8km east of the Storms

River Bridge ☎042 280 3802, ⓦwww .tsitsikamma.com. Thirty cosy A-frame cabins with their own decks and connected by boardwalks that traverse beautifully kept gardens. Most cabins have their own Jacuzzi, and there are a number of forest walks, including the lodge's famous nudist hiking trail along the river. There's also a restaurant serving South African cuisine. R1350 per cabin.

Tsitsikamma Village Inn Along the road into the village and left at the T-junction ☎042 281 1711, ⓦwww.village-inn.co.za. A charmingly old-fashioned hotel – part of the huge Protea chain – in the village with 49 rooms in eleven cottages, each differently themed and surrounding a manicured garden. Doubles R900.

Tube 'n Axe On the corner of Darnell and Saffron sts ☎042 281 1757, ⓦwww .tubenaxe.co.za. A wacky place that works hard to compete with the bright lights of Knysna and Plett by offering backpackers drumming nights, a pool table and loads of laughs. Dorms R80; two-person elevated tents R90 per person; and double rooms R220 per room.

19

Route 62 and the Little Karoo

One of the most rewarding journeys in the Western Cape is an inland counterpart to the Garden Route (see Chapter 18) – the **mountain route** from Cape Town to Port Elizabeth, largely along the R62, and thus often referred to as **Route 62**. Nowhere near as well known as the coastal journey, this trip takes you through some of the most dramatic passes and *poorts* (valley routes) in the country and crosses a frontier of *dorps* and drylands. This "back garden" is in many respects more rewarding than the actual Garden Route, being far less developed, with spectacular landscapes, quieter roads and some great small towns to visit. The central point is

▲ Karoo scenery

Oudtshoorn, but it's particularly worth breaking your journey before then, to explore the pretty towns of **McGregor**, **Montagu** and **Barrydale**, while **Worcester** and Robertson can safely be missed, unless you want to look at the excellent botanic gardens at Worcester, or stop off to buy wine at Robertson.

Continuing east from Barrydale, the R62 the landscape becomes more spare as you get into the **Little Karoo** (or Klein Karoo), a vast, khaki-coloured hinterland (the name is a Khoi word meaning "hard and dry") with low, wiry scrub and dotted with flat-topped hills. One unsung surprise along the way is **Calitzdorp**, a rustic little *dorp*, five hours' solid driving from Cape Town, down whose backstreets a few unassuming wine farms produce some of South Africa's best port. By contrast, the well-trumpeted attractions of **Oudtshoorn**, half an hour further on, are the ostrich farms and the massive **Cango Caves**, one of the country's biggest tourist draws. Less than 70km from the coast, with good transport connections, Oudtshoorn marks the convergence of the mountain and coastal roads and is usually treated as a leisurely day-trip away from the Garden Route. From Oudtshoorn, over the most dramatic of all passes in the Cape – the unpaved **Swartberg Pass**, 27km of spectacular switchbacks and zigzags through the Swartberg Mountains – is **Prince Albert**, a favourite Karoo village whose spare beauty and remarkable light make it popular with artists; the village boasts a worthwhile gallery of the artists' work and some excellent accommodation.

Worcester to McGregor

Worcester, the large functional hub of the region, is on the N1 just 110km from Cape Town, and worth a stop if you are interested in Cape flora. As you enter Worcester from Cape Town, signs point to the **Karoo Botanic Gardens** (daily 7am–7pm; R16; ☏023 347 0785), a sister reserve to Kirstenbosch in Cape Town (see p.93), known for its show of indigenous spring flowers and succulents. Looking out over the gardens onto an attractive mountain backdrop, the pleasant **restaurant** here (daily 9am–5pm) serves light meals.

South from Worcester, the R60 slithers past **Robertson**, a dull little town, but centre of an excellent wine route and a good place to stock up on reds. If you're not stocking up on wine, press straight on from Robertson to **McGREGOR**, fifteen minutes to the south at the end of a minor road signposted off the R60, and 180km from Cape Town. Don't be tempted by an approach from the south which may look like a handy back route – you'd need a 4WD for this.

McGregor

McGregor is an attractive place, with whitewashed cottages glaring in the summer daylight amid the low scrub, vines and olive trees, and a quiet, relaxed atmosphere that has attracted a small population of spiritual seekers and artists. Residents are urged to build in harmony with existing style and thus maintain the town's character. It makes a great weekend break from Cape Town, with a couple of decent restaurants, plenty of well-priced accommodation and a beautiful retreat centre with reasonably priced massage and other body-work. Spending a day wine-tasting around McGregor and Robertson is another drawcard, as long as it's not a Sunday when almost everything is closed.

McGregor gained modest prosperity in the nineteenth century by becoming a centre of the whipstock industry, supplying wagoners and transport riders with long bamboo sticks for goading oxen. There aren't too many ox–drawn wagons today, and tourism, though developing, is still quite limited. One main reason people come here is to walk the **Boesmanskloof Traverse** (see box, p.203), which starts 14km from McGregor and crosses to Greyton on the other side of the mountain. From McGregor you can walk a section of trail, hiking to the main waterfall and back to the trailhead, which is a three- to four-hour round hike of exceeding beauty through the river gorge, or *kloof* in Afrikaans.

You'll find most of what you want down Voortrekker Street, McGregor's main thoroughfare, dominated by a Dutch Reformed church. In the same street you'll also find the small, clearly signposted **tourist office** (Mon–Fri 9am–1pm & 2–4.30pm, Sat & Sun 9am–1pm; ☎023 625 1954, ⊛www .tourismmcgregor.co.za), which can book you accommodation, and issue permits for walking the whole Boesmanskloof Traverse or simply for the waterfall section (R25). Staff will also direct you to artists' studios in town, and to complementary health practitioners offering massage and yoga, and give you times of the daily meditation sessions at Temenos Reatreat Centre.

Accommodation

All the central **accommodation** is on Voortrekker Street or clearly indicated off it along the town's gravel roads. The switched–on tourist office (see above) offers a free booking service and has a list of accommodation on its website.

Lady McGregor Voortrekker St; book through the tourist office. Cheapest accommodation in town, offering thoroughly decent and clean rooms and a dorm above the Jack and Grape pub and restaurant. All linen provided, with good self-catering facilities, pool and satellite TV. Doubles R275.

McGregor Country Cottages Voortrekker St ☎023 625 1816, ⊛www.mcgregor.org.za /countrycottages.php. Tranquil self-catering in a complex of cottages with traditional reed ceilings and fireplaces, surrounded by gardens, orchards and vegetable patches. There's also a pool. A separate honeymoon house is available and worth the price. Wheelchair- and child-friendly. From R545 per cottage.

Old Mill Lodge On the southern outskirts of town, at the end of Voortrekker St ☎023 625 1841, ⊛www.oldmilllodge.co.za. A set of appealing two-bedroomed cottages at a historic country lodge, with a tranquil ambience, surrounded by vineyards and gardens. There's also a swimming pool and a good restaurant. The lovely dining area has the best views in town and log fires in

winter, and the engaging wine-buff host will make sure you drink something memorable for dinner and direct you to the latest finds in the Robertson winelands. B&B doubles R345.

Temenos Country Retreat On the corner of Bree and Voortrekker streets ☎023 625 1871, ⊛www.temenos.org.za. Retreat centre with cottages dotted about beautiful gardens and walkways, a lap-length swimming pool, a library and meditation spaces. Safe and peaceful, it's ideal for lone women. Self-catering available, or B&B. Doubles R650 per room.

Whipstock Farm 8km from the centre on the southerly continuation of Voortrekker St ☎023 625 1733, ⊛www.whipstock.za.net. Restored cottages on an old citrus, almond and grape farm in the mountains. *Whipstock* is 5km from the McGregor side of the Boesmanskloof Traverse (see box, p.203), and the owners will pick you up from the trail for free if you're overnighting. Swimming, bikes and canoes are available free to guests. Minimum stay two nights. Great for kids. Full board R330.

Eating and drinking

All the establishments mentioned here are along or off Voortrekker Street. Pick of the bunch is *Tebaldi's at Temenos* (Tues–Sun 9.30am–4.30pm, dinner Thurs–Sat from 7pm), with tapas, cheeses, Italian fare and local wines served in a tranquil garden setting or at streetside tables. *Villagers* (Mon–Sat 9am–4.30pm) sells its own olives, preserves and organic fruit nectars and is good for daytime snacks and teas, with a veranda from which to watch the passing scene. Opposite, *DeliGirls and Bistro* (Mon & Wed–Sat 9.30am–4.30pm, Sun 9.30am–2.30pm) is best for picnic supplies with home-made bread, cheese, chocolate and other tempting goodies; it also serves coffee and light lunches.

At *Old Mill Lodge* you can splash out on a four-course set evening meal (though make a reservation for this by lunchtime). You can sit by the fire in the winter, or enjoy its veranda's views on summer evenings. Decidedly convivial is the *Green Gables Country Inn*, for well-priced three-course dinners, including offerings such as roast lamb with Mediterranean vegetables, plus coffee and cake during the day; there's also a friendly **pub** here.

Montagu

Some 190km from Cape Town, and 47km from McGregor, is **MONTAGU**, a major peach- and apricot-growing region, whose soaring mountains with twisted red and ochre strata dominate the town with its pleasing Victorian architecture.

The town was named in 1851 after **John Montagu**, the visionary British Secretary of the Cape, who realized that the colony would never develop without decent communications and was responsible for commissioning the first mountain passes connecting remote areas to Cape Town. Montagu is best known for its **hot springs**, but serious **rock climbers** come for its cliff faces, which are regarded as among the country's most challenging. One of South Africa's top climbers runs *De Bos Guest Farm* (see below) which you could use as a base for climbing. You can also explore the mountains on a couple of trails or, easiest of all, on a tractor ride onto one of the peaks. Montagu is also conveniently positioned for excursions along both the Robertson and Little Karoo **wine routes**.

Arrival, information and accommodation

Buses to Montagu are restricted to a service from Belville in Cape Town via Paarl and Worcester, operated by Munniks (℡021 637 1850), departing Cape Town on Friday, Saturday and Sunday. Montagu's useful **tourist office** is at 24 Bath St (Mon–Fri 8.45am–4.45pm, Sat 9am–5pm, Sun 9.30am–noon & 3–5pm; ℡023 614 2471).

Even if you're here for the springs, it is far nicer to find somewhere to **stay** in town rather than at the spa, which amounts to little more than a large crowded resort, especially at weekends and school holidays.

Guesthouses, B&Bs and hotels

Aasvoelkrans 1 Van Riebeeck St ℡023 614 1228, ⓦwww.aasvoelkrans.co.za. Three exceptionally imaginative garden rooms at a guesthouse situated on a Arabian stud farm, in a pretty part of town. R350 per person.
Cynthia's 3 Krom St ℡023 614 2760, ⓦwww.cynthias-cottages.co.za. Seven self-catering cottages dotted around the west side of

town, all in old houses, with gardens and braai areas, and near the starting point for hiking trails. Cottages are R270–650 depending on the size of the accommodation needed.
De Bos Guest Farm Brown St ℡023 614 2532, ⓦwww.debos.co.za. Camping, dorms and basic doubles on a farm at the western

edge of town, where the well-known climber and author Stuart Brown can take you on guided climbs, though you need to have your own gear. Even if you're not a climber, you'll meet more people here and have more fun than staying at the caravan park next door, and you can go on hikes right from your doorstep. From R100 per person.

Montagu Springs Signposted off the R62, west of town T 023 614 1050, W www.montagusprings.co.za. Large resort with fully equipped self-catering chalets, some more luxurious than others, sleeping four. Prices start at R475 per chalet during the week, and R725 at weekends or school holidays.

Seven Church Street 7 Church St T 023-614 1186, W www.sevenchurchstreet.co.za. A central Victorian house, offering a very comfortable stay. Enticements include embroidered pure cotton linen and a gorgeous garden popular for bridal photography. Friendly and well run. From R300 per person.

Squirrel's Corner On the corner of Bloem and Jouberts sts T 023 614 1081, W www.squirrelscorner.co.za. B&Bs with four comfortable, spotless en-suite rooms in a friendly family house, as well as a garden suite which is two blocks from the main road. From R250 per person.

The town and around

Highly photogenic, Montagu is ideal for seeing on foot, taking in the interesting buildings or simply enjoying the setting, with its mountains, valleys and farms. There are also a couple of museums, neither of which is outstanding. The best thing about the **Montagu Museum**, 41 Long St (Mon–Fri 9am–noon & 2–4pm, Sat & Sun 9am–noon; R5), housed in a pleasant old church, is its herbal project, which traces traditional Khoisan knowledge about the medicinal properties of local plants. Work is being done in conjunction with the Pharmacology Department at the University of Cape Town and you can buy their booklet *Herbal Remedies: Montagu Museum*, which details some of the findings. The herbs themselves are also on sale, some of them grown in the gardens of the **Joubert House Museum** (Mon–Fri 9am–noon & 2–5pm, Sat 9am–noon; R5), one block west at 25 Long St. Built in 1853, this was one of the first houses standing in a vast plot which was originally a town farm, and has peach-pip floors fixed with beeswax, characteristic of the area, and period furniture on display in each of the rooms.

On Saturday mornings, don't miss the local **farmers' market** at the church, where you can get olives and olive oil, bread, cheese, almonds and dried fruit from the surrounding farms – all exceptionally well priced.

Montagu's main draw is the **Montagu Springs Resort** (daily 8am–11pm; R50, children R30; W www.montagusprings.co.za), about 3km northwest of town on the R318 (or reached on foot by following the Keisie River, which flows along the north edge of town). Several chlorinated open-air pools of different temperatures and a couple of Jacuzzis are spectacularly situated at the foot of cliffs – an effect slightly spoilt by the neon lights of a hotel complex and fast-food restaurant. It's a fabulous place to take kids, but the weekends become a mass of splashing bodies. If you want a quiet time, go first thing in the morning or last thing at night. The temperatures in winter are not hot enough to be entirely comfortable, when you're better off heading to the springs at Caledon (p.202) or Warmwaterberg (p.256), which are much hotter, and in many respects preferable.

Eating and drinking

Montagu has a couple of very good **restaurants** (evening meals must be reserved in advance); two farm stalls along Bath Street to pick up fresh and dried fruit, *biltong* and *boerewors*; a pleasant out-of-town tea garden; as well as a couple of coffee shops along Bath and Long Streets. Try *Sixty on Route 62*, on Long Street, for breakfasts, coffee and a big TV, or *Rambling Rose* on Bath Street, a wayside farm stall with fruit juices and local produce.

BellaMonta 4 Market St ☎023 614 2941.
Inexpensive family restaurant with pizza, burgers and a couple of fish and seafood dishes. Dinner only Mon–Sat.
Jessica's 28 Bath St ☎023 614 1805. Small and friendly, named after the proprietors' boxer dog and decorated with period dog prints. Here you'll get fairly pricey, refined, cosmopolitan bistro-style dishes and a top selection of Robertson wines; the

cajun-roasted baby chicken on wild rice with *peri-peri* cream is recommended. Daily eves, except Sun during winter.
Templetons@Four Oaks 46 Long St ☎023 614 2778. Pub and restaurant with meat and fish dishes, and a nice shady courtyard. Vegetarians can choose from goats' cheese ravioli or mushroom gnocchi. Lunch & dinner daily, but Sat lunch and all day Sun. Moderate.

Barrydale and around

BARRYDALE, 240km from Cape Town, is perfect for a couple of days of doing very little other than experiencing small-town life in the Little Karoo, with good, reasonably priced accommodation, hot springs at **Warmwaterberg**, 30km to the east, or if you're spiritually inclined, walking the **Labyrinth** at Lemoenshoek, 15km east of town. West of town you'll find big game – and correspondingly high rates – at the magnificent **Sanbona Wildlife Reserve**.

Not yet on the tourist route, Barrydale nonetheless has a number of restaurants and decent places to stay, and the sixty-kilometre drive from Montagu offers spectacular mountain scenery. There's a distinct rural feel about Barrydale: vineyards line the main road, farm animals are kept on large plots of land behind dry-stone walling, and you'll find fig, peach and quince trees thriving in the dryness. A couple of wine outlets are worth a visit for tasting and buying, particularly the Southern Cape Winery in Van Riebeeck (Mon–Fri 8am–5pm, Sat 9am–3pm; ☎028 572 1012).

Practicalities

The R62 swings past the village, whose entrance is marked by a tiny **visitor information centre** (Mon–Fri 8.30am–1.15pm & 2–5pm; ☎028 572 1572). Turning off the R62 takes you along Van Riebeeck Street, the main drag, with more pedestrians than cars, dominated by the ivory church and one supermarket, which houses an ATM and post office.

The best **accommodation** is the gay-owned *Tradouw Guest House* (☎028 572 1434, ⓦwww.home.intekom.com/tradouwguesthouse; R195 per person), with four rooms opening onto a courtyard shaded by vines and two onto the large garden. Rates are extremely reasonable, and the owners can pack you up a picnic lunch if you want to explore the river or, further afield, the spectacular Tradouw Pass, linking Barrydale with Swellendam. For **self-catering** go for *Sandy's Place* (☎028 572 1415; R100 per person) – the three small hotel-style units have TV, microwave and no character, but are extremely reasonably priced.

Most of Barrydale's **eating** options are strung along the R62. Pick of the bunch are the colourful, decorative *Jam Tarts*, on whose veranda you can enjoy tapas, pizza, some health foods and divine cakes, and *Clarke of the Karoo*, for good

ROUTE 62 AND THE LITTLE KAROO | Barrydale and around

steaks and *bobotie*, with a starter provided on the house. It's also open in the evening (weekends only), a rarity in Barrydale; otherwise at night *A Place in Time* (nightly except Wed; ☎028 572 1393) is recommended for its pizzas, game dishes, spare ribs and *crème brûlée*.

Sanbona Wildlife Reserve

Twenty kilometres west of Barrydale, **Sanbona Wildlife Reserve** (☎028 572 1365, Ⓦwww.sanbona.com; R2560–3350 per person per night all-inclusive) is the amalgamation of 21 farms that together create a massive wilderness area. The landscape is gorgeous – rocky outcrops, mountains and semi-desert vegetation – and there are two utterly luxurious **lodges**, *Tilney Manor*, which has a spa, and *Khanni Lodge*. The price includes two game drives a day, but, owing to the vegetation, the game is far sparser here than in the major game-viewing areas such as the Kruger National Park. Having said that, it is the only place in the Western Cape with free-roaming lions and cheetahs, which you have an excellent chance of seeing, and there's a herd of elephants. Sanbona is definitely worth considering if you are set on seeing some big game and don't have time for Kruger park, five hours' drive east of Johannesburg. A two-night stay is recommended and day visitors are not allowed.

The Labyrinth and Warmwaterberg Spa

The **Labyrinth**, 15km east of Barrydale on a small farm at Lemoenhoek, (☎028 572 1643; donation), is a beautiful outdoor maze based on one at Chartres Cathedral; the circuit is demarcated by rose quartz stones and allows you to gaze at the mountains as you move through. It can be privately booked if you want a meditative walk in peace; donations go to the farm's animal rehab project.

Another 15km east, beyond *Ronnie's Sex Shop*, a pub and well-known jokey landmark in the middle of nowhere, is **Warmwaterberg Spa** (☎028 572 1609, Ⓦwww.warmwaterbergspa.co.za), a Karoo farm blessed with natural hot water siphoned into two, unchlorinated hot pools (closed Wed) and surrounded by lush green lawns and lofty palms. Primarily aimed at South Africans, it gets rather crowded and noisy during school holidays and over weekends. Accommodation is basic and self-catering – in wooden cabins or rooms in the main farmhouse where you rent linen, and are given your own key to an indoor spa bath (from R360–600). There are also some campsites, a bar and a restaurant serving dinners and breakfasts if you want a break from doing it all yourself. While day visitors from Barrydale can be accommodated, most people stay over, to make the most of the baths at night, when the steam rises into the cold, starry Karoo sky.

Oudtshoorn and around

From Barrydale, vineyards and orchards give way to arid mountains and rocky, treeless plains vegetated with low, wiry scrub, making for a dramatic journey onwards. **OUDTSHOORN**, 420km from Cape Town and 180km from Barrydale, has been called the "ostrich capital of the world"; the town's surrounds are indeed crammed with ostrich farms, several of which you can visit, and the local souvenir shops keep busy dreaming up 1001 tacky ways to recycle ostrich parts as comestibles and souvenirs. But Oudtshoorn has two other big draws: it's the best base for visiting the nearby **Cango Caves** (see p.260), and the town is known for its sunshine and pleasant climate. Only 63km of tar and a range of mountains separate Oudtshoorn from Wilderness on the coast, yet the weather couldn't be more different; this is especially good news in winter, when a cold downpour along the Garden Route can give the lie to the idea of "sunny South Africa". It's boiling hot in summer, though, so make sure you have access to a pool, and nights in winter can freeze.

Some 50km west of Oudtshoorn, **Calitzdorp** is a delightfully unassuming Victorian village that can be seen as part of a circular excursion incorporating the scenic **Groenfontein Valley**. Its wineries and one or two tea shops offer the chance of a breather if you're travelling on the R62 through the Little Karoo.

ACCOMMODATION		RESTAURANTS	
141 High Street	E	Avocado Pierre	3
Backpacker's		Buffelsdrift Game	
Paradise	D	Lodge	A
Buffelsdrift Game		Godfather Restaurant	4
Lodge	A	Jemima's	2
De Oue Werf	B	Kalinka	1
Kleinplaas Holiday			
Resort	C		

Some history

Oudtshoorn started out as a small village named in honour of Geesje Ernestina Johanna van Oudtshoorn, wife of the first civil commissioner for George. By the 1860s **ostriches**, which live in the wild in Africa, were being raised under the ideal conditions of the Oudtshoorn Valley, where the warm climate and loamy soils enabled lucerne, the favourite diet of the flightless birds, to be grown. The quirky Victorian fashion for large feathers had turned the ostriches into a source of serious wealth, and by the 1880s hundreds of thousands of kilogrammes of feathers were being exported, and birds were changing hands for up to £1000 a pair – an unimaginable sum in those days. On the back of this boom, sharp businessmen made their fortunes, ignorant farmers were ripped off, and labourers drew the shortest straw of all. The latter were mostly coloured descendants of the Outeniqua and Attaqua Khoikhoi and trekboers, who received derisory wages supplemented by rations of food, wine, spirits and tobacco – a practice that still continues on some farms. In the early twentieth century, the most successful farmers and traders built themselves "feather palaces", ostentatious sandstone Edwardian buildings that have become the defining feature of Oudtshoorn.

Arrival, information and accommodation

Intercity buses pull in at Queens Mall, off Voortrekker Street where you'll also find the Pick 'n Pay supermarket and an Internet café. Oudtshoorn's **tourist**

office (Mon–Fri 8am–5pm, Sat 9am–1pm; ☎044 279 2532, ⓦwww .oudtshoorn.com), next to the *Queens Hotel*, Baron van Reede Street, is good for information about the caves, ostrich farms and local accommodation. *Backpacker's Paradise* rents out **bikes** and also arranges spectacular **adventurous cycling trips** down the Swartberg Pass, chaperoned with motor vehicle backup.

Oudtshoorn has a number of large **hotels** catering mainly to tour buses, plus plenty of good-quality B&Bs and guesthouses, a centrally located campsite with chalets, and one of the country's best-run backpacker lodges. Some of the nicest places to stay are in the attractive countryside en route to Cango Caves. The tourist office offers a free accommodation-booking service. **Rates** fall dramatically during the winter months following the week-long **Klein Karoo Nasionale Kunstefees** (KKNK; ⓦwww.absaknk.co.za), a major arts festival, mostly in Afrikaans, and street party in the March/April Easter holidays when people from all over the country take every bed in town.

Guest houses, backpacker lodges, B&Bs and hotels

141 High Street 141 High St ☎044 279 1751. Four large and reasonably priced rooms in a centrally located, handsome two-storey sandstone Dutch Reformed Church parsonage that's still in use, and has a very pleasant garden. Doubles R400.

🏃 **Backpacker's Paradise** 148 Baron van Reede St ☎044 272 3436, ⓦwww .backpackersparadise.net. A friendly and well-run two-storey hostel along the main drag, which makes an effort to go the extra few centimetres with three-quarter beds, en-suite doubles and family rooms as well as three small dorms – and, in season, a portion of ostrich egg on the house for breakfast. There are nightly ostrich, or veg-friendly, braais too and a daily shuttle from the Baz Bus drop-off in George to the hostel. The on-site adventure centre organizes cycle trips in the Swartberg Pass and there's a daily shuttle to the caves, ostrich farm and wildlife ranch. Doubles from R240.

Buffelsdrift Game Lodge 7km from town on the road to the caves ☎044 272 0106, ⓦwww .buffelsdrift.com. The town's top stay, in luxurious en-suite safari tents overlooking a large dam with hippo in it, and a grand

thatched dining area. Game drives or horseback rides to view rhino, buffalo, elephant, giraffe and various antelope are included in the price. No kids under 12 can be accommodated, though families can visit during the day for a meal or game activity. From R900–R1220 per person.

De Oue Werf Signposted off the R328 to Cango Caves, 12km north of Oudtshoorn ☎044 272 8712, ⓦwww.ouewerf.co.za. Luxurious and well-priced garden rooms on a working farm, run by the very welcoming sixth generation of the family. Green lawns run down to a dam which has a swinging slide and raft to play on, and lots of birdlife. Light lunches and teas can be had at the gazebo by the pool, with dinners in the candlelit dining room, presided over by family photographs. A great option if you're visiting the caves and want to stay in the country. R370 per person.

Kleinplaas Holiday Resort 171 Baron van Reede St ☎044 272 5811, ⓦwww.kleinplaas .co.za. Well-run, spick-and-span shady camping and fully equipped self-catering brick chalets, conveniently close to town, with a swimming pool and launderette. The owners know the town well and will show you the ropes. Doubles R140–470.

The town and around

Oudtshoorn's town centre is a pretty straightforward place to negotiate, and has little more than a couple of museums worth checking out if you've time to kill. The town's main interest lies in its Victorian and Edwardian sandstone buildings, some of which are unusually grand and elegant for a Karoo *dorp*.

The **C.P. Nel Museum** (Mon–Sat 8am–5pm, Sat 9am–5pm; R15), on the corner of Baron van Reede Street and Voortrekker Road, is a good place to start your explorations. A handsome sandstone building, it was built in 1906 as a boys' school, but now houses an eccentric collection of items relating to ostriches. Nearby, **Le Roux Town House**, on the corner of Loop and High streets (Mon–Fri 9am–1pm & 2–5pm; R15), is a perfectly preserved family townhouse, and the only way to get a glimpse inside one of the much-vaunted feather palaces. The beautifully preserved furnishings were all imported from Europe between 1900 and 1920, and there is plenty to stroll around and admire.

Many people come to Oudtshoorn to see, or even ride, **ostriches**. You don't actually have to visit one of the ostrich farms to view Africa's biggest bird, as you're bound to see flocks of them as you drive past farms in the vicinity or past truckloads of them on their way to the slaughterhouse (feathers being no longer fashionable, these days ostriches are raised for their low-cholesterol flesh). A number of show farms offer **tours** (45–90min) costing around R20 a person, which include the chance to sit on an ostrich and the spectacle of jockeys racing the birds. Best of the bunch is Cango Ostrich and Butterfly Farm on the main road between Oudtshoorn and the Cango Caves, which takes only one group of visitors (or individuals) at a time.

More exciting, though less traditional for Oudtshoorn, is the opportunity to feed and touch **elephants**, 7km out of town on the Cango Caves road at **Buffelsdrift Game Lodge** (☎044 272 0106; R120). Book ahead for a really worthwhile experience where you get to stroke elephants under the guidance of their handlers, and watch them at training and play throughout the day. From the lodge's **restaurant** on the large dam, you are likely to see hippos, and may be lucky enough to see other animals coming to drink.

The other "wildlife" activity around Oudtshoorn is the **Cango Wildlife Ranch** (daily 8am–6pm; R80, children R50, under 4s free; ☎044 272 5593), just outside town on the Cango road. Guided tours lead you past white tigers and cheetahs, crocodiles and other amazing creatures from other parts of Africa, and you can pay extra to be photographed touching the animals and reptiles, and even get into the pool with the crocodiles. Don't expect it to be thrilling, though; you'll be lucky if a crocodile so much as flicks its eyes while you're in there. The ranch offers a spectacle rather than authentic wildness, but it caters well for children who can frolic in water fountains or on climbing frames while you eat lunch.

Eating and drinking

Oudtshoorn has a choice of several places to eat, mostly strung out along Baron van Reede Street and catering to the tourist trade, with the obligatory ostrich on the menu. *Kalinka's* and *Jemima's* vie for the top position with excellent and imaginative fare and you can eat out of town on a game ranch.

Avocado Pierre 6 Baron van Reede St, opposite the museum. A central coffee shop that does nice salads, sandwiches, burgers, pitta pockets and decent coffee. Daily 8.30am–10pm, though closed Sun eves.
Buffelsdrift Game Lodge 7km out of town towards Cango Caves ☎044 272 0106. Have a great breakfast or lunch on a wooden deck overlooking the waterhole, and do a spot of game-viewing at the same time. The lodge is open to non-guests for meals, and you

could combine it with an elephant encounter or other game activity. Moderate.
Godfather Restaurant 61 Voortrekker Rd ☎044 272 5404. A popular eating place with a huge menu, noted for its medium-priced pizzas, venison and ostrich steaks; also good just for a drink. It's an excellent spot in winter, when there's a roaring fire. Closed Sun.
Jemima's 94 Baron van Reede St ☎044 272 0808. An imaginative and good-value menu including *boerewors*-stuffed ravioli, butternut

cheesecake, game dishes and tasty, light food. Open daily 6pm till late, plus Tues–Fri 11am–2pm. Expensive.
Kalinka's 93 Baron van Reede St ☎ 044 279 2596. Sandstone house with a fountain outside, specializing in game dishes, with Russian black bread at every meal, and imported vodka. Service is good and food well presented, delicious and expensive. The baked cardamom and date brandy pudding is great. Daily 6–10pm.

Cango Caves

The **Cango Caves** number among South Africa's ten most popular attractions, drawing a quarter of a million visitors each year to gasp at their fantastic cavernous spaces, dripping rocks and rising columns of calcite. In the two centuries since they became known to the public, the caves have been seriously battered by human intervention, but they still represent a stunning landscape growing inside the Swartberg foothills. Don't go expecting a serene and contemplative experience, though: the only way of getting inside the caves is on a guided tour accompanied by a commentary.

San hunter-gatherers sheltered in the entrance caves for millennia before white settlers arrived, but it's unlikely that they ever made it to the lightless underground chambers. **Jacobus van Zyl**, a Karoo farmer, was probably the first person to penetrate beneath the surface, when he slid down on a rope into the darkness in July 1780, armed with a lamp. Over the next couple of centuries the caves were visited and pillaged by growing numbers of callers, some of whom were photographed cheerfully carting off wagonloads of limestone columns.

In the 1960s and 1970s the caves were made accessible to mass consumption when a tourist complex was built, the rock-strewn floor was evened out with concrete, ladders and walkways were installed and the caverns were turned into a kitsch extravaganza with coloured lights, piped music and an indecipherable commentary that drew hundreds of thousands of visitors each year. Even apartheid put its hefty boot in: under the premiership of Dr Hendrik Verwoerd, the arch-ideologue of racial segregation, a separate "non-whites" entrance was hacked through one wall, resulting in a disastrous through-draft that began dehydrating the caves. Fortunately, the worst excesses have now ended; concerts are no longer allowed inside the chambers, and the coloured lights have been removed.

Practicalities

The **drive** here from Oudtshoorn involves heading north along Baron van Reede Street, and continuing 32km on the R328 to the caves. The visitors' complex includes an interpretive centre with quite interesting displays about geology, people and wildlife connected with the caves; the decent *Marimba* **restaurant**; and a souvenir shop. Below the complex you'll find shady picnic sites at the edge of a river that cuts its way into the mountains and along which there are hiking trails. Two **tours** leave every hour (daily 9am–4pm; ☎ 044 272 7410, ⓦ www.cangocaves.co.za). The one-hour Standard Tour (on the hour; R52, children R28) gets you through the first six chambers, but if you're an adrenaline junkie, the ninety-minute Adventure Tour (on the half-hour; R66) is a must; this takes you into the deepest sections open to the public, where the openings become smaller and smaller. Squeezing through tight openings with names like Lumbago Walk, Devil's Chimney and The Letterbox is not recommended for the overweight, faint-hearted or claustrophobic, and you should wear oldish clothes and shoes with a grip to negotiate the slippery floors. The caves are open every day of the year, bar Christmas Day.

Calitzdorp

The tiny Karoo village of **CALITZDORP** hangs in a torpor of midday stillness, with its attractive, unpretentious Victorian streets and handful of wineries. There's nothing much to do here, apart from have tea, taste some wine and wander through the streets.

The low-key **tourist office** at the Shell Garage in Voortrekker Street (Mon–Fri 9am–5pm; ☎044 213 3775, ⓦ www.calitzdorp.co.za) has some brochures about the village and its surroundings, as well as information about the wineries and accommodation. Some of South Africa's best ports are produced at the three modest wineries signposted down side roads, a few hundred metres from the centre. The most highly recommended is **Die Krans Estate** (Mon–Fri 8am–5pm, Sat 9am–3pm; free), where you can sample its wines and ports (its vintage reserve port is reckoned to be among the country's top three), and stretch your legs on a thirty-minute vineyard walk in lovely countryside.

The best **guesthouse** in town is the friendly *Port-Wine Guest House* (☎044 213 3131, ⓦ www.portwine.net; from R400 per person), in a renovated early nineteenth-century homestead on the corner of Queen and Station streets and overlooking the Boplaas Estate. Airy rooms that offer exceptional value are available at *Die Dorpshuis* (☎044 213 3453, ⓦ www.diedorpshuis .co.za.co.za; B&B R185 per person), which is centrally located at 4 Van Riebeeck St, opposite the church, and also has self-catering and mountain bikes for rent. *Die Dorpshuis* is a good place to **eat** (Mon–Sat), serving reasonably priced sandwiches, teas, light meals and heavier traditional Karoo food, such as stews and lamb.

The Groenfontein Valley

A circuitous minor route diverts just east of Calitzdorp and drops into the highly scenic **Groenfontein Valley**. The narrow dirt road twists through the Swartberg foothills, past whitewashed Karoo cottages and farms and across brooks, eventually joining the R328 to Oudtshoorn. Winding through these back roads is also an option to reach the Cango Caves and Prince Albert, one of the best drives you'll ever do in South Africa. Many of the roads are unsealed but are perfectly navigable in an ordinary car if taken slowly.

An excellent reason to take this back route is to spend a couple of nights at the highly recommended ⚹ *Retreat at Groenfontein* (☎044 213 3880, ⓦ www.groenfontein.com; R600 per person half-board), 20km from Calitzdorp and 59km from Oudtshoorn. This isolated Victorian colonial farmstead borders on the 2300-square-kilometre **Swartberg Nature Reserve**, an outstandingly beautiful area of gorges, rivers and dirt tracks. Accommodation is in comfortable en-suite rooms, each with its own fireplace, and rates include a very good dinner, with vegetarians well catered for, and you'll leave feeling a friend of the family. Winter rates are thirty percent lower than those in summer.

Two good self-catering establishments are *Red Stone Hills* (☎044 213 3783, ⓦ www.redstone.co.za; from R580 for four people), which has four lovely period-furnished Victorian cottages on a working farm 6km off the R62 (turn off 14km east of Calitzdorp), and the cheaper, homely *Kruis Rivier Guest Farm* (☎044 213 3788, ⓦ www.kruisrivier.co.za; R280 for two people), further along the same road. The owners will do breakfast on request, and provide braai packs.

Prince Albert and around

Isolation has left intact the traditional rural architecture of **PRINCE ALBERT**, an attractive little town 70km north of Oudtshoorn, and 400km from Cape Town, across the loops and razorbacks of the **Swartberg Pass** – one of the most dramatic drives and entries to a town imaginable. Although firmly in the thirstlands of the South African interior, on the cusp between the Little and Great Karoo, Prince Albert is all the more striking for its perennial spring, whose water trickles down furrows along its streets – a gift that propagates fruit trees and gardens. Visitors mostly come to Prince Albert for the drive through its two southerly gateways – the Swartberg Pass on the R328 and **Meiring-spoort** on the N12 – generally driving in one way, spending the night in town, and driving out the other.

Prince Albert is small enough to explore everywhere on foot, people are friendly, and you'll find everything you want on the main road. Supremely old-fashioned displays make window-shopping as much fun as the interior of any country museum, but the essence of Prince Albert is in the fleeting impressions that give the flavour of a Karoo *dorp* like nowhere else: the silver steeple of the Dutch Reformed church puncturing a deep-blue sky, residents sauntering along or progressing slowly down the main street on squeaky bikes. The town's beauty has attracted a number of artists to live here, and you'll find the excellent **Prince Albert Gallery** in an airy Victorian building at 57 Church St (Mon–Fri 10am–4pm, Sat & Sun 10am–1pm), where you can browse or purchase paintings, sculpture, beadwork, jewellery, ceramics and etchings by local artists. Right next door, with the same opening hours, be sure not to miss Kevin Hough's marvellous wrought-iron sculptures, created from found objects, inside the **Kevin Hough Gallery** where more of his work in different media is also for sale.

Staying firmly in the realm of the handmade, Prince Albert is known for its **mohair products**: rugs, socks, scarves and other garments. Browse in the Prince of Africa craft shop next to the *Prince Albert Hotel* on the main road or at Wolskuur Spinners, further down. *Gay's Guernsey Dairy* at the southern end of town sells fantastic, award-winning **home-made cheeses**, which you can taste before buying, yogurts and cream. If you're travelling with children, you can take them to watch the milking at sunrise, and walk around the farm looking at other farm animals and activities (daily 7am–9am & 4–6pm; free).

One of the most exciting things you can do in Prince Albert, if not in South Africa, is to watch the **night skies** with resident astronomer Hans Daehne (weekends & school holidays only; R150 for a lecture and viewing; ☎072 732 2950). The Karoo sky is heaven for astronomers, with no pollution and few lights, and you get some of the Southern Hemisphere's sharpest views of the firmament from here. Since 2005 South Africa has had the biggest telescope in the Southern Hemisphere at Sutherland, deeper in the Karoo.

You can also visit **rock-art sites** with one of the country's top paleontologists and archeologists, the now retired Dr Judy Maguire (☎023 541 1713, ✉questar@icon.co.za). In the studio/museum on her farm, twenty minutes' drive outside Prince Albert at the start of the Swartberg pass, she'll run through the fundamentals and let you handle all sorts of fascinating artefacts, then walk you up a mountainside to see the paintings. It's a highly recommended way to spend an afternoon, but you'll need to book beforehand to arrange a time, and get directions to the farm, and find out her current rates. Donations to the town's museum are part of the deal.

Prince Albert is one of the best places to begin a trip into **Die Hel** (also known as Hell, The Hell or Gamkaskloof), a valley that's part of the Swartberg Nature Reserve. Die Hel is not on the way to anywhere and, although it doesn't look very far on the map, you'll need to allow two and a half hours in either direction to make the spectacular but tortuous drive into it along a dirt road. A 4WD vehicle isn't needed, but you should definitely not attempt the drive in the killing heat of December or January without air conditioning. Before attempting the trip, call Nature Conservation (℡044 802 5310, ℮george@cnc.org.za) for an update on the condition of the roads.

The attraction of the place is the silence, isolation and birdlife. If you don't want to go it alone, contact Lisa from *Onse Rus* B&B, who organizes tours, for a minimum of two people, for R750. She'll cater for you, and you can get picked up if you want to hike a section of the road (4–12km), instead of driving it.

There's **accommodation** here in the form of two restored farm cottages (℡023 541 1107,℮www.diehel.com; R150 per person per day), run by a third-generation Kloof dweller, Annetje Joubert. The cottages can sleep up to eight people, and there are seven caravans for R80 per person per day, with camping facilities also available. The valley has no electricity supply, and no facilities, though you can order picnic baskets and cooked breakfasts and dinners from Annetje, who also has a shop selling her baked and bottled goods.

19

Mountain biking and hiking trips are offered at reasonable prices (R150, plus R65 a day for bike rental) by *Dennehof Guest House*; you're driven up one of the mountains, and descend the 18km on your own two wheels.

Practicalities

Most people get to Prince Albert through the mountains by **car**, a 420-kilometre trip from Cape Town, but you can get off the Cape Town–Johannesburg **train** at Prince Albert Road station, 45km from the hamlet, and arrange to be collected by *Onse Rus* B&B (even if you don't intend to stay with them). The trains are often late, and Prince Albert Road Station has absolutely no facilities. The **tourist office** in Church Street (Mon–Fri 9am–5pm, Sat 9am–noon; ℡023 541 1366, ℮www.patourism.co.za) has maps with accommodation, restaurants and craft shops, and can point you to other activities in the area; at weekends, its phone calls are diverted to the Prince of Africa craft shop at the *Swartberg Hotel*, where you also go for help. For Internet access, head to the *Lazy Lizard* in Church Street which also does good light lunches at reasonable prices.

Accommodation

There's plenty of stylish accommodation in Prince Albert, mostly in historic limewashed and thatched Karoo cottages, Cape Dutch homesteads or colonial Victorian houses.

Cactus Blue Cottages Behind the National Centre opposite the *Swartberg Hotel* ℡072 464 1240, ℮www .cactusbluecottages.co.za. Two modern, funky cottages full of space, light and pleasing colours, overlooking a small vineyard. There is a stripey day bed to loll on, a collection of DVDs to watch, and a double mattress on an outside deck if you fancy a night under the stars. Doubles R500–750.

Dennehof Guest House Off Christina de Wit St, on the outskirts of town ℡023 541 1227, ℮www.home.intekom.com/dennehof. Three self-contained cottages and suites in a homestead that is a National Monument. The owner does hiking and mountain-biking trips. B&B from R285 per person.

Hoogenoeg Holiday Houses ☏ 023 541 1455. The cheapest accommodation in town is run by Tannie ("Aunt") Alta, who rents out a number of sparsely furnished but adequate, if none too clean, old houses in Prince Albert. R50 per person.

Karoo Lodge 66 Church St ☏ 023 541 1467 or 082 692 7736, ⓦ www.karoolodge.com.

Reasonably priced, spacious accommodation in a B&B run by keen hosts who'll show you the ropes. From R295 per person.

Onse Rus 47 Church St ☏ 023 541 1380, ⓦ www.onserus.co.za. Cool, thatched B&B rooms attached to a restored Cape Dutch house, with welcoming and informed owners who serve you tea and chocolate cake on arrival, and do great breakfasts too. They also run tours to Gamkaskloof and into the Swartberg range. From R295 per person.

Eating

Celestino's Next to the *Swartberg Hotel*. Inexpensive steakhouse-style food every evening from 7pm. Good for families.

Karoo Kombuis 18 Deurdrift St ☏ 023 541 1110. Traditional, inexpensive fare from this part of the country, with a home-cooked feel and meat galore. Mon–Sat eves only, closed Sun.

Koggelmander 61 Church St ☏ 023 541 1900. Modern, moderately priced Karoo food, including lamb and ostrich. Vegetarians will

be happy here too, and it's a great place to have a beer on the terrace, lounge on the sofas inside, or wander about looking at the paintings on the wall. Tues–Sun 9am–4pm & daily 7pm till late.

Sampie se Plaasstal At the south end of the main road. A great place for snacks, with excellent dried fruit and rusks, as well as local olives which are among the best in South Africa. Open for breakfast, light lunches and tea. Inexpensive.

Port Elizabeth, Addo and the private reserves

Port Elizabeth, the Eastern Cape's commercial and industrial centre, is for many visitors a place to start or end a trip along the Garden Route. On the western end of Nelson Mandela Bay (formerly Algoa Bay), the city is the transport hub of the Eastern Cape, well served by flights, trains, buses and car rental companies. Around an hour's drive inland is Port Elizabeth's biggest draw, **Addo Elephant Park**, the closest Big Five reserve to Cape Town, with virtually guaranteed sightings of elephants, and a good prospect of seeing other big game.

You can drive around Addo yourself, but if you want to be taken around in open-topped Land Rovers and given a pampering safari experience, stay in one of the nearby **private reserves**. On the N2 highway between PE and Graham-stown, alone, there are three: **Shamwari**, **Amakhala** and **Lalibela**, while **Schotia**, a kilometre off the N10/N2 interchange, has exciting night drives. Further east, in the vicinity of the colonial settlement, are several other reserves including the pricey but outstanding **Kwandwe Private Game Reserve**. One big attraction of Addo and these private reserves is that, unlike the country's other major game parks, they benefit from the fact that the Eastern Cape is **malaria–free**. And if you've driven out this way along the Garden Route and don't fancy heading back exactly the way you came, you've the option of returning to Cape Town via the inland **Route 62** (covered in Chapter 19), branching off the N2 not far west of Port Elizabeth.

Port Elizabeth

As a city, **PORT ELIZABETH** (often referred to as **PE**) is pretty functional and easy enough to navigate. The industrial feel is mitigated by excellent and safe beaches, and should you end up killing time here, you'll find diversion in

20

◄ Cape Town, East London & Grahamstown

PORT ELIZABETH

N

Govan Mbeki Street

Harbour

GOVANMBEKI STREET

Train Station

See Central Port Elizabeth map

CENTRAL

St George's Park

SETTLERS PARK NATURE RESERVE

Humewood Road Station

Port Elizabeth Airport

Apple Express Narrow Gauge Railway

0   1 km

HUMEWOOD

King's Beach

Humewood Beach

Hobie Beach

Dolphinarium Oceanarium

Bay Tourism

Brookes Pavilion

Snake Park & Museum

HUMEWOOD

HAPPY VALLEY

See Humewood map for detail

A B C

D

E

1

2

3

F G

Humewood Road Station Apple Express Terminal

CENTRAL PORT ELIZABETH

N

S T R A N D

Train Station

Market Square Bus Depot

Intercape Bus stop

City Hall

Translux bus terminal

GOVAN MBEKI

City Library

Publicity Association **ⓘ**

Elizabeth Donkin Memorial

Nelson Mandela Metropolitan Art Gallery

RUSSELL ROAD

4

5

6

H

BRICKMAKERS KLOOF

0   300 m

Nelson Mandela Bay

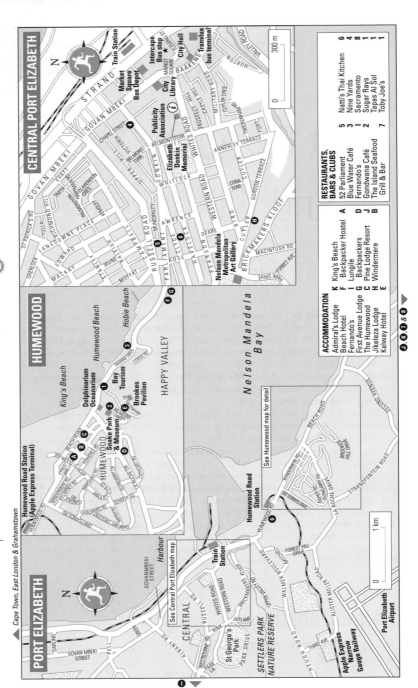

BROOKES HILL DRIVE

BEACH ROAD

STRANDFONTEIN ROAD

WINDERMERE RD

LA ROCHE DRIVE

FOREST HILL DRIVE

ALISTER MILLER

BEACH ROAD

WALMER

HEUGH ROAD

THIRD AVE

SECOND AVENUE

6

ⓘ

ACCOMMODATION
Admiral's Lodge	K
Beach Hotel	F
Fernando's	G
First Avenue Lodge	I
The Humewood	C
Jikeleza Lodge	H
Kelway Hotel	E
King's Beach Backpacker Hostel	A
Lungile Backpackers	D
Pine Lodge Resort	J
Windermere	B

RESTAURANTS, BARS & CLUBS
52 Parliament	5
Blue Water Café	3
Fernando's	I
Gondwana Café	2
The Island Seafood Grill & Bar	B
Natti's Thai Kitchen	6
Nine Yards	4
Sacramento	8
Sugar Rays	1
Tapas Al Sol	1
Toby Joe's	7

Ⓙ, Ⓚ, 7 & 8 ▶

beautiful **coastal walks** a few kilometres from town and in the small **historical centre**. A couple of classically pretty rows of Victorian terraces still remain in the **Central** suburb on the hill above the bay, where there are some decent accommodation and eating options, as there are also in the beachfront suburbs of **Humewood** and **Summerstrand**.

Arrival, information and city transport

Port Elizabeth's **airport** (☎041 581 2984) is conveniently situated on the edge of Walmer suburb, 4km south from the city centre. Taxis rank outside the airport and the fare to the city centre is around R35.

The **train station** (☎041 507 2662) is centrally located, with buses departing from the rank directly across the road. The **Baz Bus** will drop you off at any central location or accommodation. Arriving by **intercity bus**, you alight at Greenacres shopping mall in Newton Park suburb, 3km from the centre, served by Translux, Greyhound and Intercape.

The extremely helpful **Nelson Mandela Bay Tourism** office (Mon–Fri 8am–4.30pm, Sat & Sun 9.30am–3.30pm; ☎041 585 8884, ⓦwww.nmbt.co.za) is in the Donkin Lighthouse Building (a National Monument with a good view from the top) on the Donkin Reserve in Belmont Terrace, Central suburb.

City transport

If you're staying in Central, exploring the city **on foot** is a realistic possibility – try the self-guided **Heritage Walk**, shown on a map available at the tourist office. However, for any serious exploration of PE, or for getting to and from the beachfront, **renting a car** is your best option (see "Listings", p.272), as the city's transport system leaves much to be desired. **Buses** operated by the municipal Algoa Bus Company (☎041 404 1200, ⓦwww.algoabus.co.za) are infrequent, running from the Market Square bus depot to the suburbs, the beaches and Greenacres shopping mall. PE's **minibus taxis** run from town to the beachfront regularly, but are the least recommended way to travel. **Metered taxis** don't have ranks so you'll need to phone to find a taxi (see "Listings" p.272); if you're going to the airport or the bus or train stations, it's advisable to book ahead.

Accommodation

The obvious place to stay is the **beachfront**, with a vast choice of hotels, self-catering suites and hundreds of B&Bs. During the December and January peak holiday period the beachfront becomes the focus for most of the city's action, while February, March and April are much quieter yet offer perfect beach weather. Note that PE can be subject to excoriatingly **strong winds**, especially between September and December, which makes going to the beach unpleasant. Although you'll find *Jikileza Lodge* in **Central PE**, the area is gently sliding into a state of neglect, and B&Bs and restaurants have been moving out to the beach-front or into the **suburbs**, such as Mill Park.

If you fancy a slice of **African township life**, *Fundani Lodge* (☎041 454 2064 or 082 964 6563; from R360 per room) offers an opportunity to enjoy football matches, traditional ceremonies and good African cooking, while you stay with a family in the New Brighton or KwaMagxaki townships.

Admiral's Lodge 47 Admiralty Way, Summerstrand ☎041 583 1894 or 083 455 2072, ⓦwww .admiralslodge.co.za. Spacious and stylish rooms at a good B&B, at the far end of

Summerstrand about 7km from the centre. There's a braai area, communal lounge, pool and trampoline for the kids. Airport transfers are available. Doubles R1160.

Beach Hotel Marine Drive, Humewood ☎ 041 583 2161, ⓦ www.south-african-hotels.com /beach-hotel.php. Across the road from popular Hobie Beach, and sited at the centre of the beachside action, the hotel has a great patio bar overlooking the sea, offering snacks, cocktails and cold beer, and *The Bell*, a very decent à la carte restaurant. Recent renovations have included a sun deck and pool. Ask about the weekend specials. Breakfast extra. Doubles from R1000.

Fernando's Guest House & Grill 102 Cape Rd, Mill Park ☎ 041 373 2823. Purportedly South Africa's oldest guesthouse, in three separate Victorian houses decked out with period furniture and offering good value and a warm atmosphere. Doubles R450 with continental breakfast.

First Avenue Lodge 3 First Ave, Summerstrand ☎ 041 583 5173. Sixteen en-suite rooms close to the beach with their own entrances, offered on a B&B or self-catering basis, in a popular and pleasant establishment with a pool and entertainment area. Doubles R600. **The Humewood 33 Beach Rd, Humewood** ☎ 041 585 8961, ⓦ www.humewoodhotel.co.za. A large, old-fashioned hotel that reeks nostalgically of 1950s family seaside holidays. The rooms are large and feature wicker furniture and summery floral prints. Service is excellent and includes laundry facilities and babysitting. There's a good bar and sun deck. Airport transfers available. Doubles from R620.

Jikeleza Lodge 44 Cuyler St, Central ☎ 041 586 3721, ⓦ www.highwinds.co.za. Friendly backpacker place with dorms, doubles and a family room. Its adventure centre can help you sort out tour and travel bookings. Dorms R70, doubles R180.

Kelway Hotel Brookes Hill Drive, Humewood ☎ 041 584 0638, ⓦ www.thekelway.co.za. Stylish hotel kitted out with timber panelling, seagrass chairs and handcrafted wooden

tables. Standard, luxury and family rooms available. Breakfast included. Doubles from R1150.

King's Beach Backpacker Hostel 41 Windermere Rd, Humewood ☎ 041 585 8113, ⓔ kingsb@agenet.com. Spotless, well-established hostel, a block away from the beach, with camping facilities, dorms and double rooms, plus an outside bar and braai area. Although principally for self-catering, it lays on tea, coffee, bread and jams in the morning. The travel desk can book township, game park and other tours. Dorms R70, doubles R170, en-suite doubles R200.

Lungile Backpackers 12 La Roche Drive, Summerstrand ☎ 041 582 2042, ⓦ www .lungilebackpackers.co.za. Large and popular beachfront hostel where you can party indoors or step out into the heart of PE's beachfront nightlife strip. Perched on a hill, it has facilities for camping, a large lawn to relax on, sea views, a pool table, bar and swimming pool. Self-catering only. Dorms R70, doubles R180, en-suite doubles R250.

Pine Lodge Resort Off Marine Drive, Humewood ☎ 041 583 4004, ⓦ www.pinelodge .co.za. Right on the beach near the wonderful historic lighthouse and next to the Cape Recife Nature Reserve, where owls, mongooses and antelope make appearances. Offers various log cabin units, some with full kitchens, sleeping from four to eight people. Besides a popular bar and restaurant, the lodge boasts a swimming pool, a gym and a games room. Cabins for four from around R350.

Windermere 35 Humewood Rd, Humewood ☎ 041 582 2245, ⓦ www.thewindermere.co.za. Stylish hotel with just eight suites, given an almost Zen-like feel through the subtle use of off-white to oaty colours contrasted with dark hues, such as chocolate brown, and materials that include timber and granite. Doubles R2600.

The City

Port Elizabeth's **city centre** is marred by a network of freeways that cuts a swath across the south of town, blocking off the city from the harbour. The city's white population retreated to the suburbs some time ago, leaving the centre to African traders and township shoppers, who are slowly resuscitating its commercial spirit. The **suburbs** offer little to draw you away from the beachfront, unless you're a shopaholic, in which case you should make a beeline for **Newton Park**, 5km west of the centre and home to **Greenacres** and **The**

Bridge, vast shopping malls to which the city-centre department stores have relocated en masse. Further afield in **New Brighton**, you'll find Port Elizabeth's most important museum, the **Red Location Museum of the People's Struggle**, housed in a building that has won several awards.

Central

The city's main street, which runs parallel to the freeway as it sweeps into town, has been renamed **Govan Mbeki Avenue** in honour of the veteran activist (father of Thabo Mbeki, South Africa's president), who died in 2001. African traders dealing a pretty standard line in crochet tat and leather goods line up along the pavements giving the precinct a lively feel, but it's not safe after dark. The symbolic heart of town is the **City Hall**, standing in **Market Square**, a large empty space surrounded by some striking mid-Victorian buildings, adjacent to the train and bus stations on the edge of the harbour. But the dejection of the quarter, under the grimy shadow of a flyover, conspires against it ever pumping any real life into the district.

Heading west up hilly **Donkin Street**, you'll come upon a curious stone pyramid commemorating **Elizabeth Donkin**, after whom PE was named. Elizabeth was the young wife of the Cape's acting governor in 1820, Sir Rufane Donkin; she died of fever in India in 1818. As you stroll up Donkin Street, you could be forgiven for thinking you were in the wrong country, the wrong continent – the raked terrace of Victorian double-storey houses would look completely at home in any town on England's south coast. The nineteen **Donkin Houses**, built in the mid-nineteenth century and declared National Monuments in 1967, reflect the desire of the English settlers to create a home from home in this strange, desiccated land.

Further west, you reach St George's Park and the **Nelson Mandela Metropolitan Art Museum**, 1 Park Drive (Mon–Fri 8.30am–5pm, Sat 9am–4.30pm, Sun 2–4.30pm; free), which has a collection of contemporary local work, visiting exhibitions and a small shop selling postcards and local arts and crafts.

▲ Donkin Street

The beachfront and around

PE's wonderful **beaches** are its main attraction. The protection provided by Algoa Bay makes them safe for swimming (that said, it's best to do so between the lifeguard beacons), and clean enough to make **beachcombing** a pleasure.

The beachfront strip, divided from the harbour by a large wall, starts about 2km south of the city centre. En route to the beaches, the **South End Museum** on the corner of Humewood Road and Walmer Boulevard (Mon–Fri 9am–4pm, Sat & Sun 2–5pm) is worth a visit. Based in the old Seamen's Institute, it recalls the bygone days of the South End, a vibrant multicultural neighbourhood whose growth had much to do with PE's then booming harbour. As a result of the Group Areas Act it was razed street by street in the 1960s, save for a handful of churches and mosques. Today, the area is full of pricey town houses.

The first of the beaches is beautiful, wide **King's Beach**, somewhat marred by a jumble of coal heaps and oil tanks behind it. To the southeast lies **Humewood Beach**, across the road from which is a complex housing **Bayworld Museum, Oceanarium and Snake Park** (daily 9am–4.30pm; R35, children half-price); the Oceanarium (performing dolphin and seal shows 11am & 3pm) brings huge pleasure to hordes of excited children during the holidays. **Brookes Pavilion** next door and **Dolphin's Leap** nearby are complexes of restaurants, pubs and clubs with great views. Beyond, to the south, **Hobie Beach** and **Summerstrand** are great for walking and sunbathing, with one dive operator based at the latter (see "Listings", p.272). Summerstrand's **Boardwalk Casino Complex** has some pleasing shops, including an indigenous crafts market, cinemas and some reasonable eating places.

Marine Drive continues 15km down the coast as far as the village of **Schoenmakerskop** (Schoenies to the locals), along impressive coastline that alternates between rocky shores and sandy beaches. From here you can walk the eight-kilometre **Sacramento Trail**, a shoreline path that leads to the huge-duned **Sardinia Bay**, the wildest and most dramatic stretch of coast in the area. To get there by road, turn right at the Schoenmakerskop intersection and follow the road until Sardinia Bay is signed, on the left.

Red Location Museum of the People's Struggle

Situated in the suburb of New Brighton, 7km north of central Port Elizabeth, the **Red Location Museum of the People's Struggle**, at the corner of Olof Palme and Singaphi streets (Tues–Fri 10am–4pm, Sat & Sun 9am–3pm; R12), is dedicated to recalling the experiences of the residents of Red Location, Port Elizabeth's oldest African township, established in 1902. The settlement took its name from the rusted corrugated iron barracks – around which New Brighton developed – that had housed troops till the end of the Anglo-Boer War. A significant site of anti-apartheid resistance, New Brighton was the stomping

---

The Apple Express

Just southeast of the harbour, on Humewood Road, **Humewood Road station** is the starting point for the **Apple Express**, a beautifully restored steam train that, during the holiday season, usually runs at 9.30am on weekends to **Thornhill** village and other destinations. En route it stops on Van Staden's River Bridge, the highest narrow-gauge railway bridge in the world. After a leisurely lunchtime break at Thornhill, the train trundles back to Humewood, arriving at 4pm. Tickets (R130 return for adults, R65 for children) can be booked through Nelson Mandela Bay Tourism Office (☎041 583 2030).

ground of a number of significant South Africans, including Govan Mbeki, ANC stalwart and father of South Africa's president, artist George Pemba, and internationally feted actor John Kani. Red Location was the first place in South Africa to stage a passive resistance campaign against the pass laws (see p.286) and was the birthplace of the first cell of MK (the ANC's armed wing).

The museum is housed in a striking building awarded the 2006 Royal Institute of British Architects' **Lubetkin Prize** for the most outstanding work of architecture outside the European Union. Described by the judges as a "tour de force", the building wears an industrial-style saw-toothed roof that evokes the area's strong association with trade unionism. Inside, a dozen twelve-metre monumental rusted **"memory boxes"** contain exhibits exploring different themes related to the anti-apartheid struggle. The structures are inspired by the containers migrant workers used to carry their most prized possessions. Four **permanent exhibitions** trace a century of Red Location's history from 1900.

Eating, drinking and nightlife

Port Elizabeth has no great culinary reputation, but there are some decent **eating places** to suit most budgets, especially along the beachfront. Apart from the hotel bars mentioned in the accommodation section, there are a few other passable joints for a drink, and a couple of **nightclubs**.

Many of the **bars** listed below feature lively local bands playing jazz, rock and pop. The hub of the pub and club universe is Brookes Pavilion on Humewood Beach. The daily *Herald* lists the occasional **concerts** at the PE Opera House, next to the Donkin Memorial, and the odd **cabaret** event, most notably Centre-stage at the Boardwalk Casino (☎041 368 3093, ⓦwww.centrestage.co.za).

A reasonable range of popular **films** is screened at the Kine Park Cinema, 3 Rink St. For the usual Hollywood fare, try Nu Metro, Walmer Park Shopping Centre, Walmer; Ster Kinekor in The Bridge shopping complex; or Cinema Starz at the Boardwalk Casino Complex – check the *Herald* for programme details.

Restaurants

Blue Water Café Hobie Beach
☎041 583 4110. Great sea views, good pasta and moderately priced light snacks at this pleasant eating place. Daily 8.30am–11pm.
Fernando's Guest House & Grill 102 Cape Rd, Mill Park ☎041 373 2823. The best steaks in town as well as lamb and pork loin, lamb shank and calamari, all moderately priced and served with home-made chips. Mon–Sat noon–2pm & 5.30–10pm.
The Island Seafood Grill & Bar Pine Lodge Resort, Marine Drive ☎041 583 3789. A patio bar with an indoor restaurant serving a decent range of snacks and full meals. Every dish is named after an island, though the food is in fact fairly predictable pastas, burgers and so on, all nicely presented. Moderately priced.
Natti's Thai Kitchen 5 Park Lane ☎041 373 2763. Excellent restaurant serving reasonably

priced authentic Thai cuisine in a relaxed atmosphere. Evenings only.
Sacramento Marine Drive. Noted for its terrific views rather than its fare, this inexpensive eatery offers a range of less than exceptional pastas, steaks and toasted sandwiches along a stunning piece of coastline. Closes 5pm.

Bars and clubs

52 Parliament 52 Parliament St, Central. Late-night bar in a Victorian building decked out with interesting metal sculptures. DJs play house and other sounds, with occasional live music. Food is available. The R30–40 entrance fee deters impecunious teenagers. Wed, Fri & Sat.
Gondwana Café 2 Dolphin's Leap, Main Rd, Humewood. Relaxed, racially mixed eatery by day that doubles up as a club by night. Tues–Sun 9am–late.

Nine Yards Chapel St, Central. Cocktail and dance place with lots of drinks specials. Wed, Fri & Sat.

Sugar Rays, Tapas Al Sol & Toby Joe's Brookes Pavilion, Marine Drive. Brookes is a multilevel complex where you can dine, drink and party, the hub of late-night beachfront clubbing. The dance floors can be packed, but there are wooden decks with sea views to provide relief.

Listings

Airlines 1time ℡0861 345 345; kulula.com ℡0861 585 852; SAA ℡041 507 1111.

Car rental All at the airport: Avis ℡041 501 7200; Budget ℡041 581 4242; Hertz ℡041 508 6600; Imperial ℡041 581 1268; Tempest ℡041 581 1256.

Diving Although the Indian Ocean around PE isn't tropically clear and warm, the diving here is good, especially for soft corals. For dive courses, try Pro Dive, at 189 Main Rd, Walmer (℡041 581 1144, ⓦwww.prodive .co.za), which offers a one-day scuba-diving course and refresher courses.

Emergencies Fire ℡041 585 1555; see also p.163.

Hospitals St George's (private), 40 Park Drive, Settlers Park ℡041 392 6111; Provincial (state), Buckingham Rd, Central ℡041 392 3911.

Pharmacy Mount Road Pharmacy, 559 Govan Mbeki Ave, is open daily until 11pm (℡041 484 3838).

Post office Brookes Pavilion, Humewood (Mon–Fri 9am–3.30pm & Sat 8.30–11am).

Taxis Hurters ℡041 585 5500.

Addo Elephant National Park

Addo Elephant National Park (daily 7am–7pm; R100; ⓦwww .addoelephantpark.com) is just 73km north of Port Elizabeth, and should be your first choice for a relaxing few days' excursion from PE, though it is close enough to town to take in on a day-trip. A Big Five reserve, it is undergoing an expansion programme that will see it become one of South Africa's three largest game reserves, and the only one including coastline. Its PR people are talking in terms of a "Big Seven" reserve, as the denizens of the future coastal section (adjoining the Alexandra State Forest/Woody Cape section of the park) include whales and great white sharks. **Elephants** remain Addo's most obvious drawcard, but with the re-introduction in 2003 of a small number of **lions**, in two prides (big cats last roamed here over a century ago), as well as the presence of the rest of the Big Five – **buffalo**, **hippos** and **leopards** – it has become a game reserve to be reckoned with. **Spotted hyenas** were also introduced in 2003 as part of a programme to re-establish predators in the local ecosystem. Other species to look out for include **cheetah**, **black rhino**, **eland**, **kudu**, **warthog**, **ostrich** and **red hartebeest**.

The Addo bush is thick, dry and prickly, making it difficult sometimes to spot any of the 450 or so elephants and other game; when you do, though, it's often thrillingly close up. The best strategy is to ask where the pachyderms and the other four of the Big Five have last been seen (enquire with staff at the park reception), and also to head for the water hole in front of the restaurant to scan the bush for large grey backs quietly moving about. It also makes sense to go on a **guided game drive** in an open vehicle with a knowledgeable national parks driver. Two-hour outings leave throughout the day and cost R160 a person for day drives, R240 for sunset trips (including snacks and drinks), and R180 for night drives; book at Main Camp. The vehicles used are higher off the ground than a normal sedan to improve viewing opportunities.

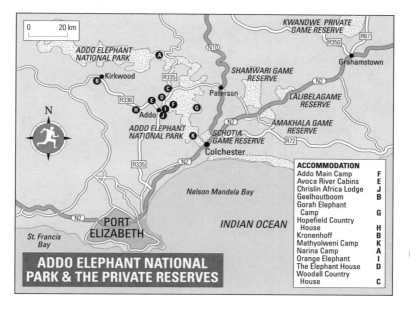

ACCOMMODATION	
Addo Main Camp	F
Avoca River Cabins	E
Chrislin Africa Lodge	J
Geelhoutboom	B
Gorah Elephant Camp	G
Hopefield Country House	H
Kronenhoff	B
Mathyolweni Camp	K
Narina Camp	A
Orange Elephant	I
The Elephant House	D
Woodall Country House	C

ADDO ELEPHANT NATIONAL PARK & THE PRIVATE RESERVES

Addo also offers a couple of **activities** to spice up your visit, with more in the pipeline. Two-hour **horse-rides**, suitable for the not-so-experienced (8am; R160), and three-hour rides for experienced equestrians (2pm; R210) leave from just outside the main gate and run along the exterior of the park fence (book at Main Camp). **Elephant-back safaris** are operated from a farm abutting the northern boundary of Addo (☎042 235 1400, ⓦwww .addoelephantbacksafaris.co.za), 90km from Port Elizabeth, off the R335. Excursions last two to three hours and cost R720 per person, with air transfers possible from Port Elizabeth or nearby private lodges.

Practicalities

By far the most straightforward way of getting to Addo is via the southern gate, which is accessed off the N2 at the village of Colchester, 43km northeast of Port Elizabeth. The gate is about 5km from **Matyholweni Camp**. It's worth noting, though, that at present there is no big game in the southern section of the park, which is currently fenced off from the northern section to prevent game moving between the two, although humans can drive through a gated checkpoint.

To get to **Main Camp**, Addo's older and more established base, which is north of Matyholweni, you can either take a slow, scenic drive through the park, which will take at least an hour, or use the R335 road that runs outside the western flank of the park – take the N2 from Port Elizabeth east towards Grahamstown for 5km, branching off at the Addo/Motherwell/Markman signpost onto the R335 through Addo village. Narina bush camp is 22km north of Main Camp along a gravel road. The network of roads within the section of the park between Main Camp and Matyholweni is untarred, but in good condition.

▲ An Addo elephant

Maps of the park are available at reception and indicate the location of **picnic** and braai sites. A **restaurant** (daily 6am–8pm) at Main Camp offers three meals a day, while the shop is well stocked with food and drink. Until the park is consolidated (expected to be completed by 2010), you won't be able to reach the coastal section that includes the Alexandria State Forest from inside the national park.

Accommodation inside the park

Addo's two major public restcamps, **Main** and **Mathyolweni**, provide comfortable national park accommodation in a range of thatched, fully equipped self-catering units, while **Narina bush camp** has four safari tents. **Reservations** are essential in the high season, and can be made through SANParks or, less than 72 hours in advance, directly with Addo (☎042 233 8600, ⓦwww.sanparks.org/parks/addo). In addition to the national parks accommodation, there are some **luxury private lodges** inside the park – most notable of which is *Gorah Elephant Camp*.

Gorah Elephant Camp 9km west along the Addo Heights road leading from the N10 to Addo village ☎ 044 532 7818, ⓦ www.gorah.com. Ultra-luxurious outfit based around a Victorian homestead decked out with the appropriate paraphernalia (mounted antelope skulls above the fireplace, evocative African landscapes, and polished tabletops you can see your reflection in) to play up those colonial-era safari fantasies. The suites are plush, there are opportunities to dine under the stars and there's a beautifully landscaped swimming pool. The steep price tag includes exclusive conducted game-viewing trips. Doubles R9440, including all meals and game drives.

Main Camp The oldest and largest of the National Parks camps. Besides camping facilities, there are forest cabins (R395) that sleep two people and share cooking facilities in communal kitchens; and more luxurious two-person chalets (R605) with their own kitchenettes. Some of these units sleep up to four people (but the minimum charge is for two occupants). Also available are well-designed, spacious safari tents (R300), perfect for summer, with decks right next to the perimeter fence; and for up to six people there are larger standard (R640) and luxury (R1760 for first four people, then R200 per person) family units. Two chalets have been adapted to accommodate the disabled.

Mathyolweni Camp National Parks accommodation in a dozen fully equipped self-catering chalets (R605) with showers, each sleeping two. Set in a secluded valley surrounded by thicket that supports a wealth of birdlife, the chalets have decks from which you will be able to view game once a planned water hole is completed. There is no restaurant, but Colchester, a 15-min drive away, has shops and basic places to eat.

Narina Camp Small National Parks bush camp in the mountainous Zuurberg section of Addo with four safari tents that sleep four people (R640) and share ablution and cooking facilities; bring your own provisions. Horse-riding is available.

Accommodation just outside the park

Outside the park, but within easy striking distance, private B&Bs and guesthouses are in abundance around Addo, especially among the citrus groves of the Sundays River Valley. Many offer day and night drives in the game reserve.

Avoca River Cabins 13km northwest of Addo village on the R336 ☎ 042 234 0421 or 082 677 9920, ⓦ www.gardenroute.co.za/addo/avoca. Reasonably priced B&B and self-catering accommodation on a farm in the Sundays River Valley. Budget cabins go for R200, more comfortable thatched huts (some on the banks of the river) from R450, and a timber chalet on stilts nestled among trees, which sleeps seven, for R750; canoes are available to rent. B&B doubles R500.

Chrislin Africa Lodge 12km south of Addo main gate, off the R336 ☎ 042 233 0022 or 082 783 3553, ⓦ www.africanhuts-addo.co.za. Quirky B&B with thatched huts built using traditional Xhosa construction techniques, with a lovely *lapa* (courtyard) and pool, and hearty country breakfasts, as well as dinners on request. Doubles from R750.

The Elephant House 5km north of Addo village on the R335 ☎ 042 233 2462 or 083 799 5671, ⓦ www.elephanthouse.co.za. Just minutes from Addo is one of the Eastern Cape's top places to stay, a stunning thatch-roofed lodge filled with Persian rugs and antique furniture that perfectly balances luxury with a supremely relaxed atmosphere. The nine bedrooms, two of which are in garden cottages, open onto a lawned courtyard. Candlelit dinners available, as are massages and game drives (R550 per person) into Addo and the surrounding reserves. Doubles R2700, Stable Cottage R1100.

Geelhoutboom 26 Market St, Kirkwood ☎ 042 230 1191, ⓦ www.geelhoutboom.co.za. Homely B&B with a/c rooms, a 20min drive from Addo main gate and shaded by a large yellowwood tree. Good value. Doubles from R520.

Hopefield Country House 20km southwest of Addo main gate ☎ 042 234 0333, ⓦ www.hopefield.co.za. Atmospheric 1930s farmhouse set in beautiful English-style gardens on a citrus farm. The five bedrooms are imaginatively furnished with period pieces in a style the owners (a pair of classical musicians who occasionally give impromptu concerts for guests) describe as "farmhouse eclectic". Doubles from R800.

Kronenhoff On the R336 as you enter Kirkwood ☏042 230 1448, 🌐 www.kronenhoff.co.za. In a small farming town, this is a hospitable, high-ceilinged Cape Dutch-style home, with spacious suites, polished wooden floors, large leather sofas and a sociable pub. In summer the sweet scent of orange blossom carries from the surrounding citrus groves. Doubles from R750.

Orange Elephant On the R335, 8km from the National Park gate ☏042 233 0023, 🌐 www.addobackpackers.com. Budget accommodation at a comfortable hostel, whose management will help you organize outings into the surrounding game reserves. Dorms R75, two-person tents R120, two-bedroom cottages R200.

Woodall Country House About 1km west of Addo main gate ☏042 233 0128, 🌐 www.woodall-addo.co.za. Excellent luxury guest house on a working citrus farm with eleven self-contained suites and rooms. There's a swimming pool, gymnasium, spa and sauna (massages are available, and there's a resident beautician). A lovely sundowner deck overlooks a small lake full of swans and other waterfowl. Renowned for its outstanding country cuisine, its restaurant offers three- to six-course dinners. Doubles from R1980.

The Eastern Cape's private game reserves

Although self-driving through Addo can be extremely rewarding, nothing beats getting into the wild in an open vehicle with a trained guide – something the handful of **private reserves** on the N2 highway between PE and Grahamstown excel at. If you're strapped for cash or pushed for time a good option is one of the day or half-day safaris that start at R600 per person offered by **Schotia** and **Amakhala**. More luxurious than these two, and consequently more expensive, is the mid-range outfit, **Lalibela**. But if you want the works – game drives, outstanding food, uncompromising luxury and excellent accommodation, you'll find it at **Shamwari**, with prices rising over R5000 per person a day. Once you're in this league it's worth considering heading slightly further afield to **Kwandwe Game Reserve** near Grahamstown, 127km from Port Elizabeth, which is arguably the best safari destination in the Eastern Cape.

The reserves are covered below in alphabetical order.

Amakhala Game Reserve

Just 2km further along the N2 from the turn-off to Shamwari (see below), **Amakhala Game Reserve** (☏042 235 1608, 🌐 www.amakhala.co.za) is a far more affordable option than its neighbour and is family-friendly, too, offering children's programmes at some of the lodges. The area is stocked with the Big Five as well as cheetah, giraffe, zebra, wildebeest and many antelopes. The Bushman's River meanders through the reserve and you can go on a canoe safari, accompanied by a ranger, and enjoy sundowner cruises on a river boat. **Accommodation** comprises six independently owned lodges that make use of the existing farmhouses on the reserve, as well as a camp where there are beds inside restored ox-wagons with private bathrooms – all with wonderful views. Rates start at R1000 per person (May–Aug), R1495 (Sept–April).

Day safaris (daily noon–6pm; booking essential) include two game drives, a river cruise and lunch and cost R720 per person.

Kwandwe Private Game Reserve

On the R67, 34km north of Grahamstown and 160km from Port Elizabeth, is the Eastern Cape's top wildlife destination, the very exclusive 🏇 **Kwandwe Private Game Reserve** (☎011 809 4300, 🌐www.kwandwereserve.com; first week of Jan, Feb, March & Oct–Dec R5740 per person per night, last three weeks of Jan & April–Sept R2605), with 30km of Fish River frontage and the Big Five in attendance. There are four lodges, two of which, *Uplands Homestead*, a beautifully restored Victorian homestead which accommodates six adults, and *Melton Manor*, a modern villa with four bedrooms set back 100m from a river, are for the exclusive use of single parties, with butlers, chefs and dedicated game rangers at guests' disposal. Of the other two, the fabulous *Kwandwe Great Fish River Lodge*, close to the water, is the quintessential traditional luxury safari lodge with nine suites and thatched roofs, wooden walkways and French windows that afford panoramic views of the surrounding countryside, while the ultra-luxurious and child-friendly *Kwandwe Ecca Lodge* – a funky boutique-hotel-in-the-bush – has six chalets, ingeniously designed with glass walls that allow you to lie on your bed and feel you're totally alone in the middle of the wilderness. Each unit has its own private plunge pool set into a wooden deck.

Apart from twice-a-day game drives, Kwandwe's safari activities include guided river walks, canoeing on the Great Fish, and rhino tracking, in which you follow one of the large mammals on foot. It also runs cultural tours with a resident historian who looks at the fascinating social and archeological past of the area. At *Ecca Lodge* special activities are laid on for children, including family game drives, short bush walks, and frog safaris. Service at Kwandwe is superb and highly personalized.

It's easy to drive to the game reserve, which is reached along the R67 between Grahamstown and Fort Beaufort. Road or air transfers are available from Port Elizabeth airport.

Lalibela Game Reserve

Preferable to Shamwari (see below) if you want slightly more affordable luxury and game viewing is the **Lalibela Game Reserve**, 90km northeast of Port Elizabeth on the N2 to Grahamstown (☎041 581 8170, 🌐www.lalibela.co.za). It's home to the Big Five and a diversity of flora and fauna, which you can see on the morning and evening safaris that are included in the accommodation rate (R2950 per person) along with all meals and drinks. There are three fabulous **lodges** with private viewing decks, swimming pools and *bomas* to choose from: *Tree Tops* offers luxury safari tents on thatched platforms; *Lentaba Lodge* houses visitors in thatched chalets; while *Mark's Camp*, the largest of the three (it takes up to twenty people), consists of stone and thatch cottages. You can dine on terrific Eastern Cape fare and contemporary cuisine.

Schotia Private Game Reserve

Schotia Private Game Reserve (☎042 235 1436, 🌐www.schotia.com), on the eastern flank of Addo, is the smallest but possibly the busiest of the private reserves, on account of the excellent value it offers. While Schotia is not a Big Five reserve, it is able to offer a Big Five experience with packages that include excursions to Addo Elephant National Park. **Full-day safaris** (R1200 per person) involve a game drive through Addo followed by lunch and an evening game drive and dinner at Schotia, after which guests are returned to their accommodation. **Overnight stays** (R1800 per person) include all this plus accommodation at Schotia in one of the three chalets or eight double rooms. If you're pushed for time or money you can opt for the **afternoon game drive** (R600 per person) in Schotia, which kicks off at 3pm and ends at 9pm. The evening excursions are full of shining eyes caught by powerful lamps, with dinner cooked on an open fire in a thatched courtyard.

Schotia's **wildlife** includes six **lions**, giraffes, rhinos, hippos, zebra and a dozen or so species of antelope. Visitors can arrange to be collected from Port Elizabeth or anywhere in the Addo vicinity; if you're driving, you're collected from a secure car park 2km up the N10 from the N2/N10 intersection.

Shamwari Game Reserve

The largest and best known of the Eastern Cape's private Big Five reserves, **Shamwari Game Reserve**, 65km north of Port Elizabeth on the N2 (☎042 203 1111, ⓦwww.shamwari.com), has cultivated an image as a jetsetter destination, hosting the rich and famous, such as Tiger Woods and John Travolta. The reserve has a diverse variety of landscapes, the requisite animals in sufficient numbers and high standards of game-viewing – which justifies its reputation as one of the leading wildlife destinations in the southern half of South Africa.

Accommodation is in the colonial-style, family-friendly *Long Lee Manor* and five other attractive lodges which don't take youngsters, dotted around the reserve and furnished with every conceivable comfort: restored Victorian homestead *Bushman's River Lodge*, overlooking a valley; the modernist stone and glass *Eagle's Crag*; ethnically decorated *Lobengula*; hotel-like *Riverdene*; and luxury tented camp *Bayethe*. Rates start at R3250 per person (May–Sept), R5250 (Oct–April).

Contexts

Contexts

A brief history of Cape Town

Cape Town's history is complex and what follows is only a brief account of major events in the city's past. For more detailed coverage on both Cape Town's and South Africa's history in general, see the list in "Books".

Hunters and herders

Rock art provides evidence of human culture in the Western Cape dating back nearly 30,000 years. The artists were hunter-gatherers, sometimes called bushmen but more commonly **San**, a relatively modern term from the Nama language with roots in the concept of "inhabiting or dwelling", to reflect the fact these were South Africa's aboriginals. San people still maintain a tenuous survival in tiny pockets, mostly in Namibia and Botswana, making theirs the longest-existing culture in the subcontinent. At one time they probably spread throughout sub-Saharan Africa, having pretty well perfected their **nomadic lifestyle** – the men hunting and the women gathering – leaving them considerable time for artistic and religious pursuits. People lived in small, loosely connected bands comprising family units and were free to leave and join up with other groups.

About two thousand years ago, this changed when some groups in territory north of modern South Africa laid their hands on fat-tailed sheep and cattle from northern Africa, thus transforming themselves into **herding communities**, known as **Khoikhoi** or simply Khoi. The introduction of livestock had a revolutionary effect on social organization and introduced the idea of ownership and accumulation. Animals became a symbol of both wealth and social status, and those who were better at acquiring and holding onto their herds gradually became wealthier. Social divisions developed, and political units became larger, centring around a chief, who had important powers, such as the allocation of pasturage.

The Cape goes Dutch

Portuguese mariners, under the command of **Bartholomeu Dias**, first rounded the Cape in the 1480s, and named it Cabo de Boa Esperança, the **Cape of Good Hope**. Marking their progress, they left an unpleasant set of calling cards all along the coast – slaves they had captured in West Africa and had cast ashore to trumpet the power and glory of Portugal with the aim of intimidating the locals. Little wonder then, that the first encounter of the Portuguese with the indigenous Khoikhoi along the Garden Route coast was not a happy one. It began with a group of Khoikhoi stoning the Portuguese for taking water from a spring without asking permission, and ended with a Khoikhoi man lying dead with a crossbow bolt through his chest. It was another 170 years before any European settlement was established in South Africa.

In 1652, a group of white employees of the **Dutch East India Company** (Verenigde Oostindische Compagnie or **VOC**), which was engaged in trade between the Netherlands and the East Indies, pulled into Table Bay to set up a refreshment station to revictual Company ships trading between Europe and the East. There were no plans at this time to set up a colony; in fact, the Cape post was given to the station commander **Jan van Riebeeck** because he had been caught with his hand in the till. Van Riebeeck dreamed up a number of schemes to keep "darkest Africa" at bay, including the very Dutch solution of building a canal that would cut the Cape Peninsula adrift. In the end he had to satisfy himself with planting a **bitter almond hedge** (still growing in Cape Town's Kirstenbosch Gardens) to keep the natives at arm's length.

Despite Van Riebeeck's view that the indigenous Khoikhoi were "a savage set, living without conscience", from the start the Dutch were dependent on them to provide livestock, which were traded for trinkets. As the settlement developed, van Riebeeck needed more **labour** to keep the show going, and bemoaned the fact that he was unsuccessful in persuading the Khoikhoi to discard the freedom of their herding life for the toil of ploughing furrows for him. Much to his annoyance, the bosses back in Holland had forbidden Van Riebeeck from enslaving the locals, and refused his request for slaves from elsewhere in the Company's empire.

Creeping colonization

Everyone at the Cape at this time was under stringent contract to the VOC, which effectively had total control over their activities and movements – a form of indentureship. But a number of Dutch men were released from their contracts in 1657 to farm as **free burghers** on land granted by the Company; they were

▲ The Castle of Good Hope

now at liberty to pursue their own economic activities, although the VOC still controlled the market and set prices for produce. This annexation of the lands around the mud fort, which preceded the construction of the more solid Castle of Good Hope, ultimately led to the inexorable process of **colonization**.

The only snag was that the land granted didn't belong to the Company in the first place, and the move sparked the first of a series of **Khoikhoi–Dutch wars**. Although the first campaign ended in stalemate, the Khoikhoi were ultimately no match for the Dutch, who had the tactical mobility of horses and the superior killing power of firearms. Campaigns continued through the 1660s and 1670s and proved rather profitable for Dutch raiders, who on one outing in 1674 rounded up eight hundred Khoikhoi cattle and four thousand sheep.

Meanwhile, in 1658, Van Riebeeck had managed successfully to purloin a shipload of **slaves** from West Africa, whetting an insatiable appetite for this form of labour. The VOC itself became the biggest slave owner at the Cape and continued importing slaves, mostly from the East Indies, at such a pace that by 1711 there were more slaves than burghers in the colony. With the help of this ready workforce, the embryonic Cape colony expanded outwards and trampled the peninsula's Khoikhoi, who by 1713 had lost everything. Most of their livestock (nearly 50,000 animals) and most of their land west of the Hottentots Holland Mountains had been gobbled up by the VOC. Dispossession, and diseases like smallpox, previously unknown in South Africa, decimated their numbers and shattered their social system. By the middle of the eighteenth century, those who remained had been reduced to a condition of miserable servitude to the colonists.

Kaapstad

During the early eighteenth century, Western Cape Khoikhoi society disintegrated and **slavery** became the economic backbone of the colony, which was now a rude colonial village of low, whitewashed, flat-roofed houses. Passing through in 1710, Jan van Riebeeck's granddaughter, Johanna, commented contemptuously that the settlement was "a miserable place. There is nothing pretty along the shoreline, the Castle is peculiar, the houses resemble prisons" and "one sees here peculiar people who live in strange ways".

Dutch global influence began to wane in the early 1700s, but by midcentury the Cape settlement had developed an independent identity and some little prosperity based on its pivotal position on the European–Far East trade route. People now began referring to it as "**Kaapstad**" (Cape Town) rather than "the Cape settlement", and by 1750 it had a thousand buildings, with over three thousand diverse inhabitants. Some of these were indigenous Khoikhoi people, but the largest number were VOC employees, dominated by an elite of high-ranking Dutch-born officials. The lower rungs were filled by the poor from all over Europe, including Scandinavia, Germany, France, England, Scotland and Russia, while slaves came from East Africa, Madagascar, India and Indonesia. There was also a transient population from passing ships, which by the second half of the century were largely manned by Indian, Javanese and Chinese crews. If nothing else, the constant **maritime traffic** injected some life into this intellectual desert, which couldn't boast a single printing press, let alone a newspaper. Entertainment consisted mainly of carousing, whoring and gambling.

Britain takes the Cape

By the 1790s the VOC was more or less bankrupt, and its control over the restive Cape burghers had become decidedly tenuous. As Dutch maritime influence declined, Britain and France were tussling for domination of the Indian Ocean. The outbreak of the French Revolution in 1789 and the establishment of a Francophile republic in the Netherlands a few years later made the **British** distinctly jittery about their strategic access to Cape Town. In August 1795, Rear-Admiral George Keith Elphinstone was sent in haste with four British sloops of war to secure Cape Town; by mid-September the ragtag Dutch garrison had capitulated.

The British occupation heralded a period of **free trade** in which exports from the Cape lifted off as tariffs were slashed, with the result that Cape wines, the largest Cape export, were meeting ten percent of British wine consumption by 1822. The tightly controlled and highly restrictive Dutch regime was replaced with a more tolerant government, which brought immediate **freedom of religion**, the abolition of the slave trade in 1808, and the **emancipation** of slaves in 1834.

Although British-born residents were a minority during the first half of the nineteenth century, their influence was huge, and Cape Town began to take on a British character through a process of cultural, economic and political dominance. **English** became the language of status and officialdom and by 1860 there were eight newspapers, six of them in English. A vibrant press fed a culture of **liberalism** which led Capetonians to thwart British attempts to transport convicts to the Cape (see box, p.55) – the first time since the American Revolution that an outpost of empire had successfully defied Whitehall. This gave the colonists the confidence to demand **self-government** and, in 1854, males, regardless of race, who owned property worth £25 or more won the right to vote for a lower house of parliament, which was based in Cape Town. A significant development of the second half of the nineteenth century was the rapid growth of **communications**, both within Cape Town and also into the interior, which reinforced the city's status as the principal centre of a Cape Colony that by now extended 1000km to the east. The road from Cape Town to Camps Bay across Kloof Nek was started in 1848, a telegraph line between Cape Town and Simon's Town was laid in 1860, but most significant of all was the introduction of steam. The first **rail line** from central Cape Town to Wynberg was completed in 1864, opening up the southern peninsula to the development of **middle-class suburbia**.

From backwater to breakwater

The development of an urban infrastructure wasn't enough to lift Cape Town from its backwater provinciality. That required the discovery in 1867 of the world's largest deposit of **diamonds** around modern-day Kimberley. Coinciding with this, the city's breakwater was started and the **harbour** was completed just in time to accommodate the massive influx of fortune-hunters, immigrants and capital into Cape Town en route to the diggings. More significant still was the **discovery of gold** around Johannesburg in the Boer-controlled South African Republic in the 1880s, which gave Cape Town a new significance as the gateway to the world's richest mineral deposits.

From the 1870s, growing middle-class self-confidence was reflected in the erection of grand **Victorian frontages** to the city centre's shops, banks and offices. Echoing Victorian London, this prosperous public facade hid a growing world of poverty, inhabited by immigrants, Africans and coloureds (people of mixed race: see p.52) who made up a cheap labour force. The degradation and vice that thrived in Cape Town's growing slums were disquieting to the Anglocentric middle class, which would have preferred Cape Town to be like a respectably homogenous Home Counties town, rather than a cultural melting pot.

As the twentieth century dawned, the authorities attempted to achieve a closer approximation to the white middle-class ideal by introducing laws to stem **immigration**, other than from Western Europe, while other statutes sought to protect "European traders" against competition from other ethnic groups. Racial segregation wasn't far behind, and an outbreak of bubonic plague in 1901 gave the town council an excuse to establish **Ndabeni**, Cape Town's first black location, near present-day Pinelands.

Industrialization and segregation

Apart from contributing to Cape Town's development as a trading port, the discovery of gold had more significant consequences for the city. By the end of the nineteenth century, a number of influential capitalists, among them **Cecil John Rhodes** (prime minister of the Cape from 1890 to 1897), were convinced that it would be a good idea to annex the two Boer republics to the north to create a unified South Africa under British influence. In 1899 Britain marched on the Boer republics, in what was rashly described by Lord Kitchener as a "teatime war", but became known internationally as the **Anglo-Boer War**, Britain's most expensive campaign since the Napoleonic Wars. Eventually, three years later, the Anglo-Boer War ended with the Boers' surrender. What followed was nearly a decade of discussions, at the end of which the two Boer republics (the South African Republic and the Orange Free State) and two British colonies (the Cape and Natal) were federated in 1910 to become the **Union of South Africa**, Cape Town gaining a pivotal position as the **legislative capital** of the country.

Africans and coloureds, excluded from the cosy deal between Boers and Brits, had to find expression in the workplace, flexing their collective muscle on the docks in 1919, where they formed the mighty **Industrial and Commercial Union**, which boasted 200,000 members in its heyday. Cape Town began the process of becoming a modern industrial city and, with the building of the South African National Gallery, promoted itself as the urbane cultural capital of the country. Accelerated **industrialization** brought an influx of Africans from the rural areas and soon Ndabeni was overflowing. Alarmed that Africans were living close to the city centre in District Six and were also spilling out into the Cape Flats, the authorities passed the **Urban Areas Act**, which compelled Africans to live in what were named "locations" and empowered the city council to expel jobless Africans – measures that preceded apartheid by 25 years. In 1927, the new location of **Langa** (which ironically means "sun") was opened next to the sewage works. Laid out along military lines, with barrack-style dormitories for the residents, it was surrounded by a security fence.

World War II

During the 1930s Cape Town saw the growth of several fascist movements, the largest of which was the **Greyshirts**, whose favourite meeting place was the Koffiehuis (coffee house) next to the Groote Kerk in Adderley Street. Its members included Hendrik Verwoerd, a Dutch-born intellectual who became a fanatical Afrikaner Nationalist and South African prime minister from 1958 to 1966. When **World War II** broke out there was a heated debate in parliament, which narrowly voted for South Africa to side with Britain against Germany. Members of all South African communities volunteered for service, the **ANC** (founded in 1912) arguing that their support should be linked to full citizenship for blacks. Afrikanerdom was deeply divided and **Nazi sympathizers**, among them John Vorster (Verwoerd's successor as prime minister), were jailed for actively attempting to sabotage the war effort. *Die Burger*, Cape Town's Afrikaans-language newspaper, backed Germany throughout the war.

The war brought hardship, particularly to those at the bottom of the heap, leading to an increased influx of Africans and poor white Afrikaners from the countryside to the cities. This changed the demography of the city of Cape Town, which lost its British colonial flavour and, for the first time in 150 years, had more black (mostly coloured) than white residents. To accommodate the burgeoning African population, Langa was extended and new townships were built during and after the war at **Nyanga** and **Guguletu**.

By the end of hostilities, Cape Town was a mixed bag of ad hoc official **segregation** in some areas of life while in others, such as on buses and trains, there was none. Coloureds in the Cape, in contrast with residents of the former Boer republics, still had the franchise provided they qualified on the grounds of property ownership.

Apartheid and defiance

In postwar South Africa, ideological tensions grew between those pushing for universal civil rights and those whites who feared black advancement. In 1948 the **National Party** came to power, promising its fearful white supporters that it would reverse the flow of Africans to the cities. In Cape Town it introduced a policy favouring coloureds for certain unskilled and semi-skilled jobs, admitting only African men who already had work and forbidding the construction of family accommodation for Africans – hence turning the townships into predominantly male preserves.

During the 1950s the National Party began putting in place a barrage of laws that would eventually constitute the structure of apartheid. Early **onslaughts on civil rights** included the Coloured Voters Act, which stripped coloureds of the vote; the Bantu Authorities Act, which set up puppet authorities to govern Africans in rural reserves; the Population Registration Act, which classified every South African at birth as "white, Bantu or coloured"; the Group Areas Act, which divided South Africa into ethnically distinct areas; and the Suppression of Communism Act, which made anti-apartheid opposition (communist or not) a criminal offence. Africans, now regarded as foreigners in their own country, had at all times to carry **passes** – one of the most hated symbols of apartheid.

The ANC responded in 1952 with the **Defiance Campaign**, whose aim was the granting of full civil rights to blacks. A radical young firebrand called **Nelson Mandela** was appointed "volunteer-in-chief" of the campaign, which had a crucial influence on his politics. Up to that point he had rejected political association with non-Africans, but the campaign's interracial solidarity brought him round to the conciliatory inclusive approach for which he is now famous. The government swooped on the homes of the ANC leadership, resulting in the detention and then banning of over a hundred ANC organizers. Unbowed, the ANC pressed ahead with the **Congress of the People**, held near Johannesburg in 1955. At a mass meeting of nearly three thousand delegates, four organizations – representing Africans, coloureds, whites and Indians – formed a strategic partnership.

From within the organization, a group of Africanists criticized cooperation with white activists, leading to the formation in 1958 of the breakaway **Pan Africanist Congress** (PAC) under the leadership of the charismatic **Robert Mangaliso Sobukwe**. Langa township became a stronghold of the PAC, which organized peaceful **anti-pass demonstrations** in Johannesburg and Cape Town on March 21, 1960. Over a period of days, work stayaways spread to all Cape Town's locations, achieving a temporary nationwide suspension of the pass laws – the calm before the storm. As the protests gathered strength, the government declared a **State of Emergency**, sent the army in to crush the strike, restored the pass laws and banned the ANC and PAC. Nelson Mandela continued to operate clandestinely for a year until he was finally captured in 1962, tried and imprisoned – together with most of the ANC leadership – on **Robben Island**.

Soweto and the Total Strategy

With resistance stifled, the state grew more powerful, and for the majority of white South Africans, business people and foreign investors, life seemed perfect. The panic caused by the 1960 uprising soon became a dim memory and confidence returned. For black South Africans, poverty deepened – a state of affairs enforced by apartheid legislation.

In 1966 the notorious **Group Areas Act** was used to uproot whole coloured communities from many areas, including District Six, and to move them to the soulless **Cape Flats** where, in the wake of social disintegration, gangsterism took root (see box, pp.100–101). It remains one of Cape Town's most pressing problems. Compounding the injury, the National Party stripped away coloured representation on Cape Town city council in 1972.

The **Soweto Revolt** of June 16, 1976, signalled the start of a new wave of anti-apartheid protest, when black youths took to the streets against the imposition of Afrikaans as a medium of instruction in their schools. The protests spread to Cape Town where, as in Jo'burg, the government responded ruthlessly by sending in armed police, who killed 128 and injured 400 Capetonians.

Despite naked violence, protest spread to all sections of the community. The government was forced to rely increasingly on armed police to impose order. Even this was unable to stop the mushrooming of new liberation organizations, many of them part of the broadly based **Black Consciousness movement**. As the unrest rumbled on into 1977, the government responded by banning all the new black organizations and detaining their leadership.

From the mid-1960s to the mid-1970s Prime Minister **John Vorster** had relied on the police to maintain the apartheid status quo, but it became obvious that this wasn't working. In 1978 he was deposed in a palace coup by his minister of defence, **P.W. Botha**, who conceived a complex military-style approach he called the **Total Strategy**. The strategy was a two-handed one of reforming peripheral aspects of apartheid, while deploying the armed forces in unprecedented acts of repression. In 1981, as resistance grew, Botha began contemplating change and moved Nelson Mandela and other ANC leaders from Robben Island to Pollsmoor Prison in mainland Cape Town. At the same time he poured ever-increasing numbers of troops into the townships.

In 1983 Botha concocted what he believed was a master plan for a so-called **New Constitution** in which coloureds and Indians would be granted the vote – in racially segregated chambers with no executive power. The only constructive outcome of this project was the extension of the Houses of Parliament to their current size.

Apartheid suffers a stroke

As President Botha was punting his ramshackle scheme in 1983, 15,000 anti-apartheid delegates met at Mitchell's Plain on the Cape Flats, to form the **United Democratic Front (UDF)**, the largest opposition gathering in South Africa since the Congress of the People in 1955. The UDF became a proxy for the banned ANC, and two years of strikes, boycotts and protest followed. As the government resorted to increasingly extreme measures, internal resistance grew and the international community turned up the heat on the apartheid regime. The Commonwealth passed a resolution condemning apartheid, the US and Australia severed air links, Congress passed disinvestment legislation and finally, in 1985, the Chase Manhattan Bank called in its massive loan to South Africa.

Botha declared his umpteenth **state of emergency** and unleashed a last-ditch storm of tyranny. There were bannings, mass arrests, detentions, treason trials and torture, as well as assassinations of UDF leaders by sinister hit squads. At the beginning of 1989, **Mandela** wrote to Botha from prison describing his fear of a polarized South Africa and calling for negotiations. An intransigent character, Botha found himself paralysed by his inability to reconcile the need for radical change with his fear of a right-wing backlash. When he suffered a stroke later that year, his party colleagues moved swiftly to oust him and replaced him with **F.W. de Klerk**.

Faced with the worst crisis in South Africa's history, President de Klerk realized that repression had failed. Even South Africa's friends were losing patience, and in September 1989 US President George Bush Snr told de Klerk that if Mandela wasn't released within six months he would extend US sanctions. Five months later, de Klerk announced the un-banning of the ANC, PAC, the Communist Party and 33 other organizations, as well as the release of Mandela.

On February 11, 1990, Cape Town's history took a neat twist when, just hours after being released from prison, **Nelson Mandela** made his first public speech from the balcony of City Hall to a jubilant crowd spilling across the Grand Parade, the very site of the first Dutch fort.

▲ First picture of Nelson Mandela after his release from prison

Democracy

Four protracted years of negotiations followed, leading eventually to South Africa's current constitution. Following the country's first-ever democratic elections in 1994, Mandela became South Africa's president. One of the anomalies of the 1994 election was that while most of South Africa delivered an **ANC landslide**, the Western Cape, supposedly the most liberal region of the country, returned the **National Party** as its provincial government. Politics in South Africa were not, it turned out, divided along a faultline that separated whites from the rest of the population as many had assumed; the majority of coloureds had voted for the very party that had once stripped them of the vote, regarding it with less suspicion than the ANC. During the ANC's first term, affirmative action policies and a racial shift in the economy led to the rise of a

black middle class, but even so this represented a tiny fraction of the African and coloured population, and many people felt that transformation hadn't gone far enough.

Despite several years of non-racial democracy, Cape Town entered the twenty-first century largely a divided city, with whites and a few middle-class blacks enjoying a leafy existence in the suburbs along the two coasts and the slopes of Table Mountain, while most Africans lived (and still do) in deprived townships. The **2000 local elections** proved once again just how divided Cape Town remained. The liberal Democratic Party, which for decades had been the only vociferous parliamentary opposition to the apartheid government, joined its former enemy, the New National Party or NNP (the renamed and freshly laundered party of apartheid, the National Party), to form the **Democratic Alliance** (DA) under the leadership of the Democratic Party's chief Tony Leon: the DA's slogan for the 2000 campaign was "Keep the ANC Out", which many read as a thinly disguised reversion to the National Party's apartheid-era catchphrase of "Swart Gevaar" (Black Peril), only this time the tactic aimed not to preserve "white purity", but to unite coloured and white voters against Africans. The scheme worked and the alliance won control of the city and the province, but the two parties swiftly fell out with one another.

Two years later, in a curious twist to national politics, the NNP then chose to become incorporated into the ANC. Formerly the bitterest of adversaries – the NNP's predecessors had, after all, locked up the ANC's leadership on Robben Island – they made unlikely bedfellows. Stranger still, the ANC welcomed them. Nevertheless, in the Western Cape, this had the desired effect of delivering the province – and the Mother City – into the hands of the ANC. In October 2002 Cape Town got its first-ever African (and first-ever woman, and first-ever ANC) mayor in **Nomaindia Mfeketo**.

On taking charge, Mfeketo promised to tackle **poverty** in Cape Town, where, according to a council report, nearly a third of all families had difficulty feeding themselves; in the shanty towns this figure rose to over seventy percent. The first **ANC municipal budget** for Cape Town allocated funds for upgrading the so-called "informal settlements" (shanty towns), with proposals to introduce proper sanitation, water supplies and floodlighting. But Mfeketo's mayorship ended in 2006, when the ANC lost the **municipal elections** and the Democratic Alliance, which in Cape Town was led by Helen Zille, formed a governing coalition, making Cape Town the only city in the country not under ANC control. Mfeketo later faced investigation for unauthorized spending of over R275m.

Despite ANC accusations that her policies were racially divisive, **Helen Zille**, who delivered her inaugural mayoral speech fluently in Cape Town's three main official languages – English, Afrikaans and Xhosa – is critically aware that only through widening her party's appeal to all communities can the DA garner support. On taking over as executive mayor, the veteran anti-apartheid activist echoed the words of her defeated predecessor in announcing that her core focus would be on alleviating poverty, which is at the root of many of Cape Town's major problems. These include inadequate housing, poor health (notably HIV, AIDS and tuberculosis) and drug-related crime, which had tripled over the previous four years.

The drug of choice in the Mother City is *tik*, or methamphetamine, which Zille identified as a particularly serious social threat, along with a "rising tide of corruption in the police", who appeared to be protecting the drug lords. Early into her term, Zille led members of the Cape Flats community in a legal anti-drug march to the house of a suspected drug dealer. The marchers (but not the alleged dealer) were arrested. In a press interview afterwards she asked: "How is it possible that dealers can continue to ply an illegal trade that is destroying an entire generation of young people, under the very noses of the police?" Charges against her were quickly dropped and she in turn laid charges of wrongful arrest against the police.

In 2007 Zille continued to hold her post as mayor of Cape Town when she was elected leader of the DA on the resignation of its national leader Tony Leon, investing her party's control of Cape Town with a significance that goes well beyond the city limits. Given that Cape Town is the only notable place in the country not run by the ANC, her performance here is critical to the national future of her party. Cape Town is a showcase for Zille to demonstrate whether the DA can deliver on poverty alleviation, efficient administration and clean government, or whether her promises are just empty words.

Books

For a country with a relatively small reading public, South Africa generates a huge number of books, particularly politics and history titles. Some of the South African published books may be tricky to find outside the country, but almost all those listed below are in print and should be available from the larger bookshops listed on p.150. Books that are especially recommended are indictated by a 🏃 symbol.

Fiction

Tatamkhulu Afrika *The Innocents*. Set in the struggle years, this novel examines the moral and ethical issues of the time from a Muslim perspective.

Andre Brink *A Chain of Voices*. Superbly evocative tale of Cape eighteenth-century life, exploring the impact of slavery on one farming family, right up to its dramatic and murderous end.

🏃 **J.M. Coetzee** *Disgrace*. A subtle, strange novel set in a Cape Town university and on a remote Eastern Cape farm, where the lives of a literature professor and his farmer daughter are violently transformed. Bleak but totally engrossing, this won the Booker Prize in 1999. See the box below for more on Coetzee.

J.M. Coetzee

To read a **J.M. Coetzee** novel is to walk an emotional tightrope from exhilaration to sadness, with a sense throughout of being guided by a strong creative intellect and an exceptionally careful observer of human experience.

Coetzee's taut, measured style strikes some readers as cold and bloodless; he is relentlessly unsentimental, and plots tend to end on an unsettling note. But despite his reputation as a "difficult" writer, Coetzee never fails to involve us absolutely in the fates of his characters; in the words of Nadine Gordimer, Coetzee "goes to the nerve-centre of being".

Born in Cape Town in 1940, and trained as a linguist and computer scientist in South Africa and the US, Coetzee began to write fiction in the early 1970s. *Dusklands* and *In the Heart of the Country*, his first two novels, were dense and often over-wrought dissections of settler psychology, but his prose reached a soaring maturity with *Waiting for the Barbarians* (1980), in which an imaginary desert landscape is the setting for a chilling exploration of the dynamics of imperial power.

In 1983 *The Life and Times of Michael K*, following the wanderings of a reclusive refugee across a future South Africa ravaged by civil war, won the Booker Prize. The novel ends with a passage of extraordinary beauty and subtlety, and stands as a postmodern masterpiece that now bears ironic testimony to South Africa's actual future. After *Michael K* came the novels *Foe*, *Age of Iron* and *The Master of Petersburg*, an anthology of criticism, *White Writing*, and a moving childhood memoir, *Boyhood*.

When Coetzee won an unprecedented second Booker Prize for *Disgrace* in 1999, he became famous beyond literary circles for the first time. This has meant exasperation for soundbite-hungry media hounds, since Coetzee abhors publicity – he chose not to attend the Booker Prize award ceremony and is notoriously cagey in social interactions. In 2002 Coetzee emigrated to Australia, where he lives in Adelaide.

Achmat Dangor *The Z Town Trilogy* and *Bitter Fruit*. One of the best writers from Cape Town, Dangor sets his trilogy in a town much like it, during one of apartheid South Africa's many states of emergency, which have started to burrow in intricate ways into the psyches of his characters. *Bitter Fruit* is the story of the son of two anti-apartheid activists, and of an act of violence and injustice threading two generations, which is resurrected by the Truth and Reconciliation Commission. The book portrays a brittle family, a dysfunctional society, and how we address – or fail to address – the past's deepest wounds.

Rayda Jacobs *The Slave Book*. A carefully researched historical novel dealing with love and survival in a slave household in 1830s Cape Town, on the eve of the abolition of slavery.

Ashraf Jamal *Love Themes For the Wilderness*. The inhabitants of a bohemian subculture are lovingly observed in this funny and free-spirited novel set in mid-1990s Observatory.

Pamela Jooste *Dance with a Poor Man's Daughter*. The fragile world of a young coloured girl during the early apartheid years is sensitively imagined in this hugely successful first novel.

Alex La Guma *A Walk in the Night*. One of the truly proletarian writers that South Africa has produced, La Guma, before his long exile in Cuba, focused on the conditions of life in Cape Town, particularly the inner-city areas like District Six. His social realism is gritty yet poignant and it gives us many indelible portraits of Cape Town in the mid-century. A real historian of the city.

Anne Landsman *The Devil's Chimney*. A stylish and entertaining piece of magic realism about the Southern Cape town of Oudtshoorn in the days of the ostrich-feather boom.

Sindiwe Magona *Mother to Mother*. Magona adopts the narrative voice of the mother of the killer of Amy Biehl, an American student murdered in a Cape Town township in 1993. The novel is addressed to Biehl's mother, and is a trenchant and lyrical meditation on the traumas of the past.

Patricia Schonstein Pinnock *Skyline*. Set in a crumbling apartment block in central Cape Town, Pinnock's novel examines a young girl's coming of age, her encounters with immigrants and refugees from Nigeria, Zimbabwe, Sudan and elsewhere in Africa, and the rising xenophobia in South Africa.

Richard Rive *Buckingham Palace, District Six*. The unique urban culture of District Six is movingly remembered in this short novel about the life of a now-desolate street and its inhabitants.

Linda Rode (ed) *Crossing Over*. Collection of 26 stories by new and emerging South African writers on the experiences of adolescence and early adulthood in a period of political transition.

Martin Trump and Jean Marquard (eds) *A Century of South African Short Stories*. A selection of South Africa's finest short stories, including contributions from Can Themba (writer of *Drum*), Charles Bosman and Nadine Gordimer.

Jann Turner *Heartland*. A white farmer's daughter and a black labourer's son are childhood companions on a Boland fruit farm; a betrayal occurs, and years later the boy returns from political exile, ready to stake his claim to the land. A hefty and ambitious popular novel.

Zoe Wicombe *You Can't Get Lost in Cape Town*. The author of a book of primarily short stories with a compelling title, Wicombe is remarkable for her sense of realism and the subtle way in which she produces work where social concern is transparent, humour is demonstrable, and yet which consents to none of the heavy-handed treatment anti-apartheid protest literature usually follows.

Guides and reference books

G.M. Branch *Two Oceans.* Don't be fooled by the coffee-table format; this is a comprehensive guide to southern Africa's marine life.

Shirley Brossey *A Walking Guide for Table Mountain.* Not hard to find in South Africa, this is an inexpensive guide to trails around Table Mountain, with useful hand-drawn maps and down-to-earth text.

Duncan Butchart *Wildlife of the Cape Peninsula – Common Animals and Plants.* Compact, well-illustrated pocket guide to the living world of the Cape Peninsula. Covers mountain, seashore and garden environments.

Richard Cowling and Dave Richardson *Fynbos: South Africa's Unique Floral Kingdom.* Lavishly illustrated coffee-table book. A fascinating layman's portrait of the *fynbos* ecosystem.

Mike Lundy *Best walks in the Cape Peninsula.* An invaluable, not-too-bulky book for casual walkers, offering plenty of possibilities for an afternoon's stroll. *Weekend Trails in the Western Cape* is the best guide to outings in the Cape, with good maps, good advice and notes on flora and fauna.

L. McMahon and M. Fraser *A Fynbos Year.* Exquisitely illustrated and well-written book about the Western Cape's unique floral kingdom.

South African National Parks *Mountains in the Sea: Table Mountain to Cape Point.* Beautifully produced and comprehensive pocket guide covering everything you need to know about the natural history of the Table Mountain National Park, including information on ecology, a handy colour wildlife- and plant-spotting section and hiking routes.

Ursula Stevens *The Winelands Explorer.* Describes a number of wine routes in the Stellenbosch, Paarl and Franschoek areas, with some interesting historical background about the different estates.

Philip van Zyl (ed) *John Platter South African Wines.* One of the best-selling titles in South Africa – an annually updated pocket book that rates virtually every wine produced in the country. No aspiring connoisseur of Cape wines should venture forth without it.

History, politics and society

Vivian Bickford-Smith, Elizabeth van Heyningen and Nigel Worden *Cape Town: The Making of a City* and *Cape Town in the Twentieth Century.* The first book is richly illustrated and exhaustively researched, and recounts the growth of Cape Town, from early Khoisan societies to the end of the nineteenth century. The second volume is a thorough and elegant account of modern Cape Town, which interweaves rich local history with international events.

Emile Boonzaier, Candy Malherbe, Andy Smith and Penny Berens *The Cape Herders: A History of the Khoikhoi of Southern Africa.* This accessible account of the Khoikhoi successfully explodes the many prejudices and myths that surround them and explores their way of life, their interaction with Europeans, and what remains of them today.

Richard Calland *Anatomy of South Africa: Who Holds the Power.* An incisive dissection of politics and power in South Africa today, from one of the country's most respected commentators.

Hermann Giliomee and Bernard Mbenga *A New History of South Africa.* A comprehensive, reliable and entertaining account of South Africa's history, published in 2007, making it the first new major work on the topic in a decade.

Barbara Hutton *Robben Island: Symbol of Resistance.* A straightforward, illustrated account of Robben Island from prehistoric times to the present, with a good overview of prison conditions in the apartheid years.

Antjie Krog *Country of My Skull.* An unflinching and harrowing account of the Truth and Reconciliation Commission's investigations. Krog, a respected radio journalist and poet, covered the entire process, and skilfully merges private identity with national catharsis.

Candy Malherbe *Men of Men.* A brief, simple and highly readable primer on the Khoikhoi.

Hein Marais *South Africa, Limits to Change.* A readable assessment of why the privileged classes remain just that, and why the new government has followed relatively conservative economic policies.

Alan Mountain *An Unsung Heritage: Perspectives on Slavery.* An account of the nature of slavery in the Cape, and the contribution imported slaves made to the fabric of the area today. Best of all is the guide to slave heritage sites in the Cape Peninsula, Winelands and West Coast, and along Garden Route, with attractive photos and illustrations.

Mike Nicol *Sea-Mountain, Fire City: Living in Cape Town.* One of the most recent books in that rare category, a documentary on living in Cape Town at the beginning of the new millennium. Hinging his narrative on the apparently prosaic business of moving house from one part of the city to another, Nicol maps many of those fissures, not to say abysses, that make Cape Town the divided city that it is.

Dougie Oakes (ed) *Illustrated History of South Africa.* Physically weighty, but written in a delightfully light style, this illustrated volume is essential for anyone seriously interested in the rise of apartheid and the country's turbulent passage to democracy.

Nigel Penn *Rogues, Rebels and Runaways.* A hugely entertaining collection of essays on deviant types in the eighteenth-century Cape. Tragi-comic and written in a wry, engaging style.

Robert C-H Shell *Children of Bondage.* Definitive social history of Cape slavery in the eighteenth century – a compelling academic text that is accessible to the lay reader.

Allister Sparks *The Mind of South Africa.* An authoritative journalist and historian traces the rise and fall of the apartheid state; a lively, economical and serious work. *Beyond the Miracle: Inside The New South Africa* examines the prospects for South Africa, looking beyond the initial buoyancy of democracy to emerging patterns in its government.

Desmond Tutu *No Future Without Forgiveness.* Tutu's gracious and honest assessment of the Truth Commission he guided. An important testimony from one of the country's most influential thinkers and leaders.

Frank Welsh *A History of South Africa.* Solid scholarship and a strong sense of overall narrative mark this publication as a much-needed addition to South African historiography.

Biography and autobiography

J.M. Coetzee *Boyhood.* A moving and courageous childhood memoir by South Africa's greatest novelist. Written in the third person, it depicts the thoughts of a young boy with profound attentiveness.

Sindiwe Magoma *To My Children's Children.* A fascinating autobiography – initially started so that her family would never forget their roots – that traces Magoma's life from the rural Transkei to the hard townships of Cape Town, and from political innocence to wisdom born of bitter experience.

Nelson Mandela *Long Walk to Freedom.* Superb best-selling autobiography of the former president and national icon, which is wonderfully evocative of his early years and intensely moving about his long years in prison. A little too diplomatic, perhaps, on his love life and on the inside story behind the negotiated settlement that spelt the end of apartheid.

William Plomer *Cecil Rhodes.* There are countless books on Rhodes and his huge influence on South Africa in the nineteenth century. Most of these books feed the legend, though some historians now regard him as a flawed colossus. Plomer, a South African poet–novelist, went against the grain several decades ago, when he pulled no punches in presenting Rhodes as an immature person driven by his weaknesses.

Benjamin Pogrund *How Can Man Die Better? The Life of Robert Sobukwe.* Long overdue story of one of the most important anti-apartheid liberation heroes, the late leader of the Pan Africanist Congress and a contemporary of Nelson Mandela, feared so much by the white government that they passed a special law – The Sobukwe Clause – to keep him in solitary confinement on Robben Island after he'd served his sentence

Anthony Sampson *Mandela, The Authorised Biography.* Released to coincide with Mandela's retirement from the presidency in 1999, Sampson's authoritative volume competes with *A Long Walk to Freedom* in both interest and sheer poundage. Firmly grounded in the author's long association with his subject, as well as exhaustive research and interviews, it offers a broader perspective and sharper analysis than the autobiography.

The arts

Marion Arnold *Women and Art in South Africa.* Comprehensive, pioneering study of women artists from the early twentieth century to the present.

Basil Beakey *Beyond the Blues: Township Jazz of the Sixties and Seventies.* Portraits, in words and pictures, of the country's jazz greats such as Kippie Moeketsi, Basil Coetzee and Abdullah Ibrahim (Dollar Brand).

S. Francis and Rico *Madam and Eve.* Various volumes of telling and witty cartoons conveying the daily struggle between an African domestic worker and her white madam in the northern suburbs of Johannesburg, these cartoons say more about post-apartheid society than countless academic tomes.

Z.B. Molefe *A Common Hunger to Sing.* Large format, well-illustrated tribute to the country's black women singers and the obstacles they have overcome.

Sophie Perryer (ed) *10 Years, 100 Artists.* Substantial coffee-table book showcasing the work of a hundred top South African artists.

Sue Williamson *Resistance Art in South Africa* and *Art in South Africa: The Future Present.* Taken together, these two volumes map the course of South African art from the early 1980s to the present day, accompanied by a commentary that's both thoughtful and concise enough to let the artworks speak for themselves.

Zapiro *Da Zuma Code.* In a country where satire is in notoriously short supply, Zapiro is the leading cartoonist, consistently exposing what needs to be exposed. This book is the eleventh in a series, containing work originally published in a number of dailies as well as the *Mail & Guardian* and *Sunday Times.*

Poetry

Ingrid de Kok *Transfer.* Technically adroit and always moving work from probably the most intelligent of South Africa's feminist poets.

Denis Hirson (ed) *The Lava of this Land: South African Poetry 1960–1996.* This most recent and comprehensive anthology of South African poetry includes work from the oral period, as well as translations from Afrikaans and other languages. The most useful introduction to date.

Ingrid Jonker *Selected Poems.* One of the few Afrikaans-language poets to be in print in an English translation that does justice to her work. The poems display a remarkable rawness in depicting the outrage of 1960s apartheid, as well as a grief-stricken lyricism from a poet who drowned herself off Sea Point in 1965.

Stephen Watson *The Other City.* No one better evokes Cape Town's changeable beauty, though Watson also writes of the heart and the great universal themes that make him a first-rate poet of the world, rather than just of his native city.

Travel writing

Richard Dobson *Karoo Moons: A Photographic Journey.* If you need encouragement to explore the desert interior of South Africa, these enticing images should do the trick.

Sihle Khumalo *Dark Continent, My Black Arse.* Insightful and witty account by a black South African who quit his well-paid job to realize a dream of travelling from the Cape to Cairo by public transport.

Ben Maclennan *The Wind Makes Dust: Four Centuries of Travel in South Africa*. A remarkable anthology of fascinating travel pieces, meticulously unearthed and researched.

Dervla Murphy *South from the Limpopo: Travels Through South Africa*. A fascinating and intrepid journey – by bicycle – through the new South Africa. The author isn't afraid to explore the complexities and paradoxes of this country.

Paul Theroux *Dark Star Safari*. Theroux's powerful account of his overland trip from Cairo to Cape Town, with a couple of chapters on South Africa, including an account of meeting writer Nadine Gordimer.

Music

espite the slow pace of the Cape Town music scene, which is a lot less lively than Jo'burg's, a steady stream of quality records has been produced, particularly by jazz artists. The city's greatest musical treasure is Cape jazz, and its greatest exponent is Abdullah Ibrahim (known as Dollar Brand before his conversion to Islam). Born and raised in District Six, Ibrahim is a supremely gifted pianist and composer, who for decades has produced a hypnotic fusion of African, American and Cape Muslim idioms. Other Cape Town jazz legends include three saxophonists – Robbie Jansen, Winston "Ngozi" Mankunku and the late Basil Coetzee – plus guitarist Errol Dyers, pianist Hotep Galata and bassist Spencer Mbadu. Two young stars stand out as heirs to the Cape jazz tradition, the astronomically cool guitarist Jimmy Dludlu and subtle, mellow pianist Paul Hanmer; catch them live if you can.

A handful of adventurous independent recording studios for jazz, *kwaito* and hip-hop music have sprung up in recent years. Of the established labels, Melt2000 (⊛www.melt2000.com) is the most innovative and intelligent, but all the titles mentioned here should be available at one of the music shops listed on p.151 or can be ordered through them.

In the reviews below, items marked with an asterisk are international releases. Other items are South African releases, issued either by local labels or by the South African operations of international labels.

Essential Cape Town sounds

Basil Coetzee *Monwabisi* (Mountain). Smoky, intensely energetic jazz record from the greatest of Cape jazz saxophonists.

Dantai *Operation Lahlela* (Nebula BOS). R'n'B-flavoured *kwaito* from one of Cape Town's up-and-coming dance acts.

Jimmy Dludlu *Essence Of Rhythm* (Universal). Dludlu is the essence of smooth jazz, and is arguably the single most popular representative of what is in turn the most commercially successful jazz style in South Africa.

Brenda Fassie *African Princess Of Pop* and *Memeza* (CCP). The former is a posthumous survey covering the entire career of South Africa's very own Madonna; the latter, featuring the massive hit "Vul'Ndlela", was Brenda's most commercially successful effort and holds the all-time sales

record (600,000 plus and still rising) for a locally produced album.

Paul Hanmer *Trains To Taung* (Sheer Sound). This album is constructed around Hanmer's dreamy, piano-based compositions. Now considered a classic and one of the first expositions of the new jazz of the post-apartheid era.

Abdullah Ibrahim *African Marketplace* (Discovery/WEA). Ibrahim's best album – a wistful, nostalgic, other-worldly journey.

Robbie Jansen *Nomad Jez* (EMI). Great, if slightly flawed, album from veteran saxophonist Jansen, playing with other luminaries of the local jazz scene including Hilton Schilder and Errol Dyers.

Winston Mankunku *Crossroads* (Nkomo/Sheer). Sinuous, upbeat township jazz from the veteran Cape Town saxman.

Prophets of Da City *Ghetto Code* (Universal). South Africa's rap supremos' finest release, full of tough but articulate rhymes and some seriously funky backing tracks, all in true Cape Flats style.

Ringo *Sondelani* (CCP). A superb modern reworking of traditional Xhosa sounds by this bald Capetonian heart-throb, including the hit track "*Sondela*", which has become one of South Africa's most popular love songs.

Springbok Nude Girls *Afterlife Satisfaction* (Sony Music). One of South Africa's most popular white bands before they disbanded, here delivering a powerful, if not particularly original, belting rock set.

Essential South African sounds

Bayete *Umkhaya-Lo* (Polygram). A seminal fusion of South African sounds with laid-back soul and funk, blended by lead singer Jabu Khanyile's unique mixing talent and spiced with his beautifully soothing vocals.

Gloria Bosman *Tranquillity* (Sheer/Limelight★). A young and compelling jazz vocalist, Bosman juggles African and American styles with consummate ease. Paul Hanmer arranges and tickles the ivories.

Lucky Dube *Prisoner* (Gallo). Originally a township jive singer, the late Dube made a switch to reggae that was both artistically and commercially inspired. *Prisoner* was South Africa's second bestselling album ever, full of stirring Peter Tosh-style roots tunes.

Sibongile Khumalo *Ancient Evenings* (Sony Music). Though a classically trained opera singer, Khumalo takes on both jazz and a variety of traditional melodies on this wonderful album, demonstrating why she is currently one of South Africa's best-loved singers.

Ladysmith Black Mambazo *Heavenly* (Gallo/Spectrum★). An inspired and commercially successful foray into Afropop, featuring solo versions of various pop classics as well as vocal collaborations with Dolly Parton and Lou Rawls.

Vusi Mahlasela *Silang Mabele* (BMG). Lush harmonies and lilting melodies from this sweet-voiced township balladeer.

Mfaz'Omnyama *Ngisebenzile Mama* (Gallo). The title means "I have been working, Mum", and is amply justified by this superb set, featuring some of the best *maskanda* ever recorded.

Pops Mohamed *How Far Have We Come?* (Melt2000). An exciting celebration of traditional African instruments: mbiras, koras, mouthbows and various percussion instruments are supplemented by bass and brass in this ethereal but funky album.

Moses Taiwa Molelekwa *Genes and Spirits* (Melt 2000). Fascinating jazz/drum 'n' bass fusion by a talented young pianist, who died tragically in 2001.

Language

Language

Language

S outh Africa has eleven official languages, all of which have equal status under the law. In practice, however, English is the *lingua franca* that dominates politics, commerce and the media. In Cape Town and along the Garden Route you'll rarely, if ever, need to use any other language. **South African English** is a mixed bag, one language with many variants. Forty percent of whites are mother-tongue English speakers, many of whom believe that they are (or at least should be) speaking standard British English. In fact, South African English has its own distinct character, and is as different from the Queen's English as Australian is. Its most notable characteristic is its huge and rich vocabulary, with unique words and usages, some drawn from Afrikaans and the indigenous African languages, of which Xhosa (see below) is one of the most widely spoken. The hefty *Oxford Dictionary of South African English* makes for an interesting browse.

Afrikaans, although a language you seldom need to speak, nevertheless remains very much in evidence and you will certainly encounter it on official forms and countless signs, particularly on the road; for this reason we give a comprehensive list of written Afrikaans terms you could come across – see below.

The other main language spoken in Cape Town is **Xhosa**, the predominant mother tongue of the city's African residents. It is also Nelson Mandela's mother tongue, which he shares with seven million other South Africans, predominantly in the Eastern Cape.

The glossary below is far from comprehensive, but it does include some of the commoner words that are unique to South African English. Words whose spelling makes it hard to guess how to render them have their approximate pronunciation given in italics. Where *gh* occurs in the pronunciation, it denotes the **ch** sound in the Scottish word lo**ch**. Sometimes we've used the letter "r" in the pronunciation even though the word in question doesn't contain this letter; for example, we've given the pronunciation of "Egoli" as "*air-gaw-lee*". In these instances the syllable containing the "r" is meant to represent a familiar word or sound from English; the "r" itself shouldn't be pronounced.

Glossary

African In the context of South Africa, an indigenous South African

Afrikaner Literally "African": a white person who speaks Afrikaans

Aloe Family of spiky indigenous succulents, often with dramatic orange flowers

Apartheid (*apart-hate*) Term used from the 1940s for the National Party's official policy of "racial separation"

Arvie Afternoon

Baai Afrikaans word meaning "bay"; also a common suffix in place names eg Stilbaai

Bakkie (*bucky*) Light truck or van

Bantu (*bun-too*) Unscientific apartheid term for indigenous black people; in linguistics, a group of indigenous Southern African languages

Bantustan Term used under apartheid for the territories such as Transkei, reserved for Africans

Bergie A vagrant living on the slopes of Table Mountain; a hobo on the streets of Cape Town

Big Five A term derived from hunting that refers to the trophy animals hunters most want to bag: lion, leopard, buffalo, elephant and rhino; often now used generically to indicate top big game country (as opposed to game reserves that only have antelope and other small mammals)

Black Imprecise term that sometimes refers collectively to Africans, Indians and coloureds, but more usually is used to mean Africans

Boer (*boor*) Literally "farmer", but also refers to early Dutch colonists at the Cape and Afrikaners

Boland (*boor-lunt*) Southern part of the Western Cape

Bottle store Off-licence or liquor store

Boy Offensive term used to refer to an adult African man who is a servant

Bundu (approximately *boon-doo*, but with the vowels shortened) Wilderness or back country

Burgher Literally a citizen, but more specifically a member of the Dutch community at the Cape in the seventeenth and eighteenth centuries; free burghers were VOC employees released from contract to farm independently on the Cape Peninsula and surrounding areas

Bush See *bundu*

Bushman Southern Africa's earliest, but now almost extinct, inhabitants who lived by hunting and gathering

Cape Doctor The southeaster that brings cool winds during the summer months

Cape Dutch Nineteenth-century, whitewashed, gabled style of architecture

Cape Dutch Revival Twentieth-century style based on Cape Dutch architecture

CBD The Central Business District of Central Cape town.

Coloured Mulattos or people of mixed race

Dagga (*dugh-a*) Marijuana

Dagha (*dah-ga*) Mud used in indigenous construction

Dassie (*dussy*) Hyrax

Disa (*die-za*) One of twenty species of beautiful indigenous orchids, most famous of which is the red disa or "Pride of Table Mountain"

Dominee (*dour-min-ee*) Reverend (abbreviated to DS)

Dorp Country town or village (Derived from Afrikaans)

Drostdy (*dross-tea*) Historically, the building of the *landdrost* or magistrate

Fundi Expert

Fynbos (*fayn-boss*) Term for vast range of fine-leafed species that predominate in the southern part of the Western Cape (see *Going wild in Cape Town* colour section)

Girl Offensive term used to refer to an African woman who is a servant

Gogga (*gho-gha*) Creepy crawly or insect

Griqua Person of mixed white, Bushman and Hottentot descent

Group Areas Act Now-defunct law passed in 1950 that provided for the establishment of separate areas for each "racial group"

Homeland See *bantustan*

Hottentot Now unfashionable term for indigenous Khoisan herders encountered by the first settlers at the Cape

Indaba Zulu term meaning a group discussion and now used in South African English for any meeting or conference

Is it? Really?

Jislaaik! (*yis-like*) Exclamation equivalent to "Geez!" or "Crikey!"

Jol Party, celebration

Just now In a while

Kaffir Highly objectionable term of abuse for Africans

Karoo Arid plateau that occupies a large proportion of the South African interior

Khoikhoi (*ghoy-ghoy*) Self-styled name of South Africa's original herding inhabitants

Khoisan A conflation of the terms "Khoikhoi" and "San" used to collectively refer to South Africa's aboriginal inhabitants; the two were socially, but not ethnically, distinct, the Khoikhoi having been herders and the San hunter-gatherers

Kloof (*klo-ef*) Ravine or gorge

Knobkerrie Wooden club

Koppie Hillock

Kramat (*crum-mutt*) Shrine of a Muslim holy man

Krans (*crunce*) Sheer cliff face; plural *kranse*

Lapa Courtyard of group of Ndebele houses; also used to describe an enclosed area at safari camps, where braais are held

Lekker Nice

Lobola (*la-ball-a*) Bride price, paid by an African man to his wife's parents

Location Old-fashioned term for segregated African area on the outskirts of a town or farm

Madiba Mandela's clan name, used affectionately

Malay Misnomer for Cape Muslims of Asian descent

Mbira (*m-beer-a*) African thumb piano, often made with a gourd

MK Umkhonto we Sizwe (Spear of the Nation), the armed wing of the ANC, now incorporated into the national army

Mlungu (*m-loon-goo*) African term for a white person, equivalent to honkie

Moffie (*mawf-ee*) Gay person

Mother City Nickname for Cape Town

Muti (*moo-tee*) See *umuthi*

Nek Saddle between two mountains

Nkosi Sikelel' iAfrika "God Bless Africa", anthem of the ANC and now of South Africa

Pass Document that Africans used to have to carry at all times, which essentially rendered them aliens in their own country

Pastorie (*puss-tour-ee*) Parsonage

Platteland (*plutta-lunt*) Country districts

Poort Narrow pass through mountains along river course

Protea National flower of South Africa

Raadsaal (the "d" is pronounced "t") Council or parliament building

Robot Traffic light

Rondavel (*ron-daa-vil*, with the stress on the middle syllable) Circular building based on traditional African huts

SABC South African Broadcasting Authority

San An alternative term for Bushmen (see above)

Sangoma (*sun-gom-a*) Traditional spirit medium and healer

Shebeen (*sha-bean*) Unlicensed township tavern

Southeaster Prevailing wind in the Western Cape

Spaza shops (*spa-za*) Small stall or kiosk

Stoep Veranda

Strandloper Literally "beach walkers"; Bushman or San social group who lived along the shores of the Western Cape and whose hunting and gathering consisted largely of shellfish and other seafood

Tackies Sneakers or plimsolls

Township Area set aside under apartheid for Africans

Transkei (*trans-kye*) Now-defunct homeland for Xhosa speakers

Trekboer (*trek-boor*) Nomadic Afrikaner farmers, usually in the eighteenth and nineteenth century

Umuthi (*oo-moo-tee*) Traditional herbal medicine

Vlei (*flay*) Swamp

VOC Verenigde Oostindische Compagnie, the Dutch East India Company

Voortrekkers (the first syllable rhymes with "boor") Dutch burghers who migrated inland in their ox wagons in the nineteenth century to escape British colonialism

Food and drink

Amarula Liqueur made from the berries of the marula tree

Begrafnisrys (*ba-ghruff-niss-race*) Literally "funeral rice"; traditional Cape Muslim dish of yellow rice cooked with raisins

Biltong Sun-dried salted strip of meat, chewed as a snack

Blatjang (*blutt-young*) Cape Muslim chutney that has become a standard condiment on South African dinner tables

Bobotie (*ba-boor-tea*) Traditional Cape curried mince topped with a savoury custard and often cooked with apricots and almonds

Boerekos (*boor-a-coss*) Farm food, usually consisting of loads of meat and vegetables cooked using butter and sugar

Boerewors (*boor-a-vorce*) Spicy lengths of sausage that are *de rigueur* at braais

Bokkoms Dried fish, much like salt fish

Braai or **braaivleis** (*bry-flace*) Barbecue

Bredie Cape vegetable and meat stew

Cane or **cane spirit** A potent vodka-like spirit distilled from sugar cane and generally mixed with a soft drink such as Coke

Cap Classique Sparkling wine fermented in the bottle in exactly the same way as Champagne; also called Méthode Cap Classic

Cape gooseberry Fruit of the physalis; a sweet yellow berry

Cape salmon or **geelbek** (*ghear-l-beck*) Delicious firm-fleshed sea fish (unrelated to Northern-hemisphere salmon)

Cape Velvet A sweet liqueur-and-cream dessert beverage that resembles Irish Cream liqueur

Denningvleis (*den-ning-flace*) Spicy traditional Cape lamb stew

Frikkadel Fried onion and meat balls

Geelbek See Cape salmon

Hanepoort (*harner-poort*) Delicious sweet dessert grape

Kabeljou (*cobble-yo*) Common South African marine fish, also called kob

Kerrievis (*kerry-fiss*) See pickled fish

Kingklip Highly prized deepwater fish caught along the Atlantic and Indian ocean coasts

Kob See *kabeljou*

Koeksister (*cook-sister*) Deep-fried plaited doughnut, dripping with syrup

Maas or **amasi** or **amaas** Traditional African beverage consisting of naturally soured milk, available as a packaged dairy product in supermarkets

Maaskaas Cottage cheese made from *maas*

Mageu or **mahewu** or **maheu** (*ma-gh-weh*) Traditional African beer made from maize meal and water, now packaged and commercially available

Malva Very rich and very sweet traditional baked Cape dessert

Mampoer (*mum-poor*) Moonshine; home-distilled spirit made from soft fruit, commonly peaches

Mealie See *mielie*

Melktert (*melk-tairt*) Traditional Cape custard pie

Mielie Maize

Mielie pap (*mealy pup*) Maize porridge, varying from a thin mixture to a stiff one that can resemble polenta

Mqomboti (*m-qom-booty*) Traditional African beer made from fermented sorghum

Musselcracker Large-headed fish with powerful jaws and firm, white flesh

Naartjie (*nar-chee*) Tangerine or mandarin

Pap (*pup*) Porridge

Peri-peri Delicious hottish spice of Portuguese origin commonly used with grilled chicken

Perlemoen (*pear-la-moon*) Abalone

Pickled fish Traditional Cape dish of fish preserved with onions, vinegar and curry; available tinned in supermarkets

Pinotage A uniquely South African cultivar hybridized from Pinot Noir and Hermitage grapes and from which a wine of the same name is made

Potjiekos or potjie (*poy-key-kos*) Food cooked slowly over embers in a three-legged cast-iron pot

Putu (*poo-too*) Traditional African mielie pap (see above) prepared until it forms dry crumbs

Rooibos (*roy-boss*) **tea** Indigenous herbal tea, made from the leaves of a particular *fynbos* plant.

Rooti A chapati

Rusks Tasty biscuits made from sweetened bread that has been slow-cooked

Salmon trout Freshwater fish that is often smoked to create a cheaper and pretty good imitation of smoked salmon

Salomie Roti

Sambals (*sam-bills*) Accompaniments, such as chopped bananas, green peppers, desiccated coconut and chutney, served with Cape curries

Samp Traditional African dish of broken maize kernels, frequently cooked with beans

Skokiaan (*skok-ee-yan*) Potent home-brew

Smoorsnoek (*smore-snook*) Smoked *snoek*

Snoek (*snook*) Large fish that features in many traditional Cape recipes

Sosatie (*so-sah-ti*) Spicy skewered mince

Spanspek (*spon-speck*) A sweet melon

Steenbras (*ste-en-bruss*) A delicious white-fleshed fish

Van der Hum South African *naartjie*-flavoured liqueur

Vetkoek (*fet-cook*) Deep-fried doughnut-like cake

Waterblommetjiebredie (*vata-blom-a-key-bree-dee*) Cape meat stew made with waterlily rhizomes

Witblits (*vit-blitz*) Moonshine

Yellowtail Delicious darkish-fleshed marine fish

Afrikaans street signs

Derde	Third
Doeane	Customs
Drankwinkel	Liquor shop
Eerste	First
Geen ingang	No entry
Gevaar	Danger
Goof	Main
Hoog	High
Ingang	Entrance
Inligting	Information
Kantoor	Office
Kerk	Church
Kort	Short
Links	Left
Lughawe	Airport
Mans	Men
Mark	Market
Ompad	Detour
Pad	Road
Padwerke voor	Roadworks ahead
Perron	Station platform
Polisie	Police
Poskantoor	Post office
Regs	Right
Ry	Go
Sentrum	Centre
Singel	Crescent
Stad	City
Stad sentrum	City centre
Stadig	Slow
Stasie	Station
Strand	Beach
Swembad	Swimming pool
Verbode	Prohibited
Verkeer	Traffic
Versigtig	Carefully
Vierde	Fourth
Vrouens	Women
Vyfde	Fifth

LANGUAGE | Glossary

Travel store

Visit us online
www.roughguides.com
Information on over 25,000 destinations around the world

- **Read** Rough Guides' trusted travel info
- **Access** exclusive articles from Rough Guides authors
- **Update** yourself on new books, maps, CDs and other products
- **Enter** our competitions and win travel prizes
- **Share** ideas, journals, photos & travel advice with other users
- **Earn** points every time you contribute to the Rough Guide
  community and get rewards

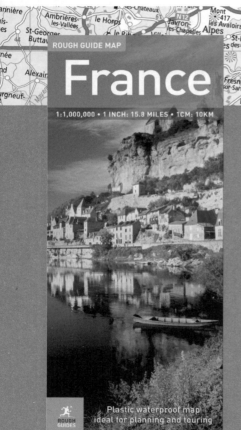

NOTES

NOTES

NOTES

NOTES

NOTES

NOTES

NOTES

NOTES

Small print and

Index

A Rough Guide to Rough Guides

Published in 1982, the first Rough Guide – to Greece – was a student scheme that became a publishing phenomenon. Mark Ellingham, a recent graduate in English from Bristol University, had been travelling in Greece the previous summer and couldn't find the right guidebook. With a small group of friends he wrote his own guide, combining a highly contemporary, journalistic style with a thoroughly practical approach to travellers' needs.

The immediate success of the book spawned a series that rapidly covered dozens of destinations. And, in addition to impecunious backpackers, Rough Guides soon acquired a much broader and older readership that relished the guides' wit and inquisitiveness as much as their enthusiastic, critical approach and value-for-money ethos.

These days, Rough Guides include recommendations from shoestring to luxury and cover more than 200 destinations around the globe, including almost every country in the Americas and Europe, more than half of Africa and most of Asia and Australasia. Our ever-growing team of authors and photographers is spread all over the world, particularly in Europe, the USA and Australia.

In the early 1990s, Rough Guides branched out of travel, with the publication of Rough Guides to World Music, Classical Music and the Internet. All three have become benchmark titles in their fields, spearheading the publication of a wide range of books under the Rough Guide name.

Including the travel series, Rough Guides now number more than 350 titles, covering: phrasebooks, waterproof maps, music guides from Opera to Heavy Metal, reference works as diverse as Conspiracy Theories and Shakespeare, and popular culture books from iPods to Poker. Rough Guides also produce a series of more than 120 World Music CDs in partnership with World Music Network.

Visit www.roughguides.com to see our latest publications.

Rough Guide travel images are available for commercial licensing at www.roughguidespictures.com

Rough Guide credits

Text editor: Ann-Marie Shaw
Layout: Ankur Guha
Cartography: Alakananda Bhattacharya
Picture editor: Mark Thomas
Production: Vicky Baldwin
Proofreader: Susannah Wight
Cover design: Chloë Roberts
Photographer: Alex Wilson
Editorial: **London** Ruth Blackmore, Alison
Murchie, Andy Turner, Keith Drew, Edward
Aves, Alice Park, Lucy White, Jo Kirby, James
Smart, Natasha Foges, Róisín Cameron, Emma
Traynor, Emma Gibbs, James Rice, Kathryn
Lane, Christina Valhouli, Monica Woods, Mani
Ramaswamy, Joe Staines, Peter Buckley,
Matthew Milton, Tracy Hopkins, Ruth Tidball;
New York Andrew Rosenberg, Steven Horak,
AnneLise Sorensen, April Isaacs, Ella Steim, Anna
Owens, Sean Mahoney, Paula Neudorf, Courtney
Miller; **Delhi** Madhavi Singh, Karen D'Souza
Design & Pictures: **London** Scott Stickland,
Dan May, Diana Jarvis, Nicole Newman, Sarah
Cummins, Emily Taylor; **Delhi** Umesh Aggarwal,
Ajay Verma, Jessica Subramanian,

Pradeep Thapliyal, Sachin Tanwar, Anita Singh,
Nikhil Agarwal
Production: Rebecca Short
Cartography: **London** Maxine Repath, Ed
Wright, Katie Lloyd-Jones; **Delhi** Jai Prakash
Mishra, Rajesh Chhibber, Ashutosh Bharti, Rajesh
Mishra, Animesh Pathak, Jasbir Sandhu, Karobi
Gogoi, Swati Handoo
Online: Narender Kumar, Rakesh Kumar,
Amit Verma, Rahul Kumar, Ganesh Sharma,
Debojit Borah, Saurabh Sati, Ravi Yadav
Marketing & Publicity: **London** Liz Statham,
Niki Hanmer, Louise Maher, Jess Carter, Vanessa
Godden, Vivienne Watton, Anna Paynton, Rachel
Sprackett, Libby Jellie, Jayne McPherson, Holly
Dudley; **New York** Geoff Colquitt, Katy Ball;
Delhi Ragini Govind
Manager India: Punita Singh
Reference Director: Andrew Lockett
Operations Manager: Helen Phillips
PA to Publishing Director: Nicola Henderson
Publishing Director: Martin Dunford
Commercial Manager: Gino Magnotta
Managing Director: John Duhigg

Publishing information

This second edition published October 2008 by
Rough Guides Ltd,
80 Strand, London WC2R 0RL
345 Hudson St, 4th Floor,
New York, NY 10014, USA
14 Local Shopping Centre, Panchsheel Park,
New Delhi 110017, India
Distributed by the Penguin Group
Penguin Books Ltd,
80 Strand, London WC2R 0RL
Penguin Group (USA)
375 Hudson Street, NY 10014, USA
Penguin Group (Australia)
250 Camberwell Road, Camberwell,
Victoria 3124, Australia
Penguin Group (Canada)
195 Harry Walker Parkway N, Newmarket, ON,
L3Y 7B3 Canada
Penguin Group (NZ)
67 Apollo Drive, Mairangi Bay, Auckland 1310,
New Zealand
Cover concept by Peter Dyer.

Typeset in Bembo and Helvetica to an original
design by Henry Iles.

Printed and bound in China

© Tony Pinchuck and Barbara McCrea 2008

No part of this book may be reproduced in any
form without permission from the publisher except
for the quotation of brief passages in reviews.

336pp includes index

A catalogue record for this book is available from
the British Library

ISBN: 978-1-85828-864-2

The publishers and authors have done their best
to ensure the accuracy and currency of all the
information in **The Rough Guide to Cape Town
the Winelands & the Garden Route**, however,
they can accept no responsibility for any loss,
injury, or inconvenience sustained by any traveller
as a result of information or advice contained in
the guide.

1   3   5   7   9   8   6   4   2

SMALL PRINT

Help us update

We've gone to a lot of effort to ensure that the
second edition of **The Rough Guide to Cape
Town, the Winelands & the Garden Route** is
accurate and up to date. However, things change
– places get "discovered", opening hours are
notoriously fickle, restaurants and rooms raise
prices or lower standards. If you feel we've got it
wrong or left something out, we'd like to know,
and if you can remember the address, the price,
the hours, the phone number, so much the better.

Please send your comments with the
subject line "**Rough Guide to Cape Town,
the Winelands & the Garden Route Update**"
to ©mail@roughguides.com. We'll credit all
contributions and send a copy of the next edition
(or any other Rough Guide if you prefer) for the
very best emails.

Have your questions answered and tell others
about your trip at
⊛ community.roughguides.com

Acknowledgements

Tony Thanks to our editor Ann-Marie Shaw for her deft editing and for being a pleasure to work with. Thanks, too, to my co-author Barbara McCrea for her usual conscientiousness and for her enormous contribution to the book, and to Gabriel Pinchuck for being an appreciative and entertaining travelling companion. I am also grateful to the scores of readers who took the time write to us, the dozens people who hosted us and shared their local knowledge and to anyone I may have omitted to mention.

Barbara Thanks to our editor Ann-Marie Shaw for her steady hand and for being a pleasure to work with; Tony Pinchuck for his ability to be on track and finish projects; the overworked contributors and researchers Nicky Joubert-Van Doesburgh, Carolyn Howell, Liz Mackenzie and Christine Morling; my brother Robert McCrea for driving us around the Kruger area; Stanley Singer

for Cape Town restaurant tips; Vanessa Berger for Grahamstown student hang-outs; my mother Pat McCrea for Eastern Cape back-up; the many unmentioned and generous people who gave us information, meals and help along the way; my travelling partner Hillel Braude who made all the research trips worthwhile; and finally my lively son Gabriel Pinchuck who has been doing Rough Guide research since he was born. Thanks also to all the people and fabulous accommodation establishments who hosted or helped us.

Finally, the editor would like to thank the authors for their patience and forebearance over many months, Ankur Guha for his flexible and patient typesetting, Mark Thomas for longsuffering picture editing, Alex Wilson for the photos, Alakananda Bhattacharya for great maps, Susannah Wight for eagle-eyed proofreading, and Monica Woods for her enthusiastic support.

Readers' letters

Thanks to all the readers who have taken the time to write in with comments and suggestions (and apologies if we've inadvertently omitted or misspelt anyone's name):

Renee Ambito, Skye Aspden, Pieter Badenhorst, Lucy Barker and Philip Normington, Irene and Rienzi Beckett, Keith Beelders, Liza Botha, Jo Brink, Anthony Crawford Brunt, Bertus and Juliet Britz, David Broadbent, Dick Butler, Barbara Clark, Kathleen Clay, Elliot Cahn, Mike Cavanagh, Emily Charles and Alex Hatch, Mike and Eileen Christie, Robin Christie, Jill Clark, Fiona Cole, David Cooknell, Erin Conradie, Aidan and Heather Corr, Meg Cowper-Lewis, Marianne Crane, Erika Cule, Carisa Cunningham, David and Tina Davies, Ruth Denton, Herbert Drewniok, Dave and Melanie Dudley, Moira Dunworth, Jannie du Toit, Audrey and Melvyn du Valle, Christine Duxbury, Laurence Elton, Simon Eriksen, Huw Evans, Jill Foster, Chris Frean, Tanja Gehren, Barbara Giacomin, Heather Giannandrea, Kathy Gie, Tony Gloster, Meg Goodare, Hana Hall, Carol Hamilton, Cathy Harris, Haley Harvey, Gavin Heath, Niels and Margret Hendriks, Rod Hirst, Nigel Hollington, Jane Holman, Clive Hooper, Simon Hoten, David Hoult, Joy Hull, Bob Hyde, Ran Jan, Decima Jones, Laurence Jones, R. A. Kastell, Carole and Alan Kenyon, Uli Kress, J.R.W Kronfield, David Land,

Annie Lavery, Eddy le Couvreur, Robby Letsholo, Grant Lindsay, Yolande Lombard, Rodney Lord, Kim McConkey and Chandra Ramarao, Peter and Lois McDonald, Stella and John Macdougall, John Major, Linda Mannheim, Genevieve Marshall, Shelley Mason, John Miller, Jo Moskon, Darragh Morgan, Dr David Murphy, Dwight Newman, Alex Nikolic, Stuart and Sue Nuttal, Jarl Olsen, Alan Palmer, David Pearson, Barbara Pellow, Lloyd Perry, Joyce Plotnikoff and Richard Woolfson, Tessa and Harry Rajak, Stephen and Mary Rea, John Read, Dallas Reed, Laurent Ribes, Neil Richmond, Carolyn and Julia Rigg, Hazel Rofe, Su Roxburgh and Steve Parkes, Joanne Rushby, Edmund Salomons, Noam Schimmel, Nicholas M Schmidt, Amanda Sebestyen, Nick Sebley, Dave Short, Daan and Zena Smit, Xolile Speelman, Angela Speight, Mike Tayler-Smith, June Taylor, Chris and Jenny Tily, Amiene van der Merwe, Adrie van Doorn, Helen & Martin Vegoda, Hans Verstrate, Marie Verwey, Dominique and Brigitte Vigliotti, Angela Warren, Nigel Watson, Helmut and Christian Wilderer, Richard and Ying Wiseman, Thomas Wiser, Judge R.H. Zulman.

Photo credits

All photos © Rough Guides except the following:

Covers
Front cover: Table Mountain from Blouwberg Beach © Frans Lemmens/Getty
Back cover: Bo-Kaap district © Nicholas Pitt/Alamy
Inside back cover: City Hall and Table Mountain © Alex Wilson

Introduction
Camps Bay © Ian Cumming/Axiom
View from Table Mountain © Chris Coe/Axiom
Trekking along the Lions Head © Ian Cumming/Axiom
Aquarium © Getty Images
Film crew © Peter Titmus

Things not to miss
04 Cape Minstrels © Mike Hutchings/Corbis
06 Sandboarding © Dave Richardson/iAfrika Photos
11 Mother City Queer Projects © Mike Hutchings/Corbis
12 Bottlenose Dolphins © Steve Bloom Images/Alamy
13 South African National Gallery © Hemis/Alamy
19 Chapman's Peak drive © Martin Harvey/Alamy
22 Robben Island © Jean Miele/Corbis

Cape colonial Colour Section
Victoria street arcitechture © Ian Cumming/Axiom
Dutch Reformed Church, Calitzdorp © Robert Hollingworth/Alamy
The hamlet of Ladysmith © Images of Africa Photobank/Alamy
Oudtshoorn feather palace © Images of Africa Photobank

Going wild in Cape Town Colour Section
Zebra © DK Images
Cape girdled lizard © Bernard O'Kane/Alamy
Bontebok © Getty Images
Common dolphins © Mike Parry/Getty Images

Black and whites
p.188 Whale at Hermanus © Hoberman Collection UK
p.201 De Hoop Nature Reserve © DK Images
p.212 Mossel Bay © Images of Africa/Alamy
p.229 Kysna Quays © Nicholass Pitt/Alamy
p.269 Donkin Street © Peter Titmuss/Alamy
p.274 Elephant © Redmund Durrell/Alamy
p.289 Mandela's release from prison © Sipa Press/Rex Features

Index

Map entries are in colour.

INDEX

INDEX

Map symbols

maps are listed in the full index using coloured text

‐‐‐‐	International boundary	★	Public transport stop
‐‐‐	Chapter division boundary	♦	Place of interest
‐‐ ‐‐	Provincial boundary	⊼	Picnic site
N2	National road	☀	Lighthouse
R62	Regional road	❦	Winery
M6	Metropolitan road	⊠	Gate
	Minor road	⊠	Post office
	Pedestrianized street	✈	Airport
	Untarred road	⊞	Hospital
	Steps	P	Parking
‐○‐	Railway line and station	⚑	Golf course
•‐‐‐•	Cable car	⬤	Swimming pool
‐‐‐‐‐	Path	⌂	Public gardens
‐‐/‐‐	River and dam	⊥	Monument
⌣	Bridge	✡	Synagogue
■ ■ ■	Wall	☪	Mosque
⌂⌂	Mountain range	☸	Shipwreck
▲	Peak	⊞	Church
⋝	Mountain pass		Building
ᴙᵘᴌᴙᴙ	Rocks	◯	Stadium
⬇	Viewpoint		Park
◔	Cave		Beach
☥	Windmill		National park/nature
ⓘ	Tourist office		reserve

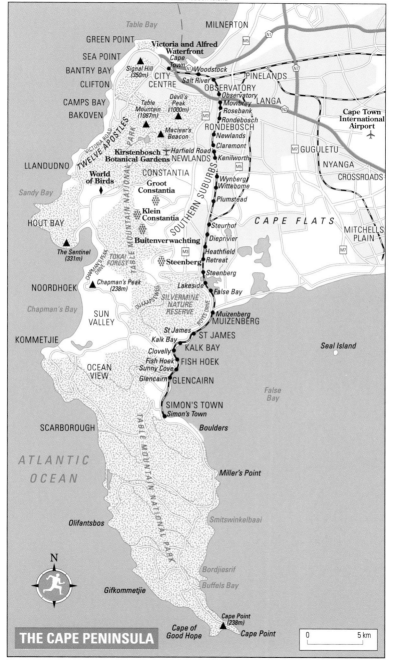

THE CAPE PENINSULA

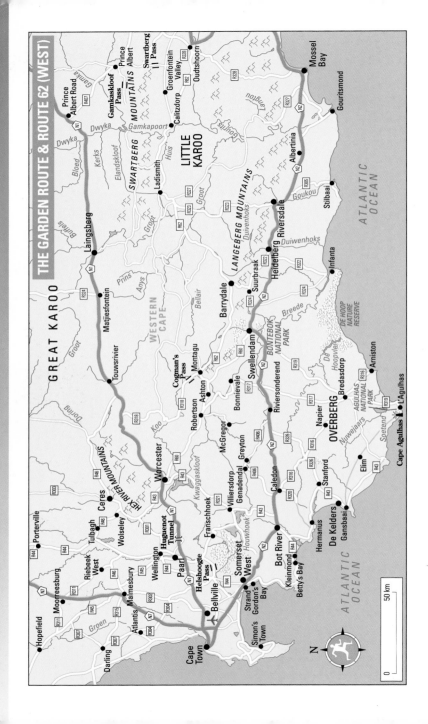

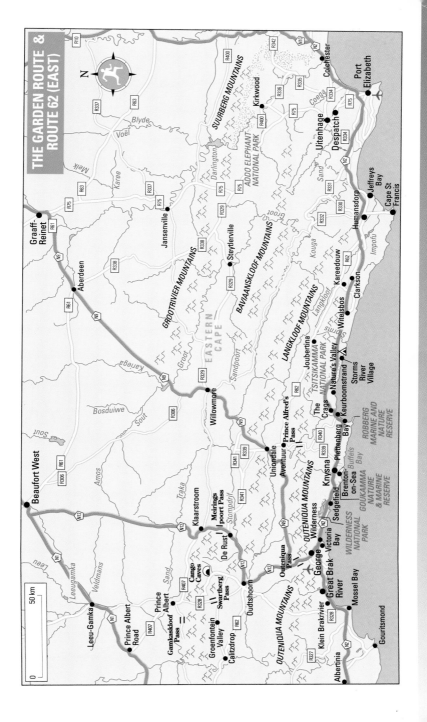

THE GARDEN ROUTE &
ROUTE 62 (EAST)

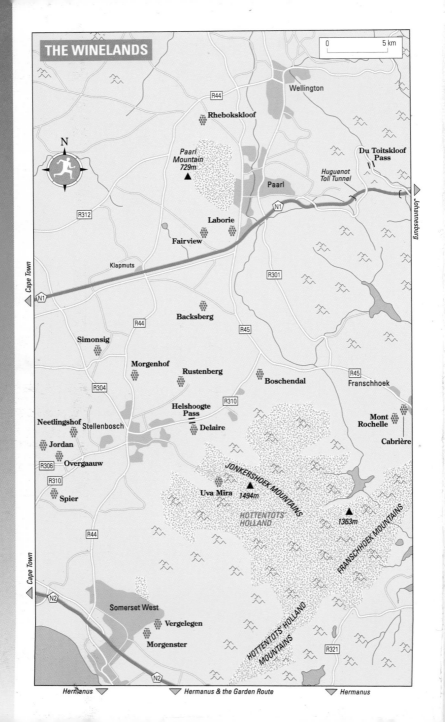

THE WINELANDS

0   5 km

N

Wellington

R44

Rheboskloof

Paarl
Mountain
729m ▲

Du Toitskloof
Pass

Huguenot
Toll Tunnel

Paarl

Johannesburg

N1

R312

Laborie

Fairview

Klapmuts

R301

Cape Town

N1

R44

Backsberg

R45

Simonsig

Morgenhof

Rustenberg

Boschendal

R45

Franschhoek

R304

Helshoogte
Pass

R310

Mont
Rochelle

Neetlingshof

Stellenbosch

Delaire

Cabrière

Jordan

R306

Overgaauw

R310

Spier

JONKERSHOEK MOUNTAINS

Uva Mira

1494m ▲

1363m ▲

HOTTENTOTS
HOLLAND

FRANSCHHOEK MOUNTAINS

R44

Cape Town

N2

Somerset West

Vergelegen

Morgenster

HOTTENTOTS' HOLLAND
MOUNTAINS

R321

N2

Hermanus ▽   ▽ Hermanus & the Garden Route   ▽ Hermanus